Governing
Dive...

Contributors to this volume

James Anderson, School of Geography, Queen's University Belfast.

Salvador Giner, Sociology Department, Faculty of Economics, University of Barcelona.

Montserrat Guibernau, Faculty of Social Sciences, The Open University.

Zig Layton-Henry, Department of Politics and International Studies, University of Warwick.

Josep R. Llobera, University College London and Pompeu Fabra University (Barcelona).

Catherine Lloyd, Gender and Development Unit, Queen Elizabeth House, University of Oxford.

Eugene McLaughlin, Faculty of Social Sciences, The Open University.

Denis McQuail, Department of Politics, University of Southampton.

Karim Murji, Faculty of Social Sciences, The Open University.

Mark J. Smith, Faculty of Social Sciences, The Open University.

Readers should note that references to other books in the series appear in bold type.

Governing European Diversity

edited by Montserrat Guibernau

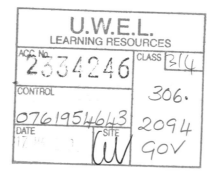

SAGE Publications
London • Thousand Oaks • New Delhi

in association with

The Open
University

This publication forms part of the Open University course DD200 *Governing Europe*. The other books that make up the *Governing Europe* series are listed on the back cover. Details of this and other Open University courses can be obtained from the Call Centre, PO Box 724, The Open University, Milton Keynes MK7 6ZS, United Kingdom: tel. +44 (0)1908 653231, e-mail ces-gen@open.ac.uk

Alternatively, you may visit the Open University website at http://www.open.ac.uk where you can learn more about the wide range of courses and packs offered at all levels by The Open University.

For availability of other course components, contact Open University Worldwide Ltd, The Berrill Building, Walton Hall, Milton Keynes MK7 6AA, United Kingdom: tel. +44 (0)1908 858785; fax +44 (0)1908 858787; e-mail ouwenq@open.ac.uk; website http://www.ouw.co.uk

Sage Publications Ltd
6 Bonhill Street
London EC2A 4PU

Sage Publications Inc.
2455 Teller Road
Thousand Oaks
California 91320

Sage Publications India Pvt Ltd
32 M-block Market
Greater Kailash - 1
New Dehli 110 048

British Library Cataloging in Publication Data
A catalogue record for this book is available from The British Library.

Library of Congress catalog record 133451.

Edited, designed and typeset by The Open University.

Printed and bound in the United Kingdom by The Bath Press, Bath.

ISBN 0 7619 5464 3 (hbk)
ISBN 0 7619 5465 1 (pbk)

1.1

Contents

PREFACES   ix

CHAPTER 1   INTRODUCTION: UNITY AND DIVERSITY IN EUROPE   1

Montserrat Guibernau

1   Introduction   1

2   The cultural frontiers of Europe: inclusion and exclusion   2

3   What divides Europeans?   14

4   What unites Europeans?   19

5   Self-organization and social regulation   27

6   Book contents and structure   31

References   33

Further reading   34

CHAPTER 2   THE RISE OF REGIONS AND REGIONALISM IN WESTERN EUROPE   35

James Anderson

1   Introduction   35

2   The diversity of regions and regionalisms   38

3   The growth of regionalism and its causes   44

4   Regionalism in the EU   50

5   Toward a 'Europe of the Regions'?   55

6   Has the future already arrived?   59

7   Conclusion   61

References   62

Further reading   64

CHAPTER 3   MIGRANTS, REFUGEES AND CITIZENSHIP   65

Zig Layton-Henry

1   Introduction   65

2   The origins of post-war migration   69

3   The responses of Britain, France and Germany   72

4   Strategies for integration   73

5   Case study I: Britain   74

6	Case study II: France	80
7	Case study III: Germany	84
8	The challenge of managing diverse societies	90
9	The impact of the EU	97
10	Conclusion	100
	References	101
	Further reading	102

**CHAPTER 4   SOCIAL MOVEMENTS IN EUROPE:
THE RISE OF ENVIRONMENTAL
GOVERNANCE   103**

Mark J. Smith

1	Introduction	103
2	Social movements as self-organizing networks	104
3	Trade unions as social movements: 'you can't touch me I'm part of the union ...'	111
4	New social movements and the environment	121
5	Toward European eco-corporatism: the new environmental governance	130
6	Conclusion	134
	References	136
	Further reading	138

**CHAPTER 5   THE TRANSFORMATION OF FAMILY
LIFE AND SEXUAL POLITICS   139**

Catherine Lloyd

1	Introduction	139
2	Recent trends in households and family life	141
3	What are the factors influencing these trends?	150
4	What do these changes tell us about governance?	157
5	Conclusion	164
	References	166
	Further reading	168

CHAPTER 6   WHAT UNITES EUROPEANS?   **169**
Josep R. Llobera

1   Introduction   169

2   Measuring European identity: the role of the
    Eurobarometer   173

3   Being in Europe, being European   176

4   The role of European élites in the unification of Europe   180

5   European identity   183

6   High culture and education in the making of Europe   184

7   Toward a European civil society?   188

8   The future of the EU   190

9   Conclusion   192

References   193

Further reading   194

CHAPTER 7   THE MEDIA IN EUROPE   **195**
Denis McQuail

1   Introduction   195

2   General aspects of media structure in Europe   196

3   The regulation of mass media in Europe   203

4   Trends and changes in European media   206

5   Issues of European cultural autonomy and dependency   210

6   National media policy in Europe   213

7   The media policies of the EU   215

8   Media at the European level?   218

9   Media and politics in Europe   220

10 Issues of language   222

11 Europe in the news   223

12 Conclusion   225

References   227

Further reading   228

CHAPTER 8   DRUGS AND EUROPEAN GOVERNANCE   **229**
Eugene McLaughlin and Karim Murji

1   Introduction   229

2   Assessing the state of drug use in Europe   231

3   Drug control and legal diversity within the EU   234

4   Governance from above: the international drug-control
    system   239

5   Governance from above: the European law-enforcement
    complex   242

6   Governance from below   247

7   Conclusion   256

References   257

Further reading   258

CHAPTER 9   CONCLUSION: ONE EUROPE? THE
DEMOCRATIC GOVERNANCE OF A
CONTINENT   **259**
Salvador Giner and Montserrat Guibernau

1   Introduction   259

2   Unity and diversity   261

3   On European citizenship   264

4   Toward a governable Europe?   265

5   Toward a European civil society?   267

6   The tradition of the new   269

7   From conflict to consensus   271

8   A conclusion   273

References   274

Further reading   274

INDEX   **275**

ACKNOWLEDGEMENTS   **292**

Series preface

The three volumes that appear in this series are part of the course *Governing Europe* from the Faculty of Social Sciences at The Open University. The course is, in the main, the product of the Politics Discipline within the Faculty, but it has benefited from the participation of a number of academic colleagues from other areas of the University, notably from the Economics, Sociology, Social Policy and Geography Disciplines and from the Arts Faculty. The interdisciplinary approach fostered by this co-operation carries on a long tradition of courses originating within the Faculty of Social Sciences that have tried to preserve a broadly based academic output across the social sciences. The Open University remains almost unique in its ability to foster and preserve such an approach, despite moves toward stricter discipline lines across the academic world more generally. The three books in this series, while specializing in particular aspects of the issue of governing Europe, maintain an interdisciplinary style throughout. The fact that the books still stand together as a coherent series, and work for the course as a whole, is testament to the ability, enthusiasm, and sheer hard work of my colleagues on the Course Team. I thank them all.

To mention all of the people associated with the project by name would create an impossibly long list, but I must record my special thanks to a number of individuals. First, without the other two editors of the books, Simon Bromley and Montserrat Guibernau, life would have been impossible in the three years that it took to prepare the course. Their role has been central to the successful outcome of the project. With clear and penetrating analytical skills and patient attention to detail, they have accomplished the successive drafting and redrafting of chapters with cheery good humour, even while working under impossibly tight schedules. I would also like to extend very special thanks to the course manager for *Governing Europe*, Eileen Potterton. Seldom has someone so new to the OU grasped the tasks at hand so quickly, so firmly and to such good effect. Her expert managerial skills and unflappable manner have calmed the nerves and smoothed the brows of many a fraught academic. Other key members of the Course Team – Paul Lewis, Richard Heffernan, Mark Smith, Will Brown, Chris Brook and Mark Pittaway – made their own invaluable contribution to the collective discussions that helped frame the books and establish their content. Rob Clifton and Bob Kelly, ably assisted by two OU Associate Lecturers, Brenda Martin and Graham Venters, added the final touches as they constantly reminded us of the primary teaching objectives of these texts. Dianne Cook, Anne Hunt, June Ayres and Fran Ford typed and formatted three drafts of each chapter with their usual good-natured efficiency.

Added to this have been the meticulous editorial skills of Mark Goodwin and Lynne Slocombe, the graphic design skills of Caroline Husher, who designed the striking covers for the books, and Jonathan Hunt and Gill Gowans from the Copublishing Department, who helped to launch the series with Sage. And in this respect I would like to thank Lucy Robinson of Sage, both for her early enthusiasm for the project and for her later support and guidance as the books moved through the production process and into the public domain.

The Open University could not operate as successfully as it does without contributions from academics and others from outside the institution. The *Governing Europe* series has relied upon a wide range of academic input from specialists in European politics and economics from a number of universities in the UK and mainland Europe. This refreshing additional scholarship has only added to the quality of the product. Special mention must also be made of the external assessor of *Governing Europe*, Mike Smith of the University of Loughbrough. As one of the UK's ablest and wisest European Studies academics, his careful and thoughtful assessment of the chapter drafts and his expert advice more generally on matters European have been warmly appreciated.

Finally, two colleagues who have now left The Open University, David Held and Anthony McGrew, were instrumental in getting the course up and running, along with the then Head of the Discipline, Richard Maidment. The fact that I inherited a course structure and a set of book proposals from these colleagues that did not change to any great extent after they had left the project is a testament to the originality and robustness of their early proposals.

Grahame Thompson
Chair, *Governing Europe*
Milton Keynes, August 2000

Book preface

I would like to thank all those who have been involved in the production of this book. In particular, I am grateful to all the contributors for their commitment and good work. I am also grateful to the Course Team, especially to Grahame Thompson. The advice I received from David Held, Richard Maidment and Anthony McGrew when I first joined The Open University and started to work on this project has proved invaluable.

Eileen Potterton, the course manager, has done an excellent job and deserves a very special mention. Mark Goodwin and Gareth Williams have edited the book in a highly professional manner. Anne Hunt, June Ayres, Dianne Cook and Fran Ford have efficiently dealt with successive drafts of each chapter and have been very supportive throughout.

Montserrat Guibernau
Editor, *Governing European Diversity*
Milton Keynes, March 2001

Chapter 1
Introduction: Unity and diversity in Europe

Montserrat Guibernau

1 Introduction

In several respects the European Union (EU) represents both a novel system of quasi-supranational governance and a novel form of political community or polity. But it is also a fragile construction, for it remains a community in the making. It has an ambiguous sense of identity and powerful forces are at work within it. This chapter identifies forces of convergence and divergence, and considers the meaning of governance as applied to the study of European social and cultural diversity.

The main aims of this chapter are as follows.

1 To stress the shifting nature of Europe's geographical frontiers and assess whether cultural frontiers have remained more stable throughout time. In particular, it will examine the origins of the cultural frontiers of Europe and the main criteria that have traditionally been employed in deciding who should be included and excluded from Europe. A different question concerns the requirements for EU membership and the EU's monopoly of the adjective 'European'.

2 To explore contemporary sources of European cultural diversity by examining the main features that unite and divide Europeans in terms of culture and identity at a time when EU politicians have decided on further European integration and enlargement.

3 To examine emerging forms of collective identity in the EU. This will entail assessing whether conflict or consensus defines the relationship between new and traditional identities. It will also involve assessing the impact of the Enlightenment and the Industrial Revolution as potent forces that radically challenged traditional European societies and fostered a profound social, political and economic transformation.

4 To consider the meaning and relevance of novel forms of governance for the study of social and cultural diversity in Europe.

2   The cultural frontiers of Europe: inclusion and exclusion

Europe is a cultural reality that spreads well beyond the boundaries of the EU. In recent times, it has become common practice to identify Europe with the EU. When people refer to 'European integration', 'European citizenship and laws', 'European institutions' or the generation of a 'European identity', they usually employ the term 'European' to refer to the processes of consolidation and integration associated with the EU.

This section explores the meaning of the idea of Europe before the creation of the EU and, in so doing, it seeks to identify some of the cultural attributes shared by those to be defined as the peoples of Europe, some of whom are currently engaged in the consolidation of the EU as a political institution. Sections 3 to 5 are concerned with the study of unity and diversity within the EU, and they also examine the meaning of governance as applied to the analysis of social and cultural diversity in the EU.

2.1   Geographical boundaries

Europe is generally understood to include the western portion of the Eurasian landmass, together with a number of islands not far from the mainland (Iceland, Corsica, Malta, Sardinia, Sicily, Crete and Ireland – as well as Great Britain), but this definition does not provide a clear-cut idea of where Asia stops and Europe begins.

Precisely where the division between Europe and Asia lies is a matter of some debate. To understand Europe as a geographical area involves an awareness of Europe's shifting boundaries. The Greeks thought of a water-bound Europe, whose borders lay on the Black Sea and its northern extension, the Sea of Azov, as far as the banks of the River Don. From the eighteenth century, though, Europe has often been understood to end (or begin) with the Ural Mountains and the river that takes its name from them and flows into the Caspian Sea. But this divide has its ambiguities. With the dissolution of the Soviet Union in 1991, it leaves the Transcaucasus and the newly independent states of Armenia, Azerbaijan and Georgia in an uncertain position with regard to Europe, while Turkey also lies to the west of the Urals.

The geographical boundaries of Europe have suffered dramatic changes over time, and even the recent past offers examples of the shifting character of European borders, including the post-1989 reunification of Germany, the separation of Czechoslovakia, the break-up of Yugoslavia, the independence achieved by the Baltic republics and the dismembering of the Soviet Union.

Further to this, we should consider the claims of countries such as Turkey, Hungary, Poland, Romania, the Czech Republic and the Slovak Republic, to mention but a few, which are currently asserting their European character and demanding the right to be included within the EU. The eventual enlargement of the EU to include, among others, some of the countries I have just mentioned strengthens the idea that the boundaries of Europe are not fixed, and that the boundaries of the EU, which is often identified with 'Europe', are not fixed either. It follows from this that the meaning of Europe and decisions about who is included and who is excluded from Europe tend to change over time. A description of Europe, or any other territory, as 'just a geographical expression' invariably implies a diminished status and the absence of the more elevated claims associated with the embodiment of some general values.

At this point, we could ask about how useful geographical boundaries are in defining Europe. Is Europe a merely geographical space? In the light of the evidence provided above, the answer to this question seems to be a negative one. The geographical boundaries of Europe are fluid, as the maps in Figures 1.1 to 1.4 demonstrate.

But what about history? Is it possible to identify any clear elements of historical continuity that point at a pre-existent idea of Europe? It would be extremely difficult to find any such elements. Confrontation, war and the effort to establish clear differences between peoples dominate the history of Europe.

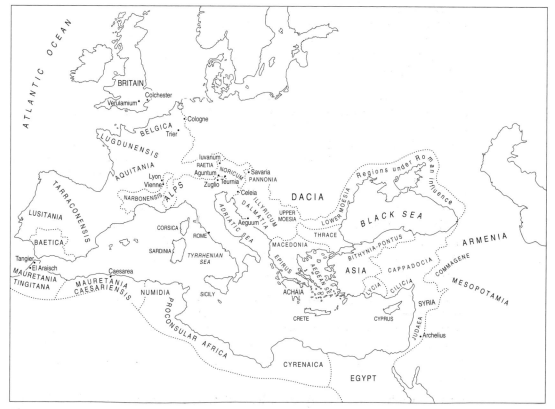

Figure 1.1   Europe at about 54 AD

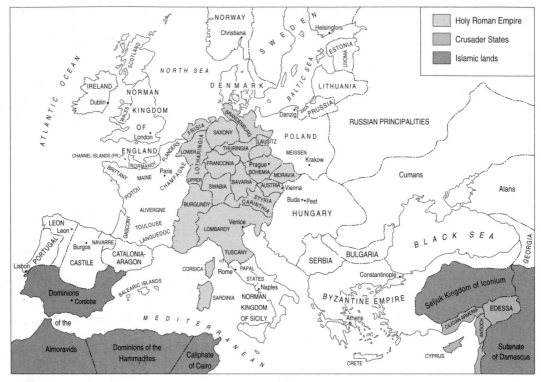

Figure 1.2   Europe at about 1140 AD

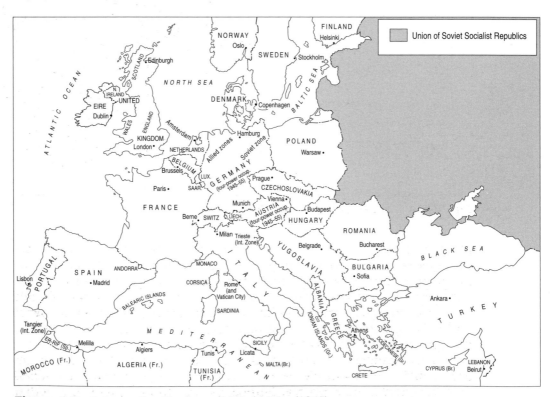

Figure 1.3   Europe after the Second World War (1945)

Figure 1.4   Contemporary Europe (2001)

All of this might lead us to conclude that geography and history are insufficient criteria in deciding who should and who should not be included in Europe. What other criteria might be applied to shed some light onto such a controversial matter? In seeking to respond to this question, many scholars and politicians have turned to the idea that what unites Europeans is the sharing of a certain culture and values, which differentiate them from other peoples, especially from the peoples of the East. This argument is based on the assumption that 'there has always been a different way of life between East and West, between the full and half European ... between real Europeans, and those caught in a nether world between the European and Asian' (Burgess, 1997, p.67). Perhaps

Europe can be defined as a system of values, with Christianity and the rise of a set of ideas, including freedom, humanism and material progress, as the key elements in the construction of an incipient European identity.

The 'idea of Europe' did not begin by reference to geographical or historical divisions. Instead, it emerged as a term connected to a specific cultural and political heritage embodied in Athenian democracy. It was not until the nineteenth century that George Grote, a radical banker and historian, located the origin of European civilization in Greek democracy, rather than in the establishment of Christianity towards the end of the Roman Empire.

But if the idea of Europe has a cultural basis connected to Athenian democracy and some common traditions and a common consciousness, is it possible to refer to the 'cultural frontiers' of Europe? What are the main criteria in deciding where to draw the line? Furthermore, if we were to agree on the existence of a certain European culture, no matter how incipient this might be, would this be sufficient to account for the existence of some incipient European identity?

2.2   Culture

Culture is formed by values, beliefs, customs, conventions, habits and practices, which give rise to a particular identity that unites those who have been socialized within a particular society (Guibernau, 1996, p.75). From a symbolic perspective, 'culture is the pattern of meanings embodied in symbolic forms, including actions, utterances and meaningful objects of various kinds, by virtue of which individuals communicate with one another and share their experiences, conceptions and beliefs' (Thompson, 1990, p.132). The process of identification with the elements of a specific culture implies a strong emotional investment. Individuals are born within cultures that determine the way in which they view and organize themselves in relation to others and to nature.

This has two major implications for an analysis of whether we can refer to a distinctive European identity based upon a shared culture. First, a common culture favours the creation of solidarity bonds among the members of a given community and allows them to imagine the community they belong to as separate and distinct from others. Solidarity is then based upon the consciousness of forming a group, outsiders being seen as strangers and potential 'enemies'. Second, a common historical past, which includes memories of war, deprivation, victory, repression and success, and a common project for the future reinforce the sense of a shared identity among members of a given community. There is a strong connection between history and culture, since crucial elements in the culture of any given community, such as symbols, language, sacred places, heroes, anthems, legends and traditions, are inextricably bound up with the community's history.

In the light of this, we should ask whether there are some key cultural elements that have united Europeans from an immemorial past and distinguished them from 'others'. Is there a sense of solidarity among Europeans that goes back to medieval times? Where are the symbols, holy places, heroes, and traditions that unite Europeans? What are Europe's shared values? In a nutshell, what are the criteria for establishing the cultural frontiers of Europe?

At present, there is a substantial body of literature that examines the historical origins of contemporary Europe and argues that some common 'traditions' and a somehow unspecified sense of a common 'conscious-ness' have united the peoples of Europe since the Middle Ages. In so doing, it seeks to highlight European unity over the diversity which has traditionally characterized European peoples. The search for a common past and common traditions responds to the need to find or invent some elements that could prove useful in the construction of a shared sense of European identity – an identity that, ideally, should go hand-in-hand with greater EU integration. In spite of considerable efforts to define the elements that may account for some unspecified and still incipient European identity, it is still quite difficult to determine the content of these 'shared' traditions and values, particularly as the history of European peoples is fraught with memories of war. The status of Europe as a cultural unit and a system of values at the dawn of the twenty-first century remains problematic. There is a clear contrast between Europe's developing institutional structures and more intensive processes of governance (at least as far as the EU is concerned) and the relative weakness and uncertainty of the values that underpin the EU. We shall come back to this theme later on in this chapter and discuss it at length in Chapter 9.

In what follows I shall begin by examining whether religion might act as an inclusion/exclusion mechanism in deciding who belongs to Europe, and continue by assessing the impact of secular elements in the construction of an incipient cultural frontier of Europe. In particular, I shall analyse the influence of the Enlightenment and the Industrial Revolution in setting up the basis for the contemporary idea of Europe, which culminated in the creation of the EU. Let's begin by assessing whether Christianity might be used as the chief criterion in defining who might be included in Europe.

2.3 Religion as an inclusion/exclusion mechanism

Samuel Huntington, in his most celebrated book *The Clash of Civilizations and the Remaking of World Order* (1996), argued that religion provides the best common means of historically distinguishing between Europeans and the rest, especially in terms of the confrontation between the Judeo-Christian tradition and Islam. This argument, however, seems to ignore the fact that, in the Middle Ages, most intra-European wars had a religious character. Of course, it could be argued that such wars did not imply the existence of different civilizations within Europe, rather they consisted of wars between countries that defended different and revised 'versions' of a religion with a unique origin. It is precisely from this perspective that it seems plausible to point at religion as a key feature in constructing what we now term an embryonic European identity. Following this line of argument, Anthony Smith stresses that 'there is a clear sense, going back at least to the Crusades and probably even to Charles Martel, in which Europeans see themselves as not Muslims or as not Jews' (quoted in Burgess, 1997, p.67). Should we then conclude that European culture is based upon Christianity, and that the cultural boundaries of Europe are determined by religion? This raises two main issues.

First, is the appeal to a shared religion a recent invention? Were Charles the Great and the crusaders convinced that the religious divide between those who believed in the Christian God and those who did not was to reflect a further division between Europeans and the rest? Would they have defined themselves as Europeans? Probably not. In addition, early Europe as Christendom already contained significant religious minorities (Jews and Muslims) – and it barely included the rural masses, whose peasant status was closely linked with a 'pagan' (and thus non-Christian) outlook that presented a constant challenge to the consolidation of any regional Christian realm.

Second, if we were to assume that religion, and Christianity in particular, is the key criterion for inclusion in Europe, what do we make of the religious wars fought between European countries since the Middle Ages? Reflecting on these issues, Adam Burgess argues that:

> ... it is only with the Ottoman challenge, coupled with the social and religious crises of the fourteenth and fifteenth centuries, that Europe became the Christian continent, and therefore distinct limits were drawn. ... Significantly, however, this unity was more apparent than real. Christian Europe was moving into the schisms of those centuries, and the heresies of the sixteenth.
>
> (Burgess, 1997, p.69)

A further point concerns the extent to which religion operates as an inclusion/exclusion mechanism in contemporary Europe. This raises some interesting questions. For instance, if religion were to be considered as the key criterion in determining a particular country's European character, could it be argued that Turkey's entry into the EU is being delayed because of its Muslim allegiance? This argument has never been employed by the EU in considering Turkey's application, and religion has not been raised as a condition for EU membership in EU documents. This undermines the validity of religion as the most important inclusion/ exclusion mechanism with respect to the EU and reinforces the idea that contemporary Europe is not based upon a religious divide arising from a pre-modern religious outlook. Yet this is not to deny that religions play a significant part in the cultural make-up of their followers or that most of the elements of Europe's secular culture have, at some point, developed in opposition, debate, confrontation or dialogue with prevailing religions in different European countries.

2.4 Europe's secular culture: the impact of the Enlightenment and the Industrial Revolution

But if religion is not an appropriate criterion in defining Europe, are there any alternative secular traditions that might be relevant in deciding where to draw the cultural boundaries of Europe? Machiavelli's work offers an incipient notion of Europe based upon secular principles, but the idea of Europe did not acquire real meaning until the age of the Enlightenment in the eighteenth century. Enlightenment humanism emerged in France and involved establishing a distinction between those parts of the world engaged in the pursuit of the ideals of rationality and progress, which lie at the heart of the Enlightenment, and those enmeshed in pre-rational practices and beliefs.

During the Enlightenment, a consciously European identity came to the fore. This 'European' consciousness retained a Christian outlook but was associated with other values, particularly those of the civilization under-stood to be embodied in a rapidly developing Europe. This in turn evoked principles of freedom, humanism and the growing ideas of material progress. According to den Boer, it was not until the nineteenth century, and after the break with tradition prompted by the revolutionary years, that the concept of Europe was historicized and politicized.

> At the beginning of the nineteenth century the idea of Europe was projected back much further in history. A search was instigated for the roots of European civilization. Europe, which in the Middle Ages had in fact hardly existed as a geographical expression, became an accepted historical category. The historical writings of the nineteenth century romantics made it appear that in the Middle Ages there had been a conscious idea of Europe. The notion gained ground that out of the ruins of the Roman empire (the Latin element), the Barbarian peoples (the Germanic element), led by the Christian church, had been amalgamated to form the true European civilization.
>
> (den Boer, 1995, p.70)

The ideas embodied in the Enlightenment took a specific political form in the democratic explosion of the French Revolution. Napoleon's dissemi-nation of revolutionary ideas throughout the European mainland contributed further to the radical transformation of European societies by prompting a series of dramatic changes that would progressively affect the peoples of Europe. These transformations challenged the so-called

ancien régime and contributed to the emergence of an incipient convergence among those belonging to the different European cultural, political
and economic élites, which emphasized the wide gap separating the mass
of the population from these élites. The transformations involved the
following processes.

- The decline of the aristocracy and the advent of the bourgeoisie, which
  was to turn into the leading component of élites throughout Europe.

- The separation of state and church, which in turn was to initiate a
  process characterized by the weakening of mass allegiance to traditional religions and the rise of secular values grounded upon
  humanist principles.

- The rise and consolidation of the nation state as the main political
  institution, with its power rooted in popular consent and its aim the
  cultural homogenization of its citizens. This framework made possible
  the rise of modern nationalism, a device that proved to be exceedingly
  useful for refocusing a people's loyalty away from the monarch. The
  nation, personified through symbols and rituals that symbolically
  recreate a sense of 'people', became the focus of a new kind of
  attachment.

- The emergence of the concept of citizenship as a mechanism for
  translating ideas of popular sovereignty into universal adult suffrage.
  Citizenship had to be struggled for and, although ideally embracing all
  inhabitants of a given nation state, in most European countries
  enfranchisement was limited to male citizens owning a certain amount
  of property. In 1830, France had a population of some 30 million, but
  an electorate of a mere 90,000. Religion could also disenfranchise
  inhabitants, particularly in the case of Catholics in Protestant states, or
  Jews. In Britain, Catholics had to wait until 1829 for the right to vote,
  and Jews had to wait until 1858. Full enfranchisement often did not
  take place until well into the twentieth century. For instance, in most
  European nation states universal suffrage was achieved after the First
  World War. And women usually acquired democratic rights some time
  after men, and not until 1971 in Switzerland.

- A great emphasis on the importance of universal education, reflected
  in most nation states' decision to create national education systems
  capable of ensuring the cultural and linguistic homogenization of an
  otherwise diverse population. Further to this, education should teach
  the population how to become good citizens, loyal to the nation state.

Recent literature suggests that the Enlightenment opened a fracture
between the 'civilized' West and the 'uncivilized' or 'barbarian' East. It
would be misleading, however, to ignore the fact that the empires of
Central and Eastern Europe were also affected by the Enlightenment, a
feature which once more stresses the difficulty of drawing a clear-cut
cultural boundary around Europe.

Enlightenment ideas triggered dramatic socio-political transformations in
European societies, but they also prompted the adoption of rationality as
a method and progress as an objective. It is in this sense that a connection

between the Enlightenment and the Industrial Revolution can be established. Rationality involved the end of alchemy and magical arguments and fostered a scientific revolution, which culminated in the Industrial Revolution. Both the Enlightenment and the Industrial Revolution challenged traditional social, political and economic patterns and prompted profound transformations in European societies.

The Industrial Revolution originated in England and Scotland in the mid-eighteenth century and expanded to the continent. By 1850, more people in England were working in industry than in agriculture, a situation that would be matched in southern Europe, including France, only a century later (Crouch, 1999, p.20). The social and economic development prompted by the Industrial Revolution transformed the West and established a radical division between industrializing countries and those primarily based around rural economies, as was the case in most of Central and Eastern Europe, but also in Greece, Portugal, most of Spain (excluding Catalonia and the Basque Country) and Italy.

> With European development, especially through the nineteenth century, the Ottoman Empire, a part of which later came to constitute the border of 'the East' of today, became not only 'the sick man of Europe' in Western eyes, but the embodiment of torpor and decay. The change here was not so much in the Ottoman Empire. Certainly it had stagnated, but it was hardly unrecognizable. Rather, the change was relative to the newfound dynamism of the West.
>
> It was the vantage point of the great powers that had really been transformed. They now looked down on those who had failed to reproduce their own astonishing rate of progress and innovation.
>
> (Burgess, 1997, p.91)

Industrialism presumes the use of inanimate sources of material power in production or in processes affecting the circulation of commodities. It involves the mechanization of production and other economic processes, and assumes the prevalence of manufacturing production understood as the manner of production rather than simply the creation of goods as such. The advent of industrialism transformed national landscapes. It created large factories, prompted rural migration to urban centres, reshaped and enlarged cities, greatly improved transport and communications, developed the media, especially in terms of the proliferation of newspapers and magazines, and resulted in a huge range of mass-produced goods.

Industrialism signalled a turning point in European societies by causing massive social change. It was based on the division of labour and the separation of home and the workplace. In many instances, industrialism was associated with the spread of capitalism, but a fundamental difference between the two should be established. Industrialism is based on the mechanization of mass-produced goods, but remains 'neutral' in respect of wider institutional alignments; capitalism is a type of production system dominant in a given society that presupposes an alignment of the 'economic' and the 'political' through private property and the commodification of wage-labour (Giddens, 1985, p.140). Only when the conjunction between capitalism and industrialism is well advanced does it become plausible to speak of the existence of 'capitalist societies', and it is precisely the constitution of such capitalist societies that could be taken as a point of reference in distinguishing between European societies and those that remained outside the industrialized world.

To sum up, after the Enlightenment competing versions of Europe emerged: liberal and conservative, for or against revolution, constitutional or absolutist forms of government. The process of incipient European convergence initiated by the Enlightenment was greatly enhanced by the almost simultaneous emergence and spread of the Industrial Revolution. From that moment onwards European societies began to share certain features that would accentuate the differences between them and the societies 'toward the East' that remained untouched by industrialism.

In spite of this, it is not until the twentieth century, after the devastating effects of two world wars, that we can locate the emergence of a coherently defined idea of Europe, an idea that has served to inspire the EU. In this process, the division of Europe into two halves during the Cold War contributed dramatically to redefining its cultural boundaries. In most cases, the contemporary criteria for inclusion and exclusion are connected to the roles played by countries during and after the Second World War, and even more crucially to the positions they held within or without the area of Soviet influence.

> Inclusion or exclusion on the basis of historical traditions is therefore an essentially arbitrary process. These 'traditions' are very recent ... Any attempt to define who merits inclusion and exclusion from Europe only highlights the impossibility of doing so. To attempt the appropriation of human achievement for the cause of 'Europe' might boost authority, but it does not stand up to scrutiny – particularly at a time when there is such anxiety about all forms of identity. We are left with essentially arbitrary cultural exclusion.
>
> (Burgess, 1997, p.73)

So far we have pointed to the dramatic transformations brought about by the spread of Enlightenment ideas and the socio-economic impact of the Industrial Revolution, and of the scientific revolution that made it possible, as crucial elements in the generation of an evolving sense of cultural distinctiveness among European peoples. We have also stressed the fact that the idea of a common cultural frontier of Europe is a relatively recent phenomenon, rooted in the twentieth-century experience of two world wars, the division of Europe into two halves by the

Cold War and the creation of a series of European institutions and organizations designed to avoid military confrontation and seek economic development. After the development of the European Economic Community, growing pressure emerged at an élite level to further European integration, and this movement culminated in the replacement of the label 'European Economic Community' with the label 'European Union'.

At a time when the EU is moving toward further political and economic integration, we are confronted with the question of whether Europe is becoming more united in cultural and social terms or whether greater divisions are emerging. At present, some commentators are arguing that any new Europe has to be imagined afresh and constructed as a conscious plan of action, rather than deduced from existing values. There are, undoubtedly, a number of different 'projects for Europe'. Again, Europe is often conflated with the EU, and although some non-EU countries claim their European credentials, the EU seems to monopolize the idea of Europe as a project, albeit one that remains largely undefined.

The aim of the next two sections is to explore contemporary sources of European cultural and social diversity by examining the main features that divide and unite Europeans at the dawn of a new millennium. Section 3 explores differences in religion, wealth, social class, welfare provision, culture, gender, family life and national and ethnic diversity. Section 4 focuses on those elements that signal the rise of a common European culture, which could eventually lead to the emergence of a shared European identity. The elements considered include memories of two world wars, the legacy of the Cold War, the emergence of a common European political culture, the rise of new social movements and the progressive cultural homogenization of Europe under the influence of the USA.

Summary

- The geographical boundaries of Europe have undergone dramatic changes over time.

- Geography and history seem to be insufficient criteria in deciding who should and who should not be included in Europe. Instead, the 'idea of Europe' emerged, as a term connected to a specific cultural and political heritage embodied in Athenian democracy.

- It has been argued that religion provides the best means of historically distinguishing between Europeans and the rest, but this assertion ignores Europe's internal religious differences and the fact that, for centuries, most intra-European wars have had a religious character.

- The emergence of an incipient cultural frontier for Europe may be found in two secular events that challenged tradition and instigated dramatic transformations in Europe's socio-political and economic make-up: the Enlightenment and the Industrial Revolution.

● It is not until the twentieth century, after two world wars and the division of Europe by the Cold War, that we can identify the emergence of the coherently defined idea of Europe that has served to inspire the EU.

3   What divides Europeans?

3.1   Religion

European societies have traditionally had a restricted range of religious and ethnic diversity, which has often resulted in one or two dominant, established Christian churches. At present, religion seems to be in decline, although at different speeds, throughout Western Europe, perhaps with the exception of Belgium and Ireland. This contrasts with church membership and participation in the USA and other parts of the world, where religion plays a key role in the day-to-day life of citizens and has a strong influence over politics. It could be argued that Europe's secularization became one of the defining features of the continent in the twentieth century. Even traditionally Catholic Ireland provided some evidence of religious decline, as exemplified in recent constitutional changes allowing divorce and birth control.

In spite of the decline in the authority of religion over people's lives, it is important to note that, traditionally, religion has been a major source of conflict between European countries. The separation of Eastern Orthodox Christianity and West European Christianity has, for a long time, been crucial in establishing a division between Western and Eastern Europe, a division that was partially reinforced by the Cold War. Further divisions within Western Christianity between Catholicism and Protestantism have determined, to a certain extent, the separation between North and South, although France and Germany are significant exceptions to this divide. France is traditionally Catholic, but the Catholic church has been excluded from public life for much of the past two centuries, and the country has witnessed the rise of Protestantism as a private religion. In contrast, Germany, which is predominantly Protestant in its origins, drifted toward Catholicism during the first four decades of the West German republic after the Second World War (Crouch, 1999, p.397). The Catholic character of Ireland and Belgium and the divided religious structures of the Netherlands and Switzerland also further the North–South divide.

Another aspect of religion is its influence in shaping European political parties, such as the Christian Democrat parties, which once created seek to appeal to large sectors of the population beyond those who identify with the religious allegiance.

3.2 Socio-economic diversity

The traditional division of Europe into a wealthy and industrialized North, including Britain, Germany, Belgium, the Netherlands and France, and a poor and underdeveloped South, including Portugal, Spain, Greece and Italy, has been challenged in recent years. Italy has become one of the richest countries in the world and a member of the G8, while Spain and Portugal have registered a faster growth in income since joining the EU. These countries share an agricultural basis and are heavily subsidized by the Common Agricultural Policy (CAP). In spite of this, their farming populations are rapidly declining as individuals seek employment in urban areas, where a dramatic and necessary modernization of the industrial landscape has generated high rates of unemployment. Ireland, a poor country with an economy traditionally based on agriculture, has also benefited enormously from EU membership. In recent years, it has managed to transform its economic base and has turned into one of the most economically dynamic European countries.

Mediterranean countries have paternalistic and poor welfare-state models rooted in the dictatorships that Spain, Greece and Portugal had to endure until the 1970s, when they initiated their individual transitions to democracy. A common feature of these countries is a steadily rising level of investment in their welfare systems since the early 1980s, when they prepared for accession into the EU.

In contrast, Scandinavian countries are characterized by strong economies dependent on world markets and universalist welfare-state systems, which share some features with British welfare-state models. The Scandinavian model guarantees minimum security and status maintenance. The German model is also based on status maintenance and assumes employment-related coverage and benefits, which include an old-age pension, disability pension, sick pay, unemployment benefits and health services (**Grahl, 2001**).

To address socio-economic inequalities, Western European countries have developed different welfare models. Crouch establishes a contrast between European countries showing a preference for welfare at the cost of high unemployment (resulting from the high indirect labour costs needed to pay for welfare and labour-market regulation as well as reduced work incentives) and the US preference for high employment levels at the expense of limited welfare provision (Crouch, 1999, p.399). This is a pattern that has been reversed in recent years. Thus, at present most European countries seem to have altered their egalitarian preferences under the influence of the US model; for instance, Scandinavia has witnessed significant changes in what used to be one of the most generous welfare systems in Europe. Hence a common trend in Western European countries is growing intra-state inequality and poverty resulting in sharper class divisions.

Differences in wealth are generally connected with different degrees of industrialization, which in turn produce different patterns of employment. Thus only some Southern European countries (Greece, Spain) and

Ireland have more than 5 per cent of their population working in agriculture and mining, while Belgium and Britain employ less than 2 per cent of their population in this sector.

3.3   Culture and social class

A feature that has historically characterized most Western European countries is the division of culture along social class lines. In this sense, class boundaries have tended to coincide with cultural boundaries and form the basis for the distinction between 'élite' or 'high' culture and 'popular' or 'low' culture. The sharp class divisions typical of the industrial period crystallized into well-organized trade unions and political parties representing the working class.

The advent of post-industrialism, or what some authors have defined as 'advanced societies', and the emergence of the middle classes have broken traditional class boundaries and have tended to replace a clearly defined 'working-class' culture with a standardized 'popular' culture, which is predominantly of US origin and is transmitted through the means of mass communication.

The major trends that unite Europeans beyond these class and wealth divisions are as follows.

- The range of goods available to the working class now compared with the range in other historical periods, especially compared with the situation in early twentieth-century Europe.
- The weakening of the working class and the predominance of a highly diversified middle class in all European countries.
- The concentration of the European population in cities. A network of cities, which have become financial, political, cultural and artistic centres, characterizes much of Europe.

3.4   Gender and family life

Major changes in traditional gender and family structures have transformed the day-to-day life of Europeans since the Second Word War. The most important of these changes is the political and social emancipation of women, involving enfranchisement, access to the labour market and the possibility of separating sexual activity from reproduction through birth control techniques.

The percentage of women in paid work varies in different countries. Northern countries have a higher percentage of women in the labour market than Southern countries, where strong family ties and weak welfare systems have traditionally resulted in women staying at home to look after children, the old and the sick. But at present the rise in the numbers of women who have access to higher education and expect to go into work is challenging these patterns.

When considering birth rates, it is quite striking to compare the high birth rates registered in Northern Europe, predominantly Lutheran with weak family links and strong welfare systems, with the low birth rates in countries such as Spain and Italy, Catholic countries with weak welfare systems and strong family ties. Differences in divorce rates also seem to follow the North–South divide. Northern Protestant countries, Britain and the Nordic countries in particular, record higher divorce rates than Southern Catholic countries such as Italy and Spain. France, Germany and the Netherlands are somewhere in between.

The number of births outside marriage is also higher in Northern Europe than in the South. In the North there is a significant difference between the Nordic countries and Britain. In the former, children tend to be born to mothers over 30 years old in settled partnerships; in Britain, children are more likely to be born to single mothers under 20 years old.

3.5 National and ethnic diversity

National and ethnic minorities are key components of the European socio-cultural landscape. Most so-called nation states are not constituted by a single nation that is coextensive with the state: internal diversity is the rule. 'Nations without states' are nations that, in spite of having their territories included within the boundaries of one or more states, by and large do not identify with those states. The members of a stateless nation maintain a separate sense of national identity, generally based upon a common culture and history, attachment to a particular territory and the explicit wish to rule themselves (Guibernau, 1999).

The nations or parts of nations included within a single state do not always share similar levels of national awareness. What is more, while some define themselves as nations, retain strong memories of a time when they were independent political units and share a common identity, as is the case with Scotland, Catalonia, Flanders and the Basque Country, others have a rather weak sense of identity and are content to be referred to as regions, as is the case in Brittany, Occitanie and Cornwall. It is important to note that the term 'region' as employed by the EU does not establish a distinction between geographical regions, economic regions, regions with a feeble or absent cultural specificity and regions endowed with a strong sense of identity and cultural distinctiveness.

Most national minorities have organized themselves and created social movements and political parties to defend their cultural specificity and their right to self-determination. This self-determination is sometimes understood to mean political autonomy, although in other cases it stops short of independence and involves only the right to secede. There are also crucial differences between national minorities, such as the Catalans or the Scots, which have opted for peaceful means in their claim for socio-political recognition, and other minorities which have turned to violence, as is the case in the Basque Country, Corsica and Northern Ireland. I should emphasize that most stateless nations are not homogeneous and contain different ethnic minorities, which may or may not identify with the nationalist claims put forward by the different social movements and political parties that claim to represent them. In some cases these minorities are marginalized, but in others they are encouraged to participate in the political life of the community.

Ethnic minorities, I argue, are primarily formed by people of migrant origin who, in some cases, have been living in the host country for several generations. Ethnic minorities also include migrants who have recently moved to the host country, as well as refugees and asylum seekers. In the light of this, it could be argued that Britain's national minorities are formed by the Scots, Welsh and Irish, while Britain's largest ethnic minorities include people of Asian and Caribbean origin, most of whom hold British passports and were born in the UK. British ethnic minorities also include migrants from other Commonwealth countries, the EU and Eastern Europe.

Between 1950 and 1975, economic prosperity brought large numbers of migrants from Southern European countries such as Spain, Italy and Portugal to Northern European countries such as Germany, the Netherlands and France. To supplement the labour force, large numbers of migrants from outside Europe were also attracted to work in the most dynamic European economies. Caribbeans and Indians flowed into Britain, Algerians into France, Turks and Italians into Germany, and Surinamese and Moluccans to the Netherlands. The recession that followed the economic boom of the 1950s and 1960s was replaced by a deep depression, which started in the mid-1970s and considerably worsened the situation of these immigrants.

In the late 1990s, the largest immigrant communities in the EU were to be found in Germany, France and the UK, although rising numbers of migrants from Africa were flowing into Italy, Portugal and Spain. Since 1989, the disintegration of the Soviet Union and political and economic instability in Asia, Africa and the Middle East have resulted in large numbers of migrants into the EU. Immigrants increase cultural diversity within the EU and have often been subject to social exclusion in the labour market, education, access to housing and the fundamental rights of citizenship.

The nation state's cultural diversity, which is grounded on the co-existence of various national and ethnic minorities with distinct identities and cultures, is further challenged by the presence of illegal migrants, refugees and asylum seekers. The rising cultural diversity within the EU has resulted in a number of opposing reactions. Some extreme right-wing movements defend the 'purity' of the nation and stand against immigrants, but other movements defend multiculturalism as a mechanism that could facilitate the co-existence of culturally different communities within a shared territory.

Summary

- The separation between Eastern Orthodox Christianity and Western variations of Christianity has, for a long time, been crucial in establishing a division between Western and Eastern Europe, a division that was partially reinforced by the Cold War. Divisions between Catholicism and Protestantism have, to a certain extent, determined the separation between North and South, although France and Germany represent exceptions to this rule. At present, the decline in church attendance is a significant characteristic, and one that seems to be constant in most European countries.

- The traditional division of Europe into a wealthy and industrialized North, including Britain, Germany, Belgium, the Netherlands and France, and a poor and underdeveloped South, including Portugal, Spain, Greece and Italy, has been partially challenged in recent years. Italy has become one of the richest countries in the world and a member of the G8, while Spain and Portugal have registered a fast growth in income since joining the EU in the 1980s. Varying degrees of industrialization and wealth have resulted in the adoption of strong welfare systems in Northern European countries, which contrast with the weak and paternalistic welfare models in the South.

- In Western Europe, class boundaries have tended to coincide with cultural boundaries and formed the basis for the distinction between 'élite' or 'high' culture and 'popular' or 'low' culture.

- The emancipation of women is probably the most important social revolution in Europe since 1945. It was led by women in Northern countries and has progressively extended into Southern Europe. Higher numbers of women in work, divorce rates and birth rates outside marriage differentiate Northern from Southern European countries.

- National and ethnic minorities challenge the notion of the nation state from a cultural as well as a political perspective. The rise of regional nationalism and the growing numbers of migrants, refugees and asylum seekers entering the EU hold the potential to substantially transform the cultural map of Europe.

4   What unites Europeans?

So far, we have considered some of the main features that account for diversity among European peoples. Now I shall focus on the features that unite Europeans in terms of culture. In so doing I shall explore what might become the foundations of a future European identity, an identity that is closely connected to the idea of furthering European integration and strengthening the EU. Five main characteristics have united Europeans and distinguished them from other peoples:

- specific memories of two devastating world wars and the experience of the Cold War, which fixed European borders for over 40 years

- the end of colonial empires after the Second World War
- the rise of a specific European political culture
- the emergence of new social movements, which reflect new concerns
- the progressive cultural homogenization of Europe under the influence of the USA.

Castellers (human towers) in Vilanova i la Geltrú (Barcelona)

4.1   Memories of war and the legacy of the Cold War

European countries were deeply affected by the two world wars. In particular, the Second World War and its legacy, the division of Europe into two different areas of influence, capitalist and communist, generated a sense of unity among those Europeans living in countries to the west of the Berlin Wall. Even countries that were not directly involved in the Second World War, such as Spain, could participate to a certain extent in this division of Europe between West and East. The division was primarily defined by Western connections with the USA and the capitalist model, and the Eastern association with the Soviet Union and the communist model.

During the Second World War, the political systems of Western Europe were largely destroyed. Over 30 million people were killed in battle or in atrocities against civilians, and the economies of the countries involved suffered tremendous losses. The war was the catalyst for a new surge of interest in European unity, which led to negative assessments of the pre-war political situation and economic practices.

The USA emerged from the war as the strongest military and economic power. Its involvement in Western Europe became crucial in the political, economic and military recovery of an area that had been devastated by two world wars.

The so-called Truman Doctrine outlined by President Harry Truman in March 1947 and the American announcement of the Marshall Plan later the same year were critical in the shaping of Western European economies and political systems. The Truman Doctrine stressed the USA's determination to defend democracy, resist the advance of communism and guarantee American security. It represented the pledge of a firm political relationship between the USA and Western Europe and provided strong support for the evolution of Western democracies. The Marshall Plan offered economic aid to all European states, although the Soviet Union rejected the offer (**Thompson, 2001**). The Marshall Plan was economically as well as politically motivated, and was a necessary part of President Truman's expressed intention to organize Western Europe into an ideological alliance against the Soviet Union and communism (Urwin, 1993, p.18).

The USA's relationship with Western Europe was enhanced by the creation of the Atlantic Pact in April 1949. The USA and Canada entered into a military arrangement for the collective defence of Western Europe with Belgium, Britain, Denmark, France, Italy, Iceland, Luxembourg, the Netherlands, Norway and Portugal. During the early 1950s, the founder members were joined by Greece, Turkey and the new state of West Germany to give rise to the North Atlantic Treaty Organization (NATO).

The Cold War consolidated a firm relationship between the USA and Western Europe, and this relationship had a large impact upon the political, social, economic and military restructuring of Western Europe.

It impinged upon government systems, party structures and political and social élites, and contributed to the Americanization of industry in Western Europe.

The Cold War contributed to some sense of unity among the peoples of Western Europe. But what about Eastern Europe? Did the experience of two world wars and the Cold War foster a sense of unity in those post-communist Eastern countries that are currently applying for EU membership? What arguments might account for a future unity between the peoples of Western and Eastern Europe? Most Central and Eastern European countries argue that they were integrated by force into the Eastern Bloc, which was dominated by the USSR, and that the end of communism provided an opportunity for them to return to where they belonged: 'Europe'. And by 'Europe', they mean the Europe that, since the end of the Second World War, has managed to create a common and prosperous economic space and generate a supranational political institution: the EU.

The attachment to liberal-democratic political systems is a feature that has come to unite Europeans, and it is one of the most distinctive aspects of the EU. From this perspective, what unites Eastern and Western Europe is shared experiences of the suffering and divisions caused by war and, above all else, the desire for the prosperity and progress embodied by the EU. There is a real possibility that conflicts of interests, life-styles, political ideas and economic models, which dominated the relationship between Eastern and Western Europe during the Cold War, may be superseded by consensus.

The end of the Cold War, which was marked by the collapse of the Soviet Union between 1989 and 1991, prompted significant changes in both Western and Eastern Europe. In the West, it fostered the transformation of socialist and communist parties and opened up the search for new political ideologies that could thrive in a world characterized by global capitalism and the absence of communism. It also gave renewed strength to the idea of greater EU political integration, with Germany as the leading power. In addition, the fall of the Berlin wall triggered a process of further EU enlargement to include countries in Eastern and Central Europe.

In the East, the end of the Cold War resulted in some former Soviet republics regaining their independence, the reunification of Germany and the search for new political ideologies, party systems and government structures to replace communism. But it has also brought capitalism and the social dislocations associated with it, and ignited ethnic conflict and confrontation in Georgia, Chechnya and the former Yugoslavia.

4.2 The end of the 'European Empire'

From the fifteenth century onward, Europeans began to explore previously uncharted seas and landmasses. They conquered and subdued native populations through superior military strength, and sought to exploit their new territories by establishing colonies. Many European states, including Belgium, France, the Netherlands, Portugal, Spain and Britain, built empires by acquiring territories outside Western Europe.

For most of the period of European expansion, the colonists saw themselves as the agents of civilization. They exported Western political ideas, cultures, manners, languages and religions, while establishing a power relation between the metropolis and the colonies that was fraught with inequality and discrimination. The early period of colonialism coincided with the rise of racism, and since then racism has almost invariably permeated many of the relations between the colonizers and those they, and their descendants, considered to be 'non-white'. To give a potent and relatively recent example, the slave trade was abolished in the British Empire in 1807, but as late as 1925 the Special Restrictions (Coloured Alien Seamen) Order prohibited black British sailors from working on British ships and forced some black sailors out of the country.

The process of dismantling the 'European Empire' accelerated after the end of the Second World War. Most former colonies had turned into independent nation states by the 1960s, although a notorious exception was Portugal's African colonies, which were not granted independence until the 1970s. During the First World War, some European states promised concessions to their colonies in return for help against their enemies. As the war drew to a close, events were to influence the development of national liberation movements in these colonies. Lenin, who led the Bolshevik Revolution in Russia in November 1917, launched an anti-imperialist propaganda campaign. And in 1918 many of the colonies called for the right to self-determination in response to the human and material effort that had been demanded from them during the war. Woodrow Wilson, then President of the USA, issued the 'Fourteen Points' defending the right of peoples to self-determination, principles that were applicable to the colonies as much as to anywhere else.

The European powers reacted in different ways to the decolonization process. Britain granted independence to most of its former colonies in response to the claims of strong national liberation movements and sought to maintain some special relationship with them through the creation of the Commonwealth. French colonies had to fight for independence. Only military defeat, as in Indochina, and guerrilla warfare, as in Algeria, forced France to abandon its colonial possessions.

The end of the 'European Empire' signaled a turning point in European politics and economics. It had a tremendous effect on the nation states, which passed from the power, prestige and economic privilege associated with the status of colonial powers to a period in which they found themselves struggling to feed their own populations. Instead of looking toward their former Asian and African possessions, they decided to concentrate on building some institutional agreements designed to prevent another war and to contribute to Europe's economic recovery. The seeds of the EU are to be found in the thoughts and deeds of the political leaders and intellectuals committed to the reconstruction of Europe. That particular generation was the first to dream about a united

Europe, although in the years after the Second World War it would have excluded the Central and Eastern Europe countries within the Soviet Bloc.

4.3 European political culture

The roots of European political culture may be found in the secular ideas disseminated by the Enlightenment. These ideas contributed to the foundation and development of the nation state as a political institution. They involved the acceptance of parliamentary democracy as a form of government, the separation of state and church, the desire for progress and the creation of the concept of citizenship, with all the rights and duties associated with it.

These principles are reflected in the Maastricht Treaty (1992), which marked a new stage in the process of European integration undertaken with the establishment of the EU. The Treaty recalls 'the historic importance of the ending of the division of the European continent and the need to create firm bases for the construction of the future Europe'. It signalled the desire to replace conflict with consensus. From this perspective, it is plausible to assert that what unites Europeans in terms of political culture is embodied in the text of the Maastrich Treaty (1992), which proclaims the attachment of EU member states to 'the principles of liberty, democracy and respect for human rights and fundamental freedoms and of the rule of law' and their 'desire to deepen solidarity between the peoples of Europe while respecting their history, their culture and their traditions'. The Treaty also emphasizes the member states' desire to further enhance the democratic and efficient functioning of EU institutions and their determination to promote economic and social progress for Europeans. Another key contribution of the Treaty was the resolution to establish a common European citizenship.

The EU member states' determination to pursue social and economic progress through the strengthening of democratic institutions within a single institutional framework based on the principle of subsidiarity is the most important feature that unites Europeans. It responds to a top-down process initiated by national élites determined to turn a rather vague idea of Europe into a well-defined political institution that will, in time, acquire a culture and identity.

4.4 New social movements

All social movements struggle for recognition, whether they are concerned with equality between men and women, the rights of gays and lesbians, animal rights or environmental issues. The main objective of social movements is to bring attention to a particular issue, to make it relevant, to denounce the unfairness and ill-treatment suffered by somebody or something (people, animals or the environment), and to put forward a set of measures to reverse the situation (Guibernau, 1999, p.25). The incipient specificity of the European socio-cultural and economic space brought about by the Enlightenment and the advent of industrialization set up a framework for the emergence of social movements within Europe.

The rise of trade unionism, the suffragette movement and the anti-slavery campaign are examples of movements that would expand and exert a wide influence across national boundaries. In the twentieth century, especially after the Second World War, European countries generated a number of powerful new social movements; for example, the 'revolution' in Paris in May 1968, which stood against conservatism and capitalist values and morals, and the so-called 'Prague Spring' of the same year, which stood against communist domination in Czechoslovakia. A number of other social movements have since emerged in European countries and expanded to the USA, or have been imported from the USA and flourished in Europe, including the Green movement, the feminist movement and the gay–lesbian movement. An exclusively European social movement in its origins that has exhibited renewed strength in the last twenty years is the rise of regional nationalism, in which particular communities identify themselves as culturally distinct and demand the right to self-determination.

4.5   The cultural homogenization of Europe: high culture versus low culture

The distinction between high culture and low culture reflects the division between the élite and the mass in EU states. I shall argue, however, that it is possible to identify some convergence at both levels. Unity at the élite level emerged earlier than unity among the masses. The influence of French culture during the Enlightenment was contested and resented by German élites. Germany displaced France and turned into the leading cultural centre of Europe in the nineteenth century, when German Romanticism expanded throughout Europe and replaced the cultural predominance exerted by the Enlightenment in the eighteenth century. British influence became strong in the second part of the nineteenth century and was attached to the rise of the Industrial Revolution.

After the Second World War, capitalism confronted communism in political terms, and high art was contrasted with national and regional popular culture, which was being eroded by the mass media and the influence of the USA. High culture, or élite culture, sees art's role as ennobling; its realm is the nation; its organizational form is the institution; its repertoire is the established canon and those works aspiring to join it; and its audience is the cultural élite. In contrast, popular culture regards entertainment as its main objective; its realm is the marketplace; its organizational form is the business; and its audience is the mass (Edgar, 2000).

The two realms of élite and popular culture are not completely isolated, and the connections between them can be illustrated by two examples. First, there is the commodification of works of art that belong to high culture. Consider, for instance, the popular appeal achieved by selected works of Van Gogh, Picasso, Renoir or Monet, which are present in their millions on postcards, posters or even T-shirts. Consider also the popular use of classical music, originally composed for kings, emperors and popes, but now common as background music in tube stations and TV and radio advertisements. Mozart would surely be amazed to see thousands of mobile-phone owners responding to a few notes of his most famous works! Second, most European governments pursue a strategy aimed at widening the audience for the traditional high arts. In Britain, this strategy has informed the BBC, and it defined the ethos of the Arts Council from its foundation by John Maynard Keynes to its high point in the mid-1960s.

In the 1960s and 1970s the new left, inspired by a number of new social movements, sought to challenge high culture. The '1968' influence brought hostility to high culture and a rejection of the 'patrician' principles associated with extending the reach of high art. Instead, grass-roots activity for subversive purposes was encouraged, although this movement itself became the privilege of selected élites. The 1980s witnessed a reversal of this trend and registered a deepening of the already wide gap between élite and popular culture.

In the post-war period, the main source of external cultural influences was the USA, partly from choice, as a breath of fresh air and democracy, and partly from necessity, given the poor state of Europe's cultural industries. The rise of television increased the reliance on imports from the USA. As Europe prospered, concerns about this dependence were widely expressed, especially in the smaller European countries.

The 1980s witnessed a new phase, prompted by the accelerating pace of the 'European project'. For the first time, certain cultural goals of a supranational kind were openly discussed and the concept of a 'European cultural identity' was raised in European élite circles. Commitment to the development of a European project has prompted European élites to take some measures to protect national specificity while at the same time taking steps in the construction of a European identity. The recently created European flag and anthem, the promotion of European sports events, the EU-sponsored exchange programmes for European students and the encouragement and financial support of European scientific networks are all cases in point.

Summary

- The Second World War and its legacy, the division of Europe into two areas of influence, capitalist and communist, generated a common sense of unity among those Europeans living in countries to the west of the Berlin Wall.

- Most Central and Eastern European countries now seeking EU membership argue that they were integrated into the Eastern Bloc by force, and that the end of communism is an opportunity for them to return to where they belong: Europe.

- At present, the peoples of Eastern and Western Europe are united by the desire for the prosperity and progress embodied by the EU. They wish to live and thrive within the prosperous economic space generated by the EU, a supranational institution grounded on democratic principles.

- In post-war Europe, new social movements emerged in European countries and expanded to the USA, or were imported from the USA and flourished in Europe, including the Green movement and the feminist movement.

- Mass communication has favoured the rise of some connections between high culture and low culture, although the division between élites and masses within the EU remains strong.

- Mass communication is also progressively increasing the standardization of a European popular culture that is heavily influenced by the USA.

- The consolidation of the EU and the generation of a 'European identity' are part of a European élite project that has already been initiated.

5   Self-organization and social regulation

So far, we have examined different criteria for inclusion and exclusion in Europe and concluded that the idea of Europe is a modern phenomenon, although heavily influenced by the ideas of the Enlightenment and the dramatic socio-economic changes brought about by the Industrial Revolution. We have also considered a wide range of features that account for unity and diversity within the EU. Some other aspects of social and cultural diversity are examined in the remaining chapters of this book, including national and ethnic minorities, new social movements, the media, changes in gender and family life, and developments in élite and popular culture across the EU.

5.1   Conflicting identities in the EU

Tension and conflict reflect the dynamic nature of society, but differences in the mechanisms employed to deal with conflict clearly distinguish democratic from authoritarian regimes. The EU defines itself as democratic and this determines, to a certain extent, the mechanisms that may be employed in seeking consensus as an alternative to tension and conflict. In the following chapters of this book we shall consider the tension between regional movements that seek greater autonomy and nation states that seek to maintain their power and integrity; the conflict associated with migrants and refugees demanding the right to become EU citizens and the EU's unwillingness to grant them the right to participate in EU politics; the tension between tradition and transformation in the emergence of new social movements; the divide between the idea of Europe as an élite project and the apathy, enthusiasm and resistance of Europe's masses; the debate about how to regulate drug consumption; the discussion about how to regulate a heavily US-influenced media while protecting national cultures and encouraging the development of a European identity; and the conflict between traditional gender roles and family structures and new movements and patterns that question these roles and structures.

A common feature of these issues is the tension between the different identities and cultures that coexist within the EU. Conflict is a constant theme, and this raises two key questions for the future of the European project: How can we manage conflict? What mechanisms will allow us to achieve consensus? These questions lead us to an even more important issue, namely whether new social modes of governance are emerging in the EU as a consequence of bottom-up processes. In what follows we shall introduce the concept of 'governance' and distinguish it from the concept of 'government', and consider the relevance of governance processes in the study of European social and cultural diversity.

5.2   On governance

Governance and government are two different concepts. The term 'government' refers to the formal institutions of the state and their monopoly of legitimate coercive power. Government is defined by the ability to make decisions and the capacity to enforce them, and it operates at the level of the nation state (see **Bromley, 2001**). In contrast, 'governance' seeks to describe shifting patterns in styles of governing and points at new processes of governing that are not exclusively grounded on the nation state as a political institution. So governance, for instance, takes account of new political actors such as Greenpeace, Oxfam, Caritas or *Médécins sans Frontières* and assesses their role in awakening the population to certain concerns and mobilizing them to put pressure on nation states or the EU to change or create new legislation. Governance is concerned with creating the conditions for ordered rule and collective action, but the processes used are different from those employed by governments.

The major difference between government and governance is the relevance conferred upon non-governmental actors, which range from pressure groups to new social movements. By including these actors, the process of governing is transformed and the boundaries between and within the public and private sectors become blurred. For example, take the March 2000 Rover car plant sell-off in the UK Midlands (at Longbridge) and think about the consequences of this for the thousands of workers who became redundant. Who should take the responsibility for helping these workers: the government, trade unions, non-governmental organizations or supranational institutions such as the EU? At present, we do not know the answer, but it is possible that a combination of these socio-political actors will be called upon. In this way, the actors are engaging in a governance process that is characterized by the blurring of the boundaries between the public and the private and the blurring of the responsibilities for tackling social and economic issues.

The consequence of this blurring of responsibilities is a growing degree of 'ambiguity and uncertainty in the minds of policy makers and public about who is responsible and can lead to government actors passing off responsibility to privatized providers when things go wrong' (Stoker, 1998, p.22). It could also turn into a mechanism for scapegoating. Who should be made ultimately responsible for looking after these workers?

Governance changes the balance between state and civil society because the latter becomes directly involved in service delivery and strategic decision making. As Stoker argues, 'The governance perspective demands that these voluntary sector third-force organizations be recognized for the scale and scope of their contribution to tackling collective concerns without reliance on the formal resources of government' (Stoker, 1998, p.21).

At this point, I should explain why the concept of governance is relevant to the study of society and culture in the EU. The answer is closely connected to the growing complexity of the governing processes and the number of actors involved. Governance involves the emergence of autonomous self-organizing networks of actors. These self-organizing networks come to centre stage as a result of the shift from government to governance, and include regions, ethnic minorities, feminist groups, Green groups, labour movements, élites, pressure groups, family associations, media organizations and many other social actors.

A 'network' is generally defined as a specific type of relation linking a defined set of persons, objects or events (**Lintner, 2001**). Different types of relations result in different networks that may include some of the same individuals. For instance, some members of a pro-devolution political party may also be members of an environmental organization. Network approaches seek to offer an analysis of the social context in which actors participate.

According to Streeck and Schmitter, 'associations' should be considered as a type of network model, which contributes to the study of the systems of bargained interest accommodation and policy concertation that emerged in Western societies in the 1960s and 1970s (Streeck and Schmitter, 1991, p.228). An 'association' is defined as a distinctive institutional basis of order that is capable of making a lasting and autonomous contribution to rendering the behaviour of social actors reciprocally adjustive and predictable. It could be argued that some political scientists and public lawyers have regarded associations as a threat to liberal democracy, parliamentary rule and state sovereignty. This perspective ignores the crucial role that associations play within civil society as actors engaged in the new governance processes. Associations represent a wide range of interests that are somehow connected with defending the right of individuals to express some aspects of their identity and make 'life choices'.

In governance processes, to assign a distinct role to associations, somewhere between the state and 'civil society' (market and community), so as to put to public purposes the type of social order that associations can generate and embody, can contribute to enlarging the repertoire of policy alternatives of both nation states and supranational organizations such as the EU.

The main advantage of encouraging the emergence of governance processes is that self-organizing networks are seen as more effective than government-imposed regulation, and they have the potential to enhance democratic practice through greater contact between the state and civil society. It is in this sense that governance can be defined as a mechanism that enables people to participate in governing processes.

The relevance of the governance approach to the study of society and culture in the EU is directly concerned with the assessment of the relationship between self-organizing networks, national governments and the EU. Throughout this book we shall explore the extent to which bottom-up mechanisms, which correspond to self-organizing networks, are able to influence and determine national and EU social regulation. The key questions addressed in the following chapters are: What are the connections between self-organization and social regulation? Do they influence each other? To what extent? Do new forms of self-organization clash with social regulation? Are new forms of governance emerging within the EU as a consequence of bottom-up processes? The remainder of the book also considers whether diversity is likely to be maintained in a greatly integrated Europe or whether the EU will contribute to the homogenization of European peoples. We shall come back to these issues in Chapter 9, but before that we invite you to explore different forms of diversity in Europe and various governance mechanisms defining the relationship between self-organizing networks, the state and the EU.

Summary

- Tension and conflict reflect the dynamic nature of society, although differences in the mechanisms employed to deal with conflict clearly distinguish democratic from authoritarian regimes.

- 'Government' refers to the formal institutions of the state and their monopoly of legitimate coercive power. 'Governance' seeks to describe shifting patterns in styles of governing and identifies new processes of governing that are not exclusively grounded on the nation state as a political institution.

- The major difference between government and governance concerns the relevance conferred upon non-governmental actors, which range from pressure groups to new social movements.

- Governance changes the balance between the state and civil society because the latter becomes directly involved in service delivery and strategic decision making.

- Governance involves the emergence of autonomous self-organizing networks of actors.

- The relevance of the governance approach to the study of society and culture in the EU is directly associated with the assessment of the relationship between self-organizing networks, national government and the EU.

6   Book contents and structure

This book explores the contested nature of the governance of 'life politics', as individuals, households and communities seek greater control over their destinies while the boundaries between the public and private spheres continue to shift. The study of what is 'new' and what is 'different' about European society and culture is approached from four different perspectives.

First, there is the study of diversity versus unity, examining bottom-up as well as top-down governance mechanisms to defend diversity or favour homogeneity, as well as examining the origins and objectives of those pressing for further European social and cultural integration.

Second, there is the study of the emerging European culture as a system of shared meanings, involving social practices that produce, regulate and organize those meanings. The study of European culture is connected with the eventual emergence of a sense of common identity among the citizens of Europe.

Third, there is the study of processes of governance as opposed to structures of government. In particular, the book focuses on the notion of governance as a set of self-organizing networks that reflect how communities and collectivities co-ordinate their activities through the construction of common interests, identities, ideologies and socio-political projects. This involves renegotiating power to avoid conflict as well as seeking new principles on which to base consensus.

Fourth, there is the study of identity through an analysis of emerging inclusion and exclusion mechanisms and an examination of the tensions arising from a confrontation between tradition and transformation in European cultural and social life.

In the following chapters, various authors examine areas that exemplify some of the tensions between unity and diversity, inclusion and exclusion, conflict and consensus and tradition and transformation in

Europe's social and cultural life. In Chapter 2, 'The rise of regions and regionalism in Western Europe', James Anderson considers the changes affecting the nation state and the intensification of globalization as key elements in the rise of sub-state nationalism. The tension between social and cultural unity and diversity is at the centre of this chapter, in which the author examines the prospect of a Europe of the regions. In Chapter 3, 'Migrants, refugees and citizenship', Zig Layton-Henry assesses the key debates on citizenship within the EU. He analyses the role of citizenship as an inclusion/exclusion mechanism and examines its impact on the governance of the EU. The status and treatment of migrants in France, Germany and Britain are analysed, as are policies encouraging multi-culturalism to accommodate cultural differences. In Chapter 4, 'Social movements in Europe: the rise of environmental governance', Mark Smith looks at the conditions that have favoured the emergence of social movements that cut across state boundaries. The chapter establishes a distinction between old and new social movements and uses a detailed analysis of trade unions and environmental movements to illustrate this distinction.

Radical changes in traditional family structures are regarded by some as a threat to a coherent society. Does this make sense? What new family structures are emerging? How is tradition being transformed? In Chapter 5, 'The transformation of family life and sexual politics', Catherine Lloyd examines the impact of divorce, low birth rates, ageing populations and the progressive recognition of the rights of children, as well as some of the transformations prompted by women entering the labour force.

In Chapter 6, 'What unites Europeans?', Josep R. Llobera looks at emerging trends in the production of culture and the arts that might lead to a sense of commonality among certain sectors of the European élites. In so doing he explores the commonalities that bind European citizens together and make the European project possible. In Chapter 7, 'The media in Europe', Denis McQuail analyses media diversity and regulation throughout the EU. He considers a number of different European reactions to the invasion of American products and asks whether the media influences cultural and social life while contributing to the perpetuation of traditional forms of governance, or whether it prompts the emergence of novel processes of governance. He also analyses whether there is room for a specifically European media and what its main attributes might be.

In Chapter 8, 'Drugs and European governance', Eugene McLaughlin and Karim Murji map the emergence and development of a pan-European governmental project to regulate and co-ordinate the suppression of drug trafficking. The chapter also considers the role of the spread in the use and acceptance of illicit drugs, particularly among young people, as a source of discord within the EU, suggesting that moves toward state and supranational regulation have been accompanied by a significant de-regulation at the individual and personal level.

Finally, in Chapter 9, 'Conclusion: One Europe? The democratic governance of a continent', Salvador Giner and Montserrat Guibernau bring together the different themes of the book and examine the prospects for further European integration and expansion. Is European cohesion possible? Is the EU governable? Are we heading toward a European identity?

References

Bromley, S.J. (ed.) (2001) *Governing the European Union*, **London, Sage/The Open University**.

Burgess, A. (1997) *Divided Europe*, London, Pluto Press.

Crouch, C. (1999) *Social Change in Western Europe*, Oxford, Oxford University Press.

den Boer, P. (1995) 'Europe to 1914: the making of an idea' in Wilson, K. and van der Dussen, J. (eds) *The History of the Idea of Europe*, London, Routledge.

Edgar, D. (2000) 'The perils of populism', *The Guardian*, 19 February, Saturday Review, p.1.

Giddens, A. (1985) *The Nation-State and Violence*, Cambridge, Polity Press.

Grahl, J. (2001) '"Social Europe" and the governance of labour relations' in Thompson, G. (ed.) *Governing the European Economy*, **London, Sage/The Open University**.

Guibernau, M. (1996) *Nationalisms*, Cambridge, Polity Press.

Guibernau, M. (1999) *Nations Without States*, Cambridge, Polity Press.

Huntington, S.P. (1996) *The Clash of Civilizations and the Remaking of World Order*, New York, Simon & Schuster.

Lintner, V. (2001) 'The development of the EU and the European economy' in Thompson, G. (ed.) *Governing the European Economy*, **London, Sage/The Open University**.

Stoker, G. (1998) 'Governance as theory: five propositions', *International Social Science Journal*, no.155, March, pp.17–28.

Streeck, W. and Schmitter, P.C. (1991) 'Community, market, state and associations? The prospective contribution of interest governance to social order' in Thompson, G., Frances, J., Levačić, R. and Mitchell, J. (eds) *Markets, Hierarchies and Networks*, London, Sage/The Open University.

Thompson, G. (2001) 'Governing the European economy: a framework of analysis' in Thompson, G. (ed.) *Governing the European Economy*, **London, Sage/The Open University**.

Thompson, J.B. (1990) *Ideology and Modern Culture*, Cambridge, Polity Press.

Urwin, D.W. (1993) *The Community of Europe*, London, Longman.

Further reading

Burgess, A. (1997) *Divided Europe*, London, Pluto Press.

Crouch, C. (1999) *Social Change in Western Europe,* Oxford, Oxford University Press.

Duina, F.C. (1999) *Harmonizing Europe,* New York, State University of New York Press.

Guibernau, M. (1996) *Nationalisms*, Cambridge, Polity Press.

Chapter 2
The rise of regions and regionalism in Western Europe

James Anderson

1 Introduction

How and why have Europe's regions and their relations with states been changing in recent decades? What roles are regions playing and likely to play in the emerging governance structures of the European Union (EU)? These structures, still in the process of formation, raise strongly contested normative as well as empirical questions, and regions occupy a central position in debates about past trends and possible futures. For instance, in debates about the EU's 'democratic deficit', is the answer a reassertion of liberal democracy in nation states, a return to a 'Europe of Nations' in the revealing misnomer of traditionalists opposed to regionalism and wedded to the so-called 'nation state'? Alternatively, should democratic reconstruction involve a 'Federal Europe' super-state? Or does the future lie with sub-state identities in a decentralized 'Europe of the Regions'? Which of the three models represents the most likely future? And which is the most desirable one? All three models have been widely touted and all three reflect elements of current reality; yet none on its own captures the complexities of a regionalizing Europe. Instead, should we perhaps expect 'more of the same', with regions playing an increasingly important role in complex multi-level structures which continue to involve the nation states, the EU's central institutions, and other transnational political actors (see **Bromley, 2001**)? Perhaps in a sense the future has already arrived.

This chapter offers some responses to these questions by outlining the variety of regions and regionalisms, their recent growth and its causes, their development in the EU context, and different future scenarios. Section 2 attempts to define 'region' and 'regionalism' in the face of their extreme cultural, economic and political diversity. Regions come in all shapes and sizes, some clearly demarcated by a long history, others little more than figments of a central bureaucrat's imagination. Regionalisms likewise range from an almost non-existent sense of regional identity to fully-fledged sub-state nationalisms, a form of identity politics which sees the 'region' as a potentially separate, independent country. The terms 'region' and 'regionalism' thus mask a range of quite different phenomena which vary not only from state to state but also within particular states, as is demonstrated very clearly in the cases of the UK and Spain (Figures 2.1 and 2.2).

Section 3 then sketches how regions in their various senses have increasingly become more important since the zenith of the centralized nation state in the Europe of the 1930s and 1940s. Regions have become more prominent in the economic, political and cultural life of virtually all European states (Harvie, 1994). There are a variety of reasons for this, including uneven economic development (and the lack of it), regional languages and cultures being threatened with terminal decline, and federalization as a means of reducing the power of central states or, alternatively, a means of containing separatist aspirations and conflicts.

The increased salience of regions as units for economic, political and cultural development is not in doubt, but what is its overall significance? Despite the diversity of its expressions and causations, there are a number of unifying factors which give the regionalizing of Europe some coherence. Particularly since the 1970s, sub-state regions in general have been subjected to many of the same pressures from accelerated globalization. These pressures have both curtailed the independent economic power of supposedly sovereign nation states, and simultaneously put a greater premium on regional and local authorities presenting themselves as attractive locations for multinational investors. Regions have been forced or encouraged, as the jargon has it, to 'think globally and act locally', rather than simply relying on nation states to do their 'thinking and acting' for them, as was often the case formerly. This is especially true of regions in the EU where these developments have advanced furthest, and the EU now has an increasingly important regional dimension (Jeffery, 1997).

Section 4 considers the EU itself as a product of more globalized competition and one of the most advanced political, as distinct from simply economic, expressions of globalization. Here the impacts of globalization, and particularly the encouragement of regionalism, are experienced in more heightened form than in the other major economic blocs in North America and East Asia, or in countries which have remained outside these blocs. For Western Europe's regions, economic integration in the Single European Market (SEM) since the late 1980s has brought additional threats and opportunities which have indirectly fostered regionalism, and increasingly this extends beyond Western Europe as the EU enlarges eastwards. In straightforward political terms, the member states have lost some of their individual sovereign powers to the EU collective, and the EU provides an institutional 'umbrella' for regions, and for would-be states, as well as for the existing member states. In focusing on regionalism in the EU, Section 4 studies EU regional policies, regional networking and alliances.

This is the context within which rosy scenarios of a 'Europe of the Regions' were propagated in the 1990s. Traditional nation states were seen as generally too small for global competition but too big and remote for cultural identification and active, participatory citizenship. States were apparently being eroded from above by the EU and from below by regionalism – a pincer movement transforming traditional conceptions of the so-called 'nation state' and the national basis of territorial sovereignty and identity. Europe's future seemed to lie with a loose, decentralized federation of regions. Furthermore, while traditionalists defend their misnamed 'Europe of Nations' (that is, the existing nation states), the conflicts generated by the unachievable ideal of the homogeneous 'nation state' in places like Ireland or the Basque Country are a further argument for the emergence of a 'Europe of the Regions', or so the story goes. But, as we shall see in Section 5, there are good empirical and normative reasons for questioning the benign ideology of regionalism and its assumption that 'small' is necessarily 'beautiful'. While global economic competition and the SEM may indeed lead to a more federalized and regionalized Europe, the EU's integration is still largely controlled by the existing member states and they continue to define the regions within their national territories. Besides, the strongest regional threats to nation states, far from being opposed in principle to the nation state ideal, are themselves nationalist in inspiration: they come from 'nations without states' (Guibernau, 1999) where nationalist movements (in, for example, Scotland, Wales or Catalonia) reflect and foster strong cultural and political identities, and typically the ultimate (if not immediate or practical) objective is their own 'nation state'. However, such nationally inspired or 'national' regionalisms are the exception in Europe's regions, and indeed the great diversity of regions constitutes a major reason why they are unlikely to become *the* basis for a 'new Europe'.

On the other hand, reversing the rise of regionalism and returning to a traditional 'Europe of Nations', as advocated by an extreme nationalistic faction in the British Conservative Party since the 1980s, seems at least equally unlikely. Yet a fully federal European super-state, whatever its advantages in terms of democratic transparency and formal represen-tation at different territorial levels, is also implausible – the process of federalization is likely to be arrested long before giving birth to a 'United States of Europe' on the North American model. Section 6 considers different future scenarios and stresses that the future, like the present, will probably be more complex than any of these models suggests. But if a 'Europe of the Regions' is ruled out, how will increasingly important regionalisms relate to other 'possible Europes' – of cities, cultures, nations, states and transnational institutions? Rather than neatly displacing nation states or other forms of political and cultural identity, it seems more likely that enhanced regionalisms will have to coexist with them.

The regional question in Western Europe is thus inextricably bound up with wider empirical and normative debates about nation states and the EU, and issues of culture, politics, development, identity and democracy (Newman, 1996). Regions and regionalism can be understood thematically in terms of individual 'diversity' within the transnational 'unity' of a global and European context and the 'conflict' of region versus state, or the submergence of regionalism in a state-wide consensus. The battle for states or regions, as distinct from a more widely conceived 'multi-level' politics, can be seen as a fight between 'tradition' and 'transformation'.

2   The diversity of regions and regionalisms

'Region' here refers to any piece of continuous territory, bigger than a mere locality or neighbourhood, which is part of the territory of a larger state (or states), and whose political authority or government, if it has any specific to itself, is subordinate to that of the state(s). Conventionally, most such 'sub-state' regions, and particularly most regions defined in terms of political authority, have fallen wholly within the borders of a single state. However, in situations where those borders are contested, as for instance in national separatist or irridentist conflicts, the relevant regions may straddle state borders; and in contemporary conditions of globalization and transnational integration, as in the EU, cross-border regions can play a special integrative role. The related term 'regionalism' has perhaps even more varied meanings. It can refer to the top-down imposition (or 'regionalization') of administration or government based on regional territory; or it may denote an active bottom-up identification with the region in social, cultural or political terms, a regionalist movement seeking more autonomy for a region, or a regionally-based nationalist movement which seeks a separate state; or indeed it may refer to any combination of these.

To attempt more precise definitions would run the risk of arbitrarily excluding many of the phenomena we need to address. In fact the intentionally loose, multifaceted nature of these definitions reflects the reality of regional diversity, which has many dimensions. The differences start with the states which in practical political terms largely define regions, for they are themselves very different in area and population size, in economic strength, in cultural homogeneity or heterogeneity, and in political structure. A diversity of state forms – unitary (for example, France, Portugal, Republic of Ireland), federal (Germany, Austria, Belgium), and 'quasi-federal' or with non-uniform limited regional autonomy (Spain, Italy, the UK) – produces a diversity of regions. In a fully federal state (for example, Germany), governmental activities are divided between the centre and the regional units (for example, *Länder*) so that each level has the right to make final decisions in some fields of activity. There is a wide spectrum between this and the extremes of authoritarian centralism (for example, in Spain under Franco's dictatorship – see below). Likewise, there are many gradations on the identity spectrum, from full national separatism based on a distinct culture and language to, at the other extreme, the absence of any popular identification with a purely administrative division that lacks any historical basis or cultural significance. Furthermore, while the *formal* equality of 'independent sovereignty' tempers the diversity of states and gives them a qualified comparability (notwithstanding huge differences in their size, wealth and so on), there is no equivalent 'common denominator' in the case of regions.

Thus Europe's regions display huge variations not only in their economic development, but also in their degrees of political organization and autonomy (if any), their status with respect to central state institutions, their historical basis or lack of it, their cultural distinctiveness, and so forth. Germany's federal region of North Rhine Westphalia with some 15 million people is over three times bigger than a member state such as the Irish Republic, while the latter's centralism has generally precluded effective regionalism (see below). Some regions are administrative concoctions with little or no popular identity, and while some of the strongest are 'national' regions comprising historic nations (for example, Scotland and Catalonia which once had separate statehood), other strong regions, such as Baden-Württemberg and Lombardy, are not based on a national history or any very marked cultural distinctiveness.

There may, though, be some convergence between the 'national' regions and the stronger 'non-national' ones: the former may experience a 'regionalizing' of sub-state nationalisms (settling for autonomy rather than full independence within the EU framework), while the latter may undergo a '(quasi) nationalizing' with further development of their autonomist identities and growing distinctiveness. Baden-Württemberg and Lombardy with Rhône-Alpes, Wales and Catalonia (see Figure 2.3) together formed the 'Four Motors' cross-border alliance of regions, all city-focused and examples of what Harvie (1994) calls economically successful 'bourgeois regionalism'. (Wales was not one of the original four members.) We shall come back to the 'Four Motors' as an example of regional networking later on in the chapter. In contrast, other regionalisms mobilize support around the problems of economic or cultural decline. Furthermore, many regions, whatever their problems, also have the problem of lacking a basis for regional mobilization – they may have little or no cultural identity, or a weak and fractured geographical structure, or they may be riven politically by local rivalries and internal divisions between competing local authorities.

Distinctions must be drawn between, on the one hand, the bottom-up development or resurgence of sub-state nationalist and populist movements, often based on the identity politics of long-established regional cultures and languages which often pre-date the state, and, on the other hand, the top-down imposition of administrative or economic regionalization, or the designation of 'problem regions' and 'regional problems' by central state bureaucracies. However, as in the Napoleonic system of regions administered by centrally-appointed 'prefects', top-down regionalism can be long established, and in some cases imposed regions can later become the basis for popular 'bottom-up' regionalism.

Figure 2.1 Regions in Ireland and the UK

(adapted from Butt Philip, 1999; Government of Ireland, 2000)

There is no simple or necessary correspondence between types of region and types of regionalism. But clearly-demarcated and long-established regions are a more likely basis for strong regionalist or nationalist movements, while top-down regionalization often results in regions with little popular identity or awareness of the region by its own inhabitants. Pre-existing regional diversity provides an uneven basis for regionalizing a whole state. For example, regionalizing the UK is relatively easy in the case of Scotland, Wales and Northern Ireland, but extremely problematical for English regions (Figure 2.1). This is perhaps especially so in the central 'Midlands' area where there are no clear boundaries. But even in the relatively strong Northern Region there are problems: the 'Campaign for a Northern Assembly' was transmuted into a 'Campaign for a North-East Assembly' which now covers only the eastern half of the region, much to the annoyance of remaining campaigners to the west. Similarly, in recently regionalized Spain, there are 'strong' pieces in the jigsaw, such as the 'national' regions of Catalonia, the Basque Country and Galicia, with their own specific cultures and languages and memories of a time when they were independent or had autonomous political institutions and laws; but there are also small newly created regions such as Murcia and tiny La Rioja which filled awkward gaps between more established regions (see Figure 2.2). The diversity of 'region' and 'regionalism' – in terms of history and geography, economics, culture and politics – is exemplified by Portugal and Spain (see Box 2.1 below).

Figure 2.2 Regions in Portugal and Spain

(adapted from del Río, 1999, p.168)

Box 2.1 Portugal and Spain

The Iberian Peninsula clearly exemplifies the historical influences behind sub-state regionalism, recent changes in an EU context, and the large variations in regionalism both between states (Portugal and Spain) and within states (in the Spanish case). Portugal is one of the most unified and culturally homogeneous nation states in Europe, with long-established, stable borders and only very weak separatist tendencies in some of its Atlantic islands. In contrast, Spain – revealingly referred to in the plural as 'the Spains' in the fifteenth, sixteenth and seventeenth centuries – experienced four waves of separatist movements between the time of the French Revolution and the victory of Franco's highly centralist regime in 1939. Today's Spanish constitution still emphasizes the territorial inviolability of the Spanish state but in addition to Castilian – regularly spoken by about three-quarters of the population – it recognizes five regional languages: Catalan, Basque, Galician, Valencian and Mallorcan. The Catalans, Basques and

Galicians constitute three historic 'national minorities' with their own regional governments, and the state comprises a further fourteen 'autonomous communities' with weaker but nonetheless real powers at regional level. Mainland Portugal on the other hand has long been and still is a unitary state. Its five administrative regions are controlled from Lisbon; 'decentralization' is encouraged by the EU but is still largely aspirational, though in the Azores and Madeira some power has been devolved to regional governments.

These variations are rooted in contrasting histories of state formation, and particularly Spain's history of 'reconquest' – the *Reconquista*. This long, piecemeal process – stretching from the northern victory over Islamic forces at Covadonga in Asturias in AD 727 to the taking of Granada in Andalusia in 1492 – involved the creation of separate, independent kingdoms, some of which roughly correspond to today's regions, and it was only in the late nineteenth century that the remaining vestiges of separate regional powers were removed. But by then separatist nationalist movements were emerging, particularly in Catalonia and the Basque Country, which had never fallen under Islamic domination in the way that the rest of the peninsula had done for seven centuries. Both Catalans and Basques could draw on local histories of opposition to central authority in Madrid (for example, Basque involvement in the nineteenth-century Carlist wars; a Catalan rebellion in the 1640s, referred to in Catalonia's official anthem). Belated political centralization meant that many other regions also retained a distinctiveness and coherence in cultural terms which would provide a basis for the present partly 'federalized' or regionalized state structure.

By contrast, the Portuguese *Reconquista* was completed much earlier: Portugal by the thirteenth century was a single kingdom ruled from Lisbon, the state was efficiently centralized by absolutist regimes, and culturally it was dominated by Lisbon and the university town of Coimbra. There was little political or cultural ground for regionalist or separatist movements, even in the Atlantic islands, and none emerged until a short-lived separatism developed in the Azores in reaction to Portugal's political revolution which ended right-wing dictatorship in the early 1970s. Within 'mainland' Portugal, opposition to the revolution was relatively strong in the politically conservative *minifundias* or rural smallholdings of the North region, which contrasted with strong support from the rural proletariat of the *latifundias* or big estates of the southern Alentejo region (Figure 2.2). But this regional contrast – a legacy of different land-holding patterns established during the *Reconquista* – led to differences in support for national political parties rather than to separate, much less separatist, regional politics.

In Spain the historically much stronger regional pressures were further fuelled by uneven industrialization from the late nineteenth century, with development heavily concentrated in Catalonia and the Basque Country, in contrast to a more 'backward' centre and south. The consequences of this uneven development included resentments about subsidizing poorer regions, and fears that the influx of Castilian speakers to growth areas would weaken minority regional languages and cultures. In the 1930s the Republican Government granted regional autonomy to Catalonia, belatedly to part of the Basque Country, and also to Galicia, but this decentralization was quickly reversed by Franco's Spanish nationalist (Castilian) regime which established itself in power by 1939 and lasted up to his death in 1975. The main facets of regional distinctiveness – cultural as well as political – were repressed, with non-Castilian languages effectively outlawed (the Basque and Catalan languages were 'fit only for dogs' in Franco's choice phrase). Regional opposition was generally met with a severe state response, particularly brutal in the Basque Country where ETA waged armed opposition from the 1960s. While repressive centralism was initially effective in stamping out regional movements, it ultimately proved counter-productive for it encouraged the very things it sought to crush – regionalism and separatism – and it enabled anti-Spanish nationalists to make common cause with the wider array of anti-Franco, pro-democracy forces both within their own regions and in other areas of the Spanish state. After 1975, regional devolution became a key ingredient in Spain's democratization and the partial dismantling of Franco's still powerful centralist legacy.

The 1978 constitution, while stressing the unity of the Spanish state, allowed for substantial devolution to regionally elected parliaments. Although ostensibly an 'across-the board', state-wide response, it has been interpreted as primarily a way of containing the oppositional regional nationalisms, mainly those of the Basque Country and Catalonia, to prevent them pushing for total separation from Spain. Being seen to grant 'favoured treatment' to these two already economically-advantaged regions would have been highly problematic in the rest of Spain, and not least with Francoists, still strong in the army and police and strongly opposed to any regional movements they deemed a threat to the territorial integrity of the Spanish state. So the 1978 plan was intentionally state-wide. However, its regionalization of Spain was inevitably uneven. It included multi-province regions such as Castilla-Leon with an area larger than several EU member states, but also much smaller single-province regions like Cantabria or Asturias. It meant that devolution was imposed on parts of Spain which not only had no nationalist or regionalist movements but in some cases had little or no pre-existing sense of regional identity. On the other hand, the three main contenders for regional self-government, the Basque Country, Catalonia and Galicia, were granted higher levels of autonomy than the other regions, which themselves had varying degrees of autonomy, while regional governments were granted few financial powers except in Catalonia and the Basque Country. These variations were to create further tensions between the regions and with central government in Madrid.

Summary

- 'Regions' and 'regionalism' in Western Europe display great diversity in economic, social, cultural and political terms, varying not only between states but also within particular states (as exemplified by Spain and the UK).

- Regions vary widely in their size, population, levels of economic development, historical origins, contemporary identity, cultural distinctiveness and political activism (or in some cases the lack of distinctiveness and activism).

3   The growth of regionalism and its causes

Regionalism has grown remarkably since the high point of state centralism in the Second World War period. A succession of factors have come into play – uneven economic development, threats to regional cultures and languages, the decentralization of some states, and more recently the impacts of globalization and European integration. The effects have been cumulative, with old factors continuing to operate while new ones were added, including, as we shall see later, the ideology that 'small' regions must be good in themselves and better than 'big' states or larger entities.

3.1   Nationalisms and federalization

In the 1960s and 1970s some states, including the UK, contributed to politicizing regional economic development by first defining 'problem regions' (for example, Central Scotland) and then failing to solve their problems. Here central states were still setting the agenda, but increasingly the lead was taken within the regions themselves, especially in regions with past experience of autonomy or their own nationalist tradition.

Nationalism had a 'bad press' from the 1930s and 1940s, thanks partly to the extreme nationalism of Nazi Germany, and this was a low point for national separatist movements in Britain and elsewhere in Europe, though in Spain regionalism was directly weakened by Franco's repressive centralism (see Box 2.1). In contrast, by the 1960s there were autonomist and separatist movements active in varying degrees across Western Europe, from Ireland, Scotland and Wales in the north-west, through Brittany, Flanders and Wallonia, to the Basque Country, Catalonia, Corsica and parts of Italy (Figure 2.3). Most of these regions had their own distinctive history and culture, often including their own 'minority' languages. However, there were contemporary reasons for the nationalist or regionalist resurgence, including economic and cultural problems and changes in the power and authority of central state administrations. In some cases (for example, in Ireland and the Basque Country) inspiration was derived from the example of anti-colonial liberation struggles and newly independent (often small) states in the 'Third World'. In general, Europe's resurgent 'regional' nationalisms tended to be toward the left of the political spectrum (sometimes in contrast to antecedents in the 1930s, as in the Breton case), though, like all nationalisms, they encompassed a variety of views, and a small minority (for example, Flemish nationalism) was dominated by the extreme right and fascism.

The other major cleavages were between 'constitutional' nationalists who used only peaceful means of opposing the status quo and those who took up arms against the state, and (an often related cleavage) between those prepared to accept limited regional autonomy and those holding out for complete separation and a new state. Armed conflicts erupted in several regions, most seriously in Northern Ireland and the Basque Country, and the ensuing state repression generally fuelled the conflict rather than solved it. However, in no case did a nationalist movement succeed in its separatist aims. On the other hand, whether through peaceful means, armed struggle, or an uneasy co-operation/competition between the two, most of the regional nationalisms have achieved a greater degree of regional autonomy.

In some previously 'unitary' states (as in Spain) they also helped bring about a more general, though often partial or 'arrested', process of federalization or devolution. Where states had only one parliament or representative assembly, and no political institutions representing distinct regions or cultural minorities, devolving or decentralizing some political powers to regional assemblies in a more federal state structure was a means of containing separatist conflict. It might 'buy off' or deflect tendencies which threatened the territorial integrity of the entire state. This was the case not only in Spain but also in bilingual Belgium with its divergent Flemish and Walloon aspirations. To prevent the Belgian state disintegrating, there has been a continuing process of constitutional reform since the 1970s, resulting in a very high degree of autonomy for the two main regions, and also for Brussels which is inside the Flemish-speaking area but has been dominated by a francophone elite. This containment strategy can work – it has worked so far in Belgium. Out-and-out separatists may reject it as a 'sop', but they may become politically isolated if others accept that 'half a loaf is better than no bread'. Autonomists are placated while more 'moderate' separatists can present federalization as a relative gain and a 'stepping stone' or stage on a road which promises full independence. This, however, is an argument which also tends to be accepted by centralists who identify strongly with state nationalism (for example, British in the UK, Spanish in Spain), except that they see federalization not as a promise but as a threat to 'their' state. They therefore generally oppose anything but the most minimal forms of centrally-controlled administrative devolution, and where more substantial types of devolution or federalization exist they may act to curtail or remove them. But – in a further twist to the

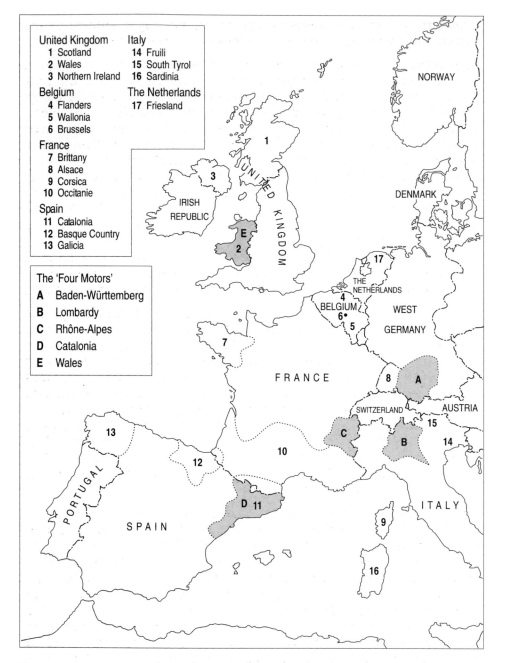

Figure 2.3 Regional and nationalist opposition movements in Western European states circa 1970 (and the 'Four Motors')

(adapted from Anderson, 1995, p.91; Bull, 1999, p.142; del Río, 1999, p.168; Stammen, 1999, p.100; Wagstaff, 1999a, p.52)

Note: The 'Four Motors' are the four main high-tech regions that came together in 1989. They were subsequently joined by Wales.

argument – this can be counter-productive, stimulating resentment in the regions and encouraging the very tendencies it is supposed to destroy.

There is thus a continuing dialectic between centralism and federalization or devolution. The various arguments about their likely effects not only separate the pro- and anti-regionalist forces, they also divide each 'camp' internally, leading to political situations of great complexity. In consequence, the historical trends are by no means all 'one-way' – as was seen for instance in Britain where the very centralist Conservative governments of Mrs Thatcher reversed the previous trend toward regionalism. However, like Franco's centralism in very different circumstances, her centralist policies were to prove spectacularly counter-productive in their own terms in some of the key regions. She provoked Scottish nationalist opposition and growth, and the decimation of the Conservative Party in Scotland, and to a lesser extent in Wales. And by what was seen as her callous treatment of dying IRA hunger-striking prisoners protesting against her attempted 'criminalization' of them, she inadvertently launched Sinn Fein as a successful electoral machine in Northern Ireland.

However, despite the complexities and reversals – mostly temporary – the dominant trend since the 1960s has undoubtedly been toward increased regionalism. Prior to 1970, the Federal Republic of Germany was the only major west European country with elected governments at a level between local municipalities and the central state (with the exception of Northern Ireland, an 'exception which proved the rule' for the UK); and even in Germany there had been some centralization of power, and federalism was weak and getting weaker (Newman, 1996). Unitary states with varying degrees of centrally-controlled regional administration then dominated the scene. But that is no longer the case, thanks in part to separatist pressures, but also to processes of democratization, globalization and European integration.

Germany's federal *Länder* were originally established as a means of reducing the power of the post-war German state, countering authoritarian centralism and rekindling democracy. Similarly motivated concerns to dismantle fascist or semi-fascist legacies of over-centralization were involved in the decentralization in Spain (and to a lesser extent Portugal) in the 1970s and 1980s, with Italy having led the way by excising some of its authoritarian legacy in 1970. It created fifteen regions, implementing regional devolution which had been envisaged in its 1945 constitution but not carried out. In these countries the process of setting up elected regional authorities reflected a general concern to revive democratic participation, as well as absorbing centripetal pressures and preventing geographical fragmentation, and their constitutions have now granted substantial autonomy to island regions and 'historic nations'.

In different contexts, Holland and Denmark have created provincial assemblies, and even in France, the epitome of Jacobin centralism, a leftish government introduced a major decentralization programme, setting up twenty-two regions and establishing regionally elected councils. True to its Jacobinism, however, France allowed these councils only limited autonomy within a fairly uniform and centralist all-France political structure; and it continued, for example, to refuse to recognize a distinctive 'Corsican people'. The statutes of Corsica's regional government allowed the expression of sub-state identity only in so far as it conformed to the state's definition of the French 'nation' (Anderson and Goodman, 1995). This trend could be reversed if plans to confer on Corsica a special status within France go ahead and the island obtains a greater degree of political autonomy and recognition as announced by the Jospin government in 2000. Although the implementation of plans for decentralizing was often slow (particularly in Portugal and Greece), and some of the regional bodies have quite limited powers (for instance in France), elected regional bodies have now established themselves as a permanent feature of political life in several of the smaller EU states and in the five largest ones, most recently in Britain.

3.2   Globalization

All this was taking place in the global context of the ending of the 'long post-war boom' in the early 1970s. Profit rates were falling and there was a return of generalized capitalist crises, an intensification of competition and a consequent acceleration in the 'internationalization' of production, as larger firms 'went global' in their search for restored profit levels. These developments not only exacerbated the problems of 'problem regions', they also led to fundamental changes in the relationships between regional, national and international economic processes.

This complex of factors, commonly referred to as 'globalization', was accompanied by a revival of laissez-faire arguments against 'state interference', and a world-wide 'privatization' of state-owned enterprises. State ownership and corporatist links between the state and 'national' capital generally became weaker and gave way to looser links with capitals of whatever 'national' origin or ownership that were located, or might potentially be located, within the state territory.

Globalization, and particularly its economic aspect (though this cannot be divorced from the political), is perhaps the main or most general and basic factor behind the recent growth of regionalism. Economic development is the policy area where states are assumed to have lost much of their former independent powers and their control over their own 'national economy'. It is also the area which provides the most widespread focus for the growth of regional and local politics as regions and localities strive to attract investment capital from external sources. Attracting external capital – 'global' in that it can in principle come from anywhere (and also might go anywhere else) – has become the touchstone of economic 'success' in more globalized markets. The social and institutional 'support systems' of local and regional economies and societies have been increasingly seen as crucial in the competition for attracting and retaining inward investment. Regional and local governments, and other regionally-based political and economic forces, became direct actors in transnational arenas, sometimes in association with central state institutions but now often bypassing them.

Particular regions became 'success stories' (for example, Emilia Romagna in Italy, which in per capita GDP went from forty-fifth to tenth richest region in the EU between 1970 and 1991). There were various attempts to explain 'success' in terms of a region's own attributes:

- regions having their own elected government which could pursue regional as distinct from 'national' priorities;
- a well-developed set of regional institutions and partnerships between the regional authorities and the private sector;
- a good physical infrastructure in the region and a social infrastructure providing training and a skilled, reliable workforce;
- regional specialization, including for niche markets, and inter-firm linkages and sourcing which maximized the 'value added' within the region.

These various factors were given different weightings in different theories, but there developed a general consensus that economic success depended on regional governance and the 'embedding' of regional economies in a dense, supportive network of institutions (**Simonetti, 2001**). It was generally assumed or asserted that the region was indeed the best spatial scale for organizing these prerequisites.

This orthodoxy or 'new regionalism' (Amin, 1999) has however been questioned by various sceptics. John Lovering points out for instance (Lovering, 1999) that it:

- tends to systematically underestimate the continuing economic importance of the state (even in federalized states);
- overestimates the coherence of most regions as a basis for development compared to the smaller scale of city or municipality;
- is theoretically weak and based on relatively few, and in many ways exceptional, examples;
- perhaps not surprisingly, has generally failed in practice to replicate 'success' in lagging regions.

Rather than being a theoretically grounded and empirically justified position, it is more an article of faith which in at least some cases is connected with a neo-liberal downplaying of nation states or concedes too much ground to this dominant ideology. It has interesting echoes in 'Europe of the Regions' ideology, as we shall see (Section 5).

Nevertheless, whatever the empirical and theoretical arguments against the 'new regionalism', regional authorities are under continuing pressure to appear attractive to investors and can hardly risk dismissing these ideas. They may be largely ideological but their sheer fashionableness gives them a material reality. Regions and regional governance are now an established part of political and economic life in Western Europe, and not least because of the EU.

Summary

- Since the heyday of the centralized nation state in the 1930s and 1940s, most of Europe's regions have grown increasingly more important in economic, political and/or cultural terms.

- This growth has been largely in response to regional inequalities in economic development, threats to traditional regional cultures, and the political federalization of states, whether to reduce their centralized power or to contain regional separatisms.

- More generally, since the 1970s, accelerated globalization has meant that attracting external sources of investment has become more crucial and this has made 'global' or at least 'international' players of regional (and local) authorities, which now deal directly with the external sources whereas previously they had usually acted through their central governments or simply relied on the central authorities acting on their behalf.

4   Regionalism in the EU

Since the ending of the long post-war boom in the early 1970s, the EU has developed in response to intensified competition in global markets, the member states have been progressively 'pooling' their sovereignty in economic matters, and globalization's political consequences have gone furthest in the EU, not least in its regions. There are thus additional, specifically EU, factors in the growth of regionalism. It has been encouraged directly by the EU's regional policies and the regional engagements of its central institutions, particularly the Commission, the Parliament and the Committee for the Regions. There is the often explicit intention of advancing the EU's own cohesion and integration via the regions, and regions are seen as a distinct 'third level' of the EU along with its central institutions and the member states (Jeffery, 1997). Less obviously but very importantly, the EU has also stimulated regionalism indirectly through forces within the regions themselves responding to general integrative developments such as the Single European Market (SEM) and Economic and Monetary Union (EMU) (Anderson and Goodman, 1995). Regions striving to become attractive actors on the international stage find 'Brussels' a helpful prop (and literally a good place to set up a 'shop-window' lobbying office); and those seeking greater autonomy or separate statehood find the EU a useful 'umbrella' in providing a trump card against arguments that they are too small and parochial. They can have 'independence in Europe', in the slogan of the Scottish National Party, with the obvious corollary that it is in fact the British nationalists defending the integrity of the UK state who are being 'parochial'. Thus while the diversity of regionalism is qualified by the common factor of globalization, the EU gives it a further overarching 'unity'.

4.1   EU regional policies

Initially, from 1957 to the mid-1970s, the European Community, in line with the dominant centralism of its member states, showed little interest in regional problems, with the exception of south-west France and the chronic 'underdevelopment' of southern Italy. Generalized regional policy only developed from 1973 when the UK and the Irish Republic joined, though ironically they have been among the most centralist of all member states. However, they wanted 'compensation' for their regional problems and their relative poverty and peripheral location with respect to continental markets, and these were major issues in the negotiations to join. In consequence, the European Regional Development Fund (ERDF) was set up in 1975, and regions in the north and west of Britain, all of Ireland, and north-west France were added to the recipients of regional aid.

However, it was only in the face of accelerated globalization, and particularly the intensified competition from the world's two other main economic blocs based on the USA and Japan, that economic and social 'cohesion' became a major EU objective. The Single European Act was passed in 1986 to establish the SEM by 1992; and it favoured cross-sectoral development strategies at regional levels and 'fine-grained' region-to-region, rather than simply state-to-state, integration. In 1988 the structural funds (the ERDF, the Social Fund and the 'guidance section' of the Common Agricultural Policy) were doubled, and there was a decision to concentrate resources in regions 'lagging behind' – the so-called 'Objective One' regions. Altogether five regional 'Objectives' were created and these subsequently became a focus for alliances, as regions of the various types, especially those with 'industrial' and 'rural' problems, sought to defend their particular interests. Though it was mainly the state governments that did the negotiating, the EU insisted that they consult their regional 'partners'. The 'region-forming' role of the Commission was clearly seen when it forced the Irish government to re-establish regional advisory bodies in 1988, one year after the government had dissolved them in a budget cut (Anderson and Goodman, 1995)! A decade later when the economic success of the 'Celtic Tiger' meant that the Republic of Ireland as a whole would lose its 'Objective One' status, the government redrew the regional map dividing the state into two regions in order to retain this status for the relatively poor counties to the north and west. But then for short-term reasons of electoral expediency, it included Counties Clare and Kerry (Figure 2.1) which did not qualify for 'Objective One' status on the standard per-capita income grounds, and again the Commission stepped in, excluded these counties and determined a regional framework.

In 1988 the Commission created the Consultative Committee of Local and Regional Authorities to strengthen its own links with these sub-state bodies. The Commission's periodic ranking of regions for aid purposes also increased the political significance of regions, and the legitimacy of regionalism was further enhanced by the Regional Policy Committee of the European Parliament which sponsored two 'Regions of the

Community' conferences in 1984 and 1991 (the 1984 conference leading to the creation of the Association of European Regions with over 170 members). The Commission also sponsored the Association of European Border Regions and in 1990 established INTERREG, which involved pooling the various structural funds available to the respective border regions in order to promote specifically cross-border economic co-operation. As well as directly furthering economic and social 'cohesion', regionalism has also been encouraged for the more political if less acknowledged objective of countering or bypassing state governments where they presented obstacles to integration. Regions and regionalism were allies or potential allies for the Commission vis-à-vis inter-governmentalism and the controlling states.

The Commission's 1991 regional discussion document *Europe 2000* (an early example of the 'new regionalism', above, which drew on optimistic versions of 'post-Fordism') argued that with 'flexible specialization' reducing the importance of scale economies, less advantaged regions could become prosperous by producing specialized products for niche markets. It argued that 'flexible production systems' were making firms more mobile and that their location decisions were increasingly influenced by qualitative life-style factors. Drawing on the experiences of 'Silicon Glen' in Scotland, Rennes in France, the Basque Country in Spain, and South Wales, and noting the potential of information technology and telecommunications for altering comparative advantage, it claimed that 'new location factors' were opening up economic opportunities for peripheral regions and more 'even' development. However, it remained the case that EU integration was mainly a market-led neo-liberal project and the redistributive measures to counter the negative effects of integration were (and still are) very limited. EU regional funds, for instance, amount to less than 1 per cent of total EU GDP (and less than the efficiency gains from the single market which largely accrue to the already better-off regions), though regional aid has been increasing and the structural funds now amount to well over a third of the EU budget compared to less than a tenth in 1980.

4.2   Regional networking and alliances

Increasingly, regions have become important players in their own right. Partly because of encouragement and legitimation from EU institutions, but also on their own initiative and in response to the threats and opportunities of the SEM, regional interests have been demanding more powers and resources. In many cases regional authorities have played a key, neo-corporatist role in stimulating economic development, linking 'Eurocrats', multinational companies, the local bourgeoisie, politicians and trade unions, and educational and training establishments. The lack or weakness of regional political structures is increasingly seen as having a debilitating effect on regional economic performance. This 'new regionalist' argument (Section 3) is widely used by regional groups seeking more autonomy or self-government.

To further these political objectives, regions have increasingly become involved in creating transnational alliances with other regions, new cross-border regional entities, and the Committee of the Regions. There was an upsurge of transnational inter-regional co-operation manifested in a multiplicity of regional groupings and associations reaching across the member states. Thus the 'Four Motors' – the 'bourgeois regionalism' or 'high-tech' association of Baden-Württemburg, Lombardy, Rhône-Alpes, Catalonia, and, recently, Wales – was established in 1989 with encouragement from the EU (see Figure 2.3). It was explicitly presented as an alliance which would enable these strong regions to take a 'pathbreaking role' in the new Europe (Harvie, 1994), while for Catalonia it was also a means of asserting its own separate national identity and pursuing its own 'European' interests rather than making common cause with poorer regions in Spain. However, while some of these alliances continue to reflect substantial economic and political linkages, many had little substance or were arbitrary and lacked identity or legitimacy (for example, the 'Atlantic Arc' linking Wales, Brittany, Aquitaine, Galicia). The diversity of regions, particularly across different states, militates against the formation of coherent regional alliances and only rarely do they link the interests of 'core' and 'periphery' or rich and poor regions. In general the new cross-border regions formed by contiguous regions from either side of a border (for example, Northern Ireland and the Republic of Ireland) are on firmer footing, though such entities often suffer from having a history of antagonism (for example, Kent and Nord Pas de Calais) rather than a history of co-operation on which to build.

4.3   The Committee of the Regions

The regions, however, have a privileged place in EU integration, and the Committee of the Regions has the status of an 'expert' which must be consulted on issues of cross-border co-operation. This Committee epitomizes both the growth of EU regionalism and the obstacles it faces from diversity and from conflicts of interest with state governments. Strong regions, particularly German *Länder*, played a key role in establishing this 'advisory committee of representatives of regional and local authorities'. In reasserting their eroded constitutional rights from the late 1980s, the *Länder* opposed the practice of the federal German government – and by extension other central administrations – of deciding how regional EU aid is distributed, and they called for some regional representation at the Council of Ministers, the EU key decision-making body. The *Länder*, the EU Commission and the European Parliament favoured the Committee of the Regions having real decision-making powers and a membership of elected regional and local politicians with democratic legitimacy. But state governments, including the German government, were less enthusiastic, and the highly centralist British and Greek representatives were openly hostile, proposing to send along unelected civil servants answerable only to central government. The then Conservative British government wanted to avoid empowering regions in the UK, seeing regionalism as a 'slippery slope' to the break-up of the UK and a harbinger of European federalism threatening British sovereignty. The compromise agreed in Maastricht was that most Committee members would be elected regional politicians but their status was only advisory. However, the Commission and Council of Ministers were obliged to consult the Committee on a range of policy areas including education, culture and economic cohesion, and the Committee could give an opinion on any EU matter whether or not asked.

The Committee was set up in 1994 and had 222 members in 1995 when Austria, Finland and Sweden joined, representation varying by size of state with 24 for the large states down to 6 for the smallest, Luxembourg. The Committee's cohesion and effectiveness is however curtailed by its heterogeneity, mirroring the diversity of the regions from which the members come. The main divisions within the membership tend to be along state lines, rather than regions of the same type (for example, all 'Objective One' regions) making common cause across different states. There are huge differences in the 'political weight' of members, reflecting the political status of their regions. There are also divergences between regional politicians and local representatives of cities and municipalities which divide the regions; to minimize this problem the Committee presidency and deputy presidency alternate between representatives of important regions (for example, Catalonia or Lombardy) and those from the big municipalities (for example, Barcelona or Milan).

The EU's 'subsidiarity' principle gives precedence to lower territorial 'levels' of government over higher ones – at least in theory. Thus the EU as a whole should take action only where individual states cannot act effectively, an idea supported by 'anti-federal' British governments and so-called 'eurosceptics'. However, on the continent subsidiarity is interpreted more positively as a federal principle which gives rights to the smaller, constituent parts of a state including sub-state regions. In 1995, a Committee of the Regions report, overseen by the Catalan President, Jordi Pujol, proposed that it should automatically extend not only to state level but to sub-state level as well:

> the Community shall take action, in accordance with the principle of subsidiarity, only if and so far as the objectives of the proposed action cannot be sufficiently achieved by the Member States, *or by the regional and local authorities endowed with powers under the domestic legislation of the Member State in question.*
>
> (Wagstaff, 1999b, p.192, emphasis added)

This was followed in 1997 by another report, 'Regions and Cities: Pillars of Europe', prepared by the leader of Bavaria's regional government and the Mayor of Oporto, and it was the basis for a Committee of the Regions 'summit conference' before the Amsterdam Treaty negotiations. The Treaty however did not extend automatic subsidiarity to the regions, but it did further increase the Committee's freedom of action; the main gain was the addition of more obligatory spheres, such as environmental and social policies, on which the Committee had to be consulted.

There has therefore been a remarkable historical trend of increasing regionalism, given a recent boost by globalization and European integration. But the question remains: what is its significance, where is it all leading?

Summary

- The EU as presently constituted is itself a product of globalization, and here the impact of globalization has been heightened by the central institutions of the EU directly encouraging regionalism and cross-border co-operation between regions to further its own political and economic integration.

- Regionalism has also been indirectly boosted by other EU policies, particularly the development of the Single European Market since the late 1980s.

5   Toward a 'Europe of the Regions'?

The significance of regionalism hinges on empirical questions about the probable future of the EU and normative questions about the (un)desirability of different models for the future. A return to the traditional 'Europe of Nations' (that is, nation states) model is improbable precisely because of the growth of regionalism, as well as the firm establishment of the central institutions of the EU. On the other hand, because of the continuing power of states and their major say in European integration, the federalization process will probably be 'arrested' long before the arrival of the 'Federal Europe' super-state model (Anderson, 1996). If so, the most plausible of the three dominant models would seem to be the 'Europe of the Regions'.

However, when it is claimed, explicitly or implicitly, that regions will replace the Europe of nation states, problems immediately arise. So here it is essential to distinguish the growth of sub-state nationalist and regionalist politics, an established reality in Western Europe, from what I consider the ultimately implausible ideology of a 'Europe of the Regions'.

5.1   The regionalism project

The regionalism project has normative as well as empirical elements – it says what *ought* to happen as well as what *will* happen – and its normative origins pre-date its contemporary usage in advocating European integration. It is open to criticism on these different grounds.

It presents a benign vision of regions and regionalism replacing or displacing nation states and nationalism. Strong versions proclaim the 'death of the nation state' and the 'end of territorially based sovereignty', while in weaker versions such ideas are only implicit, or the decline of states in favour of regions is seen as a relative, long-term matter. In EU circles weaker versions prevailed, not only because they are more plausible but also because the Commission's objective was to make allies in the regions rather than enemies in the states, which retained control over the general direction and pace of integration. However the stronger version had more resonance at a popular level.

Empirically, the regionalist project suggests that the growing importance of a level of government between the levels of local municipality and the nation state is a trend which will continue inexorably and at the expense of nation states. It exaggerates this trend, and it inappropriately sees the relationship between regions and states as a simple 'zero-sum game', where more power to regions must mean less to states as if there was a fixed amount of 'power' that they had to fight over.

Regionalism, rather than being some independent rival, continues to be conditioned by the states. They define the regions, and in most cases still set the limits within which regionalism is possible. Far from being a preferable 'alternative' to the system of states, we have seen that the great diversity of regions and regionalisms often constitutes a poor basis for unified policy or co-operation. The Committee of the Regions has, for example, been hampered by the great heterogeneity and unevenness in the interests, power and democratic legitimacy of the regional representatives. The 'death of the nation state', like that of Mark Twain, is greatly exaggerated (Anderson, 1995). The member states of the EU largely control the direction and pace of EU integration, which is still mainly harnessed to their interests, and still dominated by the meetings of Heads of Governments and the Council of Ministers. Indeed, in some respects it has strengthened rather than weakened the member states, giving them more leverage over economic forces than they would otherwise have. Nor does regionalism necessarily weaken states. Spain, for instance, is arguably stronger as a result of devolving powers to Basque and Catalan parliaments, and it would be nonsense to argue that federal Germany is a 'weak' state because of its strong regions, or that Greece and Portugal are 'strong' because they are highly centralized. States in general have lost some economic power because of globalization, but contrary to neo-liberal ideology they continue to have crucial roles in supra-state and sub-state developments.

The normative idea that regions are good in themselves and better than states or larger entities is also suspect for related reasons. The regionalist project suggests that regions in Europe express 'diversity within unity', that regions are economically efficient and powerful units yet close and cosy for politics and identity, that they express respect for cultural difference and are democratically responsive to local aspirations, and that regionalism provides a peaceful alternative to nationalism and national conflicts over sovereignty and territory. The contrast (sometimes implied rather than explicitly asserted) is with the supposedly greater economic inflexibility and inadequacy of 'distant' state institutions and policies, and a more bureaucratic Brussels where the Council of Ministers meets in secret. Such normative regionalism is not confined to the 'Europe of the Regions' project but it is well exemplified by it.

5.2 Origins and weaknesses of the regionalist project

The origins of the regionalist project can be traced back to Leopold Kohr's *The Breakdown of Nations*, first published in 1957 (Kohr, 1986). By 'nations', Kohr actually meant nation states and in particular big states, for his book was a polemic against the 'bigness' of states as the source of modern ills. Indeed he saw excessive size as the main cause of all social problems and his ideas would later be successfully popularized by E.F. Schumacher's slogan and best-seller *Small is Beautiful* (Schumacher, 1973). The more recent adaptation of this idea to regions has several different sources which may help explain its appeal.

In part, the 'Europe of the Regions' model was developed as an ideology of EU integration and legitimation. Its rhetoric served to overcome, minimize or obscure some of the problems involved in creating the SEM after 1986, and later Economic and Monetary Union (EMU) as envisaged in the 1991 'Maastricht Treaty'. For example, in 1991, the Chef de Cabinet to the Regional Commissioner argued for a new Europe where regional authorities had greater political autonomy: 'The Europe of the regions is already a cultural reality and in the new European single market there will soon be an economic one. Why not turn it into a political reality too?' (see Harvie, 1994, Chapter 5). The idea was vigorously propagated by the 'Four Motors', and it lent heavily on their reputation for 'success' and that of other exceptional regions such as Emilia Romagna, rather than on more typical cases.

In the early 1990s the EU faced a legitimacy crisis as it sought to speed up integration. The Parliament was weak and perceived to be weak, and the Commission needed additional popular support. Linking regional identity to a putative European identity suggested a new more democratic EU, and it helped counter the largely top-down nature of integration and the perception that EMU would lead to a centralization of economic power. It downplayed the difficulties faced by peripheral economies, particularly in times of economic depression when 'core' and 'periphery' generally diverge; and it provided a counter-balance (at least ideologically) to the neo-liberalism of the SEM and the threat it held for weaker regions, particularly as substantial help for them was ruled out by the dominant neo-liberalism.

Both the EU and the regions gained legitimacy by working directly together, and the normative ideology was picked up by interests in the regions themselves for their own reasons. A 'Europe of the Regions' would further the autonomy or even independence of places such as Scotland

and Wales 'in Europe'; it would help in creating regionalism in England and reforming the unwritten constitution of the British state with its archaic conception of sovereignty as the indivisible preserve of the Westminster Parliament.

The Labour government's programme of constitutional reform has involved among other things, the creation of a Scottish Parliament and a Welsh Assembly (1999). It has also made possible through the Belfast Agreement (10 April 1998) the establishment of a devolved parliament in Northern Ireland.

When EU President Jacques Delors propagated the idea of a 'Europe of the Regions' he was supported by the Northern Irish MEP, John Hume, who counterposed to the 'Europe of Nations' of De Gaulle and Thatcher 'a Europe which is much more comprehensive in its unity and which values its regional and cultural diversity while working to provide for a convergence of living standards' (Hume, 1988, pp.48,57). It was predicted that in the 1990s we would 'leave the Europe of competing nationalisms behind us'; the nation state would break up and we needed to move beyond it to 'a European federation of equal regions' (Kearney, 1988, pp.8,15–18). But a Europe of 'equal regions' is a utopian non-starter if ever there was one; and far from ending nationalism, some of the strongest regional movements – in Scotland, Ireland, the Basque Country and elsewhere – are themselves nationalisms whose core supporters seek not merely their own region but their own, reconstituted nation state.

In normative terms, as with empirical reality, regions are not necessarily more desirable than states, and in some respects could be distinctly worse. Despite the many shortcomings of existing states, it is by no mcans self-evident that regions would fare better in the face of global forces, and most regions, being significantly weaker than their states, would arguably be significantly less effective in delivering economic welfare, cultural and other rights. Such rights may be decreasing in existing states but the capability of these states is still much more substantial than that of any foreseeable regional alternatives. A 'Europe of the Regions' could indeed turn out to be a multiplicity of smaller competing units all 'beggaring their neighbours', and without the possibility of the state-organized regional transfers or cross-subsidies which are still generally much more important to disadvantaged regions than EU aid. While the German *Länder* are very powerful, it was the German state which made the crucial (albeit inadequate) resource transfers to former East Germany.

As with 'new regionalism' (Section 2), the 'Europe of the Regions' project has the same dangers of underestimating the continuing economic importance of the state, overestimating the coherence of most regions, and conceding too much ground to the dominant neo-liberal ideology which would weaken the state's intervention and redistributive capabilities. Indeed, in some richer regions (for example, in northern Italy), regionalisms have been partly motivated by opposition to transfers from themselves to despised poorer regions, and nationalism has no monopoly on supremacist racist attitudes. Contrary to the benign vision, some regionalisms can be very parochial, even xenophobic, as well as progressive – they are not inherently either one or the other. As for the question of Europe's future, the answers on empirical and normative grounds suggest that it is unlikely to be a 'Europe of the Regions'. It seems equally as unlikely as a return to the 'Europe of nation states' model, or the development of a fully-fledged federal 'United States of Europe' super-state.

Summary

- The idea that regions are replacing nation states and that the future of Europe lies in a loose, decentralized federation of regions is a misinterpretation of recent and current developments.

- This 'small is beautiful' ideology of a 'Europe of the Regions' can be rejected on empirical and normative grounds: it is still largely the existing member states which control EU integration and define the regions; the strongest regional threats to nation states come from nationalist movements wanting their own 'nation state'; most regions would be too weak to cope with the pressures of globalization; and their very diversity rules them out as a replacement for nation states.

6   Has the future already arrived?

If the 'Europe of the Regions' model is also ruled out – at least in its stronger versions which suggest that nation states are being replaced – the interesting question remains: how will significantly enhanced regionalisms relate to other 'possible Europes'? These include the traditional 'nation state' and 'Federal Europe' models, both of which also reflect some continuing elements of reality, but in addition a 'Europe' of cities, of cultures, of national and ethnic minorities, and of transnational movements and structures which extend well beyond the institutional architecture of the EU. This multifaceted Europe is not captured by any of the three 'models', most obviously because they are too simplified. But, more fundamentally, they fail because they each focus on one of three 'traditional levels' of territorial government as if the future involved simply making a choice between these levels. They counterpose them as discrete 'alternatives' rather than focusing on how they interrelate, and how particular social processes span or include the different levels. They fail to appreciate the qualitative transformation in their interrelationships that is already well underway.

Political power and government are seen very simplistically in terms of a 'zero-sum' competition between discrete territorial levels, with more power at one level automatically meaning less at another. But political restructuring cannot be reduced to this simple arithmetic – there is no 'fixed total' of power to be distributed, and power is not only distributed between political institutions at different spatial scales, it is also located in the relations between these institutions and it is found outside them in civil society. As Susan Strange pointed out, nation states may be losing some of their autonomy not because power has 'gone upwards' to other political institutions such as the EU but because it has 'gone sideways' to economic institutions and global market forces, and in some respects it has 'gone nowhere' or just 'evaporated' as political control over economic forces is simply lost (Strange, 1994). Likewise, more power for regions does not necessarily mean less for states. We have seen that states may indeed be strengthened by devolving some political processes to their regions and by 'pooling' some of their sovereignty in the EU collective. Furthermore, while states may lose some autonomous power in one policy area (for example, industrial development), they may gain new powers in other areas (for example, labour training, and controls over labour migration), and such distinctions are increasingly important given the fact that globalization is having very uneven impacts on different state functions. So the idea of the EU or the regions as alternatives to the nation state would seem to be fundamentally flawed.

The traditionalist limitations of this idea are well depicted by the metaphor of 'Gulliver's fallacy', in which new political forms can only be scale replicas of the existing nation state, either larger as in a 'United States of Europe', or smaller as in regional government (just as the two societies which Gulliver met in his Travels, one of giants, the other of midgets, were simply scale replicas of human society). This perspective sees only a change of geographical scale with no real appreciation that political processes and institutions at different scales are likely to be qualitatively (not just quantitatively) different, and no recognition that their new interrelationships may be a key factor potentially transforming the whole nature of politics. Much of the debate about Europe's future is vitiated by false polarizations between regions, states and other territorial levels.

Instead, it seems more fruitful to think of qualitative changes in the relationships within and between such levels, and to see them as being increasingly linked in 'multi-layered' or 'multi-level' structures of governance, with multiple identities and loyalties, albeit ones of varying intensity or importance (Guibernau, 1999). We also need to take into account the fact that regionalism, along with other territorial forms of politics, culture and identity, is increasingly in interaction with *non*-territorial transnational movements which cross-cut these levels.

The sovereign authority of states has not been replaced, nor is it likely to be in the foreseeable future, but it is already significantly less clear-cut than it was only some decades ago. Rather than sovereignty being based on a single territorial level, whether that of the state or a scale replica, we are more likely moving toward a situation of segmented, overlapping or shared authority, where regions are one level among several territorial and non-territorial political entities.

A fully federal 'United States of Europe' seems highly unlikely in the foreseeable future. The states would hardly agree to 'sink their differences' in a federal state, not least because of uneven regional development and the fact that the pace of cultural unification in Europe has not been at all commensurate with the moves toward economic union. All the states, and some of the regions, remain important as repositories of distinct cultures. Equally, and for similar reasons, the nation states are not about to acquiesce to a 'post-nationalist' and loosely federal 'Europe of the Regions'. The comparative importance of the different territorial levels will continue to change, perhaps in unpredictable ways, and in some policy areas both the EU and the regional levels may continue to gain relative to the states. But the broad outlines of more complex multi-level governance and multiple identities are already visible in present structures and relationships. In that sense the future has already arrived.

Summary

- None of the three models – national, federal or regional – can adequately capture the complexity of the multifaceted Europe of today. Each implies an exclusive distribution of power between the levels of territorial governance that is too simplistic.

- We need to think in terms of qualitative changes in the relationships within and between the levels and see them as being linked in multi-layered structures of governance.

- Such a complex multi-level governance system, with multiple identities and loyalties, may already be with us.

7   Conclusion

In summary, this chapter has endeavoured to substantiate a variety of related points which epitomize current trends and problems in 'governing European diversity'.

'Regions' and 'regionalism' in Western Europe display great diversity in economic, social and cultural terms, within particular states as well as between states; regions vary widely in size, population, levels of development, history, identity and politics (or lack thereof). But since the heyday of the centralized nation state in the 1930s and 1940s, most of Europe's regions have politically grown increasingly more important. This has been largely in response to regional inequalities in economic development, threats to traditional regional cultures, and the political federalization of states, whether to reduce their centralized power or to contain regional separatisms.

More generally, since the 1970s, accelerated globalization has meant that attracting external sources of investment became more crucial and this has made 'global' or at least 'international' players of regional (and local) authorities which previously had acted largely with and through their central governments. These developments have advanced furthest in the European Union, whose central institutions have directly encouraged regionalism and cross-border co-operation between regions to further the EU's political and economic integration. Regionalism has also been indirectly boosted by other EU policies, particularly the development of the Single European Market since the late 1980s.

However, the idea propagated in the 1990s that Europe's future lies in a loose, decentralized federation of regions, and that regions are replacing nation states (allegedly too small for global competition but too big for cultural identification, apparently being eroded 'from above' by globalization and the EU and 'from below' by regionalism, and inherently associated with nationalistic conflict), is very misleading. Notwithstanding the problems of nation states and nationalism, in my view this 'small is beautiful' ideology of a 'Europe of the Regions' can be rejected on empirical and normative grounds: the existing member states still largely control EU integration; they define the regions; the strongest regional threats to nation states come from nationalist movements wanting their own 'nation state'; most regions would be less able to cope with the pressures of globalization; and the great diversity of regions undermines any possibility of them replacing nation states.

Instead of the future lying unambiguously with regions, or with a European super-state, or a return to the traditional Europe of nation states, it is much more likely to resemble the multi-level present. Regions will continue to develop but through complex interactions with the EU, the member states, other regions and cities, and *non*-territorial associations which span these different territorial 'levels'.

References

Amin, A. (1999) 'An institutional perspective on regional economic development', *International Journal of Urban and Regional Research*, vol.23, no.2, pp.365–78.

Anderson, J. (1995) 'The exaggerated death of the nation state' in Anderson, J., Brook, C. and Cochrane, A. (eds) *A Global World? Re-ordering Political Space*, Oxford, Oxford University Press/The Open University.

Anderson, J. (1996) 'The shifting stage of politics: new medieval and postmodern territorialities?', *Environment and Planning D: Society and Space*, vol.14, no.2, April, pp.133–53.

Anderson, J. and Goodman J. (1995) 'Regions, states and the European Union: modernist reaction or postmodern adaptation?', *Review of International Political Economy*, vol.2, no.4, Autumn, pp.600–31.

Bromley, S.J. (ed.) (2001) *Governing the European Union***, London, Sage/The Open University.**

Bull, A. (1999) 'Regionalism in Italy' in Wagstaff, P. (ed.) *Regionalism in the European Union*, Exeter, Intellect, pp.140–57.

Butt Philip, A. (1999) 'Regionalism in the United Kingdom' in Wagstaff, P. (ed.) *Regionalism in the European Union*, Exeter, Intellect, pp.19–39.

del Río, J. (1999) 'Regionalism in Iberia' in Wagstaff, P. (ed.) *Regionalism in the European Union*, Exeter, Intellect, pp.167–87.

Government of Ireland (2000) 'EU structural funds', www.irlgov.ie

Guibernau, M. (1999) *Nations Without States: Political Communities in a Global Age,* Cambridge, Polity Press.

Harvie, C. (1994) *The Rise of Regional Europe*, London, Routledge.

Hume, J. (1988) 'Europe of the Regions' in Kearney, R. (ed.) *Across the Frontiers: Ireland in the 1990s*, Dublin, Wolfhound Press.

Jeffery, C. (ed.) (1997) *The Regional Dimension of the European Union: Towards a Third Level in Europe?*, London, Frank Cass.

Kearney, R. (1988) 'Introduction: thinking otherwise' in Kearney, R. (ed.) *Across the Frontiers: Ireland in the 1990s*, Dublin, Wolfhound Press.

Kohr, L. (1986) *The Breakdown of Nations*, London, Routledge & Kegan Paul.

Lovering, J. (1999) 'Theory led by policy: the inadequacies of the "new regionalism"', *International Journal of Urban and Regional Studies*, vol.23, no.2, pp.379–95.

Newman, M. (1996) *Democracy, Sovereignty and the European Union,* London, Hurst & Company.

Schumacher, E.F. (1973) *Small is Beautiful: Economics as if People Really Mattered,* London, Abacus.

Simonetti, R. (2001) 'Governing European technology and innovation' in Thompson, G. (ed). *Governing the European Economy***, London, Sage/The Open University.**

Stammen, T. (1999) 'Federalism in Germany' in Wagstaff, P. (ed.) *Regionalism in the European Union*, Exeter, Intellect, pp.98–118.

Strange, S. (1994) 'The power gap: member states and the world economy' in Brouwer, F., Lintner, V. and Newman, M. (eds) *Economic Policy Making and the European Union*, London, Federal Trust.

Wagstaff, P. (1999a) 'Regionalism in France' in Wagstaff, P. (ed.) *Regionalism in the European Union*, Exeter, Intellect, pp.50–73.

Wagstaff, P. (1999b) 'The Committee of the Regions of the European Union' in Wagstaff, P. (ed.) *Regionalism in the European Union*, Exeter, Intellect, pp.188–93.

Further reading

Anderson, J., Brook, C. and Cochrane, A. (eds) (1995) *A Global World? Re-ordering Political Space*, Oxford, Oxford University Press/The Open University.

Guibernau, M. (1999) *Nations Without States: Political Communities in a Global Age,* Cambridge, Polity Press.

Harvie, C. (1994) *The Rise of Regional Europe*, London, Routledge.

Keating, M. (1998) *The New Regionalism in Western Europe: Territorial Restructuring and Political Change,* Cheltenham, Edward Elgar.

Newman, M. (1996) *Democracy, Sovereignty and the European Union*, London, Hurst & Company.

Wagstaff, P. (ed.) (1999) *Regionalism in the European Union*, Exeter, Intellect.

Chapter 3
Migrants, refugees and citizenship

Zig Layton-Henry

1 Introduction

International migration, by which I mean the movement of people across the borders of sovereign states, has been a major factor in the diversification of European societies. The myth of a Europe composed of homogeneous nation states has disappeared, as over 30 million people from all over the world have moved to Western Europe since the Second World War. In the early post-war period this migration was largely a movement of men and women from neighbouring European countries seeking work in the more prosperous and expanding industrial centres close by. It was often a continuation of traditional economic migrations that had been disrupted by the recession in the 1930s and the Second World War. Thus the Irish migrated to Britain, the Finns to Sweden, the Italians and Spaniards to France, Germany and Switzerland, and the Portuguese to France. As the post-war economic boom continued and labour shortages became even more acute in the 1960s and early 1970s, migrant workers were recruited from further and further afield. People from the Caribbean and the Indian subcontinent migrated to Britain, people from Turkey, Yugoslavia and Greece migrated to Germany, and people from North and West Africa migrated to France.

The oil price crisis in 1973 caused a serious recession and a major reassessment of labour recruitment policies in all Western European countries. Large-scale labour recruitment was ended and more selective recruitment regimes were introduced. Some labour migrants were encouraged to return to their countries of origin. These immigration control policies had the unintended consequence of forcing 'guestworkers' to decide between permanent settlement or returning to their countries of origin, and then perhaps not being allowed to come back. In general, they decided to stay, and most sent for their families to join them. Large-scale family reunification thus became the cause of further migration and the foreign populations of Western European countries increased quickly. In the 1980s and 1990s the former emigration countries of Europe, including Italy, Greece, Spain and Portugal, became the recipients of migrant workers, particularly from Africa. A conflict of interest emerged in the European Union (EU) between Northern European countries, which favoured tough controls, and Southern European countries, which wanted a liberal immigration regime as a source of labour for poorly paid agricultural work such as fruit picking.

The ending of large-scale labour recruitment in the mid-1970s did not end migration flows. Attention switched from labour migration to the increasing numbers of people coming to Europe and claiming asylum and the status of 'refugee'. Under the 1951 United Nations Convention on Refugees, persons with a well-founded fear of persecution in their own country have a right to protection and rehabilitation in countries to which they flee. The suspicion in Western Europe is that many of these asylum seekers are really economic migrants using the UN Convention to gain admittance to the more buoyant job markets in Europe. The flow of refugees to Western European states was dramatically increased in the 1990s by the wars in Bosnia and Kosovo and by the movement of gypsies from the Czech Republic and Romania.

In the UK, the rising numbers of asylum applications added to a huge backlog of applications at the Home Office, which reached a peak of 105,000 early in the year 2000. The UK media, in particular tabloid newspapers, have been full of dramatic stories of lorries full of Albanians being stopped at Dover or illegal immigrants being found at motorway service stations. Gypsies have been accused of breaking the law by aggressive begging on the streets, and lorry drivers have been warned that they will be heavily fined and could have their lorries confiscated if people without travel documents are brought into the UK. The desperation of the people wishing to migrate to Western Europe was highlighted by the tragic deaths of 58 Chinese people who were found asphyxiated in the back of a sealed lorry stopped at Dover in June 2000. The Home Secretary was quick to blame the deaths on criminal gangs trafficking in illegal immigrants, rather than on the tough immigration controls that encouraged people to take extreme risks. Nevertheless, in the immediate aftermath the deaths shocked the media and politicians into taking a more considered view of immigration issues.

The foreign populations of European states, that is, those who do not have citizenship of the state in which they live, are a complicated mixture of temporary visitors, such as tourists, businessmen, students and au pairs, and temporary or permanent residents, the spouses and children of permanent residents, applicants for asylum and those with refugee status. Table 3.1 shows the foreign populations of nine major receiving countries in Western Europe in 1997.

Table 3.1 shows that Germany had by far the largest foreign population in total, although Luxembourg and Switzerland had the largest in proportional terms. In Luxembourg other EU citizens made up 90 per cent of the foreign population, while in Switzerland EU citizens accounted for 60 per cent. In the UK, EU citizens made up nearly 50 per cent of the foreign population, while in France they represented 40 per cent and in Germany 25 per cent.

Table 3.1 The foreign populations of nine major receiving countries in Western Europe, 1997

Country	Foreign population (000s)	Percentage of total population	Foreign labour (000s)	Percentage of total labour force
Austria	733	9.1	326	9.9
Belgium	903	8.9	333	7.9
France*	3,597	6.3	1,570	6.1
Germany	7,366	9.0	2,522	9.1
Luxembourg	148	34.9	125	55.1
Netherlands	678	4.4	208	2.9
Sweden	522	6.0	220	5.2
Switzerland	1,341	19.0	693	17.5
UK	2,066	3.6	949	3.6

* The figures for France are for 1990.

(OECD/SOPEMI, 1999)

These figures for foreign populations underestimate immigration to a substantial extent. In some countries, such as Belgium, France, the Netherlands, Sweden and the UK, many immigrants either have naturalized or already had citizenship as they migrated, as they came from former colonies of the countries to which they moved. In Germany, immigrants of German descent from Eastern Europe have easy access to German citizenship and so are not included in the foreign population. It is estimated that ethnic German migrants number about 4 million people.

The foreign populations of European countries have become highly diversified and this diversification is increasing. The composition by nationality of foreign or immigrant populations varies between countries, depending on geographical proximity, colonial or other historical links, migration traditions and cultural ties such as language and religion. In recent years migration has become a global phenomenon, and cities such as Berlin, London and Paris include communities from every corner of the world. Moroccans and Tunisians, who emigrated to France for historical reasons, have now spread out across the EU and have established sizeable communities in the Netherlands, Spain and Germany. Refugees from the former Yugoslavia used to flee overwhelmingly to Germany, but can now be found in all Western European countries. They have also fled to some Eastern European countries, including Bulgaria and Hungary. Refugees from Africa, Kosovo, the Czech Republic and Latin America tend to apply for asylum in Britain.

The migration of large numbers of foreign-born people to settle in European countries has presented European states with a number of challenges. It has caused them to reflect on who should be entitled to enter their countries and settle. Should priority be given to the demands of labour markets or to people related by descent to the native population? What behaviour should be expected of newcomers? Should they modify their customs and behaviour before they are accepted as members of their new society, or should multiculturalism be accepted, even encouraged, by the receiving society? Should citizenship be offered to all newcomers after a period of permanent residence as the first step toward inclusion, or should citizenship be accorded only to people who have embraced the customs, language and culture of their new country of residence? Should an oath of allegiance be required? What behaviour should be tolerated toward non-citizens? Should they have most of the rights of native citizens, or should they be kept in a second-class situation? This chapter will examine the following issues.

- The origins of post-war migration.
- The responses of the three major receiving countries, namely Britain, France and Germany.
- The strategies for integration and exclusion adopted by Britain, France and Germany.
- The challenge of managing diverse societies.

A note on terminology

The terms used to describe migrants and refugees have strong political connotations and are therefore highly controversial and contested. An 'immigrant', for example, is a person who moves into a country from another country with the intention of staying longer than a specified period, normally six months. Colloquially, an 'immigrant' is a person who moves to a new country to settle permanently. People who move to a country for less than six months tend to be described as 'tourists' or 'visitors'. An immigrant who decides to stay permanently might be described as a 'settler', although this term is rarely used except when referring to white settlers in Africa.

The intense controversy over non-white immigration into countries such as Britain and France has caused a narrowing in the everyday use of the term 'immigrant' and its use as a label for non-white people. Thus white immigrants are not called immigrants, and black people born in Britain or France are often inappropriately described as immigrants. Being described as 'immigrants' causes intense resentment in British-born black people. Describing a person as an immigrant suggests that he or she is a recent incomer who is not yet accepted as part of the community. The failure to describe white immigrants as immigrants suggests that they are quickly accepted as members of their new society.

An 'economic migrant' is a person who moves to improve his or her standard of living, usually by seeking employment. Economic migrants may move to seek work within the same country or move to another country. 'Labour migrant' is another term for an economic migrant.

'Guestworker' is a term first used in Germany to describe a worker specifically recruited from another country to work in Germany, usually recruited under labour agreements between Germany and the other country. The term implies an invitation to work for a specified period and then return to the country of origin. Like the term 'immigrant', it also implies that the individual is not fully accepted as a permanent member of his or her country of residence.

An 'asylum seeker' is a person who is claiming the status of a refugee under the 1951 United Nations Convention and the 1967 United Nations Protocol on Refugees. The 1951 UN Convention stipulated that the status of refugee would be given to persons with a well-founded fear of being persecuted for reasons of race, religion, nationality, membership of a particular social group, or political opinion. Refugee status is determined by the state to which the asylum seeker has fled, and the state is forbidden from returning the applicant to the frontiers of territories where his or her life would be threatened. The rise in asylum applications to Britain in the 1990s caused a fierce debate about how genuine some of the applicants were and the coining of the term 'bogus asylum seeker' to describe people who were assumed to be economic migrants seeking to circumvent immigration controls by claiming asylum. The term 'Convention refugee' is sometimes used to describe a person whose claim for asylum has been accepted under the 1951 UN Convention.

2 The origins of post-war migration

Migration to Western Europe in the post-war years has transformed European societies, but it has not transformed them from homogeneous societies into heterogeneous societies. Europe has always experienced considerable migration and European states have always been composed of a kaleidoscope of peoples, including both territorially based indigenous minorities and immigrants from far and wide. In the nineteenth century, European migrations included Czech and Slovak people migrating to Vienna, Poles moving to the Ruhr, and Irish people and Russian Jews coming to Britain. London, Paris and Vienna were then, as they are now, major cosmopolitan cities of great ethnic diversity. These cities all attracted immigrants from large hinterlands. By the late nineteenth century the core European industrializing countries of Britain, France, Germany and Switzerland were all recruiting workers from other parts of Europe. At the same time Britain and Germany continued to be major emigration countries, sending people to North America in particular.

The First World War and the subsequent depression greatly reduced intra-European migration and emigration overseas. In fact, many who had emigrated from Europe to other continents returned. However, the onset of the Second World War was to herald a huge upsurge in both intra-European migration and intercontinental migration.

The intra-European movements of people were on a massive scale during and immediately after the Second World War. Millions of Germans fled west before the advance of the Soviet armies and millions of Germans, Poles and Czechs were displaced by boundary changes and expulsions. These forced migrations presented European states with massive economic and social disruption, but not with political challenges. The problems were feeding, housing and finding employment for refugees who were often fellow citizens or wartime allies. They were displaced against their will and grateful to find sanctuary and security in Western Europe. Post-war reconstruction and Marshall Aid from the USA encouraged economic recovery in Western Europe. This allowed the refugees and displaced persons to be integrated into the recovering European economies, which facilitated their social and political acceptance.

As economic recovery in Europe gained pace, the 1950s ushered in a period of intense and sustained economic growth that was to last for nearly 30 years. This prolonged economic boom occurred in all the advanced industrialized countries of Western Europe, and they all quickly experienced serious labour shortages. At first, migrant workers were attracted from within Europe; Britain experienced a large migration from Ireland, while Germany and France recruited from Italy, Greece, Spain, Portugal and Yugoslavia. In the British case, it was not long before immigrants were attracted from colonies and former colonies in the West Indies, West Africa and the Indian subcontinent. The French and German governments acted vigorously to help their industrialists recruit the workers they needed. France, for example, signed recruitment agreements with Italy in 1946 and 1951, West Germany in 1950, Greece in 1954, Spain in 1961, Morocco in 1963, Mali, Mauritania, Tunisia and Portugal in 1964 and Yugoslavia and Turkey in 1966. The Federal Republic of Germany signed similar agreements with Italy in 1955, Spain and Greece in 1960, Turkey in 1961, Morocco in 1963 and 1966, Portugal in 1964, Tunisia in 1965 and Yugoslavia in 1968. Between 1956 and 1993 net immigration to the Federal Republic of Germany was 12.6 million, which represented 80 per cent of its population growth over the period (Figure 3.1).

Summary

- The notion that Europe was ever composed of homogeneous nation states is a myth.

- Nineteenth-century industrialization brought widespread migration, which was halted and then partly reversed by the First World War and the economic depression that followed.

- After the Second World War, the recovering European economies absorbed massive numbers of displaced persons. Labour shortages stimulated traditional migration patterns until the early 1970s, when the oil price crisis and a recession ended large-scale labour recruitment.

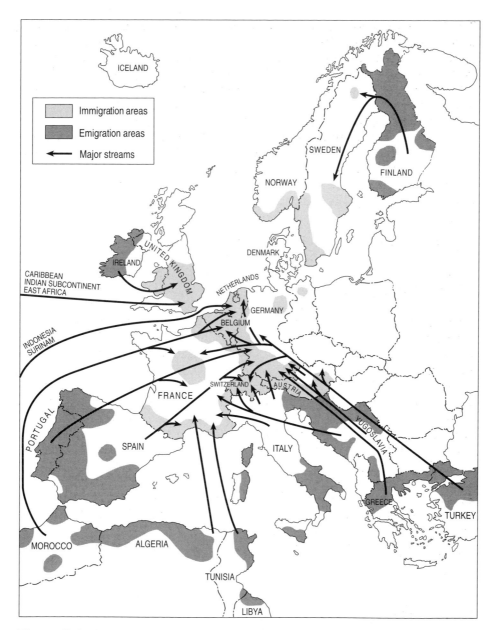

Figure 3.1 Migration to Europe, 1950 to 1974

(adapted from Hammar, 1985, p.3)

- Foreign populations now make up a significant proportion of most Western European labour forces. Immigration continues through family reunifications, asylum seekers and refugees, the recruitment of skilled workers and illegal immigration.

- Over 30 million people have moved to Western Europe since 1945.

3 The responses of Britain, France and Germany

The proactive management of migration by the French and German governments was in marked contrast to the more passive role assumed by British governments toward most post-war immigration. The French government had a long-standing concern about the size of the population, owing to a fall in the French birth rate in the nineteenth century and the enormous losses sustained by France during the First World War. The French government was thus positively disposed toward immigration both as a means of sustaining economic growth and as a method of increasing the size of the population. Even illegal immigration was encouraged as a positive contribution to the French economy. The political élites saw immigration and settlement as a benefit to the French economy and as a means to help populate a country that was relatively underpopulated, given its geographical size and resources.

Immigration to Germany was even more organized. The German government operated recruitment offices in the countries with which it had labour recruiting agreements in order to select suitable workers. These offices arranged health checks, provided work and residence permits and organized transport by train to future employers. German politicians assumed that these workers would be temporary 'guestworkers' and that they would return home in times of economic recession. In practice, and in spite of the political rhetoric that Germany was not a country of immigration, the 'guestworkers' found it easy to obtain work permits and to bring their families to Germany. German employers were against a rotation system of recruitment, which was far less efficient than retaining workers who had learnt German, acquired skills and settled into the firm's culture.

In Britain the key policy-making élites, politicians and civil servants, assumed that immigration would lead to settlement: experience of migration within the Empire and within Britain during the war had led them to this conclusion. The recruitment of Indians to work on the sugar plantations in Guyana, Fiji and Natal in the nineteenth century, or on the railways in East Africa in the twentieth century, had resulted in settlement. Many of the colonial sailors who had come to Britain before the First World War had settled in London, Cardiff, Liverpool and other ports. Colonial migrants recruited during the Second World War to work in forestry, munitions factories or the Royal Air Force had often married local women and settled down in the 'Mother Country'. Once post-war migration began, British policy makers were immediately concerned with housing the new immigrants, their employment prospects and the welcome they were likely to receive.

Summary

- France took a proactive role and encouraged immigration both for economic growth and to increase her population.

- Germany operated highly organized 'guestworker' recruitment offices in countries with which it had labour recruiting agreements.

- Britain was concerned about the implications of the settlement of non-white colonial people.

4 Strategies for integration

The flow of migrants to Western Europe reached its peak in the late 1960s. Labour recruitment ended with the oil price shock and the subsequent recession from 1973 to 1977, but the immigration of dependants continued as families reunited within their new countries of settlement, and this process raised the issue of integration.

Integration policy is closely linked to, and can be seen as another 'face' of, immigration policy. It includes a variety of direct and indirect policies that have an impact on immigrants as individuals and communities. Integration policy assumes that immigrants will remain in their new country of residence for a significant period and that they need help to enable them to function effectively as social actors in new situations. Integration policies may positively promote integration by providing language training, residence and employment protection, and access to social housing, education, social security benefits and health care. Immigrants may have legal protection from arbitrary arrest, racial harassment, discrimination on racial or national grounds and criminal activity. All countries have citizenship laws that specify the conditions under which resident non-citizens can apply to become citizens through the processes of registration or naturalization.

Integration was famously defined by Roy Jenkins as 'not a flattening process of assimilation but as equal opportunity accompanied by cultural diversity, in an atmosphere of mutual tolerance' (Jenkins, 1967, pp.267–73). It is not a process that is completely in the hands of the state authorities at either national or local level. Legislation and public policy can encourage integration or hinder it, but actions by individuals and organizations are also important. Decisions by employers, teachers, doctors, local government officers, social workers, magistrates and journalists can all have major cumulative effects on integration processes. Integration is also influenced by the decisions of individual immigrants and their associations, so decisions about establishing a business, where to live, whom to marry or whether to naturalize can all affect the degree to which integration and a commitment to the new society can be said to have taken place. Actions of the state, such as anti-discrimination legislation, can help to combat racism in the workplace and public places. But state policies are often contradictory, so that immigration-control legislation, enforcement or lack of enforcement of the criminal law, and appointments to public office may act to exclude immigrants, thus cancelling out positive integration policies. Immigrants may come to feel that integration is a form of subordination; for example, that giving up specific cultural traditions, such as the Sikh turban, is a form of surrender to pressures to conform to the norms of the host society.

Hammar (1985, pp.7–10) distinguished between two forms of integration policy: indirect and direct. Indirect integration policies are policies designed for the whole population and include immigrants in their general allocation of benefits – for example, social security policies, health policies and education policies. Direct integration policies are policies introduced specifically on behalf of immigrants – for example, affirmative action policies and anti-discrimination measures.

Summary

- The existence of an integration policy assumes that immigrants will remain and will need help to combat discrimination in employment, education and housing. They may also need help with language training, protection from racist attacks and assistance with social entitlements.

- Each country has its own laws under which immigrants can apply for citizenship after a period of residence.

- The extent of integration depends on the social environment as well as on legislation and public policy.

- Immigration control policies are often at odds with positive integration policies.

5   Case study I: Britain

5.1   Immigration

In the immediate post-war period, the immigration of British subjects from the Caribbean and the Indian subcontinent was not especially welcomed by British policy makers, despite the acute labour shortages caused by post-war reconstruction and economic recovery. Policy makers were concerned about the difficulties the newcomers might have in finding jobs and accommodation. They assumed that the newcomers would experience severe racial prejudice from employers, landlords and neighbours. The government preferred to recruit European workers, who might integrate more easily. Major sources of these additional workers were the Irish, the Poles and volunteer workers from displaced persons camps in Germany (Tannahill, 1958).

Irish people were a traditional source of workers for British employers, particularly in farming, manufacturing and construction. Irish immigration was high during the Second World War and continued unabated after the war at around 60,000 persons a year. The withdrawal of Ireland from the Commonwealth in 1948 did not affect the flow of migrants and the Ireland Act 1949 was passed specifically to continue the political rights of Irish residents in Britain, which would otherwise have been lost. The British government was determined not to discourage the flow of Irish migrants into Britain. Similarly, the establishment of the Common Travel Area, covering the UK and Ireland, meant that there were no restrictions of any kind on travel between the two countries. No specific integration policies were introduced to help Irish immigrants to settle, apart from the Ireland Act 1949, but policy makers assumed that there would be little discrimination and that, in a period of labour shortages, they would easily find work and accommodation.

A second source of European workers that the government was anxious to encourage to settle in Britain were people displaced by the war. There was a large group of Polish soldiers who had fought under British command and who did not wish to return to a Poland under Soviet occupation. The First Polish Army, which had been led by General Sikorski until his death in 1943, was already stationed in Britain, as was the Polish Government in Exile. The Second Polish Army, which had fought in Italy under General Anders, was brought to Britain and allowed to settle, although many preferred to migrate to the USA and Canada. Some 100,000 Poles settled in Britain. The Polish Resettlement Act was passed in 1947 to facilitate their integration and a Polish Resettlement Corps was established. The acute labour shortage resulted in their being rapidly absorbed into the economy, and high rates of intermarriage aided their social integration. A number of schemes were also devised to recruit workers from Austria, the Baltic States and displaced persons camps in Germany. About 140,000 of these workers were recruited under very strict conditions, and many of them migrated on to the USA.

The migration of colonial British subjects from the West Indies and New Commonwealth people from India and Pakistan was facilitated by their war experiences. Those who had served in the UK knew that jobs were easy to find and, after encountering unemployment at home, many returned to the UK. A spontaneous migration thus began in 1948 when the *Empire Windrush* docked with nearly 500 migrants from Jamaica. These migrants were not welcomed unreservedly, as policy makers were concerned about their reception both by landlords and by employers, but all quickly found jobs, and they were followed by others as the demand for labour in the UK, exacerbated by high levels of emigration, continued to attract economic migrants. Table 3.2 shows the development of New Commonwealth immigration from 1953 until the introduction of immigration controls to regulate immigration from the Commonwealth in 1962.

Table 3.2 Estimated net immigration from the New Commonwealth, 1953 to 1962

Year	West Indies	India	Pakistan	Others	Total
1953	2,000	n/a*	n/a	n/a	2,000
1954	11,000	n/a	n/a	n/a	11,000
1955	27,500	5,800	1,850	7,500	42,650
1956	29,800	5,600	2,050	9,350	46,800
1957	23,000	6,600	5,200	7,600	42,400
1958	15,000	6,200	4,700	3,950	29,850
1959	16,400	2,950	850	1,400	21,600
1960	49,650	5,900	2,500	–350	57,700
1961	66,300	23,750	25,100	21,250	136,400
1962**	31,800	19,050	25,080	18,970	94,900

* Data not available.
** First six months up to introduction of controls.

(Layton-Henry, 1992, p.13)

New Commonwealth immigration transformed Britain from a nation that thought of itself as a white Anglo-Saxon and Celtic population into a truly multiracial and multicultural society. In the 1950s and 1960s the new immigrants found work in all the major industrial centres and major industries. In London, they worked in car factories, engineering, construction, communications, the health service, transport and tourism. In Birmingham, engineering factories and foundries were avid employers, as was the textile industry in the northern towns. The health service in particular was heavily dependent on overseas doctors and nurses as well as less skilled staff. In the space of 50 years Britain had acquired a non-white ethnic minority population of some 6 per cent. It also had a substantial but 'invisible' white ethnic minority population, which included Irish, Americans, Australians, South Africans and Canadians. Table 3.3 gives an indication of the populations of non-white ethnic groups in Britain in 1999.

Table 3.3 Estimated population of Great Britain by ethnic group, 1999

Ethnic group	Population (000s)	Percentage of population
White	53,074	93.3
Black Caribbean	490	0.9
Black African	376	0.7
Black other	308	0.5
Indian	930	1.6
Pakistani	663	1.2
Bangladeshi	268	0.5
Chinese and other	770	1.3
Total	56,879	100.0

(Owen et al., 2000, p.9)

5.2 Integration policy

The focus of British integration policy in the post-war period has been on the non-white population. Black and Asian immigrants, whether migrants or refugees, have been defined as needing government intervention to combat social resentment, discrimination and racist violence. White immigrants, apart from some refugee groups such as the Hungarians in 1956 or the Bosnians and Albanians in the 1990s, have been 'invisible', and it has been assumed that they do not need assistance in dealing with discrimination or other integration issues. British policy makers have thus defined integration policy as a 'race relations' matter. Race relations is defined in dichotomous terms as relations between whites and non-whites. The definition of ethnic categories in recent censuses provides a vivid illustration of the obsession of policy makers with non-white ethnic minorities, as it provides one category for all white groups regardless of ethnicity and a number of categories – eight in all – for non-whites (Bulmer, 1996, pp.33–62).

At first, the British government defined the migration of people from its colonies and former colonies as a spontaneous, voluntary migration that did not require government assistance or intervention. Immigrants were largely left to fend for themselves in finding accommodation and jobs. Local authorities were expected to manage housing difficulties and to integrate immigrant children into local schools. As the migrants were British subjects, they had the unrestricted right to come to the UK and full political rights as well as rights to social security and health benefits.

This laissez-faire policy was shaken by the anti-black riots in London and Nottingham in 1958, and by the growing campaign in the press and the Conservative Party for controls on New Commonwealth immigration.

These events raised the political salience of the issue and caused the first Commonwealth Immigrants Act to be passed in 1962 to control immigration from the Commonwealth. The new Labour Government elected in 1964 adopted a bifurcated policy, which was neatly summed up in 1965 by Roy Hattersley, a junior Home Office Minister: 'Integration without control is impossible, but control without integration is indefensible' (*Hansard*, cols 378–85, 23 March 1965). There then followed a series of increasingly tight immigration controls designed to reduce non-white, Third World immigration, closely matched by a series of anti-discrimination measures. Thus tougher controls were included in the Government White Paper *Immigration From the Commonwealth* in 1965, in the Commonwealth Immigrants Act of 1968 and in the Immigration Act of 1971. Anti-discrimination legislation was introduced in the Race Relations Acts of 1965, 1968 and 1976. Moreover, both the immigration controls and the anti-discrimination legislation received a high degree of bipartisan support. This support across all the main parties was maintained despite Enoch Powell's campaign to break it in the late 1960s and early 1970s, the activities of the far-right National Front party in the 1970s and the anti-police riots of the early 1980s.

The tough stance on immigration controls was vigorously maintained by the Thatcher governments of the 1980s, beginning with the Nationality Act of 1981, which maintained the rights of everybody legally settled in the UK, but created two new citizenships for British subjects in colonies or former colonies, namely Citizenship of the British Dependent Territories and British Overseas Citizenship. These people had lost the right of access to the UK under the Immigration Acts, and the new citizenships did not include the rights of entry into and abode in the UK. A series of further measures in the 1980s and 1990s strengthened immigration controls and attempted to make it more difficult for asylum seekers to reach the UK by imposing visa requirements on the countries from which asylum seekers came and imposing a duty on carriers to ensure that only passengers with proper travel documents were accepted.

The strict immigration control measures of the 1980s and 1990s were not balanced, as before, by specific integration measures, but the government did respond to particular 'crises'. Thus the inner-city riots of 1981 led to the Scarman Report and increased expenditure in inner-city areas, and the Swan Report in 1985 attempted to tackle the issues involved in educating an increasingly multicultural population.

In the 1980s it was noticeable that the British black and Asian populations were becoming more prominent in all spheres of social activity, including sport, the media, business and politics. Black and Asian citizens showed high rates of electoral registration and, with the exception of young African-Caribbeans, high rates of voter turnout. The first Members of Parliament (MPs) from ethnic minorities were elected in 1987, and at the local level there was a steady rise in the number of councillors from ethnic minorities (most of them – but not all – elected as Labour Party candidates). In 1990, some 328 ethnic minority councillors were elected, and in London boroughs the numbers rose from 35 in 1974 to 202 in 1994.

Towns such as Birmingham, Blackburn, Bradford, Coventry, Leicester, Manchester, Luton, Nottingham and Slough all had impressive numbers of ethnic minority councillors. The rapid expansion of the non-white electorate meant that local and national politicians of all parties had to take account of their ethnic minority constituents. It is no accident that black political activists were prominent in the campaign for the Mayor of Greater London in 2000, as all the main candidates had to appeal to the large non-white electorate that makes up at least one-fifth of London's voters. Trevor Phillips, a prominent black journalist, became the first leader of the new Greater London Assembly.

The British government has also been forced to respond to campaigns by black and Asian people against racial violence and inadequate protection or unjust treatment by the police. There have been a number of campaigns associated with the deaths of black people while being arrested or in police custody, or with inadequate police action in response to racial violence. The most notable of these campaigns was the one led by Neville and Doreen Lawrence to bring the murderers of their son, Stephen, to justice. This campaign gained considerable public and media support and led to a major inquiry and report – the Macpherson Report (1999) – into the police handling of the case. As a result, considerable political pressure has been put on the police by the Home Secretary to be more sensitive in their dealings with the ethnic minority communities and to recruit more black and Asian people.

Summary

- Irish immigrants and other Europeans were sought to meet labour shortages after the Second World War.

- Between 1953 and the imposition of controls in 1962, nearly half a million New Commonwealth British subjects also entered Britain, and 6 per cent of the population now belong to non-white ethnic minority groups.

- These immigrants were received reluctantly by policy makers, who expected racial prejudice but took a non-interventionist stance.

- Anti-black riots in 1958 were followed by a series of immigration acts and race relations acts. Immigration controls were strengthened in the 1980s and 1990s to prevent the entry of people without a close connection to the UK and to discourage asylum seekers.

- Political participation by ethnic minorities grew in the 1980s, with small but increasing numbers becoming councillors and MPs.

- Dissatisfaction with the police response to the concerns of ethnic minorities has forced the British government to put pressure on the police to improve their relations with the ethnic minorities.

6 Case study II: France

6.1 Immigration

In contrast to most European countries, France has been a country of immigration since the second half of the nineteenth century owing to labour shortages resulting from a low birth rate and war losses. After the First World War, immigrants came mainly from Italy, Spain, Portugal and Poland – all Catholic countries with similar cultures to France. In the years immediately following the Second World War, recruitment treaties were signed with Italy, West Germany and Greece. A high priority was given to recruiting Italians, as they were considered to be hard-working and easy to assimilate into the French population, but immigrants from Algeria and Spain proved easier to recruit. Naturalization was simplified to encourage permanent settlement. The French government was keen to increase the size of the French population, as it was relatively modest given France's large territory and great power status.

During the late 1950s the war of independence in Algeria caused the return of large numbers of French repatriates, called *'Pieds Noirs'*, and Algerians who, until independence in 1962, had had French nationality and so could travel freely to France. At this time the French economy was expanding, led by a boom in construction, and the new immigrants contributed to further economic investment and growth. Even after Algerian independence the flow of migrants continued as the French economy expanded rapidly, especially in labour-intensive industries such as construction, transport, the automotive industry, textiles, chemicals and agriculture. Immigrants from Spain, Portugal, Algeria, Morocco and Tunisia were followed by migrants from francophone West Africa, especially from Mali, Senegal, the Ivory Coast and Cameroon. Most immigrants in the 1960s were 'undocumented', as the French government was happy to pursue a laissez-faire policy in which the manpower needs of employers were met in a flexible way at minimum cost. Illegal workers' positions would be legalized once they had secured stable employment, and regular amnesties were held – for example, in 1958, 1961 and 1969 – to allow these workers to be regularized.

The crisis of May 1968 caused a reconsideration of the position of immigrants, as many had taken part in the strikes and demonstrations and so had violated the ban on foreigners disrupting public order. Many were deported for this offence. There was also growing concern about the poor housing conditions of immigrants, especially the *'bidonvilles'* which had sprung up outside large towns. Concern about unemployment was also bringing pressure for state intervention to develop a more selective and controlled immigration system. The oil price crisis in 1973 and the subsequent recession caused a temporary ban on labour recruitment, including family reunions. However, these initiatives were not very successful and immigrants and their families found it relatively easy to enter France.

There was thus growing concern in the 1970s about the social problems associated with immigration, especially immigrants' poor housing, the lack of educational success in the second generation, high levels of unemployment and involvement in crime. In 1977 an attempt was made to encourage immigrants to return to their home countries by providing financial incentives, but it was unsuccessful. The offer was mainly taken up by Spanish and Portuguese workers who were probably returning anyway. The incentives were not taken up by the Africans who were the targets of the programme. In 1980 entry and residence conditions became more strict and strenuous efforts were made to bring immigration more closely under government control. However, the control of immigration could be only limited, as there was strong support for family reunions and for France to fulfil her obligations to her former colonies and because free movement of labour was allowed between members of the European Community.

During the 1980s immigration became one of the most important issues in France with its dramatic exploitation by the *Front National*. Under the charismatic leadership of Jean-Marie Le Pen, the *Front National* made significant electoral gains on an anti-immigrant platform and forced the major parties to reassess their policies. Support for the *Front National*, which was sustained throughout the next two decades, showed that a significant minority of the French electorate felt that far too many immigrants had come, and continued to come, to France.

The aim of the Socialist government under François Mitterand, elected in 1981, became to convince the electorate that immigration was under firm government control and that French national identity and culture were safe. A series of measures was introduced to take action against illegal immigration and to integrate those already in the country. New laws, for example, required immigrants to have proper travel documents and to be subject to expulsion if they failed to produce them. Expulsions rose dramatically between 1982 and 1985, so the government could claim that the policy was working. On the other hand, foreigners settled in France with valid work permits, spouses and children admitted under the family reunion scheme, refugees and foreigners married to French citizens were all given greater security. They were granted ten-year residence permits and unrestricted permission to work. At the same time stricter measures were taken to control asylum seekers and there was a significant rise in the rejection of asylum applications, especially for applicants from Asia.

The Gaullist government elected in 1986 also tightened some controls, notably by extending visa requirements to almost all countries outside the EU. Its period of office was notable for fierce debates over integration issues, such as the 'headscarf affair' (*l'affaire du foulard*) in 1989, and there were riots in many large cities in the early 1990s. Second-generation unemployment and involvement in crime were constant sources of debate and concern.

The 1990s saw a continuation of the policy of tightening immigration controls. Sanctions against employers using illegal workers were introduced in 1991 and asylum seekers lost the right to work while awaiting a decision on their application for refugee status. Further tough regulations were introduced between 1993 and 1995, but the return of a Socialist government in 1997 led to some relaxation in policy, in that the new government quickly introduced a new regularization programme for illegal immigrants.

6.2   Integration policy

As a country of immigration, France under successive governments has given a high priority to welcoming immigrants as potential citizens of France. The assumption has always been that immigrants will choose to settle in France and sooner or later choose to become French citizens. French nationality laws have thus been liberal and expansive. The Naturalization Act of October 1945, passed at the beginning of post-war recruitment policies, aimed to expand the number of French citizens by giving automatic citizenship to children born in France of foreign parents (*ius soli*, the 'law of the soil' or citizenship through birth in the territory) and to children born in France whose parents were also born in France (double *ius soli*). The former became citizens at the age of 18 years provided they had resided in France since the age of 13 years; the latter became citizens at birth. This second provision has been particularly important for young Algerians whose parents were born in Algeria before 1962, when Algeria was defined as part of France.

Naturalization is possible after five years of residence in France and 80 per cent of all applications are approved. Applications can be rejected for lack of assimilation to French culture and society or for lack of loyalty. In practice a large number of naturalizations are approved each year. In 1997 a total of 115,000 foreigners acquired French nationality; of these, approximately 60,000 were granted by formal naturalization procedures, 34,000 by formal statement claiming nationality, and 21,000 through marriage. (There were 24,000 marriages between French citizens and foreigners in 1996, and intermarriage with North Africans is becoming more common.) In addition, a further 6,000 acquired nationality at birth by being born in France to parents of foreign descent who had also been born in France. The five main groups acquiring citizenship were Moroccans, Portuguese, Algerians, Tunisians and Turks.

The main policy to assist immigrants to integrate socially and economically has been the provision of French language courses for adults. The schools, of course, have been one of the main institutions promoting the integration of young foreigners, but in the post-war period there has been great concern about the high drop-out rates of immigrant children. The housing of France's large immigrant population has also been a major problem, and many tend to be segregated in poor suburbs or temporary accommodation.

The challenge for French integration policy is to discover how a highly centralized state with such strong historical and cultural traditions – including, for example, the separation of church and state – can integrate a large and growing population of immigrants, many of whom come from cultures with very different norms and traditions. Historically, France has been very successful in assimilating large numbers of immigrants, but these have usually been Catholic Europeans. The post-war immigrants are much more diverse, including large numbers from Africa and Asia. They also include large numbers of Muslims.

The tradition of citizenship in France is that all French citizens are equal and free. They have a duty to be politically active and they are voluntarily members of the nation – 'nationality is a plebiscite that takes place every day' (Renan quoted in Favell, 1998, p.64). People who opt to become citizens therefore have an obligation to accept French customs and institutions. They have a duty to defend and promote the interests of the state to which they belong. This duty includes loyalty to the territorial integrity of France.

The present reality is more confusing. Many immigrants, including French citizens, have multiple loyalties. They are loyal to France but also to their homeland and its cultural traditions. Nations and states no longer have a monopoly over the loyalties and identities of their members. Moreover, many groups in France have high rates of unemployment, educational failure and poverty. The cutbacks in the welfare state make their position even more difficult, and the lack of recognition of minorities in France makes the creation of remedial strategies more difficult. In times of stress, support for religious fundamentalism might grow and challenge the strict separation of church and state that is central to the French republican tradition. There are advantages in living and working in a prosperous, stable state, especially given the instability in northern Africa, but the challenges of managing diversity are well illustrated in the French case. And more may have to be done to accommodate Islam, which is now the second religion of France.

Summary

- A low birth rate and war losses made France a country of immigration, mainly from other European countries, for 150 years.

- The Algerian war of independence, and a booming French economy, led to immigration from North and West Africa in the 1960s, and those who entered illegally were allowed to regularize their position through regular amnesties.

- A temporary ban on labour recruitment following the 1973 recession was ineffective and short-lived. By 1982 nearly 3.7 million foreigners were resident in France, plus many French citizens of overseas origin.

- Social problems led to unsuccessful attempts to encourage repatriation by means of financial incentives.

- In the 1980s, the *Front National* made significant electoral gains on an anti-immigrant platform. The government responded with tough action to expel illegal immigrants, reduce the number of asylum-seekers and integrate legal immigrants already settled. Legislation was introduced to tighten immigration controls.

- Integration is assisted by liberal nationality and naturalization laws, and by the provision of French language courses for adults.

- Diverse cultural backgrounds and multiple loyalties – for example, to Islam and the homeland as well as to France – make integration more difficult for Africans than for Europeans. There are also problems associated with the relative educational failure of the children of immigrants, poor housing, unemployment and involvement in crime.

7 Case study III: Germany

7.1 Immigration

In the nineteenth century the German states were, like Britain, areas of emigration. Germans migrated to the United States in particular, but also to Canada, Australia and Latin America. In medieval times Germans had migrated eastwards and German settlements were scattered across Poland, Romania, Russia and the Baltic States. These eastward migrations complicated the process of nation building in Germany, which intensified in the nineteenth century, as they made the determination of Germany's eastern borders very difficult. One goal of the nation-building project was to unite all Germans in a single nation state, but this was an impossible dream with so many German communities scattered among other nationalities. Germany's eastern borders were a particular source of conflict with Poland over Silesia, Danzig and West Prussia. There were also German minorities in Denmark, Holland, France and Czechoslovakia, and conflict was particularly acute with France over Alsace-Lorraine and with Czechoslovakia over the Sudetenland. Another nation-building issue was the status of Austria. Were the Austrians part of the German nation or a separate national group? This issue was settled only after the Second World War. The present frontiers of Germany were confirmed only in 1990, when the German Democratic Republic was incorporated into the Federal Republic of Germany (West Germany) to create a united Germany incorporating the great majority of the German people.

The overriding importance of the national question caused the history of immigration to Germany to be neglected. In the late nineteenth century labour shortages in agriculture in Prussia were met by recruiting Polish workers and Ruthenians. In 1908 some 309,000 foreign workers were employed in Prussia, the overwhelming majority of whom were Poles. Industrialization in the Ruhr also resulted in a migration of over 100,000 ethnic Poles from eastern German territories to work in the mines and factories, most of whom were German citizens. During the First World War some 700,000 'foreign' Poles were recruited to work in the German war economy, and many Hungarians and Belgians did the same. After the war the recession ended foreign immigration until a gradual economic recovery after 1934 caused it to begin again. The huge demands for manpower during the Second World War resulted in forced labour being used by the Nazi regime, and 8 million foreign workers were exploited in Germany, of whom 6 million were forced labourers and 2 million were prisoners of war.

As the war reached its conclusion, and in the aftermath, western Germany received a huge influx of people from the eastern territories of the German Reich. Some 12 million people fled westwards in advance of the Soviet armies or to escape the new communist regimes that were being established, and about two thirds of them settled in western Germany. Many thousands were also expelled from territories annexed by Poland and the Soviet Union. There was a further migration of 3 million East Germans who left the German Democratic Republic for West Germany between 1949 and 1961 until halted by the building of the Berlin Wall. These refugees and expellees were gradually absorbed into the West German society and economy as post-war reconstruction and Marshall Aid from the USA revived the economy and laid the foundations for the post-war 'economic miracle'.

By 1955, as economic expansion continued apace, German employers began to experience severe labour shortages. The German government came to their aid and negotiated a series of bilateral recruitment agreements with Italy, Spain, Greece and Turkey. These proved to be inadequate, and in the mid-1960s further agreements followed with Portugal, Tunisia, Morocco and Yugoslavia. Recruitment offices were established in major cities, including Athens, Lisbon, Madrid and Istanbul, to select suitable applicants, provide them with work and residence permits, and organize their transport to suitable employers. The demand was for less skilled workers in construction, engineering, textiles and services. In 1973 the number of foreigners reached 4 million, two-thirds of whom were workers and the rest dependants. By 1980 two-thirds of all foreigners in Germany were of Turkish origin.

As in France, the oil embargo and world economic crisis in 1973 caused a halt to labour recruitment and there was a major reappraisal of policy. Until 1973 it was easy to describe foreign workers as 'guestworkers', and to assume that they were temporary residents who would leave Germany when they were no longer needed. Unlike British policy makers, German politicians did not assume that immigrant workers would settle, and conservative politicians insisted that Germany was not a country of immigration. However, once workers had learnt German and proved their value, employers naturally wished to keep them and arranged for their work and residence permits to be renewed.

The ending of labour recruitment in 1973 did not halt immigration but contributed to a change in its composition. When confronted with the prospect of not being able to return if they left Germany, most 'guestworkers' realized that they were settlers. They therefore sent for their wives and children under the family reunification procedures, a trend encouraged by a large rise in children's allowances in 1975. The immigration of dependants rose sharply and West Germany found itself with a large, settled foreign population of some 4.6 million people by 1982.

In the 1980s there was a large increase in the number of asylum seekers coming to Germany. The right of asylum was guaranteed in the German Basic Law and was considered an important break with Germany's 'Nazi' past. The right was meant for refugees from communist countries, but in the 1980s two-thirds of asylum applications were from people from the developing world. There was a widespread feeling in Germany that economic migrants were using the liberal asylum procedures to gain entry to the Federal Republic. The asylum law was tightened up in 1993 after a massive rise in applications in 1992 to nearly 440,000 per annum (Table 3.4).

Table 3.4 Asylum applications to Germany, 1989 to 1997

Year	Asylum applications (000s)
1989	121.3
1990	193.1
1991	256.1
1992	438.2
1993	322.6
1994	127.2
1995	127.9
1996	116.4
1997	104.4

(OECD/SOPEMI, 1999)

The collapse of Soviet hegemony over Eastern Europe in 1989 had dramatic consequences for West Germany: in particular, it resulted in German reunification. West Germany had to take responsibility for the East German economy and infrastructure, and the German population rose from 60 million to over 81 million. Most of the attainable goals of nation building had been achieved by reunification, but there remained the commitment to allow people of German descent in Eastern Europe to come to Germany as citizens. This promissory note was now cashed as, with the end of the communist regimes in Eastern Europe, the right to emigrate was conceded by these countries. In 1989, some 377,000 people of German descent migrated from Eastern Europe to Germany, and in the same year some 344,000 Germans from the former German Democratic Republic migrated to West Germany seeking work and a higher standard of living.

The increased migration from Eastern Europe and the new internal migration from eastern to western Germany had two consequences. First, there was pressure for a tougher policy toward Third World people seeking political asylum and this resulted in a constitutional amendment in 1993 that restricted the scope of future grounds for claiming asylum. Second, there was a reassessment of Germany's commitments to people from Eastern Europe and the Soviet Union who claimed German descent (*Aussiedler*). Although these were regarded as good workers, eager to integrate and become good German citizens, many did not speak German or have any knowledge of German culture. They were increasingly regarded as economic migrants and an annual quota was introduced in 1993. People claiming to be ethnic Germans who wish to migrate to Germany now have to apply for entry from their home countries and have their claims verified before they are admitted. Entries of *Aussiedler* fell from 180,000 in 1996 to 100,000 in 1998.

Ironically, Germany has become the major country of immigration in Europe. It had a foreign population of well over 7 million in 1997, which was 9 per cent of the united German population of 81.6 million. The foreign population in Britain, at 2 million, was only 3.4 per cent of the population, and in France, at 3.6 million, it was 6.2 per cent of the population. The composition of the foreign population in Germany in 1997 can be seen in Table 3.5 (overleaf).

Table 3.5 Germany's foreign population, 1997

Country of origin	Population (000s)
Turkey	2,107
Yugoslavia	721
Italy	608
Greece	363
Poland	283
Bosnia	281
Croatia	207
Austria	185
Portugal	132
Spain	132
UK	115
Other	2,231
Total	7,365

(OECD/SOPEMI, 1999)

7.2   Integration policy

The first priority of German integration policy after the Second World War was to integrate the refugees and expellees from the former eastern territories. This had to be done at the same time as West Germans displaced by the war were accommodated, and in the face of a continuing influx of people from East Germany, soon to become the German Democratic Republic. The large numbers of people involved were a huge burden on the new West German state that was created in 1949 as the Federal Republic of Germany. In spite of the devastation of war, the high levels of unemployment and the great numbers of refugees, the German government used careful regional planning and a balanced dispersal policy to manage the processes of social integration and settlement with the help of the allied powers. Political integration was not an issue because under the Basic Law all Germans from territories controlled by the Reich were entitled to come to Germany as citizens. The refugees and expellees thus had full civic, social and political rights, and they came to play a prominent role in the politics of the new West German state. Despite this massive immigration and an increase in the population, West Germans did not consider their state to be an immigration country; they saw the Federal Republic as a country with a high population density that was being forced to accommodate fellow Germans displaced by the catastrophe of the war and its aftermath. Immigration was perceived to be more of a burden than an asset.

The expansion of the West German economy in the 1950s and the economic boom of the 1960s created a new situation. The rapid increase in the foreign population and the recognition of their settlement in the 1970s caused a rethinking of policy. West Germany's membership of the EU meant that citizens of other member states had substantial economic, social and civic rights and occupied a privileged position, but non-EU nationals were 'guestworkers' with no political rights. Traditionally, the West German priority had been to integrate Germans from East Germany and ethnic Germans from Eastern Europe. These people had a right to citizenship. The importance of the national project meant that it was difficult for foreigners to naturalize as German citizens. They had to be resident for a minimum of ten years, have a good knowledge of the German language, culture and politics, and have no serious criminal convictions. They also had to renounce their previous citizenship. Even if these conditions were met, citizenship was granted only if it was deemed to be in the interests of the Federal Republic of Germany. In practice, naturalization was left to the discretion of government officials and there was a wide variation between different parts of the country, with naturalization procedures being interpreted more liberally in *Länder* such as Berlin and more restrictively in Bavaria.

The German electorate was slow to appreciate that Germany had become an immigration country, and was only too willing to collude with politicians who argued that it was not one. In the 1970s there were a number of campaigns to grant long-term residents local voting rights, to aid their political integration. Some cities and towns established advisory councils for resident foreigners that advised local authorities on policy, but these were generally unsuccessful. By the 1980s there was pressure for more liberal naturalization laws, including the acceptance of dual nationality, but this liberalization was implemented only in the late 1990s and then only to a limited extent. Meanwhile, young people of foreign descent, especially those of Turkish descent, do poorly in the education system and later experience higher levels of unemployment than German young people.

Summary

- Refugees fleeing west after the war, and East Germans arriving until 1961, were integrated in West Germany society as post-war reconstruction advanced.

- Labour shortages, which were evident by 1955, prompted bilateral recruitment agreements with a number of countries around the Mediterranean, particularly Turkey.

- In the 1950s and 1960s, immigrants not of German descent entered the country as 'guestworkers'. Naturalization was difficult, and long-term residents were denied voting rights.

- Although the 1973 crisis halted immigration, many employers wished to keep trained 'guestworkers' and large numbers settled permanently. Recruitment continued in shortage areas and Germany had 4.6 million settled foreigners by 1982.

- A large influx of Eastern Europeans of German descent into West Germany following reunification and the collapse of communism in 1989 led to quotas for people claiming German descent.

- The numbers of asylum seekers from the developing world rose sharply in the 1980s and early 1990s, prompting the tightening in 1993 of hitherto liberal asylum laws framed to accommodate refugees from communist countries.

- More liberal naturalization laws were introduced in the 1990s, but educational achievement and employment rates remained relatively low among the foreign population.

- Germany is the major European country of immigration with over 7 million foreigners, that is, 9 per cent of the population.

8   The challenge of managing diverse societies

Processes associated with globalization have challenged the image of a Europe composed of sovereign nation states. An individual state, or even the EU, no longer controls its economy, but is subject to global markets and international agreements such as the General Agreement on Tariffs and Trade (GATT). Similarly, European societies have become much more cosmopolitan. International migration has transformed the social composition of European societies in the post-war period. All Western European states have substantial minority communities created by migration, and these communities are expanding through continued migration and reproduction. International travel is intensifying to support the huge demand from global business, tourism, politics, education and family reunions. The international movement of people is thus harder for states to control. International treaties, such as the Schengen Agreement, allowing free movement of people within all EU states (except for Britain and Ireland), suggest that many states are recognizing this new reality and are becoming more relaxed about border controls. Other international treaties, such as the UN Convention on Asylum and Refugees, require that people with a well-founded fear of persecution in their own country should be admitted and protected by the signatory states. This also represents a giving up of sovereignty, for good reasons, by states and it reduces their ability to control who is admitted within their borders.

8.1 Britain

European states confronted with more socially diverse and cosmopolitan societies have adopted different strategies to manage this diversity. Britain's immigrants, who have come mainly from Ireland, the colonies or Commonwealth countries, all had citizenship rights when they arrived. This was significant, as it meant that racism and informal processes of discrimination by employers, landlords, the police and neighbours were not reinforced by legal forms of discrimination against non-citizens. Citizenship implies equal treatment and equality of opportunity and to be a citizen gives one greater protection from arbitrary treatment, such as deportation.

Most countries exclude non-citizens from work in the civil service and from employment generally if qualified citizens are available and looking for work. Non-citizens are also excluded from voting and associated political activities such as standing for political office. Those immigrants and refugees who came to Britain as non-citizens from countries such as Poland, Italy and Hungary had to apply for citizenship through naturalization after five years' residence. However, most who decided to settle permanently did become naturalized citizens. Their British-born children were automatically citizens under the *ius soli* provisions of the 1948 Nationality Act. Children born after 1983 to parents legally settled in Britain are automatically entitled to citizenship if they are resident in the UK for their first ten years.

The strategy of successive British governments for managing a diverse society has been to intervene to manage relations between different ethnic groups only when social harmony and public order are threatened. When anti-immigrant feeling rose in the late 1950s the government adopted a Janus-faced strategy of, on the one hand, reassuring a xenophobic and prejudiced electorate that its concerns were being met by the introduction of tough immigration control legislation and, on the other hand, assuring anti-racists, liberals, socialists and the ethnic minority electorate that discrimination and racism within the country would be curbed by race relations legislation and laws outlawing incitement to racial hatred. This twin-track approach was pursued in the 1960s and 1970s with the clear intention of reducing the political salience of the issue. Tougher immigration controls continued to be introduced in the 1970s and 1980s in response to Enoch Powell's campaign and public support for the National Front, until its near demise in the early 1980s. This tough stance on immigration control was 'balanced' by the strong anti-discrimination legislation in the Race Relations Act 1976 and the creation of an enforcement agency, the Commission for Racial Equality.

The growth of an ethnic minority population with citizenship has protected successive governments' commitment to anti-discrimination legislation. Ethnic minorities form an important and growing part of the electorate, especially in cities such as Greater London, Birmingham and Bradford. No party can afford to ignore them. There is also continuing concern among politicians about racial violence and associated public-order issues. The anti-police riots in 1981 and 1985 forced the government to reform police training and practices, and to pay attention to black youth unemployment. The campaign against the inadequate police response to the murder of the black teenager Stephen Lawrence led to a major inquiry, the Macpherson Inquiry (1999), and reforms of the Metropolitan Police to make them more representative of, and responsive to, the Greater London population.

The problem with the British government's approach is that it is pragmatic rather than principled and proactive. It is also contradictory. Surges in public concern about immigration or asylum applications, often whipped up by the tabloid press, are quickly acted upon by politicians who argue that they must respond to genuine public concerns. They respond by introducing tighter controls which fuel public anxiety; at the same time they argue that Britain must continue to welcome genuine refugees and meet its international obligations. Far-right groups, such as the British National Party and the National Front, try to exploit the resulting confusion.

The asylum crisis in Britain in 2000 is a good example of this process. In the 1970s the level of asylum applications to Britain and other Western European countries was very low. Only 13,000 applications were made to the whole of Western Europe in 1972. The numbers rose after the halt in labour recruitment in the mid-1970s, but in 1979 Britain received only 1,563 applications. During the 1980s applications rose strongly in Western Europe, reaching a total of 232,000 in 1988, but applications to Britain remained stable at around 5,000 per annum. The British government was not complacent, however, and a rise in applications from young Tamil men in 1985 brought about the immediate imposition of mandatory visas for visitors from Sri Lanka. The visa regime was extended to India, Pakistan, Bangladesh, Nigeria and Ghana in 1986, partly to discourage applications. In 1989 the number of asylum applications rose to 15,530, with sharp rises from Somalia and Turkey, so mandatory visas were introduced for these countries too. As applications rose, so did the refusal rate: it was 40 per cent in 1980, but 75 per cent in 1988. Applications continued to rise, despite government efforts, reaching 30,000 in 1990 and 57,700 in 1991. The government responded by doubling the fines under the 1986 Carriers' Liability Act from £1,000 for each undocumented person brought into the UK to £2,000 per person. Table 3.6 shows the numbers of asylum applications to the UK, France and Germany for the period from 1987 to 1991.

Table 3.6 Asylum seekers and refugees applying to selected European countries, 1987 to 1991 (in thousands)

Country	1987	1988	1989	1990	1991
France	27.6	34.3	61.4	54.7	50.0
Germany	57.4	103.1	121.3	193.1	256.0
UK	5.2	5.7	16.5	30.0	57.7

(OECD/SOPEMI, 1992)

The British government responded to this rise by recruiting more staff to process applications, training airline staff to spot false documents and increasing the numbers of applicants held in detention centres. They also introduced an Asylum and Immigration Appeals Bill to speed up the procedures and reduce fraudulent multiple applications. This Bill became law on 1 July 1993.

The tough regime introduced by the Conservatives reduced applications from 57,700 in 1991 to 28,000 in 1993, but after this the number of applications rose again, reaching a peak of 71,160 in 1999. Local and national papers were full of stories of refugees, often from Kosovo, being found in the backs of lorries at Dover or at motorway service stations. The opposition argued that Britain was a 'soft touch' and on 1 May 2000 William Hague, the Conservative party leader, said that unless the government clamped down on the flood of asylum seekers, the National Front would become more popular. In fact, the Labour government had followed the tough line of its predecessor in introducing an Immigration and Asylum Bill which enabled asylum seekers to be dispersed in specified accommodation over the country and be given food vouchers instead of some benefits payments. There was also a huge backlog of applications to be processed, so waiting times were long. One of the most controversial measures introduced by the government was to extend the Carriers' Liability provisions to lorry drivers. In October 1998 the Home Secretary announced that haulage companies would be fined £2,000 for each illegal immigrant discovered in their lorries and that the lorries could be impounded until the fines were paid. Despite vociferous protests from the road haulage industry, the new laws were implemented. It was clear that the Home Secretary believed that some lorry drivers were smuggling in asylum seekers for cash.

The asylum seekers' lack of political rights and their small numbers make them more vulnerable than other minorities to scapegoating and stereotyping. In the local and tabloid press they are stereotyped as grasping and threatening and are portrayed as a problem that must be removed from society. The use of terms such as 'bogus asylum seekers' or 'aggressive beggars' shows the hostility that asylum seekers experience when they arrive in Britain.

8.2 France

The French stance toward immigration has been more positive than the British or the German stance. Immigration has been seen as both an asset and a necessity, as something that makes a positive contribution to the French national interest.

The preferred sources of immigrants were people from neighbouring European countries, who were encouraged to settle and naturalize. They were regarded as hard-working people from similar cultures who would easily accept and adopt French culture. The republican tradition laid great stress on equality of treatment and universal rights for all, whether citizen or non-citizen, but the assumption was that immigrants (probably), and their children (certainly), would eventually become citizens.

It was only with the immigration of Muslims from North Africa and black Africans from francophone West Africa in the late 1960s that public opinion swung against immigration, with the feeling that too many 'unassimilable' immigrants were being admitted to France. In particular, there was a fear that Muslim immigrants would not accept the strict separation of religion and politics which is a cherished tenet of the French secular republican tradition. African immigration was complicated by decolonization and the obligations the French élite felt to France's former colonies. In the case of Algerian immigration, some people's hostility was increased by memories of the bloody war of independence. Hostility to immigration was also increased by the fear of unemployment and concern about the erosion of French identity and culture. The British model of multiculturalism was strongly opposed by most people in France, who regarded it as discriminatory and divisive: immigrants, no matter what their background, should become active and equal French citizens, loyal to the culture and traditions of the French Republic.

These fears about immigration, unemployment and the erosion of French culture and identity were exploited by the *Front National*, which made dramatic electoral gains in the 1980s and the 1990s. In response to support for the *Front National*, successive governments tightened immigration controls, and measures were introduced to reform the citizenship laws, emphasizing an active choice of French citizenship rather than passive acceptance. But these measures were largely symbolic. France has remained relatively open to immigration and receives around 100,000 immigrants a year. Attempts to restrict access to citizenship have been strongly resisted and some proposals have led to vocal public opposition. There seems to be considerable public support for the liberal naturalization laws.

There is, however, some conflict between principle and practice. The French tradition of refusing to recognize minority groups and ethnic diversity and regarding everybody as an equal and participating citizen is positive in its refusal to categorize and stereotype people by their race or ethnicity. In everyday life, however, discrimination takes place in employment, in education and in police actions such as identity card checks. The lack of success of young French people of African descent in the schools and the labour market could be a potential source of frustration in the future.

8.3   Germany

Germany has been much less welcoming to labour migrants than either Britain or France. This is largely because German politicians and the German people have not regarded Germany as a country of immigration. The major concerns of West German politicians have been to provide a haven for people of German descent fleeing communist oppression in

Eastern Europe and to reunite the German people in one state by encouraging the collapse of the German Democratic Republic (East Germany). The economic recovery of West Germany after the war was not expected to be as strong or as sustained as it proved to be, so when workers were recruited from Southern Europe and from Turkey, especially in the 1960s and early 1970s, they were regarded as temporary 'guestworkers', and a myth was created that they would rotate between Germany and their country of origin. This facilitated their acceptance by the German population, but not their integration into German society. They were not regarded as potential German citizens.

By 1975 concern had grown in West Germany about 'over-foreignization.' The foreign population had reached 4 million, one-third of whom were Turkish, and many 'guestworkers' were buying houses and bringing in their families. A second generation of German-educated and German-born young people was growing up without German citizenship. Attempts to reduce the foreign population through incentives to return to their countries of origin were unsuccessful.

Opportunities for foreigners to participate in German society were limited. They could participate in the trade unions and in the advisory councils which some local authorities established as a means of consultation with foreigners, but these arrangements did not work well. The unwelcoming stance of the German state toward foreigners was reflected in the citizenship and naturalization laws. German citizenship was acquired at birth by *ius sanguinis*, that is, by descent from a citizen. People of German descent from Eastern Europe are regarded as German and have easy access to German citizenship, but young people born in Germany to foreign parents had to take their parents' citizenship and then naturalize to become German. Naturalization provisions in Germany were tough until the reforms in 2000, with considerable discretion for local officials. Applicants had to have resided in Germany for ten years, and they had to have a good knowledge of German language, culture and politics. They had to be without a criminal record, they had to renounce their previous citizenship, and their naturalization had to be in the interests of the Federal Republic of Germany. The conditions and expense of naturalization deterred many potential applicants. Now that it is clear that most of the foreign population will settle permanently, some *Länder* such as Berlin are encouraging naturalization and this is increasing the number of applications.

On 1 January 2000, Germany introduced an element of *ius soli* into its citizenship law for the first time, so that a child born in Germany to non-German parents will automatically receive German citizenship if one parent fulfils certain residence requirements. This is a major innovation in German citizenship law, and it is estimated that the children of one-third of the foreigners in Germany will qualify under these provisions (Green, 2000, p.114). The residence requirement has been reduced to eight years.

Despite their relatively long residence in West Germany, Turkish youths do poorly in the school system and tend to be segregated by housing patterns. The integration of young foreigners is a key issue, but many

Germans regard Turks as difficult to integrate because of their perceived lack of education, their Islamic religion and the extreme divisions between Islamic fundamentalists and liberal secularists in Turkish politics. Divisions between Kurds and Turks also complicate ethnic minority politics in Germany and are a source of embarrassment to the German government.

The upsurge of asylum applications in the mid-1980s was unexpected and resented by most Germans. A dispersal policy that distributed asylum seekers across the whole country in a period of recession contributed to dissatisfaction with the generous asylum provisions in the Basic Law and the associated costs to the German taxpayer. Resentment against foreigners and asylum seekers was especially high in eastern Germany after reunification and there were attacks on foreigners in Hoyenswerda and Rostock in August 1992. Eight Turks were murdered in the west German towns of Mölln and Soligen in May 1993. These acts of violence were widely condemned in Germany, but were seen as a warning that positive steps were needed to integrate Germany's large foreign population. The recession also contributed to growing resentment at the costs of integrating ethnic Germans from Russia and Eastern Europe, and a quota of 225,000 a year was imposed in 1993.

Today, German politicians and the electorate are gradually being forced to accept Germany's status as an immigration country. Germany has become the major country of immigration in Europe and the strength of its economy and demographic trends indicate a continuing need for substantial immigration which seasonal worker agreements with Poland or other forms of temporary recruitment cannot fill.

Summary

- Globalization processes and international agreements are making the movement of people harder to control.

- European states have adopted different strategies to manage the more socially diverse and cosmopolitan societies that have resulted.

- British governments have intervened to manage ethnic relations only when harmony and public order are threatened. They have used a dual strategy of tight immigration control and race relations legislation which is pragmatic rather than principled.

- The growth of ethnic minority populations – now electorally significant – protects commitment to anti-discrimination legislation, but growing numbers of asylum seekers incur hostility and remain vulnerable to scapegoating and stereotyping.

- In France, multiculturalism is seen as divisive. Immigrants are expected to become active and equal French citizens, loyal to the culture and traditions of France, without categorization or stereotyping.

- Muslim immigrants' unwillingness to accept the strict separation of religion and politics is seen as a threat to the republican secular tradition, and large numbers of immigrants have been viewed as a threat to French culture, leading to an increase in support for the *Front National*.

- The French government's response has been to tighten immigration controls and reform citizenship laws to allow an active choice of French citizenship instead of passive acceptance, while retaining relatively open access to citizenship. Despite these measures, discrimination is widespread in everyday life, in employment, education and policing, and is a potential source of unrest among young people of African descent.

- Germany is relatively unwelcoming to foreigners. It has focused on uniting the German peoples rather than coming to terms with being a country of immigration.

- The temporary status of 'guestworker' has facilitated acceptance but delayed integration, especially as citizenship is conferred by descent, and naturalization means meeting tough conditions and significant expense.

- Turkish young people underachieve at school and housing tends to be segregated.

- Violence prompted by an upsurge in asylum seekers has highlighted the need for positive steps to encourage integration, and has led to the imposition of quotas on ethnic German immigrants.

9   The impact of the EU

Britain, France and Germany have all had very different reactions to post-war immigration. The British approach has been pragmatic and reactive and has moved from imperial expansiveness and openness to greater restrictiveness and tighter immigration controls. The French approach has been more welcoming and liberal, and this has continued despite public concern and significant support over two decades for the *Front National*, support which now, at last, seems to be waning. Germany has been a reluctant country of immigration, except for people of German descent. All three countries, however, have accepted the reality of permanent settlement and all are pursuing policies of integration. Germany's policies are implemented unevenly due to the federal structure of the state and its relatively tough naturalization laws, but liberal reforms are gradually being introduced.

These three diverse states, with their differing traditions of inclusion and exclusion, are all members of the EU and are having to adjust to the need to develop common policies toward all people within their territories, both citizens and non-citizens. There are also attempts to create a common European citizenship. The first steps toward a European citizenship were made in the Treaty of Rome, which guaranteed free movement of workers (Article 48), the right of establishment (Article 52) and free movement of services (Article 59). Derivative legislation guaranteed equality in relation to employment, tax and 'social advantages', a term interpreted broadly by the European Court of Justice (Guild, 1999). The scope of free movement and the application of the principle of non-discrimination on grounds of nationality have been gradually extended, so that the Single European Act (1986) revised 'free movement of workers' to 'free movement of persons'. Despite British attempts to restrict this to nationals of EU member states, the European Commission insisted on a more generous interpretation in 1992. The Amsterdam Treaty (1997) emphasized this commitment to free movement and the abolition of internal frontiers, but recognized that this would require common policies on external border controls, especially with regard to immigration and asylum applications (Article 61a). These measures had already been foreshadowed by the Schengen Agreement and the creation of the Schengen Group, which now contains all the members of the EU with the exception of Britain and Ireland. The Schengen Agreement was signed in 1985 by France, Germany and the Benelux countries. It abolished their internal borders and allowed free movement of persons within their territories. It was signed in frustration at the slow progress toward this end in the EU in general. Its success in attracting additional adherents makes it inevitable that the Schengen model will provide a blueprint for EU policies on free internal movement and control at the external borders. This was recognized in the Amsterdam Treaty, which incorporated the Schengen Agreement within the framework of the First Pillar arrangements (**Heffernan, 2001**).

The Schengen Agreement inevitably involves a high degree of police co-operation among the member states, and the co-ordination of policies to control non-citizens. Thus non-citizens who enter a Schengen country, as well as usually requiring a visa, have to show that they have sufficient means to support themselves, and they are normally admitted for only three months. If they move from one Schengen country to another they have to register with the authorities within three days. People defined as undesirable by one state are excluded from all, and entrants who fail to comply with their conditions of stay are excluded from the whole area. As in Britain, airlines and shipping companies who carry aliens with inadequate or false documents are liable to fines. The Schengen Agreement is backed up by a computerized intelligence and information system (the Schengen Information System), which is based in Strasbourg. This provides data on people to be refused entry, such as asylum seekers who have already had their applications refused, illegal immigrants, criminals and suspected terrorists.

The idea of a European citizenship as outlined in the Maastricht Treaty is confined to the nationals of member states, who can now, for example, vote in local elections in any member state and also in elections for Members of the European Parliament. But a debate has already started about whether legally resident non-nationals should be discriminated against at all. In many respects, legally resident non-nationals do have equal rights and it is illegal to discriminate against people on grounds of nationality, but should they be entitled to European citizenship without having to become a naturalized citizen of a member state? This is a highly controversial issue and one that has not been resolved. Britain in particular is keen to maintain control of her borders and has opposed German proposals for a sharing of asylum seekers among all EU states. No states have yet proposed common naturalization procedures, although moves toward a European citizenship will undoubtedly make this an issue for discussion in the future. Finally, the proposals to enlarge the EU further by admitting Eastern European countries, such as the Czech Republic, Hungary, Poland, the Baltic States and Turkey, have huge implications for migration within the EU. The commitment to free movement of people within its territory and the abolition of internal borders may be sorely challenged if enlargement stimulates a large migration from East to West. Border controls and admittance to citizenship are issues which lie close to the heart of a state's sovereignty, and it will be interesting to see whether the momentum toward common policies continues or whether national interests reassert themselves.

Summary

- Britain, France and Germany have all accepted the reality of permanent settlement, and as members of the EU are committed by the Amsterdam Treaty (1997) to free movement of people within EU borders.

- The Schengen Agreement, which covers all EU countries except Britain and Ireland, already involves police co-operation and the co-ordination of policies to control non-citizens.

- European citizenship allows nationals of EU member states to participate in local and European Parliament elections; voting rights for resident non-nationals are under debate.

- Agreements are yet to be reached on border controls, the sharing of asylum seekers among all EU states and naturalization procedures.

- Enlargement of the EU to the east could greatly encourage intra-European migration.

10 Conclusion

This chapter has provided a comparative analysis of the different strategies employed by Britain, France and Germany in response to the increasing intra-state diversity caused by the flow of migrants and refugees which began at the end of the Second World War.

The chapter has analysed different strategies for the inclusion and exclusion of migrants and refugees. In so doing, it has raised issues about whether citizenship, for example, should be granted only to those sharing a single national identity fostered by the nation state or whether, on the contrary, citizenship should be extended to all long-term residents of a particular nation state regardless of their country of origin, ethnicity, culture and values. Individual nation states as well as the EU, as a political institution, currently face the challenge of determining how to manage internal diversity while maintaining social cohesion to a degree sufficient to prevent social disintegration.

Rising support for right-wing parties strongly opposed to the presence of migrants and refugees has been associated with the rising numbers of such individuals seeking to settle in the EU. These parties defend a unified and homogeneous image of the nation states they claim to represent. They reject diversity and perceive it to be a threat to the integrity and continuity of their societies as they wish them to be. In so doing, they oppose change and refuse to accept the fact that nation states have never been homogeneous.

The ethnic diversity of EU societies is now well established and their economic growth and success is partly dependent both on the presence of migrants and refugees, and on their continued immigration. These people should be given the opportunity to contribute to the generation of an eventual European (EU) identity. In the early years of the twenty-first century, we are witnessing a continuing conflict of opinion about how migrants and refugees should be treated and what status should be granted to them. Those who have settled legally are gradually being granted full citizenship rights, but many who have become citizens feel that legal equality does not diminish their everyday experiences of racism and discrimination. Even societies that define themselves as multicultural and claim to welcome diversity are not free from tension and conflict, a fact which may be exploited by politicians. It remains to be seen how long it will take for those perceived as 'different' to be fully integrated into European societies.

References

Bulmer, M. (1996) 'The ethnic group question in the 1991 census of population' in Coleman, D. and Salt, J. (eds) *Ethnicity in the 1991 Census, Vol. 1,* London, Office of Population Censuses and Surveys.

Favell, A. (1998) *Philosophies of Integration: Immigration and the Idea of Citizenship in France and Britain*, Basingstoke, Macmillan.

Green, S. (2000) 'Beyond ethnoculturalism? German citizenship in the new millennium', *German Politics*, vol.9, no.3, pp.105–24.

Guild, E. (ed.) (1999) *The Legal Framework and Social Consequences of Free Movement of Persons in the European Union,* London, Kluwer Law International.

Hammar, T. (ed.) (1985) *European Immigration Policy,* Cambridge, Cambridge University Press.

Heffernan, R. (2001) 'Building the European Union' in Bromley, S. J. (ed.) *Governing the European Union*, London, Sage/The Open University.

Jenkins, R. (1967) *Essays and Speeches*, London, Collins.

Layton-Henry, Z. (1992) *The Politics of Immigration*, Oxford, Blackwell.

OECD/SOPEMI (1992) *Continuous Reporting System on Migration*, Paris, OECD.

OECD/SOPEMI (1999) *Continuous Reporting System on Migration*, Paris, OECD.

Owen, D., Green, A., Pitcher, J. and Maguire, M. (2000) *Minority Ethnic Participation and Achievements in Education, Training and the Labour Market*, Research Report RR225, London, Department for Education and Employment.

Tannahill, J.A. (1958) *European Volunteer Workers in Britain*, Manchester, Manchester University Press.

Further reading

Baubock, R. (1994) *Transnational Citizenship: Membership and Rights in International Migration*, Aldershot, Edward Elgar.

Guibernau, M. and Rex, J. (1997) *The Ethnicity Reader: Nationalism, Multiculturalism and Migration*, Cambridge, Polity Press.

Meehan, E. (1993) *Citizenship and the European Community*, London, Sage.

Rex, J. (1996) *Ethnic Minorities in the Modern Nation-State*, London, Macmillan/Centre for Research in Ethnic Relations.

Roche, M. and van Berkel, R. (1997) *European Citizenship and Social Exclusion,* Aldershot, Ashgate.

Chapter 4
Social movements in Europe: the rise of environmental governance

Mark J. Smith

1 Introduction

In the half century after the Second World War, something remarkable has happened in the issues and concerns of groups and organizations involved in political representation. New groups and movements characterized by informality and yet able to mobilize considerable resources around single issue campaigns have come to play a significant role in politics. This chapter explores the emergence of social movements that cut across state boundaries and at the same time draw their vital support from particular communities aroused by local concerns. A number of questions need to be considered. Why are these movements emerging and what is their significance in European societies? Do they pose a challenge and represent a departure from traditional politics? Are they changing the way that governance is conducted or are they being changed by conventional politics? How important are global issues in the construction of these new social movements?

The chapter examines the contested nature of the governance of 'life politics' within the European Union (EU). In particular, it considers how the EU has become a new site of struggle as communities, collectivities and organizations seek to construct or pursue their own identities, lifestyles and values; and at the same time national governments, the EU and other public agencies seek to exert varying degrees of social control. We look first (Section 2) at how these two dimensions of governance (self-organizing governance from below and regulation from above) interact and combine in distinctive ways in different situations. Section 3 then focuses on the role of the trade unions and their relative decline in influencing political decisions. The subsequent sections consider the emergence of new social movements by exploring the development of the environmental or 'Green' movements in European societies and in relation to environmental governance within the EU.

2 Social movements as self-organizing networks

Why do we need a concept like 'social movement'? For a start, social movements are different from most political parties. They start out as attempts to mobilize support outside established political institutions. Sometimes they promote interests or causes that have been marginalized and neglected by mainstream forms of political representation. In short, they have oppositional origins and their organizational character is often shaped through the political struggles they face in trying to ensure that their concerns are recognized. They may organize employees in order to combat the effectiveness of employers in influencing economic policy. They may bring together consumers against producers, local residents against a company responsible for some pollutant, disabled or ethnic communities against discrimination and prejudice, feminist movements against androcentric (male-centred) cultures and so on. Social movements are as diverse as the people they mobilize.

During the early stages of their development, because social movements have been excluded from the usual ways of exerting political influence, direct action strategies are common (involving demonstrations, strikes, civil disobedience, occupations and such like). So, for instance, in the 1980s and 1990s, gay pride movements had been accompanied by groups such as Outrage! (in the UK) which exposed the sexual preferences of public figures ('outing') or engaged in flamboyant protests against institutionalized homophobia in, for example, the Roman Catholic Church. As such movements become more successful they are often incorporated into the political process and their interests are expressed in broad projects. Consequently, they usually become more formal and hierarchical in their organizational structures and can, on occasion, initiate their own political parties, as happened in the past with the Labour and Social Democratic parties or more recently the Green parties across Europe. So, we need the concept of 'social movement' to draw our attention to the way such collective actors bring the concerns of everyday life into touch with the formal institutions of government, not only to make a difference in policy making but also to change the cultural attitudes and values we hold.

2.1 Defining social movements

We will start with the assumption that old and new social movements are of different types (see Table 4.1) and then assess how far this conceptual distinction helps us understand European trade unions and environmental movements. Old social movements are typically concerned with influencing policy making in the executive and legislative institutions of the political system. This has been achieved through mainstream political parties. For example, trade unions have strong historical ties with leftist

Table 4.1 Old and new social movements: a helpful distinction?

	Old social movements	*New social movements*
Location	Polity	Civil society
Ideology and aims	Political integration Economic rights	Autonomy in civil society New values/lifestyles
Organization	Formal and hierarchical	Informal network and grass roots
Medium of change	Participation in political institutions	Direct action and cultural politics

(Martell, 1994, p.112)

parties such as the German Social Democratic Party, but have also built connections and alliances across the political spectrum with Christian Democratic parties. Moreover, trade unions have aimed to become participants or insiders in the policy-making process of economic management. While formal and hierarchical structures are a common feature of organizations with large numbers of members, for trade unions they were also necessary for securing members' compliance with successive prices and incomes policies in exchange for political influence.

If we look at the organizational structure of trade unions as an example of an *old social movement*, we can see certain characteristics that help us to distinguish them from new social movements. First, their primary task is to defend their members' interests through whatever means seem most feasible and effective, from legal action to strikes and working to rule. Industrial action is usually a defensive option when negotiations have failed. On the whole, unions secure their economic rights through participation and integration within industrial relations networks and political institutions. Since the membership of unions tends to be large, there is considerable pressure to develop a hierarchical formal organizational structure to co-ordinate members. In addition, most members do not have the time to commit themselves to participate fully in the organizational activities, ensuring that activists and officials have a disproportionate impact on the decisions made in the organized movement.

A variety of *new social movements,* such as the women's movement and the environmental and peace movements, emerged as significant forces in the 1960s. They had a different set of concerns and were quite different in terms of organization and values from many trade unions in this period. They were often informal associations with more active participation by members and in some cases without a central leadership. These new social movements sought to promote different ways of life or to defend certain groups of the population against those who exercised power. Their concern was not just with those with authority in government; it was also with any individual in a position to make authoritative decisions over others in a range of institutional contexts, such as in the criminal justice system, educational institutions and psychiatric care. And most important, these new social movements acknowledged the role of power relations in private relationships (for example, the concern with domestic violence by feminist movements). Many contemporary pressure groups concerned with gay rights, disability rights, civil rights, prisoners' rights and the welfare of psychiatric patients originated in the new social movements. The kind of social change these groups wanted was likely to be delivered not by legislation (against, say, discrimination), but from a transformation in the cultural values of the society as whole. Social movements are thus in one way or another the means of political expression for the marginalized and the 'underdogs' of civil society. So, in attempting to change the prevailing moral and ethical assumptions of a culture and in recognizing the presence of power relations in private as well as in public contexts, the new social movements involved cultural politics.

2.2 Explaining social movements

Why do social movements come into existence? The organizing principles for a social movement can be economic interest, concern about a particular hazard, promotion of a cause or moral/ethical message, collective desires to forge new identities or protect established identities, or any combination of these. So you should expect all social movements to be distinctive, complex and subject to change. In the remainder of this section we will look briefly at the explanations for the rise of social movements in general and we will return to consider the specific causes of the rise of environmental movements later in the chapter. Each approach captures an important dimension in the life of social movements, although they don't provide a complete picture.

First, social movements as the products of changes in the social and economic structure of European societies.

For example, mass labour movements have often been seen as a direct response to the emergence of assembly-line factory production with routinized and specialized working practices in industrial societies. In these working environments, especially if whole communities were largely dependent upon a single company for employment, common class identities were forged. Collective action (such as strikes) was most evident in those factories which had large-scale dissatisfied workforces engaged in monotonous semi-skilled labour characteristic of the assembly line. In the late twentieth century the shift toward less organized forms of production, more mobile workforces and flexible working practices can be seen as responsible for the fragmentation of class identity and the dispersion of the members of such working communities upon which collective action was based. Such changes in the social structure have opened up opportunities for other kinds of cultural identification with different political values.

Second, social movements as manifestations of post-materialism.

The growing affluence, improved education and growth of equal opportunities in post-war European societies also shifted attention away from
economic objectives and the quantitative measurement of human welfare
toward new post-materialist goals or values. As you can see from Table 4.2
(overleaf), this approach involves not only thinking about ways to limit
economic growth (see **Baker, 2001**), but also includes a desire for greater
accountability, transparency and participation in our decision-making
institutions (as opposed to the bureaucratic formal top-down political
institutions associated with materialism). There is an increased preoccupation in maintaining the quality of the environment and the diversification of cultural norms and alternative lifestyles (see Figure 4.1). This
approach also suggests that structural changes in the composition of
society, such as the growth of the salaried middle class and professionals
(or at least their offspring), provide a ready constituency for post-
materialism. In more recent research, Alberto Melucci (1989) suggests
that social movements are cultural laboratories for new lifestyles and
values, often existing as latent currents in cultural relations and only
manifest in visible outbursts at certain times. Melucci goes further to
argue that the preoccupation with sexuality, gender and ethnic identity
which feature in the 'submerged networks' of social movements makes
them cultural rather than political. He concludes that social movements
are both *pre-political* because they derive sustenance from everyday life
and *meta-political* because while their interests can be represented they
can never be fully captured by political parties. Bear in mind that Melucci
is defining political as primarily concerned with exercise of power in the
public sphere not in private life.

Figure 4.1   Christiania, Denmark – a post-materialist community

Table 4.2 Materialist and post-materialist goals

Materialist goals	Post-materialist goals
Maintaining a high rate of economic growth	Giving people more say in important government decisions
Making sure that strong defences are maintained	Progress towards a less impersonal and more humanitarian social order
Maintaining a stable economy	People should have more say in the decisions made on their behalf
Fighting price inflation	Progress towards a society where ideas are more important than money

(Cotgrove and Duff, 1981, p.96)

Third, social movements as insiders or challengers.
Since the late 1970s a new explanation has developed, concerned with the specific contexts within which social movements emerge and the resources they can mobilize in support of their goals. Social movements are distinguished here in a way that is reminiscent of the distinction between old and new social movements in Table 4.1. This approach, developed by Charles Tilly (1994), is more focused on whether the movements are *insiders* (polity members) or *challengers* (fighting from the outside). Collective action is thus interpreted as an attempt to stay in or to join the polity. It addresses the opportunity structures that exist within political institutions for such movements to make a difference. These opportunity structures include: the capacity of the movement to mobilize support or resources from public opinion and hence to be taken seriously; the willingness of political institutions to integrate their concerns; and the willingness and capacity of the state to establish measures which address the movements' concerns. For example, anti-nuclear protests in the UK and in France have faced the problem of public apathy (even when local communities have been subject to hazards) as well as the lack of will in the political apparatus to integrate their concerns. In Sweden and Germany the problem is less one of public support and political openness, and more one of the implementation of effective policies. This resource mobilization approach also considers how movements and counter-movements tend to emerge in waves (with all new movements producing backlash movements). For example, libertarian movements concerned to make criminal justice more accountable tend to generate 'law and order' movements in response, thus making the rights of defendants a continual battleground.

This last approach, sometimes called the resources mobilization approach, also explores how political crises are relevant for the success of a social movement in achieving its goals. The primary focus here is the way people recognize the injustice involved in the issue with which they are concerned, organize themselves, raise funds and mobilize people for direct action. It also focuses attention on the way the organizational structure affects a movement's relationship with other movements, parties and institutions. So whether the movement is old or new is less relevant than what it does and how it does it. More than the other approaches so far discussed, this account tries to explore the interconnections between governing institutions at national and European levels and the self-organized forms of governance witnessed in social movements. In this way it is possible to consider how culturally specific collective actors emerge and interact with political institutions and conventional political parties in order to achieve their goals.

2.3 Unions and environmental movements: closer ties?

As the story goes, if the period between the 1920s and the 1950s can be described as the age of the unions (as an old social movement), then the 1960s saw the birth of new social movements concerned with the operation of power in both the public domain of mainstream politics and in the private lives which political scientists tended to ignore. Actually, this is a little deceptive for we will concentrate on a variety of labour and environmental movements that are quite complex in charac- ter. The networks of alliances which can emerge between unions, environmental movements and other campaigning groups can be unpre- dictable and changing. For instance, during 1999 a wide variety of European groups took part in the demonstrations against the World Trade Organization (WTO) in Seattle. The promotion of global free trade by the WTO has been blamed for its negative impact on both the environment and those people employed in industries that were shielded from open competition by tariff barriers and other controls. Of the 1,448 non-governmental organizations from 89 countries supporting the Friends of the Earth/ASEED (Action for Solidarity, Equality, Environment and Development) petition against the trade talks in Seattle, 575 were situated in European societies. In addition to political representatives from Green parties and international environmental and union organizations, a whole variety of locally based groups and organizations signed up. To give you a feel for the variety involved in this petition consider the organizations and groups identified in Box 4.1 (overleaf).

As you can see from the way such diverse groups are able to mobilize around a common cause, the differences between class identity, regional or national affiliation and environmental concerns are not especially clear cut. The history of environmental awareness throughout Europe has been closely connected to labour movements engaging in attempts to improve the urban environment or creating greater opportunities for urban populations to have access to the countryside. Public health improve- ments were always a feature in the reformist policy platforms of trade unions as well as the political parties with which they have been aligned. The impetus for town planning and the amelioration of environmental hazards from smog to cholera have been as much a feature of centre-right political parties concerned with national efficiency as of leftist ones

---

Box 4.1 European groups petitioning against the millennium round of WTO*

Alternative Consumer Association & Fur for Animals from the Netherlands;

Association of Social and Ecological Intervention & Nea Ecologia in Greece;

Finnish Association for Nature Conservation & Grandmothers for Peace in Finland;

Comitato Scientifico Antivivisezionista, Italy;

HempLETS Local Exchange Trading Scheme;

Coventry Trades Union Council, New Economics Foundation and the Scottish Crofters in the UK;

L'Association H20 (Health Help Organization) &

Women's International League for Peace and Freedom (WILPF) in France;

Swedish Consumer Coalition & Swedish Society for Nature Conservation;

PCPE (Partido Comunista de los Pueblos de España), Movimiento Contra la Europa de Maastricht y la Globalización Económica, Ecologistas en Acción and Plataforma Rural in Spain;

Dyrebeskyttelsen Norge (Norwegian Society for the Protection of Animals), Norsk Okologisk Landbrukslag (Organic Farmers Union) and Oljearbeidernes Fellessammenslutning (Federation of Oil Workers Trade Union) from Norway.

* These groups have not been selected from the full list of signatories because of their numerical and political significance. Many are small scale, focused on specific issues or defending particular interests in a variety of cultural locations. Many more could have been selected to take their place from a list that covers most of Europe and movements within your own locality. They demonstrate the heterogeneity of groups within the environmental movement.

---

focused on social justice. Environmentalist initiatives such as organic farming (including permaculture) and forest conservation were also a feature of fascist regimes in the early twentieth century. So bear in mind that environmental movements have links and influences across party politics.

In this chapter we focus upon two commonly told stories: the decline of the unions and the rise of environmental movements within European societies. These stories are full of paradoxes that are related to the shifting patterns of governance at national and European levels. While unions have declined in importance in a number of national contexts, many of their objectives on the minimum wage and redundancy agreements have been (at least partially) achieved through European political institutions. The effects of environmental movements are also patchy and uneven and they often come into conflict with the stated objective of 'sustainable development' of the European Community (**Baker, 2001**). Both unions and environmental movements are engaged in these kinds of struggles and both have experienced the dilemmas involved in choosing to oppose or become part of the process through which policies are formulated and implemented. In the next section we focus on unions and ask whether they conform to the description of old social movements outlined earlier.

Summary

- Social movements are self-organizing networks that are produced as part of oppositional struggles against dominant economic and political interests or against specific threats or hazards.

- Old social movements have been associated with organized movements and groups which are integrated into the political system; new social movements have often been marginalized groups reacting to powerful interests. In practice, the difference is harder to identify.

- Social movements have been seen as a product of social and economic changes, shifting values or the unique effects of the mobilization of resources in specific institutional conditions.

3   Trade unions as social movements: 'you can't touch me I'm part of the union ...'

Unions emerged in specific trades and occupations as a form of collective organization in order to secure higher wages, better working conditions and reasonable working hours. They also served as a location for building mutual support through insurance schemes (against sickness, unemployment or injury), non-profit making production of necessities – both goods and services – from food to funeral services, as well as providing venues for cheap recreation such as working men's clubs and sporting events. They provided for greater security (especially where state-financed support for welfare was absent) and even served as a context for the educational improvement of their members. Unions initially represented male employees working in the same trade or industry and served to defend their common interests. Becoming a member was a life-long commitment to the group, sharing its cultural values and becoming a participant in the self-organizing networks upon which you could depend in harder times as well as the good. Those industries where the working conditions were harsh, such as in mining and/or where fraternal relations were bound through hardship (such as through insecure employment, for example, dock work), produced extremely solidaristic unions which could act as very effective collective actors. Union banners served as visible symbols (akin to the flags indicating military victories or glorious defeats) of the struggles of the labour movement and were often paraded and celebrated at annual fairs, sporting occasions, music festivals and other local cultural events (Figure 4.2). Regardless of the absence of democracy and accountability in many union structures, they served as a key site for constructing the identity of working-class communities.

The confederations of unions that attempted to co-ordinate their activities across regions and industries acquired a significant influence on government policies and, in different times and places, became quite involved in both the formulation and implementation of economic policy. In short, unions served as a major focus for cultural identity, providing an organizational and financial basis for the provision of relief in times of hardship, delivering basic incomes, providing legal support for employees, campaigning for welfare improvements and encouraging co-operative behaviour across regions and nations. Union membership included a responsibility to act on behalf of the collective; in return it offered some protection against the vagaries of economic life and the effects of social inequalities.

Yet, at the start of the twenty-first century, union membership in many European societies is lower than it has been for half a century. In addition, in many national contexts the role of unions has become less important in the formulation and implementation of policy making. Unions continue to provide a space for mutual support and a variety of activities that bind communities together. They remain strongest where all members are in the same social position and have roughly the same life chances. In a world increasingly characterized by rapid change and greater social and geographical mobility in the workforce, unions are often engaged in defensive actions to preserve communities in the face of redundancies and industrial relocation.

The question we should ask, then, is not what will take the place of trade unions in civil society but in what kinds of activities will unions be engaged and how does this relate to other ways of constructing cultural

Figure 4.2 Remembering the Tolpuddle martyrs: a customary display of union loyalty followed by all the fun of the fair

Figure 4.3 Unions have remained strong when they matter in cultural life –
Festa D'Unita, Bologna, remains one of the largest gatherings of
union members in Europe (attended by millions every year)

identity, campaigning for environmental protection and improving the
built environment. Union representatives have been involved on national
consultative committees on environmental protection in Germany and
France, and at the Earth Summit in 1992 the United Nations identified
trade unions as a crucial stakeholder in formulating and implementing
policies on sustainable development at the local and national level. So
perhaps the role of unions will be increasingly bound up with other social
movements such as those concerned with the quality of life.

3.1 Unions and national cultures: Germany, the UK and France

*To understand unions, do we start with a local or national focus or look more
broadly?* Certainly, unions developed transnational affiliations throughout
the twentieth century. Even prior to the First World War, social democratic parties and trade unions had attempted to develop fraternal support
for industrial action across European societies. However, this was
undermined by the two World Wars. In the years immediately following
the Second World War, trade unions played a part in the policy-making
processes of many national governments and remained largely committed
to national rather than transnational objectives. In the UK this was a
result of the involvement of leading members of the labour movement in
the wartime administration and subsequently in the 1945–1951 Labour
Government. In France, Italy and elsewhere, labour movements had close

links with members of national coalition governments in the initial years of reconstruction.

During the post-war economic boom, governments were concerned to avoid the industrial conflict of the early twentieth century by institutionalizing the negotiations between the representatives of capital and labour. Economic growth was based upon the successful implementation of mass production (manufacturing of the assembly-line type) supported by small-scale enterprises supplying the more specialized components. Governments sought to ensure that this was matched by steady and reasonably predictable patterns of mass consumption through three devices:

- maintaining specific levels of consumer spending through welfare provision (to prevent sectors of the population falling into a condition of under-consumption as in the industrial areas in the 1920s and 1930s);

- redistributive or progressive taxation systems (to even out the spending patterns of different groups of people);

- a consistent level of consumer spending also sustained through the maintenance of full or near to full employment through Keynesian demand management (roughly 250,000–400,000 unemployed).

When needed, direct state intervention was initiated through the nationalization of strategically important industries that would otherwise shed labour. This situation placed trade unions in a much stronger bargaining position to secure further material concessions, whether at the level of factory production or as part of the national bodies for co-ordinating economic policy. There were considerable differences of approach from country to country, which helps to explain the different roles of unionism across Europe (**Dawson, 2001; Grahl, 2001**).

In the former West Germany, unions played an important part in the industries devoted to export-oriented production of capital goods (machinery and technical support systems which enabled companies to produce manufactured products). Post-war reconstruction had created sixteen large trade unions, each based in a particular industry. These were also co-ordinated by the *Deutschegewerkschaftsbund* (a centralized and unitary federation of unions). Successive post-war German governments had encouraged extensive worker participation in the long-term investment decisions of West German companies in exchange for union compliance with government policies in other areas. The processes of collective bargaining were heavily regulated by statute and, as a result, judicial resolutions of conflicts became commonplace. Agreements were binding for two to three years and wildcat actions were made illegal. Both employers and employees developed highly organized and effectively co-ordinated organizational representation at federal, state and local levels. Negotiations over pay levels and working hours were conducted at the regional level while Works Councils were focused on working conditions in each plant. In addition, both capital and labour acknowledged the role of export growth and productivity as significant factors in establishing future agreements. As a result of this social partnership, exports increased from 8 per cent of GDP in 1955 to 25 per cent in 1980 (Hall, 1986, p.237).

In contrast, union involvement in collective bargaining in the UK was voluntary and much less organized. Many unions were rooted in craft distinctions and traditional industrial divisions had been retained from the early twentieth century. Consequently, most large plants had different unions representing the workers connected to separate parts of the productive process and these unions were as concerned with the differential payments between skills as with improving conditions and the basic level of pay. In addition, consumer-oriented mass production (rather than capital goods) has been embraced more wholeheartedly in the UK. This ensured that while growth was strong and full employment attainable in the 1950s, British industries were more vulnerable to short-term changes in market conditions. Both the Conservative and Labour governments responded to such changes with the 'stop-go' economic policy to counter stagflation, stimulating the economy when it experienced a decline in growth and using the taxation system to dampen down consumer demand when inflation began to accelerate.

In France, unions are politically fragmented as well as divided on religious grounds. The *Confédération Générale du Travail* (CGT), the most highly organized and disciplined trade union alliance, was tied to the politically marginalized French Communist Party (CPF), which had been excluded from government from 1947 to 1981. Even the moderate socialist unions (the *Confédération Française Démocratique du Travail*, CFDT) found themselves marginalized by the 1960s as successive governments opted for the technocratic approach, which involved planning economic policy solely with the managers of key industrial sectors and companies.

So, in each of these three examples we can see quite distinctive patterns:

- the incorporation of unions into a social partnership with the relationship between employers and employees regulated by statute and judicial arbitration at all levels;

- the involvement of union representatives in policy making nationally, but their effective exclusion from decision making in investment decisions at a plant level;

- the exclusion of fragmented unions from economic planning by the state and employers, resulting in running conflicts at all levels.

Nevertheless, this still presents too generalized a picture of quite uneven patterns of unionization. The distribution of trade unions tends to be governed by the location of employment. In some cases, membership can be highly concentrated, creating the potential for a highly organized workforce (such as in mining communities). Their solidarity and cohesion tends to be stronger when the communities involved are isolated from wider social networks with alternative forms of work. In these situations, union members tend to be more conscious of their collective identity, whereas elsewhere instrumental attitudes and self-interest drive collective action such as strikes. The size of any particular workforce is less important than its strategic significance. In Germany, IG Metal exerted considerable leverage due to its role in the export strategy identified earlier, and in the UK the electrical and coal workers were able to exert considerable leverage in industrial negotiations because they could affect the power supply.

Political culture also affects the ways in which unions have developed. In the UK, trade unions across industries and sectors are co-ordinated through the Trades Union Congress (TUC), an umbrella organization which represents the interests of workers in the formation and implementation of economic policy. TUC representatives actively participated in the National Economic Development Council (NEDC) where employers and unionists could establish common objectives (or at least air their grievances). These mechanisms for reconciling the interests of capital and labour were seen as tantamount to a new social order, a post-capitalist society (Dahrendorf, 1959). Whether these interests were ever really reconciled is doubtful. What they did achieve was the facilitation of medium and longer-term planning in economic policy by European governments until the 1970s.

We can say, then, that the trade unions operated as a key mechanism for collective identification and as one of the institutional means for securing improvements in the material conditions of union members (mostly male) and their families. Identification with social class position and associated political parties was also strong. Bear in mind that unions, as a reflection of the labour market, were male oriented and that the strongest unions excluded members of marginalized groups. They were often situated in geographically and socially immobile communities and viewed migrants as a threat to their improved prosperity. Unions involved the lifestyle politics of only certain sectors of the population and some unions were also heavily reliant on members from culturally homogenous working-class communities. This provided for cohesion and organization during periods of direct action, but made it hard for them to adapt. As a result, they were to find themselves increasingly out of step with the more dynamic shifting peoples of the late twentieth and early twenty-first centuries (see Chapter 3).

3.2 Europe, the labour market and the decline of unionism

What has changed since the post-war boom? By the 1970s and 1980s the virtuous cycle of growth and full employment, from which organized unionism has benefited, began to disappear. This resulted in a profits squeeze, economic rationalization and the shedding of labour. Unemployment in the UK rose above the one million mark and has remained over that figure until 2001 (although there have been changes in how the statistical figure is defined). Mass production no longer offered a secure route for growth. Changes in market conditions (with goods and services increasingly differentiated) demanded more flexible forms of production. Factory machinery had to be altered and improved to cope with smaller batches of products and the greater variety in the goods manufactured, while the labour force became more flexible. This, in conjunction with technological developments such as the application of microchip electronics (initially to consumer durables but more recently to clerical and administrative work), led to two decades of unparalleled industrial restructuring. Repeated attempts to develop a partnership between representatives of capital and labour failed in the face of austerity packages that saw public sector services cut and unemployment increase to record levels.

External factors affected European economies as commodity prices increased dramatically (especially oil prices). The effects of economic change were uneven throughout Europe, but ultimately the influence of trade unions began a dramatic decline in France and the UK. This took place against the background of the economic slump of the 1980s (the severest since the Great Depression of the 1930s). Employers took this opportunity to restructure the production process and in some cases de-unionize their workforces. The result has been the marginalization of the unions and the collapse of union membership (to below six million in the UK, from the peak of over twelve million in 1979). Belonging to a union has become an increasingly instrumental choice concerned with local pay and conditions rather than an all-embracing expression of class identity. Other aspects of individual lifestyle – ones that are focused on gender, the effects of cultural differences or environment – now play a larger role in collective action.

In West Germany, the effects of restructuring did not have such a significant immediate impact. Unlike those societies which had moved toward the Fordist production of consumer durables, the dependence on exports combined with the persistently undervalued exchange rate of the Deutschmark (so that exports were competitive and imports more highly priced than domestic manufactures) provided a cushion against the early effects of the economic downturn. In addition, the maintenance of higher wages was helped by the willingness of trade unions such as IG Metal to link negotiations over working hours, flexibility, training and productivity. This enabled Kohl's Christian Democratic government, prior to the reunification of Germany, to secure restructuring of capital and greater flexible production in many sectors of industry (without the scale of opposition and lost production associated with industrial action in the UK).

3.3 Employment rights and the labour market in Europe

What sort of labour market now exists in Europe? While there are still significant differences between working lives across national boundaries in the EU, one feature of the labour market can be said to be common within all its member societies. This is the experience of workforce fragmentation, a development also closely related to our lifestyles and cultural identities. The labour market, as before, is divided between skilled and semi-skilled/unskilled workers but this is now too simplistic to provide an accurate description of the different kinds of employment (in)security and flexibility. The privileged members of the primary labour market are generally more secure than most other workers. There is still substantial variety in this group, especially between those with and without access to profit sharing and performance-related pay, private benefits and insurance schemes, and labour market and income security.

Not all members of this primary group have fared so well. For example, civil servants and skilled unionists have seen their occupations decline in number as well as in income and labour market security. The most significant new development has been the substantial growth in the number of people employed in the secondary labour market with its multi-tier pay and variable contract systems. Such 'flexi-workers' experience some combination of irregular wages, short-term contracts, subcontracted employment through agencies (rather than as a direct company employee) and limited opportunities for career management. In France, the Netherlands and Germany, the expansion of this kind of work (such as telecomputing employment) enables employers to take advantage of lower wage costs in the peripheral regions of the single market (such as the former East Germany). The labour market is not only more fragmented, it is also more European with increased geographical mobility. At first sight, collective organization of the workforce by unions across Europe appears too difficult – if not impossible. However, unions that have become marginal in economic influence at the national level have found that some forms of co-ordination in particular sectors (such as dockworkers) can have tangible benefits (as Box 4.2 suggests).

While many trade unions have been on the defensive at the national and local level, there have been some remarkable gains in employment rights through the European institutions. In the Treaty of Rome, the improvement of working conditions and the standard of living were explicit objectives. Equal pay for equal work was legally adopted by member states in 1976 with equal access to employment, training, promotion and working conditions in 1978 (with a right of appeal to the European Court should national law fail to comply). This has improved matters, but has not eradicated the problem of discrimination in terms of gender and ethnicity. The European Foundation for the Improvement of Living and Working Conditions (based in Dublin) monitors health and safety issues and the effects of part-time employment, shift patterns and temporary contracts on the workforce. This has prompted the establishment of programmes aimed at reducing the risks of exposure to biological, chemical and physical agents and permanent monitoring bodies in specific industries such as nuclear power, mining and steel manufacturing (Esping-Anderson and Regini, 2000).

The implementation of the internal market brought with it the need to develop common rules with respect to working conditions, pay, mobility and social security. The internal market presumes that capital and labour should operate on a comparable basis throughout the EU (that a common

Box 4.2   Transnational unionism in the Euro-labour market – the dockworkers

Transnational links have been constructed between older social movements. In the 1980s and 1990s, the Coordinadora, a grass-roots and initially unofficial network of Spanish dockworkers, forged links with similarly organized dockworkers in established dockers unions in the UK and France. They also built strong ties with Works Councils in German ports (e.g. Hamburg), and circulated newsletters in Rotterdam and Antwerp as well as in Århus (Denmark). These movements were informed by anarchist and syndicalist ideas and remain fiercely independent of Social Democratic or Communist parties. The movement bypassed and challenged both employers and the official International Transportworker's Federation. Dockworkers are (with the possible exception of miners) unique in their historical commitment to solidarity with other dockworkers around the world as well as workers in other industrial sectors. Unlike unions in the same company in different countries (as in the car industry), dockworkers have often been employed by state-owned companies, municipal authorities or private corporations located solely within the ports. In Spain, especially in Barcelona and Las Palmas, dockworkers have strong collective traditions and a willingness to develop self-organizing networks and engage in economic and political action (even against the authoritarian Franco regime up to 1975).

The Coordinadora was organized with relatively open participation and a clear structure of delegates based on zones of ports, weighted to ensure that the preferences of the larger ports did not overwhelm the smaller groups of dockworkers. Prior to the 1990s, the dockworkers had engaged in working to rule, prolonged strike actions and other forms of direct action (such as street blockades) to improve pay and working conditions. They also aimed to ensure comparability of pay and conditions between ports or respond to disciplinary measures taken against dockworkers in other ports. They challenged the privatization of port facilities and boycotted the ships of companies involved in a dispute with unions within and outside the industry. This can be seen in the active support for workers in Swedish ports in 1981 and for the NUM in the coal dispute of 1984/85 as well as the British dock dispute of 1989. These actions often bypassed the official transnational union bodies such as the ITF. The action was sometimes oriented to making a political protest against human rights abuses in Latin America (such as boycotts of Chilian imports), toxic chemical and arms exports, working conditions for seamen in developing countries and so on. Such actions often drew on the support of families and communities who were economically dependent on the ports. These communities had a stable resource base, were conscious of their identity, cohesive and capable of acting decisively.

By the 1990s, employers became more organized and more willing to use legal instruments to secure solutions to industrial relations problems. The transnational activism of dockworkers became less effective so they focused on defending their own backyard. However, when 500 dockworkers were sacked by Cammell Laird (Merseyside, UK), dockworkers across the moribund network were reactivated producing a surge of financial support during 1995–1998. After two and a half years of picketing, on 26 January 1998 Jim Nolan, chair of Merseyside Port Shop Stewards, announced that with dwindling public interest and support they had no choice but to accept a 'go-away' payment of £28,000 each and the continuation of existing pension arrangements through Mersey Docks and Harbour Company. This even prompted a reassessment of the state of industrial relations by the International Dockworkers Conference (Montreal, May 1997) establishing the European Area of the IDC in Barcelona to set a permanent union across all European ports to exchange information and make collective decisions. The Coordinadora was asked to co-ordinate this development and establish links with all ports in Europe. Despite the process of de-unionization through the 1980s and 1990s, the Spanish dockers have now established themselves as the cornerstone for an officially recognized transnational union as part of the International Council of Dockers (inaugurated 29–30 April 2000) representing the European continent rather than individual nations.

(See Waterman, 1998, pp.99–110.)

market for companies presumes a common market for workers and good industrial relations). There has been agreement over the terms of collective redundancy, the employment rules relating to take-overs and mergers and the rights of workers in bankrupt companies; but attempts to develop a social partnership by introducing industrial democracy and worker participation have been less successful. The Vredeling proposals (Draft Directive on Procedures for Informing and Consulting Employees) of 1980 called for all firms with a workforce exceeding one thousand employees to keep their workers fully informed about company plans and any prospect of changes in production such as closures or alterations of working methods and techniques. This is where the national differences highlighted earlier are significant. Italy, the UK and Greece have a long history of industrial conflict and little in the way of established traditions of consultation between employers and employees. While this kind of social partnership fits well with industrial relations in West Germany, in the UK the CBI consistently opposed worker participation proposals – seeing them as a licence for industrial espionage and at odds with managerial traditions. Unions have also been worried about the way that formal institutional structures would turn unionists into employers' puppets.

In 1994, with the exception of the UK, all EU members adopted the European Social Policy resolution to promote competitiveness and job-generating growth while protecting workers' rights. Reducing the unemployment of 18–20 million throughout the EU has remained the priority. This approach combines a recognition of the need for flexibility and competitiveness with setting minimum standards for labour (such as the minimum wage), training and education (enshrined in the employment chapter of the 1997 Treaty of Amsterdam). Conservative governments from 1979 in the UK had consistently opposed the implementation of minimum workers' rights and had dismantled the Wages Councils that had advised on minimum standards. The election of a Labour government in 1997 removed the main obstacle to implementing the Social Charter, introducing workers' rights and creating the conditions for industrial partnership (**Grahl, 2001**).

Instrumental in all these EU measures has been the dialogue generated between employers, unions and public enterprises. A crucial aspect in pressing home the concerns of the unions has been the role of organized sectors of the workforce, together with the centre-left political parties in the European Parliament, in lobbying member states and the European Trades Union Federation (based in Brussels). Yet this also means that those people within the workforce but situated outside the organized unions or as members of weaker unions often find their specific employment needs marginalized or even ignored. The rights of disabled workers provide a good illustration of this. Broad support for integrating disabled people into the workforce was created as part of the Social Charter. Previously, the Social Fund contained some limited provision for vocational training and the subsidy of employers for people disabled as a consequence of work-related injury. Only in the 1990s have attempts been made by the agencies of the EU to encourage economic and educational integration as well as facilitate self-reliance (through the HELIOS programme). By the end of the twentieth century, the main development was an information-sharing exercise to facilitate action in a more co-ordinated way. In short, unions have played a role but have not been crucial in aiding the campaigns for marginalized social groups.

Summary

- Unions started out as self-organizing networks for mutual support, for representing the interests of different groups of workers and as outsiders to the policy process. However, during the mid to late twentieth century they became heavily involved in the formulation and implementation of policy making.

- Involvement in top-down governance carried the price of becoming more formal and less accountable to union members; thus unions became increasingly divided between officials and rank-and-file members.

- Unions have become less influential in political institutions and parties. To defend their collective communal identities some have returned to their role as challenging groups and have forged alliances with other social movements in order to defend communities, prevent hazards and resist social control.

4 New social movements and the environment

Since the 1960s, various social movements have emerged which are grounded in debates over cultural differences, gender, human rights, peace and, our focus here, the environment. You will recall from the early parts of this chapter that the rise of social movements as self-organized expressions of collective identities cannot be reduced simply to class location. This has prompted a rethink about the motivations for political action and why certain issues matter to people. It is useful to recap briefly on some of the key differences between old and new social movements. Whereas the unions tended to be characterized by formal and hierarchical structures, the new social movements are largely made up of informal networks and participative associations (which is why they have been linked to post-materialism, see Table 4.2). Such grass-roots organizations have sought to change public opinion and transform relationships in civil society rather than concentrating their attention on being integrated into public policy-making bodies. Indeed, until the late 1980s, such movements were often marginalized in conventional party politics and ridiculed in the media. Unions saw it as their primary duty to defend their own members' interests within political institutions; new social movements attempt to change attitudes and transform social relationships more generally.

4.1 Explaining environmental movements

Environmental organizations are quite diverse; some seek to change public opinion, others focus their attention on lobbying mainstream political parties oriented to the labour movement or the business community. Some attempt to construct broad platforms while others are fixated upon the hazard in their own backyard. Four main explanations have been developed to account for the rise of environmental movements, of which the first two are closely linked to the explanations of social movements considered earlier.

Changes in the class structure have seen the decline of the traditional working class and the emergence of a new middle class employed in professions, middle management and public services.

Changes in values within developed Western societies: the values acquired during the Depression and war years of the early twentieth century (when economic security and growth was the prevailing concern) have been increasingly supplanted by an alternative *post-materialism* of the post-war generations (notably among the children of parents with material security).

Corporatism as an institutional arrangement focused exclusively on the relations between capital and labour among political regimes in Austria, Sweden and West Germany. This has been seen as partly responsible for environmental movements becoming oppositional challenging groups in these national contexts. The state becomes their main antagonist – a direct consequence of the exclusion of environmentalists from participation in policy making (Scott, 1990). Environmental movements have thus been consistently loud and prominent in the media, for the quiet mechanisms of influence have often been closed to them. Nevertheless, the transition from oppositional movement to potent political force depends more on the electoral system than the precise environmental issues raised. In politically open societies with proportional representation (such as Germany) and financial support for electioneering, Green political representatives can secure seats in the national assemblies. Electoral systems and political institutions are especially important for accounting for variation across Europe.

The visibility of environmental deterioration (see, for example, Figure 4.4) has had the effect of generating a greater environmental consciousness in post-war Europe. This would also explain the greater intensity of environmental action in Southern Germany, Northern France and the Netherlands where direct experience of problems such as air and water pollution is more likely. In the UK, however, environmental concern is well integrated into the party political framework, with pressure groups

Figure 4.4   Some forms of environmental impacts are highly visible – the effects of acid rain on European forestry

such as the Campaign for the Protection of Rural England and the National Trust (sometimes referred to as the 'eco-establishment') providing a moderate avenue for political influence. Direct action is usually limited to issues where extensive consultation with environmental groups has been inadequate, such as on nuclear power and highway construction.

These explanations, although relevant, offer a partial account of the reasons which explain the rise of environmental movements. Recent studies consider these movements as expressions of disaffection with the alienating conditions of urban life, the impersonal social relations in twentieth-century culture and the increased state intrusion into personal lives.

4.2   Environmental movements and national cultures: the breakthrough of the German Greens

How did the environmental movement emerge and coalesce into the more formal political organizations that now make up the Green parties in national assemblies, regional assemblies and the European Parliament? One of the most prominent environmental movements originated in Germany, which had a culture that harboured a widespread concern for environmental protection in local areas (Figure 4.5). From the 1960s to the 1980s, the growing concern with the effects of industrial processes produced thousands of citizen action groups (*Bürgerinitiativen*) which had sprung up in response to town planning issues (Boehmer-Christiansen and Skea, 1991). These groups were radicalized by the experience of anti-nuclear protests and campaigns for nature conservation being ignored by established parties and political institutions. The formation of the Federation of Citizens Groups (BBU) provided a national platform for environmental politics and managed to maintain the grass-roots support of ordinary activists.

The form our cities have taken on in the industrial age no longer meets their inhabitants' basic vital and cultural requirements. The object is to work for alternative solutions in order to counteract the exodus from the cities and to make inner-city living more attractive. The Green Bridge ... is a piece of a new urban landscape, inviting and encouraging use. The bridge structure eliminates a dangerous pedestrian traffic light crossing, it provides an unbroken link from the residential area in the Neustadt ... with the local recreational zone along the bank of the Rheine, and offers a variety of stimulating recreation areas.

(Jockel Fuchs, former mayor of the City of Mainz)

Figure 4.5   Green Bridge, Mainz: environmental action in-volves changing small spaces, not just responding to big issues

By 1980, an estimated 50,000 citizen action groups had been established throughout West Germany (about 1.6 million people – equivalent to the combined membership of political parties). These citizen action groups campaigned alongside the more traditional organizations for landscape and conservation, such as the BUND (the German Federation for Nature Protection). Since the BUND was established to defend the interests of landowners (unlike the defence of cultural heritage by the National Trust in the UK), it served as a conservative force when environmental issues were raised in mainstream politics. The BUND was especially strong where the German Christian Democrats were also the dominant political party, as in Bavaria. Although still very diverse, the BBU was also considerably more radical in its objectives. Its members were heavily involved in mass protests and direct action against nuclear power stations in Whyl (near Freiburg), Brokdorf (near Hamburg) and the Wackersdorf reprocessing plant (Bavaria) as well as against American bases identified as holding cruise missiles directed at the Eastern bloc. Both protesters and police came equipped for violent confrontation, and the notion that the environmental movement would serve as a means of social and political transformation provided a significant alternative to the union movement, which remained closely affiliated to the SPD, German Social Democratic Party (Mewes, 1998).

The formation of *Die Grünen* (the German Green Party) in 1978 provided a new mechanism for environmental pressure to be brought to bear on mainstream politics (Figure 4.6 overleaf). As a political organization it had a middle-class membership and a strong appeal for those born since the 1950s. Nevertheless, the membership (approximately 40,000) is no reflection of the diversity of the 3.5 million voters it attracted in West Germany and more so since the unification of Germany. As a political party *Die Grünen* has drawn support away from all the mainstream parties, although its association with leftist politics makes it a considerable threat to the Social Democrats. It draws support from BUND members who have become so dissatisfied with Christian Democratic responses to environmental issues that they have at key moments voted for *Die Grünen* (Mez, 1998).

In addition, the strong and organizationally effective ecofeminist strand in the Greens emphasized the links between the domination of women and the degradation of nature. This part of the environmental movement sees equal rights in the workplace as a distraction from the way that the organization of work is itself part of the ecological problem. Ecofeminists celebrated the role of women in social reproduction and highlighted the inequity of unpaid domestic labour in order to draw upon the support of mothers with small children (Smith 1998, pp.82–8). Furthermore, the transformist politics of the Greens provided younger voters with a natural place for protest. This alliance of diverse interests also presented its own difficulties in co-ordination and in listening to their members' concerns.

Green political parties are caught between two imperatives. They draw from models of democratic thinking which emphasize the importance of participating in the decisions which affect our lives. But they also recognize that making a difference to policy making means that they

Figure 4.6 Green party politics provokes some
interesting confrontations

have to redirect the demands of the broader environmental movement within the confines of existing political institutions. As a result, they could continue to act as a protest movement co-ordinating a fragile alliance of movements or they could try to build a party that could make a difference to policy making.

In order to achieve influence and secure voting support, Green parties throughout Europe and within the European Parliament decided to play by the rules of the political game. This enabled them to present a clear policy line which can be assimilated easily within media sound-bite presentation as well as recruit members and voters, raise money for campaigns and so on. According to the 'realists' in *Die Grünen*, all of this could be achieved much more easily through a hierarchical party structure. However, 'fundamentalists' (which included the ecofeminist wing of the party) were willing to risk being less effective in order to maintain their identity as transformative organizations. The internal divisions that led up to and followed the realists' victory over the 'fundis' on internal structure and organization also severely harmed the electoral performance of *Die Grünen* at state and federal level (Roth and Murphy, 1998). Similar divisions and consequences were evident in the British Green Party in the early 1990s as it transformed itself from a party of protest to a professional party with the same centralized leadership and formal, hierarchical organization of mainstream parties.

In both Germany and the UK the result was a fall in membership as many activists moved on into related movements focusing on direct action on single issues. These have included the eco-warrior strategies adopted in protests against airport extensions, highway construction (such as Twyford Down) and 'The Land is Ours' movement (which occupies and builds urban villages on brown-field waste sites in protest at greenbelt developments). Environmental movements also tend to promote local initiatives, such as non-monetary exchange systems, self-sufficiency projects, producers co-operatives and other citizenship initiatives. They are more concerned with developing strategies for change in their private lives and are sceptical about the capacities of the state to find answers.

So, as with trade unions, it is more accurate to acknowledge the variety of environmental movements placed in very different cultural locations and recognize the ad hoc and informal character of these kinds of social movements throughout Europe. They do not usually exist in a pure form that fits the definitions devised by social scientists; they draw from the lived experiences of complex communities with a mix of social classes and culturally specific groups, as illustrated in the Kalamas campaign (Box 4.3 overleaf).

Summary

- Environmental movements are the product of changes in the socio-economic relations and cultural values which underpin European societies. They also indicate the failure of established parties and political institutions to acknowledge the need to respond to environmental degradation produced by industrial processes.

- Protests like that in Kalamas are often characterized as environmental movements. They are, in fact, often complex configurations of economic, political and cultural forces mobilized in response to a specific threat. Challenges to power-holders who fail to take notice of the effects of their decision making depend on the interconnections between the environmental and social issues and the motivations to organize and resist governance from above within a specific location.

Box 4.3 Environmental movements as mobilizing resources: the Kalamas campaign as a case study

Environmental movements often involve specific communities mobilizing and co-ordinating their activities against an environmental hazard or planned development. They present a sustained challenge to power-holders and state bodies through feisty demonstrations of 'commitment, unity and worthiness' (Tilly, 1994, p.7). In the Kalamas campaign, conducted by an alliance from Thesprotian communities and the island of Corfu in North West Greece, we find an example of a challenging group. Such a campaign demonstrates the interaction of opportunity structures and the mobilization of resources in specific circumstances. To understand any campaign we need to consider the context in which a movement emerges.

The Kalamas campaign was a localized environmental movement against the construction of a sewage treatment plant planned by the municipal authorities in Ioannina. In this development project, the treated effluent would be discharged into the River Kalamas and so alter the ecosystem upon which the prevailing agricultural practices and growing tourism were based. This project was instigated by the Greek central government, which had provided grants for technical and financial support as part of a longer-term programme of urban development. However, solving this problem of urbanization produced a massive backlash and extensive community mobilization to challenge the project. This was due largely to the perception that urban benefits would generate costs for the people who lived in the surrounding rural areas and on Corfu. This did not mean that the campaign was against development, but it sought a strategy that worked with rather than

disrupted existing relationships between local people and the ecosystem, and of special concern was the potential damage to fisheries and tourism.

Maria Kousis's study of the internal organization of the campaign revealed a complex decentralized committee system that emerged solely to press the case of Thesprotia and Corfu at local, regional, state and international levels, including the World Health Organization. The various tactics used – from lobbying and demonstrations to strikes, blockades and occupations – secured extensive media coverage. The campaign was grounded in local cultural knowledge and signalled a distrust of technical experts (for backing the sewage project in the first place). The campaign also built links with broader environmental movements (including RIXI in Athens and *Die Grünen*). No formal membership list existed and all participants were volunteers. Yet, through poster announcements and a limited committee structure, an extensive range of actions was successfully initiated. The Kalamas committee (chaired in rotation among its members) was more important in preventing splits in the movement than in providing a central organizational focus. Mobilization of supporters was swift and very effective, including a successful 41-day blockade of the provincial capital, Igoumenitsa. Kousis identifies the extent of cohesion that is possible in such events:

> In public referenda, all unions and associations and individual locals voted to cease all activities – even schools and hospitals were closed – and to block all routes of transportation to the city. The municipal town hall was chained and locked up by members of the Struggle Committee

and public buildings were occupied by local citizens. On a number of occasions, farm tractors were used in these mobilizations though the actions were characterized by non-violence. These mobilization tactics were also used in Athens, in front of parliament and in front of the major TV stations, by internal migrants from Thesprotia and Corfu.

(Kousis, 1997, p.249).

The state of the local economy has produced high levels of migration from Thesprotia, so the campaign could rely on 'internal migrants' to act on their behalf and organize pressure from every possible direction. The Kalamas campaign was not an isolated incident but part of a pattern of environmental movements. It coincided with the active, mobilization of communities on the island of Milos against a geothermal power-plant project and the successful Astakos campaign against the government granting a licence for a toxic-waste storage and disposal project to a European waste company. Each campaign had distinctive qualities but they shared deep routes in the collective identities of both communities. In such spontaneous self-organizing networks in defence of local interests, concerned with social justice as well as with environmental issues, we can identify many features of environmental movements throughout Europe since the 1970s. Each campaign had distinctive qualities but they shared deep routes in the collective identities of both communities.

This example highlights how environmental movements have deep routes in both the collective identities of communities and a variety of interests. There are parallels between the forces mobilized in favour of environmental protection and the attempts to defend communities through trade unions (see Box 4.2). All such projects need to be considered in terms of the wider plans for modernization and developments supported by the EU. On many occasions it will be the European regional development initiatives that will be challenged for their effects on the environment and communities. Governance involves both regulation from above and mobilization from below.

5   Toward European eco-corporatism: the new environmental governance

So far we have focused on self-organizing governance from below. However, Green parties and environmental movements have become progressively engaged in environmental policy making. Just as the objectives of unionism were promoted through governance from above, so too can those of environmental movements. In 1972, the heads of government of the then EC developed a joint statement making a clear commitment to environmental protection in the following ways:

- pollution should be prevented at source and costs should be incurred by the polluter;

- project planning has to take environmental impacts into account;

- environmental policies must work in a compatible fashion with the broad objective of economic and social development.

Ever since, European environmental policy makers have faced the difficult task of finding a balance between achieving environmental objectives and promoting open economic competition and development across the community. For instance, environmental protection legislation could be interpreted as a restriction on trade.

The 1972 declaration coincided with one of the key landmarks in the rise of environmental awareness, the Club of Rome report (*The Limits to Growth*), which contained a direct challenge to the idea that growth and environmental protection can go hand in hand. This report highlighted the ecological limits on the processes of industrial development, both in terms of the finitude of natural resources and the capacity of existing ecosystems to act as a sink for pollution. This enormously influential report combined the expertise of industrialists, business advisers, civil servants and academics in order to develop simulated predictions of the effects of resource depletion, population growth and pollution. In the various scenarios of the computer simulation developed in the report, there were definite limits to the continuation of growth. It is now widely accepted that the report was too fatalistic and underestimated the potential of technological solutions. Nevertheless, the broad view that the solutions to the effects of growth will be social rather than technical and scientific still remains a feature of environmental politics. These dilemmas between growth and environmental protection, and between finding social solutions or technofixes for problems such as resource depletion and pollution, are central to the emergence of environmental governance.

5.1 Managing development in a sustainable way?

Especially important in assessing the role of the EU are the contradictory implications of the idea of *sustainable development* that predominates in European policy – development that 'meets the needs of the present without compromising the ability of future generations to meet their own needs' (World Commission on Environment and Development; WCED, 1987, p.43). The sustainable development approach assumes that we are adversely affecting our descendants and that we should find ways of organizing our own affairs in a more sustainable way by leaving the world for our immediate successors roughly in the same state in which we found it. This is one of the most frequent justifications deployed for environmental action, yet on the development side it also assumes that problems such as poverty and disease should also be addressed.

The ongoing five-year environmental action plans that followed the 1972 declaration were primarily concerned with hazards such as chemicals, industrial accidents, agricultural practices, biotechnology and the protection of the natural heritage. Another significant step was the 1985 Directive on Environmental Impact Assessment which required member states to assess the environmental consequences of major projects such as oil refineries, steel and cast-iron plants, power stations, airports, highways and facilities for the storage and disposal of nuclear, asbestos and chemical waste. This came into full force in 1989 and carries with it the requirement that the public must be involved in prior consultation (see **Baker, 2001**).

The event that changed environmental policy making and produced an important shift in public opinion on environmental issues (as well as in attitudes to environmental movements which had often been seen as on the fringe and cranky) was the Chernobyl incident. In the night of 25/26 April 1986, following an energy experiment, the Chernobyl nuclear reactor near Kiev exploded, producing radioactive dust and gas which drifted across Europe for the next two weeks. The extent of the deposits of radioactive fallout largely depended on rainfall but the most seriously affected areas were Poland, Scandinavia (especially Sweden), Germany, Austria and finally the UK and Eire. Alongside global awareness of the problems in the supply of fresh water, pollution of riverways and the seas, ozone depletion and global warming, there was an increased recognition that environmental protection was needed against the creeping and invisible problems which were not tied to local areas in the manner of traditional industrial pollution. Increasingly, questions were raised about the top-down approach of national governments and European political institutions in addressing such complex and uncertain threats as well as the need to find appropriate solutions at the regional and local levels.

One legacy of the formation of the EC as an economic community has been the tendency of policy making to be located within centralized bodies accountable to the national governments of respective member states; thus power has resided largely in the executive bodies, creating the democratic deficit ('that decisions in the EU are in some ways insufficiently representative of, or accountable to, the nations and people of Europe', **Lord, 2001**, p.165). Until the SEA (Single European Act, which, as part of its revision of the Treaty of Rome, included environmental policy as a function of the community), environmental policies required unanimous consent from all member states. As a result, the measures were often narrow and focused on specific problems (in order to meet the least possible resistance). The SEA identified DG XI (Directorate-General for Environment, Nuclear Safety and Civil Protection) of the Commission as the institutional vehicle for environmental protection. In addition, environmental legislation became subject to qualified majority voting, with the European Parliament given the power to amend but not to veto the legislative measures (**Heffernan, 2001**). While still a top-down approach to policy making with the executive in the driving seat, this at least enabled environmental policy to move from being concerned with remedial actions toward preventative measures (for example, regulating large combustion plants in 1988). Some of the obstacles to EU-wide regulation of the environment have been removed.

The first four environmental action plans have produced a variety of concrete results leading to the improvement in the quality of bathing water, limits on sulphur dioxide emissions, restrictions on lead in petrol and in air, as well as controls on the industrial emissions and the disposal of waste. In the 1992–2000 Environmental Action Plan, the emphasis on maintaining the quality of life, access to natural resources and avoidance of lasting environmental damage did not, at first sight, suggest a radical and ambitious campaign (see **Baker, 2001**). Nevertheless, it introduced performance targets for the recycling of resources used in production and consumption. Of note, is the attempt to reduce CO_2 emissions to 1990 levels by the year 2000 and plans to harmonize energy taxation throughout the community. The regulation of energy production has now moved to a crucial stage. With the 1996 Framework Directive on Integrated Pollution Prevention and Control (IPPC), the various forms of pollution are to be considered in terms of their impact on ecosystems rather than as forms of air or water pollution. This Directive targets the production of energy, metals and chemicals as well as the manufacture of products such as paper, ink and dyes as being of immediate concern. However, the legal instruments devised are not binding for they depend on market forces, through the use of financial incentives and support (such as the provision of funds to cover investment expenses), to produce spontaneous changes in the behaviour of citizens and firms.

5.2 Responding to global initiatives: the legacy of Rio

The most significant development in the 1990s has been the ongoing effects of the resolutions of the United Nations Conference on Environment and Development (the Earth Summit in Rio de Janeiro, 1992). This international conference sought through an action plan, Agenda 21, to encourage local responses to ecological problems by mobilizing a range of groups and favouring the development of new forms of governance that could ensure their involvement as *stakeholders* in local decision-making processes. Environmental problems and political institutions in each locality or region were quite distinct and responses had to work at this level. Under Section 28 of Agenda 21, local authorities had to exchange information and co-ordinate plans with local stakeholders (representatives of municipal and environmental service providers, universities, trade unions, environmental movements, health agencies, industries, farmers and youth groups). Each area was to hold an environmental forum by 1994 and, following a consultative process, reach a consensus on a 'Local Agenda 21' by 1996, prioritizing the environmental issues in each case. The discretionary character of Agenda 21 means that implementation is enormously varied (Lafferty and Eckerberg, 1998): some countries were 'pioneers' in initiating LA21 measures (Sweden, the UK and the Netherlands); some 'adapters', modifying existing environmental policies (Finland and Norway); and others 'late-comers' (Ireland, Austria and even Germany, where citizen action groups had lost momentum in the 1990s).

The activities associated with LA21 range from fiscal measures, policy integration, public–private partnerships and local business development to ethical investment and eco-auditing. The precise effects of this initiative have also varied with culture, institutions and groups involved. In Eire, the branches of organizations such as Friends of the Earth and Greenpeace have concentrated their efforts on the national government to ensure its continued interest in global issues. *An Taisce* (The National Trust in Eire), however, with its own organizational history based on dialogue and informed discussion, has become heavily involved in the consultation process and the emerging partnership between local authorities and stakeholders (Mullally, 1998). So, it seems that some kinds of organizational cultures are also more likely to find a constructive place in this kind of consultation.

Susan Baker argues that two types of environmental policy have featured in the European context and each has definite implications for environmental movements. First, there is the traditional incremental process of European policy making, whereby general policies of environmental management and quality control emerged in a slow step-by-step manner. This approach does not challenge the prevailing economic and social objectives and adapts environmental policy to ensure that it is implemented. Second, there are the radical policies, which are directed toward the reorganization of consumption patterns in order to produce low or zero growth in a steady state economy (or by redistributing resources and reforming political and military structures along the lines suggested in the early days of *Die Grünen*). While the Green parties across Europe and many environmental groups seek to achieve the second policy option, this would not fit easily with policies in other areas (for instance, those directed toward fulfilling the Social Charter discussed earlier). In conclusion, Baker argues that a weak version of sustainable development is much more likely to be implemented in the EU (**Baker**, 1997, pp.91–106; **2001**). If the environmental movements are going to have an impact on European politics, they will have to challenge the economic and social priorities of the EU at some point.

The growing status and significance of the European Parliament has provided one way in which movements grounded in civil societies can have an impact. In the 1990s, since the Maastricht Treaty, policy making has become more inclusive through the principles of openness and subsidiarity. It was increasingly recognized that policies should not be developed at EU level when they could be more effectively delivered through national governments (Liefferink and Anderson, 1998). This creates opportunities not only for drawing in a wider range of environmental movements, but also for national governments to avoid the implementation and monitoring of environmental policy. As a result, there are greater opportunities for regional and local organizations as well as environmental NGOs to make their presence felt in formulating and implementing policy through policy review groups, dialogue groups and the general consultative forum (which brings together environmental NGOs with national and local authorities). Underpinning these developments is the belief that such policy making will foster a new social partnership based on shared responsibilities. Whether this will produce a kind of eco-corporatism, with groups from civil society working within institutionalized mechanisms for collaboration on the formulation, implementation and monitoring of environmental policy, only time will tell. What is more likely is a continual interaction of environmental regulation with environmental movements emerging spontaneously from below in response to specific problems and unanticipated hazards.

Summary

- The solution to environmental problems is as much a social and political issue as a scientific and technical one.

- The effectiveness of the EU to serve as regulator of environmental issues and problems depends on its ability to set realistic goals which secure the consent of the actors involved.

- Successful environmental decisions at the local, national, regional and European level should be regarded not only as agreements negotiated within the policy process and appropriate to the problem under consideration, but also as those which can be carried through: implementation and verification are as important as consensuality.

6   Conclusion

While the decline of the unions opens up new opportunities for broadening consultation with a wider variety of social movements, much will depend on the relations between political institutions and private corporations. In the UK and France there has been a tendency to orient policies to the generation of growth without including environmental groups, although rural campaign groups have exerted an influence on some policy areas (such as that achieved by French and British farming communities). The strategies developed by environmental movements with the emphasis on low growth and a reorganization of production toward the local level are unlikely to be warmly endorsed by private business. There have been some moves toward green consumerism, and recycling businesses have become better organized and more productive. In addition, some companies have been careful to have their productive processes audited for their environmental impact (such as The Body Shop in the UK). However, more radical change along the lines suggested by eco-activists would challenge the role of profit making and the continual accumulation of capital through which businesses measure their success.

It is important not to overemphasize the differences between old and new social movements. Certainly, there are differences in their location within the policy process, internal organization, ideology and goals. Trade unions did operate within corporate relations and have been located within political institutions (including political parties), while environmental movements have often been excluded from such privileged access. Unions have had formal hierarchical organizations promoting the interests of their members and a more equitable distribution of wealth, while environmental movements tend to be decentralized and with 'grass-roots volunteerism' expressing lifestyle politics against the regulative powers of the state. But we should remember that old social movements started out in the same way and that unions are now much less involved in economic and regional policy. Furthermore, many environmental organizations have become (or are becoming) more institutionally embedded and more hierarchical as a result of participation in policy making. For instance, Greenpeace now tends to focus on producing scientific reports and sustained lobbying rather than frequently engaging in media stunts. The door is now open in political institutions for many environmental movements. Most Green parties have compromised their ideals on participatory democracy in order to achieve some of their policy objectives; rotating spokespersons have become leaders and participatory conferences have become stage-managed events. There has been a shift from government to new forms of governance; at the same time the pressures to conform to the conventional political structures and to focus on politics at a national level have been formidable.

There remains the question of whether environmental movements are a product of the alienation with modern urban life, an underlying romanticism about the natural world within many European cultures, the emergence of new environmental hazards, the willingness of local communities to defend their own space (NIMBY – not in my backyard) or part of a broader shift toward post-materialist values which reject growth and perpetual development (NIABY – not in anyone's backyard). It is probably a little of each. What is clear is that we are witnessing the emergence of new self-regulating forms of governance which are slowly drawing in environmental groups and organizations to provide advice and possibly help in the implementation of policy. New sites of struggle have arisen in communities seeking to defend their way of life, collective identities, lifestyles and values. To understand environmental movements we have to take account of the culturally specific practices which produce, regulate and organize the meanings communities use to represent the environment (their values, beliefs, customs, conventions, traditions and habits). The self-organizing networks identified in examples such as the Kalamas campaign (Box 4.3) or the Coordinadora (Box 4.2) demonstrate how communities and collectivities can construct common interests, identities, ideologies and socio-political projects in order to challenge power-holders.

At the same time, national governments, the EU and other public agencies seek to exert greater control to realize objectives agreed upon by political representatives and civil servants across Europe. The top-down governance mechanisms seeking to co-ordinate environmental policy have had a contradictory impact on European social and cultural integration. Environmental policies devised at the centre may also be seen as intrusive, costly and likely to generate resistance (for example, the trawler fishermen who have found that their livelihoods are affected by fishing quota restrictions designed to conserve fish stocks). The emergence of environmental policy making is also a product of broader global attempts to co-ordinate environmental policies in developed and developing societies. In this context, Agenda 21 offers an important step in identifying local and regional environmental concerns within a general framework that attempts to develop environmental policies in a cohesive way. The question remains as to whether environmental movements will become heavily involved and use the opportunity to make a difference.

References

Baker, S. (1997) 'The evolution of European Union environmental policy: from growth to sustainable development?' in Baker, S., Kousis, M., Richardson, D. and Young, S. (eds) *The Politics of Sustainable Development: Theory, Policy and Practice within the European Union*, London, Routledge.

Baker, S. (2001) 'Environmental governance in the EU' in Thompson, G. (ed.) *Governing the European Economy*, London, Sage/The Open University.

Boehmer-Christiansen, S. and Skea, J. (1991) *Acid Politics: Environmental and Energy Policies in Britain and Germany*, London, Belhaven.

Cotgrove, S. and Duff, S. (1981) 'Environmentalism, values and social change', *British Journal of Sociology*, vol.XXXII, no.1, March, pp.92–110.

Dahrendorf, R. (1959) *Class and Class Conflict in Industrial Society*, London, Routledge.

Dawson, G. (2001) 'Governing the European macroeconomy' in Thompson, G. (ed.) *Governing the European Economy*, London, Sage/The Open University.

Eckerberg, K. and Lafferty, W. (1998) 'Comparative perspectives on evaluation and explanation' in Lafferty, W.M. and Eckerberg, K. (eds) *From the Earth Summit to Local Agenda 21: Working Towards Sustainable Development*, London, Earthscan.

Esping-Anderson, G. and Regini, M. (eds) (2000) *Why Deregulate Labour Markets?*, Oxford, Oxford University Press.

Grahl, J. (2001) '"Social Europe" and the governance of labour relations' in Thompson, G. (ed.) *Governing the European Economy*, London, Sage/The Open University.

Hall, P. (1986) *Governing the Economy: The Politics of State Intervention in Britain and France*, Cambridge, Polity.

Heffernan, R. (2001) 'Building the European Union' in Bromley, S.J. (ed.) *Governing the European Union*, London, Sage/The Open University.

Kousis, M. (1997) 'Grassroots environmental movements in rural Greece: effectiveness, success and the quest for sustainable development' in Baker, S., Kousis, M., Richardson, D. and Young, S. (eds) *The Politics of Sustainable Development: Theory, Policy and Practice within the European Union*, London, Routledge.

Liefferink, D. and Anderson, M.K. (1998) 'Greening the EU: national positions in the run-up to the Amsterdam Treaty', *Environmental Politics*, vol.7, no.3. Autumn, pp.66–93.

Lord, C. (2001) 'Democracy and democratization in the European Union' in Bromley, S.J. (ed.) *Governing the European Union*, London, Sage/The Open University.

Martell, L. (1994) *Ecology and Society*, Cambridge, Polity.

Melucci, A. (1989) *Nomads of the Present: Social Movements and Individual Needs in Contemporary Society*, London, Radius.

Mewes, H. (1998) 'A brief history of the German Green Party' in Mayer, M. and Ely, J. (eds) *The German Greens: Paradox Between Movement and Party*, Philadelphia, Temple University Press.

Mez, L. (1998) 'Who votes green? Sources and trends of green support', in Mayer, M. and Ely, J. (eds) *The German Greens: Paradox Between Movement and Party*, Philadelphia, Temple University Press.

Mullally, G. (1998) 'Ireland: does the road from Rio lead back to Brussels?' in Lafferty, W.M. and Eckerberg, K. (eds) *From the Earth Summit to Local Agenda 21: Working Towards Sustainable Development*, London, Earthscan.

Roth, R. and Murphy, D. (1998) 'From competing factions to the rise of the realos' in Mayer, M. and Ely, J. (eds) *The German Greens: Paradox Between Movement and Party*, Philadelphia, Temple University Press.

Scott, A. (1990) *Ideology and New Social Movements*, London, Unwin Hyman.

Smith, M.J. (1998) *Ecologism: Towards Ecological Citizenship*, Buckingham, Open University Press.

Tilly, C. (1994) 'Social movements as historically specific clusters of political performances', *Berkeley Journal of Sociology*, vol.38, pp.1–30.

Waterman, P. (1998) *Globalization, Social Movements and the New Internationalisms*, London, Mansell.

World Commission on Environment and Development (WCED) (1987) *Our Common Future*, Oxford, Oxford University Press.

Further reading

Baker, S., Kousis, M., Richardson, D. and Young, S. (eds) (1997) *The Politics of Sustainable Development: Theory, Policy and Practice within the European Union*, London, Routledge.

Esping-Anderson, G. and Regini, M. (eds) (2000) *Why Deregulate Labour Markets?*, Oxford, Oxford University Press.

Lafferty, W.M. and Eckerberg, K. (eds) (1998) *From the Earth Summit to Local Agenda 21: Working Towards Sustainable Development*, London, Earthscan.

Lowe, P. and Ward, S. (eds) (1998) *British Environmental Policy and Europe: Politics and Policy in Transition*, London, Routledge.

O'Riordan, T. and Voisey, H. (eds) (1998) *The Transition to Sustainability: the Politics of Agenda 21 in Europe*, London, Earthscan.

Chapter 5
The transformation of family life and sexual politics

Catherine Lloyd

1 Introduction

Successive governments and other bodies in Western Europe have expressed concern about changes to the family and have linked these changes to changes in sexual mores and gender roles. At the same time, there are new challenges and demands on the family in its caring role given changes in attitudes to public expenditure, critiques of a 'dependency culture' and cutbacks in welfare.

This chapter will approach this debate by addressing four main questions: What are the recent trends in household and family life in the UK compared with the rest of Europe? Can we detect signs of unified European trends or is the situation very different from one country to another? What are the factors that have influenced these trends? Finally, what do these developments tell us about issues of governance? In particular, can we say that 'life politics' constitutes a system of governance and are there any signs of the emergence of a trans-European politics in this area? Throughout this discussion we shall bear in mind the key themes of unity/diversity, conflict/consensus and tradition/transformation.

Theorists of social change broadly agree that in modern industrial society the family has become separated from the world of formal employment and paid work. Family members are not expected to calculate their relations in terms of the market but on the basis of affective ties, while at work they are expected to operate on the basis of precise calculation and objective criteria (Crouch, 1999, p.53). This division between family and paid employment is paralleled by a division in gender roles, with women heading reciprocal relations in the family and community, and the diffuse exchanges of kin and friends, while men focus on the calculating world of the market. The family is responsible for its members who cannot take paid employment, sustaining the position of the young, the elderly, the infirm and those in full-time education. Different societies organize these tasks in many different ways, but women working in the home have always undertaken this caring role. The process of the differentiation of the world of paid employment from the family and the formalization of welfare for non-workers reached a climax after the Second World War in what Crouch terms the 'mid-century compromise'. This involved a fairly strict division between adult men of working age concentrated in the paid workforce and married women engaged in work within the home. In most countries of Western Europe, the subsistence needs that could not be met in the labour market were provided through the welfare state, but there were significant differences between these arrangements, which will be important for our comparative analysis.

While this gender division is apparent in all European societies, it is still expressed differently in each one. In some it gives rise to considerable conflict, and in others there remains considerable consensus about gender roles. Post-war migration has given rise to a wider range of family forms, sometimes leading to conflict, as in situations where families operate strict control of their members or where they are separated by immigration law. In other situations, migrant families suggest a model which gives a more important place to the elderly than the privatized solutions adopted by many European family members.

Increased social acceptance of lesbian and gay relationships has led to a challenge to the assumption that families are heterosexual, and recent campaigns have drawn attention to legal anomalies arising from these assumptions. One example of this is the debate around the right of gay couples to adopt children. Pressure from these groups, coupled with the implications of reproductive technology, has given rise to new understandings of the basis of parenthood, and its associated rights and duties. Different European societies have approached this question, which expresses as a wider range of gendered diversity, in a variety of ways; in some the voices of change are more successful than in others. This highlights the complexities and the transformation affecting the family and sexual politics in Europe.

In undertaking any comparative work we need to be aware of several factors. It is important for us to bear in mind the different historical, political, socio-economic and cultural contexts. Similar trends may be explained in terms of different dynamics in different countries, and these contexts are invaluable in understanding these variations. The contexts will help us to determine how far 'traditional' family forms have been transformed in recent years, while also explaining the level of diversity between different European countries. Our discussion about issues of governance and the emergence of a trans-European politics will be informed by this approach.

The family is political in the wide sense of the term: as the primary institution of social control it determines how the individual relates to the rest of the society. The concept of governance will help us understand how society regulates the family where boundaries are blurred.

Increasingly, governments have adopted a regulatory approach to family life, attempting to identify and prevent abuse, violence and neglect. The family, then, illustrates the way that systems of governance operate in a situation where the boundaries between the public and the private are unclear.

The first section of this chapter will examine evidence that the 'mid-century compromise' model of the family has now been transcended. We shall examine the evidence for the argument that the family has been undergoing rapid change to a point where it is increasingly flexible, but rendered vulnerable by a changing economy and social change. Since 1945 demographers have become aware of major changes taking place in advanced industrial countries, characterized by later marriage, smaller families and longer lives. Governments in such industrial countries will increasingly face the challenge of an ageing population (United Nations, 2000).

2 Recent trends in households and family life

In this section we shall first look at the main trends in the UK and then more broadly at comparative European data, to understand whether there is convergence or whether there remain significant differences between countries.

In the 1950s and 1960s the majority of families in Western Europe were headed by an adult man of working age in full-time work (there were very few part-time jobs). The children, the elderly and those in full-time education were cared for at home by married women, large numbers of whom were mainly engaged in family-oriented work. It was possible to distinguish two main groups of countries: in Northern Europe unemployment rates were relatively low and many men and women from the then more agriculturally-based countries in Southern Europe came to work in the reconstruction of manufacturing and the construction industry. The largest immigrant groups in Germany, Switzerland and France at this time were from Italy and Portugal (Castles, 1972).

Today, people in the UK live in a greater diversity of forms of household than ever before. This is partly because of the impact of migration from the New Commonwealth. But for society as a whole, Table 5.1 shows that the most significant changes are the increases in the number of births outside marriage, the divorce rate and the number of lone-parent families, from the 1960s to the 1990s. However, the figures tend to obscure social differentiation: teenage pregnancies, for instance, tend to occur especially among the most disadvantaged groups. As the table shows, during the same period the average age of marriage and first motherhood rose, while the fertility rate fell. Increasing numbers of people either postpone starting a family or do not plan to have children at all. It is now quite common for couples to cohabit before marriage.

Table 5.1 Changes in family composition in Britain from the mid-1930s to the mid-1990s (n/a = data not available)

	mid-1930s	mid-1960s	mid-1990s
Mean age at first marriage	26	22	26
Mean age at first birth	26.7	23.9	26.5
Total fertility rate	1.8	2.9	1.8
Childlessness (%)	23	10	20
Divorces per 1000 marriages	n/a	2	13
Births outside marriage (%)	n/a	5	35
Cohabitation before marriage (%)	n/a	5	70
Lone-parent families	n/a	570,000	1.5 million

(McRae, 1999)

The figures in Table 5.1 also suggest that in some ways the 1960s might have been an exceptional period, sandwiched between the long-term trends indicated by the figures of the 1930s and the 1990s. In the UK, exceptionally during the 1960s, the introduction of the welfare state, and high and secure employment levels made it possible for couples to contemplate early marriage.

We can see similar trends throughout Europe, where fertility rates have fallen substantially in all countries since the 1960s, as shown by Table 5.2. Ireland, which had an extremely high fertility rate in the 1960s, is now no longer an exception. Indeed a striking feature of the fertility rates in Europe is their uniformity.

In contrast, live births outside marriage have increased in all countries, with wide differences appearing between countries (see Table 5.3). Countries fall broadly into three clusters, with Sweden, Denmark and Norway scoring the highest proportion of births outside marriage. Finland, France, Austria and the UK comprise a middle group, while the other countries (mainly in the South, but including some as diverse as Greece and Germany) register a much lower increase. We shall see later that there is no single explanation for these trends, although we can distinguish groups of countries with similar characteristics.

Table 5.2 Trends in fertility rates* in Europe, 1960 to 1990

	c.1960	c.1990
Austria	2.65	1.48
Belgium	2.58	1.56
Denmark	2.54	1.75
Finland	2.71	1.81

continued over

Table 5.2 Trends in fertility rates* in Europe, 1960 to 1990 (continued)

	c.1960	c.1990
France	2.73	1.65
Germany	2.37	1.39
Greece	2.27	1.34
Ireland	3.76	1.93
Italy	2.41	1.25
Netherlands	3.12	1.57
Norway	2.83	1.86
Portugal	3.01	1.52
Spain	2.86	1.26
Sweden	2.17	2.00
Switzerland	2.44	1.51
UK	2.66	1.79

* The fertility rate is the mean number of children for women of child-bearing age.

(adapted from Crouch, 1999)

Table 5.3 Percentages of live births out of wedlock in Europe, 1960 to 1990

	c.1960	c.1990
Austria	13.0	25.2
Belgium	2.1	8.9
Denmark	7.8	46.5
Finland	4.0	27.4
France	6.1	27.5
Germany	6.3	11.1
Greece	1.2	2.4
Ireland	1.6	18.0
Italy	2.4	6.7
Netherlands	1.4	12.5
Norway	3.7	42.9
Portugal	9.1	16.1
Spain	2.3	9.6
Sweden	11.3	49.5
Switzerland	3.8	6.7
UK	5.2	30.8

(adapted from Crouch, 1999)

2.1 The lone-parent household

High rates of births outside marriage could imply a big increase in the numbers of lone parents. Britain leads the European Union in the proportion of lone-parent families and of children raised in such families (Coleman and Chandola, 1999). The numbers have increased from 570,000 in the 1960s to 1.5 million in 1997. The UK-based single-parent charity Gingerbread has estimated that 24 per cent of all families with dependent children lived in lone-parent households in 1997. The incidence of marital breakdown and single parenthood is closely linked to poverty. The currently divorced population is more likely to be unemployed and to be living in disadvantaged housing. Lone parents are often among the poorest members of the community, twice as likely to be poor as two-parent families. They are also likely to be on benefits for longer periods of time. As a group, lone mothers find it difficult to obtain anything other than low-paid work. Over half of them have children under five years of age, so their prospects are closely tied to their ability to find childcare.

Those affected by these high rates are among the poorest and most vulnerable young people in the UK, including those in care and those who have been excluded from school. In 1997/98, the UK had the third highest proportion of children in poverty of any European country. Nearly 33 per cent of all children in the UK were living below the poverty line, compared with 13 per cent in Germany, 12 per cent in France and 24 per cent in Italy. The EU average was 20 per cent. The proportion of children with lone mothers in the UK was the highest of any country and the poverty rate of such children was among the highest (Piachaud and Sutherland, 2000). The main explanation for these figures was the combination of single parenthood and unemployment. Britain was second only to Ireland in the rates of non-employment for working-age households with children (61.2 per cent compared with 60.8 per cent). In the UK, 20 per cent of households had no adult in work compared with 8.6 per cent in Germany, 8.8 per cent in France and 7.6 per cent in Italy. The UK was also below average for the number of children staying on at school after the age of 16, with 82 per cent going on to further education compared with 95 per cent in Sweden, 92 per cent in France and 96 per cent in Germany.

There is evidence that people are tending to postpone marriage, or not to marry at all, throughout Europe (Clarke and Henwood, 1997). There has been a general rise in levels of cohabitation. This has been interpreted either as an aspect of family decline or as an attempt by individuals to re-stabilize the institution. Pre-marital cohabitation has become a relatively normal stage in France, Germany and the UK, and there is even evidence that it is being practised in countries with more conservative patterns such as Ireland and Switzerland, but there are lower levels in Italy and Spain (*Eurobarometer* 34, 1991).

From the mid-1980s onwards in the UK another change became evident: a rising curve of never-married mothers who now form about one in twelve of all families with dependent children and 80 per cent of all teenage lone-parent families (Haskey, 1996). About half of these are households formed after the breakdown of a cohabiting relationship. Approximately one in six lone mothers have never been married (Pullinger, 1998).

The UK government's Social Exclusion Unit report on teenage pregnancy published in 1999 estimates that there are nearly 90,000 conceptions a year to teenagers including 7,700 to girls under 16 and 2,200 to girls 14 or under. These UK figures are twice as high as in Germany, three times as high as in France (where there are an estimated 10,000 unwanted pregnancies every year, half of which are terminated) and six times higher than in the Netherlands, although the figures in the USA are even higher than those in the UK.

2.2   Divorce rates

Change often implies the breakdown of consensus and an increase in conflict. Within the family, conflict can often lead to divorce. Divorce has increased considerably since 1945 throughout Europe. In the past it was an expensive, demeaning and sordid business; in the UK the law only accepted a narrow range of reasons for marital breakdown, often forcing people to fabricate adultery. At the end of the twentieth century in the UK approximately 40 per cent of marriages ended in divorce. Divorce laws were liberalized in the 1960s and by the 1980s about 13 in every 100 marriages in the UK ended in divorce. There is evidence that divorces are taking place after shorter periods of marriage (Coleman and Chandola, 1999; Roberts, 1996). Research suggests that those in early marriages and very young parents are most at risk of marital breakdown (Pullinger, 1998). Children from very short-lived marriages are more likely to lose contact with their fathers. Alternatively there are increasing numbers of complicated family arrangements arising from divorce, with different forms of access to children, step-siblings and several different groups of grandparents. Lone-parent households may be more likely to rely upon grandparents for support of various kinds.

European data (see Table 5.4) suggests a general trend to increased divorce from the late 1960s onwards (Kaufmann, 1997). After the disruption of the war, in the late 1940s, there had been considerable pressures on marriages, and separation and divorce became more acceptable. In the 1960s and 1970s many countries introduced legislation facilitating divorce.

This time a smaller group of countries stand out as having exceptionally high divorce rates: Denmark, Sweden and the UK. There are also high numbers of births outside marriage in these countries. Given that the majority of divorced people remarry at some time and may have a new family, quite complex families are developing composed of different sets of parents, grandparents and half-kin (Crouch, 1999, p.210). The lowest divorce rates are in countries where the Catholic or Orthodox Church plays an important role in controlling social behaviour – Greece, Ireland, Italy, Spain and Portugal.

Table 5.4   Trends in crude divorce rates (%) in Europe, 1960 to 1990

	c.1960	c.1990
Austria	5.0	8.5
Belgium	2.0	8.4
Denmark	6.0	13.1
Finland	4.1	9.6
France	2.8	8.4
Germany	3.4	8.8
Greece	1.5	2.6
Ireland*	0.0	0.0
Italy	0.0	2.1
Netherlands	2.2	8.1
Norway	2.8	9.9
Portugal	0.4	2.8
Spain	0.0	2.1
Sweden	4.9	11.1
Switzerland	3.9	8.0
UK	2.2	12.3

* Divorce became legal in Ireland only after a referendum in 1995.

(adapted from Crouch, 1999)

Research suggests that women are more likely to become divorced when they are in paid employment than if they have no independent income. This may be because if women think there is a high risk of divorce they are more likely to sustain their employment position as insurance against the future. A high rate of divorce may have the effect of deterring couples from having children, while the absence of children may weaken the bonds keeping a couple together (Ermisch and Ogawa, 1997).

2.3   Married women's employment

One of the key features of the family in the middle of the twentieth century throughout Europe was the woman working at home. Many married women tended to withdraw from the labour market. The biggest increases in female labour market participation between the 1960s and the 1990s occurred in Austria, Greece, Ireland, Italy and Spain, countries where the agricultural sector had provided unrecorded family employment in the past.

Table 5.5 Changes in the percentages of married women in paid employment in Europe, 1960 to 1990

	c.1960	*c.1990*
Austria	58.5	54.4
Belgium	27.2	48.7
Denmark	49.3	66.8
Finland	50.9	86.1
France	38.3	59.7
Germany	44.3	52.3
Greece	38.3	40.3
Ireland	34.7	48.5
Italy	29.1	39.9
Netherlands	24.4	55.3
Norway	25.3	70.2
Portugal	18.4	54.0
Spain	19.1	39.0
Sweden	35.5	68.6
Switzerland	36.5	60.1
UK	39.4	58.3

(adapted from Crouch, 1999)

The countries with the highest proportions of married women in paid employment are Denmark, Finland, Norway, Sweden, and Switzerland, with the lowest proportions in Greece, Italy and Spain (see Table 5.5). An associated trend is the growth of service sector jobs; women are highly represented in these posts, often in part-time employment (Crouch, 1999, pp.64, 90). The informal sector is also important, explained by the insecurities of the formal economy and reductions in the scope of the welfare state. In some areas Crouch found that this had led to a revival in family solidarity and in female informal activity. This arises from measures taken by some groups to close ranks to protect themselves against insecurity resulting from a concentration of unemployment among the young, women and immigrant groups.

Crouch suggests that there are three basic patterns of married women's participation in the labour force in Western Europe. The first is the 'housewife model' in which the majority of younger married women are not in paid employment. By the 1990s this would be true only of Belgium, Greece, Ireland, Italy and Spain. The second is the 'moderate sex role pattern' in which women interrupt full-time employment or take part-time jobs while their children are young. This applied in most countries by the 1990s. The third model is the 'employed woman pattern', which mainly applied to the countries of the former Soviet bloc in the 1980s, which is outside our remit here (Crouch, 1999, p.211).

The impact of married women's employment depends on the ease with which women can combine work and motherhood. This depends on welfare provision. Research suggests that in West Germany it is particularly difficult to combine work and motherhood because of the relative scarcity of support systems for carers. This leads to a polarization of family forms – women either pursue careers or they form families and withdraw from the labour force.

There is a general tendency in Europe for women in paid employment to postpone childbearing. The increase in women's employment tends also to be positively associated with the tendency to divorce, though it is not possible to conclude a direct causal link. Swedish women for instance are more likely to combine large families, motherhood and paid employment, even if they have high levels of education (Crouch, 1999; Hoem, 1993, p.215).

2.4   An ageing population

The European population is ageing. Throughout Europe life expectancy is increasing: in the UK for instance life expectancy at birth in the 1930s was 58 for men and 62 for women, while in 1997 it was 74.6 years for men and 79.6 years for women. Life expectancy increases with age: in the UK, for a man aged 60 it is 78.8 and for a woman aged 60 it is 82.6. The European Commission estimates that by 2050 there will be nearly 100 million people of pensionable age in Europe, and that the numbers aged over 80 will have quadrupled between 1960 and 2020 (European Commission, 1999).

One third of all households in the UK are headed by a person of over 60 years, while one in six consists of one person over pensionable age living alone. Figures from other European countries vary, the highest being Sweden at 40 per cent and the lowest Spain at 14 per cent. In the UK in the mid-1990s the majority of people aged over 65 lived in private housing, with only 5 per cent living in a residential or nursing home. Of those in private housing nearly one third lived alone, a half lived with their partner and the remainder lived with other people such as a son, daughter or sibling.

Pensions in the UK depend on contributions made to the state earnings-related pension scheme (SERPS). Some receive the basic pension, which in 2000–2001 was £67.50 per week for a single person or £40.40 for a married woman who has not paid contributions. At the same time the European Commission estimates that by 2025 the elderly population will control 70 per cent of all wealth (disposable plus fixed assets). The increase in the elderly population has put pressure on the role of carers, and this is exacerbated by geographical mobility and the employment of married women. Also, modern urban housing has been built with the nuclear rather than the extended family in mind.

The benefits of experience

Summary

- There has been a unified move toward lower fertility rates in all European countries since the 1960s.

- All European countries have experienced an increase in the number of births outside marriage, divorce, cohabitation and the number of lone-parent households.

- Child poverty is particularly serious among lone-parent households in the UK where it is linked to high levels of unemployment.

- There has been an increase in the number of married women in employment, and this is linked to changes in the age of first childbearing.

- Europe has an ageing population and this has implications for the role of carers and for the control of wealth in the future.

- Some of these trends suggest that Europe is still divided along North–South lines, but that these divisions are being reduced. One of the key factors is the decline in the role of the agricultural sector, where women's work was often unrecorded.

3   What are the factors influencing these trends?

In explaining some of these trends it is important to distinguish between immediate and underlying factors. The latter take into consideration economic, political and cultural factors. The most frequently discussed change in family patterns is that of employment. This change gives rise to conflict which links to other factors, notably the growth in divorce, the numbers of lone-parent families, and welfare provisions. One of the most important underlying trends in all European countries has been the changing role and position of women.

3.1   The women's movement and reproductive rights

The status of women throughout the world has been profoundly affected by the women's movement, a social movement which swept many countries in the 1960s and 1970s and which continues to reverberate today. By the turn of the twentieth century the women's movement had international ramifications, following the UN Decade for Women (1985 to 1995), the Vienna Conference on Human Rights (1993) and the Beijing conference (1995). These developments have facilitated the formation of women's NGOs, which take advantage of the opportunities for inter-national networking. Many governments have also established special units or even departments with responsibility for equality, family life and the status of women. Women's 'issues' are bound up in different ways with the family, even though feminists have made strenuous attempts to disconnect them. Campaigns for reproductive rights, or for women's equality at work have had a major impact on changes in the family. The feminist movement has acquired a transnational character and exem-plifies the strength of a bottom-up mechanism which has become directly engaged in governance issues. It is through lobbying and the generation of potent feminist groups at a local and national scale that a transnational feminist movement operates, exerting pressure on national governments and supranational institutions.

European integration has until now focused on economics. However, economic changes have important social implications in terms of labour market regulation and social welfare systems, which in turn have an impact on the family. European institutions have been particularly active in initiatives for gender equality and against sexual discrimination in employment. The European Commission made recommendations and issued a code of practice on the protection of the dignity of women and men at work in 1991. This helped to reinforce the efforts of women's organizations against sexual harassment, although there is considerable variation in the way in which this has been implemented across Europe.

The general decline in fertility coincides with women's campaigns for reproductive rights. From the 1970s, in most European countries it became easier for women to decide not to have children, through more reliable contraception and the political campaigning that helped to make it more acceptable and freely available.

The UK women's movement developed through small 'consciousness-raising groups' discussing the limited possibilities open to women, many of whom were frustrated as they realized that they were not likely to be able to use the higher education they had received. Many parts of this movement challenged women's role in the family while rejecting hierarchical forms of organization. Their debates about women's sexuality and fertility were hugely influenced by Juliet Mitchell's famous article 'Women: the longest revolution' (Mitchell, 1966), in which she discussed the effects of new contraceptive methods on women's future. Contraception seemed to make it possible for women to dissociate their sexual experiences from biological reproduction. Abortion on demand was another important campaign, because the 1967 abortion law was extremely limited, keeping the decision-making power in the hands of doctors and only allowing limited resources to the National Health Service to cover the costs of abortions. The National Abortion Campaign (NAC) set up in 1975 was extremely active, but defensive, acting mainly in response to attempts to limit access to abortion (Rowbotham, 1990). The NAC was an important organization because it established links between the more informal parts of the women's movement and the more traditional politics of trade unions and political parties. There was much resistance to attempts to formalize the women's movement. Some parts never really identified with the 1975 Equal Pay Act or the Equal Opportunities Commission, formed to apply and regulate the law (Coote and Campbell, 1982, p.106).

In other European countries, there was a similar picture. The women's movement in France also focused on reproductive rights. In the 1940s, Vichy France forbade the supply of information about contraception, and abortion was declared a crime against national security, punishable by death (Rodgers, 1999). After the war, in a more relaxed climate, the government continued to encourage couples to have large families. In the 1970s the *Mouvement de Libération des Femmes* mobilized around the slogan 'The children we want, when we want them'. They secured the legalization of contraception in 1967, though it was not widely advertised until the early years of the AIDS epidemic. By the 1990s contraception was so widely available in France that only four per cent of women who did not want to become pregnant used no method at all (Aubin and Gisserot, 1994, p.35). The French Social Security reimburses the cost of most forms of contraception. Abortion was decriminalized in 1979 and four years later the costs became reimbursable through Social Security (Rodgers, 1999).

These developments were mirrored across Europe. It is hardly surprising then that many women are choosing either not to have children or to limit the numbers of children they have. They may postpone having children until they have established themselves in a career or job in order to guarantee themselves some autonomy.

One common factor between all countries is that women are still overwhelmingly the main group of people who take responsibility for caring for dependants. Thus a vital element in the accessibility of paid employment to many women is the availability of reliable and affordable childcare facilities.

3.2 Childcare in Europe

Behind the provisions which different European countries make for childcare lie different assumptions about the role of women and the division of labour in the family. In the UK, provisions are informed by the liberal assumption that the individual should make their own provisions, while in France the government takes a more collective responsibility for publicly funded childcare facilities. In Germany the mother is still expected to look after the child while the father is expected to be the main breadwinner. These broad differences are reflected in research which shows that British parents pay the highest childcare costs in Europe – about a quarter of one person's income in the average couple, compared to three per cent of the same in Germany and eight per cent in Scandinavian countries (Family Policy Studies Centre, 2000). In Belgium and France childcare is free regardless of earnings. In France the free *école maternelle* cares for all children between the ages of 2 and 6, after which children attend the *école primaire* where they can be looked after until six in the evening (Rodgers, 1999, p.60).

Comparing the effects of the French and (the then) West German family policies in the 1990s, Fagnani found that the birth rate is falling more slowly in France despite the fact that French mothers are more economically active. Between 1965 and 1992 fertility rates fell from 2.84 per 1,000 to 1.73 in West Germany and from 2.51 to 1.40 in France. In West Germany the family policy confirmed and strengthened the antagonism between maternity and employment while in France the model of the working mother is fully integrated into the family policy, which has always encouraged large families. The French female labour force is one of the highest in the EU at roughly 44.3 per cent of all women working, compared to 46 per cent in Denmark and 43.2 per cent in the UK. This is not new: there is a long tradition of female labour market participation in France. Even more significantly, French mothers do less part-time work than their German counterparts where, in the 1990s, 30 per cent of women were in part-time work compared with 23 per cent in France (Fagnani, 1996). This has important implications for women's careers. Full-time posts tend to be of higher status and give access to greater job security, holiday, maternity and pension rights than do many part-time jobs.

In Germany there is still considerable social pressure on mothers to devote themselves exclusively to bringing up their children: the career woman often encounters negative stereotypes, while there is much emphasis on the male breadwinner (Fagnani, 1996, p.131). In France, however, the early socialization of young children is seen as important.

The state encourages women to combine family and professional life. From quite early beginnings the French state has put in place arrangements to build families and create an environment in which the welfare of children is supported. France, Belgium and Denmark have the most generous childcare provisions in the EU.

In Germany there is a shortage of childcare facilities, with only 3 per cent of children under 3 in public day-care centres and less than 40 per cent of 3-year-olds attending nursery school, compared with French figures of 20 and 90 per cent respectively. German kindergartens are mainly run by church-based organizations and tend to be open for only part of the day, while in France local authorities provide 95 per cent of the crèches, which are open for eight hours a day. Legislation in France has moved to deduct a higher proportion of child-minding expenses from taxable income which provides a financial incentive for parents to use childcare services. An allowance of some £200 a month is payable to working mothers to enable them to arrange childcare in their own homes until their children are old enough to attend nurseries. This is intended to cover the National Insurance contributions of registered childcare workers.

In France both men and women are legally entitled to take parental leave for three years for each child in addition to maternity leave (provided that they have worked for their present employer for the past year). In the late 1980s the government encouraged parents to have a third child by giving them flat-rate benefits during parental leave if they had worked for at least two out of the preceding ten years. This compared favourably with West German provisions which gave paid parental leave for the first child regardless of previous employment (Fagnani, 1996).

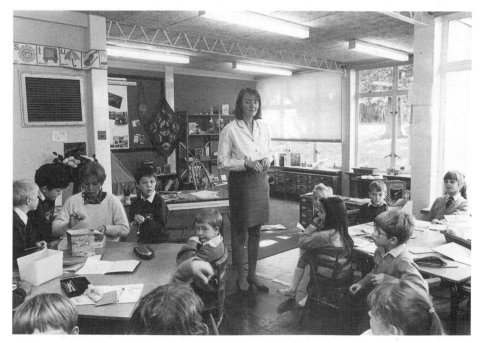

Childcare: reconciling maternity and employment

3.3   Changes in employment

To get a more complete picture of employment throughout Europe we need to look at the wider context of economic change, which has had an impact on the stability of men's employment, while opening opportunities to women. The decline in full-time employment in the 'traditional' manufacturing sector in particular has eroded the position of men as family breadwinner and head of household in all countries. At the same time the growth of jobs in the service sector has made it easier for women to be independent. In this rapidly changing situation, it seems that women have responded in a more flexible way than men. This poses particular problems for the state because family and welfare policy in the UK since 1945 has been based on the premise of the male breadwinner, with the wife earning no or very low wages. As we have already seen above in our discussion of childcare, this premise is not shared throughout Europe.

It is often argued that the main reason for the changes in family life is the increased participation of women in paid employment. This is only partly true and needs to be qualified. We need to bear in mind broader economic changes, and how these changes have affected mainly particular groups of women and men. A further consideration might be the increased choice which women have in shaping their working lives.

While women may decide to go to work for a variety of different reasons, we need to understand how these individual decisions make up a broader trend. To understand these changes from a broader perspective we need to look at other factors, in particular the impact of changes to the economic structure of the country. This development has gone further in the UK than in most other countries of Western Europe due to the economic restructuring of the 1980s and 1990s. In the UK, jobs in manufacturing industry have declined from 7 million in 1979 to 4 million in 1997 and employment in the service sector has increased from 60 per cent in 1979 to 75 per cent in 1997. In turn there has been a reduction in the number of men employed in full-time (especially unskilled) jobs. The number of economically inactive men doubled from 1.4 million in 1979 to 2.8 million in 1997.

These shifts in the UK economy have involved a loss of stable, unskilled jobs and an increase in low-waged, insecure, part-time employment in the service sector. Women have traditionally been more prepared than men to accept part-time employment, partly for convenience, but also out of necessity, and perhaps also because they have often worked part-time in the past. There are also signs of growing rates of economic inequality: between 1979 and 1995 average incomes grew by 40 per cent but those of the richest tenth grew by over 60 per cent while those of the poorest tenth grew by only 10 per cent.

In the UK by 1997 one-third of women in employment were in managerial, professional or associated occupations, compared with 1 in 5 in 1980 (Martin and Roberts, 1984; Pullinger, 1998). Such women may decide to postpone starting a family until they have established their careers. If they have children they are likely to spend less time bringing them up and return to work earlier. An increased number of women are deciding not to have children at all: population experts project that 25 per cent of women will be childless by 2010 (Office for National Statistics, 1997; Joshi, 1985; McRae, 1991).

Although they tend to be unemployed for shorter periods of time than men, the majority of women are in lower-paid jobs. For instance, in the UK 46 per cent of women are in part-time employment, compared with 8 per cent of men. There is still considerable labour market segregation, with 52 per cent of women working in jobs where 60 per cent of employees are women and 54 per cent of men in jobs where more than 60 per cent of employees are men. Across the board, women are paid lower wages than men. The Equal Opportunities Commission (EOC) reports that when it was first set up some twenty years ago, women's average hourly pay was less than 75 per cent of men's. In 1998 it was still only 80 per cent, and the gap was growing wider again. Explanations for the difference tend to focus on women's domestic role, particularly periods of maternity leave (Equal Opportunities Commission, 1998). A recent study questioned the importance of breaks for childcare. *Women's Incomes Over the Lifetime* (Rake, 2000) suggested that an average woman will earn almost £250,000 less in her lifetime than a similarly qualified man, even if she has no children.

Table 5.6 Job segregation and links to pay: the average gross weekly earnings of employees by selected occupation in Great Britain, 1998

Occupation	Women's earnings	Men's earnings	Women's earnings as percentage of men's earnings
General administration/ national government	£501.00	£563.40	88.9
Treasurers and company financial managers	£680.10	£1070.30	66.5
Medical practitioners	£767.60	£945.70	81.2
Solicitors	£597.30	£756.80	78.9
Nurses	£366.40	£391.20	93.7
Chefs/cooks	£202.70	£255.00	79.5
Bar staff	£156.50	£193.20	81.0
Care assistants	£197.30	£229.30	86.0
Sales assistants	£184.00	£229.40	80.2
Cleaners/domestics	£181.40	£221.20	82.0

(Equal Opportunities Commission, 1998, p.14)

3.4   Cohabitation and lone parents

The immediate causes of the formation of a lone-parent household may include divorce and separation as well as births to single women. The underlying causes include: changes in divorce legislation; changes in social attitudes to sex, contraception, marriage, divorce and parenthood; changes in the relative economic prospects of young men and women; and changes in the social security system and in the allocation of housing. There is considerable variation in these factors throughout Europe.

Research suggests that many people who cohabit before marriage do so in order to test their relationship. French research shows that cohabitees tend to constantly re-appraise their situation. They tend to be both in paid employment, to share many interests in common, to enjoy and expect a more intimate relationship than their parents, but also to have more conflictual relationships (Chafetz, 1995). The growth of cohabitation may indicate growing expectations about the quality of close relationships. It is a trend among people who are less traditional and more likely to support radical social movements and post-material values. They are more likely to stress tolerance and understanding, and to place the adult couple at the centre of their concept of partnership (Lesthaeghe and Moors, 1996). In comparison, a research study of the time spent by married couples with their children found that women in France still spend twice as much time with their children as do their husbands. While fathers are involved mainly in activities linked to socialization (such as visits to museums or to parks) the mother is still expected to perform most of the domestic labour such as shopping, cooking, washing and care for the personal hygiene of children and older people (INSEE, 2000).

3.5   Gay and lesbian households

The status of cohabitees varies considerably between European countries – in the UK the tax law still tends to favour the married couple and to define the family as essentially heterosexual. This disadvantages people whose family relationships do not get recognition as a legally recognized family relationship which would entitle them to rights such as financial support, inheritance, protection of housing rights, welfare benefits, pension entitlements and the right to the regulation of disputes by law (O'Donnell, 1999). This has fuelled debates about same-sex marriage and campaigns for the adoption of children by same-sex couples. Lesbian and gay rights organizations emphasize the damage done to people's self-esteem when their family relationship is not socially or legally recognized. In divorce cases involving partners who may be lesbian or gay, the courts in the UK adopt the view that it is preferable for children to be brought up in a heterosexual mould, only giving custody to the lesbian/gay partner when there is no alternative. This has exposed the law to criticisms that it has failed to keep up with changes in the way people live and adheres to an outmoded definition of marriage that arguably conceals homophobia.

One approach has been to define different formal links between people registering partnerships. Such forms of family are recognized in Denmark, Norway, Sweden and the Netherlands (O'Donnell, 1999). In France, where lesbian and gay organizations have been campaigning hard for recognition of their status, the *Pactes Civils de Solidarité* (PACS) was introduced in 1999, with a wide range of rights for unmarried couples (both heterosexual and homosexual) such as inheritance, tax benefits, employment leave to support sick partners, and adoption. A survey published in the first few months of the PACS suggests that there has been a considerable take-up of the new status, but that there are a number of legal loopholes.

Summary

- Some of the demands of the women's movement for equal rights have been taken up by the UN and the European Union but with important variations at national and regional level. They have given women greater choice in arranging their lives.

- The women's movement has acquired a transnational character. It stands as a bottom-up mechanism ready to participate in the governance of our societies.

- The development of contraceptive technology has also made it easier for women to make their own decisions about the size of their families without necessarily referring to their partners.

- Wide structural changes in employment patterns have brought about a loss of stable, unskilled jobs in manufacturing (which tended to be mainly held by men in the 1950s and 1960s). Growth tends to be in low-paid, insecure jobs in the service sector, which are more likely to be held by women. Despite substantial increases in the number of women working outside the home, they still earn considerably less than men, at all levels of employment. This is compounded by the inequitable share of household responsibilities.

- The existence of a variety of forms of household raises the need for their legal recognition in order to guarantee their rights.

4   What do these changes tell us about governance?

The family is an intensely political subject, in terms of both its internal dynamics and its implications for the way society is governed. Family arrangements are powerful determinants of the way in which social agents can act on their social or physical environment and the power dynamics within families have an important impact upon their members' life-changes.

Governance is bound up with this understanding of politics which is 'ultimately connected with creating the conditions for ordered rule and collective action' (Stoker, 1998, p.17). It involves styles of governing where boundaries between and within the public and private sectors have become blurred, using mechanisms which do not necessarily rest on the authority and sanctions of the government. It would seem that one of the most fruitful areas to look for the developments in governance would be within the family.

In his study *The Policing of Families*, Jacques Donzelot traces the development of a 'social sphere' from the collapse of the *ancien régime* in France at the time of the Revolution of 1789 (Donzelot, 1977). The family was a key issue in this development of a social sphere. Transformations in family life began with mid-eighteenth-century critiques of childcare practices. The bourgeoisie were criticized for handing over their children to wet-nurses and to the supervision of domestic servants, while the poor were reprimanded for abandoning their children to foundling hospitals or letting them run wild in the streets. There were comments from many different quarters – from what became a philanthropic movement of intellectuals, academics, clerics and the growing medical establishment. Doctors in particular sought to ally themselves in an implicit contract with bourgeois women who could be educated to take responsibility for the improvement of domestic hygiene and provide a sheltered environment in which children could grow up and be educated. This gave the bourgeois mother much more autonomy and a status independent of that of her husband. The working-class mother was seen by these philanthropists as posing more of a problem, but Donzelot argues that it was still in her interest to co-operate with philanthropic organizations in order to obtain material and social support. A different attitude was however apparent towards working-class mothers: they were subject to surveillance and tutelage rather than co-operation. These interventions were framed within a paradigm of the inadequacy of parenting roles but tended to focus on supporting women to fulfil their roles as mothers. Fathers tended to be sidelined in the new relationship between the mother and the medical adviser. In particular, these social interventions were concerned with the protection of children and sought to regulate families to ensure that future generations could be regular and useful citizens.

In the twentieth century, psychoanalysis and medical advice were increasingly used to supply a regulatory but non-coercive response to societal problems. These forms of intervention are central to the ways in which life politics can become subject to a system of governance, so that the idea of investing in families is bound up with the development of 'human capital'.

This suggests three important issues. We have already addressed the first earlier in this chapter: our discussion of transformations in the family confirms that it is a rapidly changing institution. The second issue focuses on the role of the family as the primary institution of social control, and its regulation has come about largely through concerns for the protection of children. The third arises from the fact that although we often think of the family as belonging to the private domain, there is considerable overlap between the public and private spheres. The next section explores some of the ways in which the family is regulated and then looks at ways in which these regulations have blurred the distinction between public and private spheres.

4.1 Organizations involved in the regulation of the family

As Donzelot shows, the family is surrounded by the regulatory mechanisms of the welfare state, which the women's movement has sought to influence in different ways. From the early days of the women's movement and then through the UN Decade for Women (1985 to 1995) and the Beijing conference of 1995, many women's NGOs were formed, highly conscious of the advantages of international networking. Such organizations were concerned with the position of women who were mainly charged with the burden of caring and hence often excluded from influence or participation in public life. Others were formed in the mould of the interventions described by Donzelot, to protect different members of the family from one another or to regulate the ways in which welfare benefits were dispensed.

Since the 1950s the European Commission has institutionalized the issues of gender and the family, largely by focusing on gender equity in the field of employment. At this level the social tends to be seen as serving economic policy. Underpinning the move of married women into employment, most European states now have legislation that redresses discriminatory treatment of women at the workplace, legislation sometimes forced on unwilling governments by European Commission directives or the findings of the European Court of Justice (as has happened in Ireland, Britain and Denmark). The Commission has focused particularly on the problem of reconciling occupational and family roles in the Charter of Fundamental Social Rights (Meehan, 1993).

Lobbying at European level tends to be biased towards élite groups while women's organizations have tended to be loose and networked. Policy makers are inclined to assume that women are a unified, homogenous category and in paid employment. The women's European policy network tends to exist as a diverse, fluid entity with the capacity to reach into the grassroots, but which has challenged assumptions by drawing attention to the different situation of migrant women (Hoskyns, 1996, p.171). Similar changes have not taken place at such a conscious level in the status of men, but they have been profoundly affected by some of these developments, particularly in terms of the relationship between working hours and family life.

As we have already seen with the issue of childcare, while there are unified trends, different European countries still operate from different premises. While the Scandinavian countries and France have tended to focus on women's achievement as adult worker-citizens, Germany and the UK still base their policies on a male breadwinner. National governments have also set up structures which oversee family life and regulate the position of women in the labour market. Since the 1970s most French governments have included a Secretary of State for Women or a Minister responsible for women's affairs. During the 1990s the movement for *parité* pushed for equal representation of women and men in public life. This has helped to build a growing consciousness of the need for a structure which would be responsible for the family, distinct from issues of women's rights. The 1994 French law on the family extended the family allowance for education from the birth of the second child, gave extra maternity insurance for multiple births and supported adoption. In 1998, the French government set up an Inter-ministerial Delegation for the Family, chaired by the Prime Minister, which aimed to co-ordinate all public authorities and ministries involved with the family. Its objectives are to help families in their educational role, to reconcile family life with the demands of employment, to improve housing, to respond to the needs of young adults and to improve relations between generations. In April 2000 the French government announced that this organization would be upgraded to the status of a ministry for the family and childhood, an important change because hitherto policies towards young people tended to be organized through the education system. Interventions frequently failed because they needed the support of the family; the new ministry envisaged the development of mutual support (Aubry, 1998).

In 1999, on the eve of the twenty-fifth anniversary of the Veil law on abortion, the French government launched a new information campaign on contraception emphasizing the range of contraceptives available and particularly the issue of free choice for women. It emphasized the need to reach different social, ethnic, or cultural groups by avoiding normative statements about the form of the family. This campaign brought together the Ministries of Employment and Solidarity, the Secretaries of State for Health and Women's Rights, and in a secondary role the Ministries of National Education, Youth, Sports, and Agriculture, and the Secretary of State for Overseas. A number of bodies from civil society such as the French Movement for Family Planning, the *Médecins du Monde,* the Red Cross, experts from the world of medicine and academic life, and feminist organizations, were also involved. It used leaflets, telephone hotlines, television, radio and press coverage and materials in clinics. Youth structures such as hostels, local clubs and the Federation of Discotheques were mobilized.

Similarly in the UK the Social Exclusion Unit was set up by the Blair Government in 1997 to fulfil broadly parallel functions to the French Interministerial Delegation for the Family. One of its first reports was on teenage pregnancy, which identified three main explanations for the high rates in the UK. Firstly, teenage pregnancy is more common amongst young people who have been disadvantaged in childhood and have poor expectations of education or employment. They have no incentive to take precautions against becoming pregnant. Secondly, there is widespread lack of knowledge about contraception or sexually transmitted infections. About half of under-16-year-olds use contraception when they become sexually active in the UK compared with about 80 per cent in the Netherlands, Denmark or the USA. Thirdly, young people receive mixed messages: many believe that sex is desirable but that contraception is illegal.

This was identified as a classic 'joined-up problem' requiring a multi-agency approach as in France. The government announced a national campaign involving government, media and the voluntary sector. At national level they announced a task force of ministers and an implementation unit led by the Department of Health to focus on the reduction of teenage pregnancy rates, and an independent national advisory group on teenage pregnancy to advise government. At local level the strategy involved a local co-ordinator to pull together the local services which were designed to prevent teenage pregnancy or support young people who became parents. New guidelines on 'sex and relationship education' were planned for schools (Department for Education and Employment, 2000).

There are many other issues that could be cited as similar examples of the extension of the regulation of families, which are represented across Europe. There are organizations which regulate cases of adoption and fostering, but also become involved when the family runs into problems such as child abuse or neglect, or one of its members attracts the attention of the authorities for delinquency or anti-social behaviour. Despite the rhetoric about 'joined-up government', however, policies are still often in conflict with one another. Piachaud and Sutherland cite a recent shortcoming in respect of policies to encourage lone parents to work. While the Working Families Tax Credit requires that parents work for sixteen hours a week, there is only 12.5 hours of schooling for 3–4-year-olds for 33 weeks of the year (Piachaud and Sutherland, 2000, p.39).

4.2 Public and private: increasingly blurred?

The women's movement and feminist theory have increasingly challenged the idea that the public and private spheres can be treated as though they were rigidly separated from one another. This division, it has been argued, has been pivotal to the exclusion of women from full citizenship rights and has obscured the workings of social policy in relation to the family (Pateman, 1988). As we have already seen (and as demonstrated by Donzelot), the family is not a sphere which is cut off from the rest of society. It affects and is affected by political, social and economic change.

The transformations which have been taking place in European family life discussed in this chapter draw attention to a number of important issues which are connected to the future relationships between the public and the private. We have seen that in the past the woman working in the private sphere of the family has taken responsibility for dependants and for general tasks such as housework and the production of meals. This has been mediated in different forms and to a greater or lesser extent by welfare provisions. During the 1980s there were regular debates over how publicly funded welfare could best be delivered in the UK, the rest of Europe and the USA. A discourse of governance started to emerge in which ideas of professionalism, administration and the public interest were replaced by the discourse of economics and management borrowed from the private sector. New Public Management was marked by a system of devolved management responsive to consumer pressures, using market mechanisms within the overall structure of contractual accountability. Critics of welfare stressed the negative effects of what they described as a dependency culture and established policies designed to encourage people who were not earning (including lone parents) to join the workforce, and for families and individuals to take responsibility for their dependants. The majority of carers are women and Ruth Lister has drawn attention to the dilemma contained within these contradictory imperatives (Lister, 1997). Does the future lie in arrangements where earning should no longer be privileged over caring, or should women's access to the labour market be improved to enable them to compete on equal terms with men and gain the same employment and social rights?

Measures deployed in the UK to reduce the serious problem of child poverty illustrate this dilemma well.

> Poverty affects different aspects of people's lives, existing when people are denied opportunities to work, to learn, to live healthy and fulfilling lives, and to live out their retirement years in security. Lack of income, access to good quality health, education and housing, and the quality of the local environment all affect people's well-being. Our view of poverty covers all these aspects.
>
> (Department of Social Security, 1999)

Recent government policy initiatives have linked the problems of poverty and social exclusion emphasizing that all individuals and communities need 'the opportunity to achieve their full potential and to take control of their own lives'. This idea underpins the broad strategy of welfare reform, which stresses the need to make employment available for all who can work, and to provide security for a much smaller number who cannot (Department of Social Security, 1999, p.3).

Three types of measures are deployed to reduce child poverty: direct financial support to families through the tax and benefit system, the promotion of paid work, and measures to tackle long-term disadvantage. In the UK context, Piachaud and Sutherland have analysed these measures in some detail and find that the changes have reduced the size of the poverty gap by approximately one quarter, mainly through increased levels of child benefit and means-tested benefits for children (Piachaud and Sutherland, 2000).

The system of tax credits puts resources directly into pay packets rather than through benefits which have to be claimed. This is designed to demonstrate that 'work pays' but has the disadvantage of being a long-term strategy which has little impact on people budgeting on a short-term basis (Piachaud and Sutherland, 2000, p.22).

> Our ambition is to deliver a change of culture among benefit claimants, employers and public servants, with rights and responsibilities on all sides. Those making the shift from welfare into work are being provided with positive assistance, not just a benefit payment. We are shifting the focus to include all groups – partners of the unemployed, lone parents, carers, people with a long-term illness or disability – not just the claimant unemployed.
>
> (Department of Social Security, 1999)

Recent attempts to regulate the family go further than these measures. Feminists in Europe have suggested that if the family is where early learning takes place, then a 'just family' can help to create a commitment to principles of justice (Lister, 1997, p.103; Okin, 1989). The regulation of working hours has wide implications for the future of the family. The distribution of resources within the family, including work and time, is bound up with power relationships. This may reflect economic bargaining power – women's command of independent income and relative power (Hobson, 1990). The sexual division of unpaid work and time within the home determines female and male access to the public sphere, especially the labour market, but also affects the time members of the family can spend together. Recent French research has attempted to operationalize this idea by distinguishing different types of parental activities: house-work, 'taxi services', education and socializing.

The European Union has given support for networks lobbying for changes in family policy, especially for women's rights, based on its commitment to equal opportunities in the Treaty of Rome, Article 119. These networks exemplify the strength and salience which bottom-up movements are achieving in governance processes and their effectiveness in influencing national and EU policies. This has been partly in recognition of international developments such as the UN Decade for Women in the 1980s and 1990s. Human rights within the family became an important issue following the 1993 Declaration of the UN World Conference on Human Rights in Vienna 'that the human rights of women and of the girl-child are an inalienable, integral and indivisible part of human rights', combined with the Beijing Platform for Action. Between 1991 and 1995 the third European medium-term action programme on equal opportunities for men and women focused on the development of a legal framework, integrating women into the labour market and improving their status in society. The fourth action programme (1996 to 2000) focused on: prioritizing the implementation of existing legislation; challenging the segregation of the labour market, which underpins the undervaluing of women's work; giving women greater access to decision making; and reconciling professional and family life by focusing on care for dependants. The European Social Fund, European Regional Development Fund and European Agriculture Guidance and Guarantee Fund help with crèches, kindergartens, after-school activities and the adaptation of transport in sparsely populated areas.

Summary

- The family *is* political, determining how people act on their social environment. The power dynamics within the family can affect people's chances in life.

- The family has been used as a tool of governance: as a means of improving people's physical health and domestic hygiene, and in dealing with social problems.

- Non-governmental organizations have played a prominent role in representing competing interests in this area.

- European institutions and other international institutions (such as the United Nations) have played an important role in encouraging gender equity in the field of employment, regulating discriminatory treatment of women at the workplace and setting up structures to help reconcile occupational and family roles. National frameworks may pose obstacles to this.

- There are already some parallel structures in different countries. In both Britain and France inter-ministerial committees have been established to work across different government agencies.

- The feminist movement has challenged divisions between the public and the private, which exclude women. Government interventions in the family have attempted to support women's 'traditional' role in caring for dependants and in general reproductive tasks. At the same time, attempts to end a culture of dependency have encouraged women to go out to work.

5 Conclusion

Recent trends in household and family life in the UK are similar to those of other European countries. People in the UK live in a greater diversity of forms of household than ever before. The number of births outside marriage has risen, fertility rates have fallen substantially (as in all countries since the 1960s), and there has been an upsurge in divorce rates. In 1997/98, the UK had the third highest proportion of children in poverty of any European country. Throughout Europe, the percentage of married women in paid employment has risen, and life expectancy is increasing everywhere.

Since 1945 we have witnessed dramatic changes concerning family life and sexual politics throughout Europe. As we have already mentioned, among other things, these changes respond to:

(a) the rising economic prosperity enjoyed by European peoples

(b) the integration of women into the labour market

(c) the spread of feminist ideas and the generation of a transnational feminist movement which has played a crucial role in defending women's rights

(d) the development of efficient anti-conceptive methods, which has rendered possible the separation between sex and reproduction while giving women much greater control over their bodies.

Throughout this period, however, there has been a constant tension between pressure to maintain traditional family patterns and the often unavoidable transformations brought about by economic, social and political change. Still today, we witness numerous examples of such tension: for instance many women are expected to look after children and the infirm while at the same time maintaining a paid job outside the home.

The tension between *tradition* and *transformation* almost invariably leads to *conflict* between the two, and it is only after negotiation that *consensus* can be achieved, although this is not always the case. Confrontation between feminist groups defending the right to abortion and 'pro-life' groups contesting this right illustrates this. It should be noted that, in some cases, 'anti-abortion campaigners' have employed violence against hospitals and doctors practising abortion; this highlights the fact that consensus is not always possible especially when certain positions are not open to negotiation and dialogue.

Diversity comes to the fore when considering family life and sexual politics in Europe; there are however, some signs of *unity* in the development of our societies. The European context is shifting and there is evidence that countries are being transformed broadly in the same direction, as with fertility and divorce, which are changing at slightly different rates but in a similar way. However, political and social developments in different countries have, until recently, followed very different trajectories. This accounts for the diversity of family forms still to be found throughout Europe, which was revealed in our discussion of childcare.

The idea of European integration suggests some measure of the density and intensity of the relations between parts of a system. There may be causal interdependence, consistency or coherence and co-ordination among the parts and even some structural connections. Integration may involve the development of rules and repertoires or processes of autonomous adjustment. Co-ordination may be ad hoc – the removal of internal barriers to interaction and exchange or the development of supranational institutions of governance and routine joint decision making at different levels. There may be common administrative institutions or a common public space in which European institutions can develop.

Bottom-up strategies have become crucial in pressing for the transformation of family life and sexual politics within our societies. Many networks, some of which have turned into well-organized social movements, have campaigned for issues such as the defence of the rights of women, gay and lesbian rights, the rights of children and those of the elderly. They have launched or contributed to numerous campaigns, among them those demanding equal pay for men and women, maternity and paternity leave, state-funded childcare, AIDS prevention advice, information about contraception methods, the right to abortion and euthanasia, and social security for single parents. By so doing, these networks and social movements participate in governance processes and are able to influence state as well as EU policy in these areas.

References

Aubin, C. and Gisserot, H. (1994) *Des femmes en France, 1985–1995,* Paris, Documentation Française.

Aubry, M. (1998) *Un avenir pour la paternité,* Paris, Syros.

Castles, S. (1972) 'The function of labour immigration in Western European capitalism', *New Left Review,* no.73, pp.3–23.

Chafetz, J. (1995) 'Chicken or egg? A theory of the relationship between feminist movements and family change' in Mason, K. and Jensen, A.M. (eds) *Gender and Family Change in Industrialized Societies,* Oxford, Clarendon Press.

Clarke, L. and Henwood, M. (1997) 'Great Britain: The lone parent as the new norm?' in Kaufmann, J. (ed.) *Family Life and Family Policies in Europe,* Oxford, Clarendon Press.

Coleman, D. and Chandola, T. (1999) 'Britain's place in Europe's population' in McRae, S. (ed.) *Changing Britain: Families and Households in the 1990s,* Oxford, Oxford University Press.

Coote, A. and Campbell, B. (1982) *Sweet Freedom,* London, Picador.

Crouch, C. (1999) *Social Change in Western Europe,* Oxford, Oxford University Press.

Department for Education and Employment (2000) *Sex and Relationship Education Guidance,* London, The Stationery Office.

Department of Social Security (1999) *Opportunity for All: Tackling Poverty and Social Exclusion*, London, Department of Social Security.

Donzelot, J. (1977) *The Policing of Families,* London, Hutchinson University Library.

Equal Opportunities Commission (1998) *Annual Report*, Manchester, EOC.

Ermisch, J. and Ogawa, N. (1997) *The Family, the Market and the State in Ageing Societies,* Oxford, Clarendon Press.

European Commission (1999) *Survey of the Current Status of Research into Ageing in Europe*, Brussels, European Commission.

Fagnani, J. (1996) 'Family policies and working mothers: France and West Germany' in García-Ramón, M. and Monk, J. (eds) *Women of the European Union: The Politics of Work and Daily Life,* London, Routledge.

Family Policy Studies Centre (2000) *Families and the Labour Market*, London, Family Policy Studies Centre.

Haskey, J. (1996) 'Population review (6): families and households in Great Britain', *Population Trends*, no.85, pp.7–24.

Hobson, B. (1990) 'No exit, no voice: women's economic dependency and the welfare state', *Acta Sociologica*, vol.33, no.3, pp.235–50.

Hoem, B. (1993) 'The compatability of employment and childbearing in contemporary Sweden', *Acta Sociologica*, vol.36, no.2, pp.139–66.

Hoskyns, C. (1996) *Integrating Gender: Women, Law and Politics in the European Union,* London, Verso.

INSEE (2000) *France, Portrait Social 1999–2000*, Paris, INSEE.

Joshi, H. (1985) *Motherhood and Employment: Change and Continuity in Post-War Britain*, London, OPCS (Occasional Paper no.34).

Kaufmann, J. (ed.) (1997) *Family Life and Family Policies in Europe,* Oxford, Clarendon Press.

Lesthaeghe, R. and Moors, G. (1996) 'Living arrangements, socioeconomic position and values among young adults: A pattern descriptive for France, West Germany, Belgium and the Netherlands, 1990' in Coleman, D. (ed.) *Europe's Population in the 1990s*, Oxford, Oxford University Press.

Lister, R. (1997) *Citizenship: Feminist Perspectives,* London, Macmillan.

Martin, J. and Roberts, C. (1984) *Women and Employment: A Lifetime Perspective,* London, OPCS/HMSO.

McRae, S. (1991) *Maternity Rights in Britain,* London, PSI.

McRae, S. (1999) *Economic Disadvantage and Family Change in Britain,* Oxford, Oxford Brookes University Centre for Family and Household Research.

Meehan, E. (1993) 'Women's rights in the European Community' in Lewis, J. (ed.) *Women and Social Policies in Europe*, London, Edward Elgar.

Mitchell, J. (1966) 'Women: the longest revolution', *New Left Review*, no.40, November/December, pp.11–37.

O'Donnell, K. (1999) 'Lesbian and gay families, legal perspectives' in Jagger, G. and Wright, C. (eds) *Changing Family Values*, London, Routledge.

Office for National Statistics (1997) *Population Trends*, London, HMSO.

Okin, S. (1989) *Justice, Gender and the Family*, New York, Basic Books.

Pateman, C. (1988) 'The paternal social contract' in Keane, J. (ed.) *Civil Society and the State: New European Perspectives*, London, Routledge.

Piachaud, D. and Sutherland, H. (2000) *How Effective is the British Government's Attempt to Reduce Child Poverty?*, London, Centre for Analysis of Social Exclusion, LSE.

Pullinger, J. (1998) *Social Trends*, no.28, January, London, The Stationery Office.

Rake, K. (ed.) (2000) *Women's Incomes Over the Lifetime*, London, The Stationery Office.

Roberts, C. (1996) *The Place of Marriage in a Changing Society*, London, Family Policy Studies Centre.

Rodgers, C. (1999) 'Gender' in Cook, M. and Davie, G. (eds) *Modern France, Society in Transition*, London, Routledge.

Rowbotham, S. (1990) *The Past is Before Us*, London, Penguin.

Stoker, G. (1998) 'Governance as theory: five propositions', *International Social Science Journal*, no.155, pp.17–28.

United Nations (2000) *Replacement Migration*, New York, United Nations.

Further reading

Asquith, S. and Stafford, A. (1995) *Families and the Future*, Edinburgh, HMSO.

Gittins, D. (1992) *The Family in Question*, London, Macmillan.

McRae, S. (ed.) (1999) *Changing Britain: Families and Households in the 1990s*, Oxford, Oxford University Press.

Chapter 6
What unites Europeans?

Josep R. Llobera

1 Introduction

When I went to Loughborough for the first time I was pleasantly surprised as a social scientist to see that the town was twinned with Épinal, the French town where the founder of modern sociology, Émile Durkheim, was born. In fact, as you enter any major English town you are likely to see sooner or later a plaque indicating that the town is twinned with another European town. But what is the meaning of this practice?

After the Second World War, which pitched European state against European state, a number of countries, particularly France and Germany, decided to bring the European peoples together and put an end to national rivalries and xenophobia.

The idea was to start at the local level and make sure that friendships between citizens developed. In the words of Jean Berath, one of the founders of the twinning movement, the point of linking two municipalities from two different countries was to establish diverse forms of co-operation between their peoples.

At the symbolic level, twinning was an opportunity to establish contacts between different communities, often ignorant if not altogether suspicious of each other and to exchange ideas. It was hoped that people would see what united them rather than what divided them. Politically, the twinning movement was meant to contribute to the construction of European unity. The key issue, however, was to start at a grassroots level and to involve as many citizens as possible. It was also a framework in which information could be exchanged at a number of more official levels – from matters of urban planning to racial issues, from the defence of cultural heritage to the protection of the environment.

It was in this context that the Council of European Municipalities was established in 1951. It later became the Council of Municipalities and Regions. To ratify the commitment of the partners, the ritual of signing the *twinning oath* was instituted. The form of the oath is shown in Box 6.1.

Box 6.1

Mayors of ...

- freely elected by our citizens,

- responding to the profound aspirations and real needs of our population,

- aware that the European civilization was born in our ancient 'communes' and that a sense of freedom was foremost inscribed in the franchise won by them,

- considering that history is made in an ever-expanding world, but that this world will only be truly human when men can live freely in free cities,

on this day, we take the solemn oath:

- to maintain permanent ties between our municipalities, to encourage exchanges in all domains between their inhabitants so as to develop through a better mutual understanding, the notion of European brotherhood,

- to join forces as to further, to the best of our ability, the success of this vital enterprise of peace and prosperity: THE UNION OF EUROPE.

By the end of the twentieth century there were more than 8,000 towns twinned. Not surprisingly, the densest network of twinning was between France and Germany (more than half of the twinning), but other countries belonging to the Council of Europe, including most Central European ones, have also become involved in the twinning movement. The Treaty on European Union signed in Maastricht in 1993 recognized the importance of bringing European citizens together.

Critics of the twinning movement have emphasized that the percentage of citizens involved in exchanges of one sort or another is extremely small. They have pointed out the perfunctory and bureaucratic character of many of the manifestations of the movement; this seems to be particularly the case in so far as the UK is concerned. Evidence seems to suggest, however, that Franco-German *jumelages* have been much more successful in developing lasting friendships and better understanding between the two countries.

In this chapter we shall be considering what *unites*, but also what *separates*, Europeans. It must be stated from the beginning that 'Europe' is a rather hazy concept, with no clear boundaries. In recent years, Europe and the European Union (EU) have become practically synonymous; the expression 'joining Europe', standing (at least in the British parlance) for joining the EU. Needless to say, the EU has become a disputed object: highly valuable and desirable for some, anathema to others.

The issue of whether the development of the EU has created a sense of European identity among its people is open to controversy, due to the lack of agreement as to what is meant by 'European identity' and hence the difficulty of its measurement. The problem of the issue of European identity partly stems from the assumption that the EU is, for both partisans and foes, a proto-nation state and hence the comparison between national and European identities is appropriate. If, however, the EU is envisaged as an attempt not to emulate the existing nations, but to transcend them, then it will perhaps be easier to understand its trajectory. Nonetheless, fifty years after the inception of the European Economic Community (EEC) the EU has hardly dented national identity, although in most countries an important number of people are happy to express a joint European/national identity (Section 2).

An important question that we must tackle in any approach to the study of Europe is the very ambiguity of the concept. There are no clear-cut geographical, political, cultural or historical boundaries that define Europe once and forever (see Chapter 1). It would surely be difficult to conceive of Europe without reference to a core group of countries, of which the founders of the EEC (France, Germany, Belgium, Netherlands, Luxembourg and Italy) would definitely be part. Beyond that, the ambiguity begins. Today there are arguments as to whether Russia or Turkey are European, while not so long ago it was said that Africa began at the Pyrenees. The UK is often perceived both by natives and aliens as being detached from Europe – and not only geographically. Another important issue, discussed in Section 3, is that 'being in Europe' and 'being European' are different things. Even accepting the existence of a vague feeling of belonging to Europe, that might have very few cultural and political implications because the paramount allegiance of the individual is to the nation. In any case, it would be surprising, and against the grain of what we know about the formation of national sentiments, to expect that 'Europeanness' should have flourished in a world in which the dominant actor was, and still is, the nation. In any attempt at coming to terms with the meaning of the term 'Europe' we shall have to explore the literature on the topic and ask: What is Europe? Is it a purely geographical term? Does it make sense to talk about European culture? Or is 'Europe' just a civilization or a cultural area?

Our next stage will be to ascertain the importance of the so-called European ideal. Ideas can become social forces if they capture the imagination of people. After the Second World War, with all its well-known horrors, leading European intellectuals and politicians met a number of times to find ways of avoiding future conflicts and wars. The idea of uniting the peoples of Europe was rekindled, though it was soon realized that the path was fraught with difficulties.

How different collective actors (trade unions, political parties, and so on) have reacted over the years to the idea of the unification of Europe is the object of Section 4. It must be said that the building of a unified Europe has always relied upon the initiative of, at first, a few individuals, and, later, of small élites. However, the bulk of the population, particularly in the core countries of the EEC, has agreed with the moves toward further unification. Section 5 looks briefly at some of the ways in which unity and the development of a European identity are being created through 'bottom-up' processes.

In Section 6 we shall be considering in some detail two crucial areas which are of great relevance to any attempt at 'constructing' a European identity: education and the mass media. How effective have they been in creating, across the EU, a sense of belonging to a community, not only in the material, but also in the more intangible cultural or civilizational sense?

Section 7 explores the following issue: to what extent has a European public space or civil society developed? It is fair to say that over the years a common space has been created in the economic, legal, and, to a certain extent, political spheres. However, when we come to other realities (language, culture, religion, history, memories, values and practices, and so on) the peoples of the EU have tended to maintain their national allegiances. It is only very slowly that a public space is emerging. This should not be surprising given the strength of national sentiment and the absence of a comprehensive policy of Euro-building.

Section 8 is rather more speculative in considering the main variables that are likely to affect the EU in the next ten years. The point is not so much to predict future developments, but to provide a conceptual framework with which to envisage the dynamic possibilities of the EU.

In many of the documents emanating from the EEC/EU one term that seems to crop up with regularity is *acquis communautaire*. It is rarely translated into English, perhaps because no appropriate equivalent has been found, although 'community patrimony' is perhaps the closest approximation. It refers to the legal, constitutional and other levels of agreement reached by the community over the years. At the end of the second millennium, and in the light of the *acquis communautaire* of the past fifty years, but particularly since the mid-1980s, it is possible to state that the EU has radically transformed European society at the economic and legal levels, has created a new political space and has begun to construct a sense of European identity. What is far from clear is the final outcome of these complex processes, particularly in the context of both closer union and enlargement.

To many social scientists the project of constructing a European community out of an array of different states with different languages and cultures was utopian (Shore, 1993). There is no doubt that in the mind of the founding fathers of the EEC (Monnet, Schuman, De Gasperi, Spaak, Adenauer and others), there was a clear federalist project which, for different reasons, has been realized only in part. The construction of the European community has had its ups and downs, often following the vagaries of the moment and reflecting the difficulty in harmonizing the different national perspectives. If today there is no clear picture of what the EU is, and what it wants to be, this is due to a certain extent to the often intricate language of the documents produced by the European Commission.

2   Measuring European identity: the role of the *Eurobarometer*

In 1973 the Directorate of Information of the European Commission instituted a survey of public opinion amongst the members of the EEC. So now, twice a year, a sample of about 1,000 people from each country are interviewed on topics related to European integration and EU policy and institutions. This survey of public opinion is usually referred to as *Eurobarometer*. The reports are initially published by the Commission in French and English, though they are subsequently made available in the other official languages of the community. The *Eurobarometer* presents data by individual states and also about the community as a whole. When it refers to 'European opinion' what it is in fact doing is averaging national opinions. To a certain extent the *Eurobarometer* assumes the existence of European citizenship, while at the same time some of the questions are trying to find out how committed the different nationals are to the EU. Furthermore, some of the questions in the surveys are rather consensual and not probing enough, particularly in relation to the future of the community. Perhaps the most interesting thing that the *Eurobarometer* shows is the divergence of opinions between the different member countries (Wolton, 1993a, pp.288–90).

The results of successive editions of the *Eurobarometer* show that in most EU countries only a very small percentage of people (around 5 per cent) declare having an exclusive European identity, while up to 50 per cent do not have any sense of European identity. Among the founding members of the community the sentiment of Europeanness is most developed. Although it is possible, and perhaps even justifiable, to criticize the methodological assumptions and categories used in most opinion surveys – including, for example, the dubious assumption that European identity and national identity are the same type of identity – none the less there is little doubt that the sentiment of belonging to an entity called Europe is rather limited.

In their study of European values at two different moments in time, 1981 and 1990, Ashcroft and Timms (1992) concluded that perhaps there is no such thing as 'European values' or rather that there is more disagreement than consensus. It is true that in some areas (family life, gender and attitudes toward the state and the economy) there are some broad similarities, but concerning, for example, the role of the individual and religion, the differences are staggering and do not appear to fade away. In the opinion of the authors 'national culture and opinion remain robustly diverse in spite of the increasingly close political and economic ties' (Ashcroft and Timms, 1992, p.112).

Two preliminary conclusions can be drawn from the information published by the *Eurobarometer*: European political identity is weak and there is a great variation across states. It is naive, however, to contrast national identities and European identity with the argument that the former are natural and the second is artificial. It is true that at present national identities can be envisaged as given, while European identity is only in its infancy, and hence has to be constructed, but it is a well-known historical fact that national identities are also the result of a centrally-engineered process of nation-building which in many cases is relatively recent. It is, of course, another, quite different, matter as to how far the EU would want to go along the path of constructing a European identity.

Measuring the degree of European unity might necessitate looking at the support accrued to the European community over a long period of time. However, according to the *Eurobarometer*, a number of general points can be made.

- At the affective level, support for European integration tends to be stronger among the original founders of the community (between 70 per cent and 80 per cent); among the other countries, Spain ranks as high as the original six and Denmark is the lowest of all (with less than 50 per cent).

- At the utilitarian level, support is still strong among the 'old guard' (with figures between 60 per cent and 70 per cent) and rather low for the UK (37 per cent) and Denmark (38.8 per cent); the other countries are somewhere in between.

- Between 1973 and 1992 support for membership of the EEC/EU increased in all individual countries.

- Support increased when the national economy performed well and it decreased when the economy slumped. In the oldest communitarian states this correlation is less relevant, that is, people do not envisage their membership of the EU in economic terms.

According to Inglehart and Reif (1991), it is possible to state that support for the EEC reached high levels in the 1970s and 1980s, though, as we have seen, during this period Denmark showed a lesser commitment. In surveys conducted in the late 1980s, that is, before the Maastricht Treaty, 87 per cent of the EEC people were in favour of the unification of Europe, and only 11 per cent against. However, when it came to the formation of a European government that would be responsible to a European Parliament, the results were rather different: 49 per cent in favour versus 24 per cent against, with 26 per cent of don't knows/abstentions. These figures hide, however, the fact that there was strong opposition to the idea in two countries: Denmark (with 64 per cent against it and only 13 per cent in favour) and the UK (45 per cent against and 31 per cent in favour). It would appear that for the British the main reasons were economic (a perceived 'bad deal'), while for the Danes they were political (concern about further national erosion).

Since 1992 the *Eurobarometer* has been following the extent to which the citizens of the EU define themselves as sharing a European identity. The question asked in the surveys is:

In the near future do you see yourself as:

1 Nationality only?

2 Nationality and European?

3 European and nationality?

4 European only?

The results from Spring 1992 to Spring 1998 are shown in Table 6.1.

Table 6.1 Responses to survey question, Spring 1992 to Spring 1998 (in percentages)

	Spring 1992	Autumn 1993	Autumn 1994	Autumn 1995	Spring 1996	Spring 1997	Spring 1998
Nationality only	38	40	33	40	46	45	44
Nationality and European	48	45	46	46	40	40	41
European and nationality	7	7	10	6	6	6	6
European only	4	4	7	5	5	5	5

The way in which the European Commission reads these results is instructive.

> Throughout the years that the survey has tracked the development of a European identity, there have always been more people who feel to some extent European than people who identify themselves as only having their own nationality. However, as the table above shows, the sense of sharing a common identity does not appear to have become more widespread over the years.
>
> The rank order amongst countries that had been established in previous surveys has now changed slightly. Although Luxembourg residents are at 13% still by far the most likely to feel European only, the number of people who now feel Luxembourgisch only has increased significantly (+8), so that Italians (67%) are now most likely to feel to some extent European. In Portugal (62%), the UK (60%) and Sweden (59%), people are still most likely to see themselves as their own nationality only.
>
> (*Eurobarometer* 49, September 1998, p.41)

The sense of feeling to some extent European had increased in some countries (Belgium, Denmark, Spain and Italy), while the sense of identifying with one's own nationality had also increased in Portugal, Ireland, the Netherlands and the UK. By age, people over 55 were less likely to feel European than other age groups (42 per cent, while the average was at 52 per cent). Gender differences were small: 54 per cent of men and 50 per cent of women felt to some extent European. Among those groups who felt more European than average were: well-educated people (69 per cent) and students and managers (66 per cent). Also worth mentioning is the fact that 70 per cent of those who supported the EU felt European.

In the *Eurobarometer* 50 (released in 1999) there was a question which had direct impact on the issue of European identity. It was formulated in the following way: 'Is there a European cultural identity shared by all Europeans?' It was plain from the answers that Europeans distinguished between the sentiment of being European and the issue of whether or not there was a European cultural identity. The responses obtained do not always follow the patterns that occur in other parts of the survey.

By the beginning of the twenty-first century identification with Europe in its three modalities (nationality and European, European and nationality, and European only) was at an all-time low (50 per cent) when compared with the 1990s. Not surprisingly the European Commission expressed a growing concern with this issue. It is not clear, however, whether this state of things was due to excessive centralization (the 'Brussels syndrome') or to the inability of the EU to offer an appealing European agenda.

Summary

- The results of successive editions of the *Eurobarometer* show that in most EU countries only a very small percentage of people, around 5 per cent, declare having an exclusive European identity, while up to 50 per cent do not have any sense of European identity.

- European political identity is weak and there is a great variation across states.

3   Being in Europe, being European

Is there a Europe beyond the EU? This is a question that becomes more and more difficult to answer. It is quite common for example to hear of such or such a country wishing to 'join Europe', when what is meant is that they wish to apply to join the EU.

The criteria for joining the EU were laid down in the summit of Copenhagen, 21 and 22 June 1993. Candidates must have reached an institutional stability that guarantees democracy, legality, human rights, and the respect and protection of minorities; they must have a functioning market economy and the ability to withstand the competitive pressures and forces of the Union market; and finally, candidates must be able to fulfil the economic, political and monetary obligations of the Union.

Turkey's desire to join the EU provides an interesting case study. Different Turkish governments have pursued, at least since the 1960s, the objective of being a part of first the EEC and later the EU. Not until 1999, however, did the EU give the green light to Turkey to start negotiations with a view to joining the community. (At the other end of the spectrum, the UK joined the EEC in 1973 but a variable part of the intelligentsia, politicians and public opinion still see themselves as non-European and against the idea of an EU, unless it is limited to a pure common market.)

To many Western observers Turkey is, if anywhere, on the margins of Europe. It is envisaged as an Islamic country that traditionally, in its Ottoman incarnation, was the fiercest and most important adversary of Western Christendom. The Ottoman Empire was characterized by extreme cultural heterogeneity, incorporating many ethnic groups. The sense of belonging, however, was based not on nationality but on religion, and more specifically the Muslim idea of *umma* or community of the faith. Within the Ottoman Empire the Turks were the ruling ethnic group, although they had no interest in spreading their culture through-out the Empire because Islam already cemented its fabric.

By the early nineteenth century, and in the context of European philhellenism, the romantic movement that favoured Greek independence, the Turks were vilified. The foundations of a reactive and invented Turkish nationalism were laid by the end of the nineteenth century. After the First World War modern Turkey made its appearance. Led by Kemal Attaturk, the new republic was meant to represent a clean break with past authoritarianism; it was meant to be a progressive, secular and popular-based republic, in which the state would still have the economic upper hand. An important political blunder was the idea that all those people who lived within the Turkish border were ethnically Turks, while in fact there were many ethnic groups (the Kurds being the most numerous one).

In the context of the Cold War, Turkey became a staunch American ally and the pillar of NATO's south-eastern flank. Turkish relationships with Western Europe were friendly, at least until the Greco-Turkish dispute over Cyprus tended to poison them in so far as Western countries sided mostly with Greece. Because of its Ottoman past, the perception that it is an Islamic country, its poor human rights record and the issues of Kurdistan and Cyprus, Turkey was seen as a non-European country. However, the Turkish élites, both left and right, have long seen them-selves as modernizers and failed to understand why the EU rejected them for such a long time. They also argued that the growth of Islamic fundamentalism in Turkey was partly the result of the European community's failure to accept them as a member (Keyder, 1993).

In December 1999, at a meeting in Helsinki, the EU decided to accept Turkey as a candidate for membership. However, accession was con-ditional on Turkey satisfying a number of tough conditions. Another twelve countries, from Central and Eastern Europe, are also negotiating access to the EU; most of the countries could become members between 2004 and 2010.

Accepting Turkey as a candidate raises the issue of how far the EU can extend itself. Russia also has a foot in Europe and could, in due course, apply for membership. If the only criteria are those decided at the meeting in Copenhagen in 1993, could not Morocco, or Israel or Lebanon become members as well in the future? Geographically they may not strictly be in Europe, but are not also Britain and Ireland detached from the continent? As to their past, North African countries were influenced by Greece, saw the birth and spread of Judaism and Christianity, and were part of the Roman Empire, and so on.

Any approach to the study of European unity and diversity must tackle the issue of what exactly is this entity called 'Europe' – how should we conceptualize it, and what are the distinguishing characteristics that set it apart from other regions of the world? However, we have also seen how difficult it is to delineate the external boundaries of the continent, to the point that the officials of the EU have given up this endeavour.

To say that Europe is at the same time one and diverse is a truism. Many things unite Europeans – a common civilizational heritage, the attachment to liberal-democratic values and the will to overcome past conflicts. However, the construction of Europe cannot ignore the national diversities of culture and language. Europe can only move forward if the different peoples that constitute it do not sense that they are being railroaded into becoming identikit Europeans. Furthermore, as the EU expands further east, to include even Turkey, its own identity will have to be redefined, becoming more inclusive.

In the past, one way of looking at what united Europeans was to consider who they were fighting against. Historically, Islam was the classical enemy. In the twentieth century, it was the struggle first against fascism and then against communism. At present there are three main factors which some authors maintain unite Europeans: increased economic relations between the different European states, increased information exchange through the mass media, and personal contact through tourism, study, work and so on. At the same time, it is also the case that these exchanges are intensifying at a global level. So perhaps the most significant factor to apply to Europe specifically is the increasing integration at a political level through agreements and treaties, and an increasingly vigorous drive toward legislative and institutional standardization, particularly within the EU. So, will increased integration within the EU act as a catalyst to greater homogeneity within Europe or will it exacerbate differences between EU members and non-members?

What, then, is the extent of the differences within Europe today? The general consensus is that with the collapse of Soviet communism after 1989, market economies and liberal democracy are the dominant principles of organization for Europe as a whole, independently of how long it might take for some of the Eastern economies to implement these principles. However, this begs the question of whether these changes will eventually result in significantly levelling Eastern and Western Europe and making for a more homogeneous whole. A persistent factor of differentiation within Europe is the socio-economic level of development as expressed not only in the per capita GNP but also in what is usually referred to as 'quality of life' (standard of living, level of education, state of health, access to cultural facilities and so on).

At the cultural level there are also important historical differences, although there are some indications that these may be, if not fading away, at least attenuating. For example, with respect to religion it is possible to distinguish three major historical religious groupings: Catholic, Protestant and Orthodox Christianity. Linguistically, we can isolate three major groups: the Romance, Germanic and Slavonic languages. Up to a point a correlation can be established between religion and language group, with the consequence that on the whole there is an overlap between Catholicism and Romance languages, between Protestantism and Germanic languages, and Orthodoxy and Slavonic languages.

As the historian Hugh Seton-Watson (1985) has noted, the word 'Europe' has been used and misused, and interpreted or misinterpreted from so many different perspectives, that its meanings appear to be both legion and contradictory. What is particularly interesting to note, both histori-cally and sociologically, is the way in which the 'idea of Europe' as a political ideal and mobilizing metaphor has become increasingly promi-nent in the latter part of the twentieth century. Much of the catalyst behind this has undoubtedly been the growth of the EU which has rendered even more urgent and problematic the question of defining Europe. One effect of this, which increased with the advance toward the millennium, has been a growing number of speeches and books by European leaders setting out their 'visions' of Europe. The Treaty of Rome states that 'any European country is eligible for membership to the EC', yet it fails to specify what 'European' means. Given the perceived economic and political advantages of membership, it clearly matters to some governments on which side of the 'European/non-European' divide their country falls.

To some extent, therefore, 'Europe' might be considered an example of what Victor Turner called a 'master symbol': an image that succeeds in embracing a whole spectrum of different referents and meanings. The boundaries of 'Europe' change according to whether it is defined in terms of institutional structures, historical geography, or observed patterns of social, economic and political interaction. In each case, a somewhat different 'core' area emerges. In spite of that, Europe can be defined as a distinctive civilizational entity, one united by shared values, culture and psychological identity. As has already been mentioned by Guibernau in Chapter 1, it is possible to point to Europe's heritage of classical Greco-Roman civilization, Christianity, the Renaissance, the ideas of the Enlightenment, and the triumph of science, reason, progress, liberty and democracy as the key markers of this shared European legacy. Significantly, these are all features which EU officials emphasize as being particularly representative of 'the European idea' as they see it (Goddard et al., 1994).

Summary

- The shifting character of European geographical boundaries is illustrated by Turkey and the other twelve countries from Central and Eastern Europe which are currently negotiating access to the EU.

- The boundaries of Europe change depending on whether Europe is defined in terms of institutional structures, historical geography or observed patterns of social, economic and political interaction.

4   The role of European élites in the unification of Europe

European unification was begun by the social democratic and Christian democratic leaders of the Western European states who had fought each other during the Second World War. The idea was to create a community of states that would guarantee peace and prosperity. The process turned out to be long and arduous, particularly after the federalist failures of the Congress of the Hague (1949) and the European Defence Community (1953). The main emphasis was on economic co-operation, and the project was essentially élitist (Hayward, 1996, p.253).

European unification was a process lead by top political élites. It was the decisive leadership of Konrad Adenauer in Germany, Robert Schuman and Jean Monnet in France, Alcide de Gasperi and Altiero Spinelli in Italy and Paul Spaak in Belgium that created the first institutions: the European Coal and Steel Community (1951) and the European Economic Community (1957). British political élites adopted a studiously ambiguous attitude toward European unification. Although it was favoured by Churchill in the aftermath of the Second World War, it was also viewed as a continental development excluding Britain.

The élites who participated in these developments in France, Germany, Italy and the Benelux countries were small in number but they agreed on the basics. Apart from the communists and extreme nationalists, all major political parties backed the move toward European unification. Other major social forces such as industrialists, farmers and trade unions followed suit. An important force in the original impulse toward unity came from the senior civil servants of all these countries, France being the weakest link. The progress of the EEC/EU has often been the task of a few dedicated people with a clear sense of purpose, from Jean Monnet in the 1950s to Jacques Delors in the late 1980s and early 1990s. On the other hand, the path has been anything but easy; there have been a lot of interruptions. In some periods of history the EEC/EU stood completely still, left to the vagaries of powerful politicians who aimed at blocking any progress – as was the case with de Gaulle in the 1960s and Thatcher in the 1990s (Wilson, 1999).

With the development of the EU an arena for collective action has appeared. But, as we shall see in Section 7, it is rather limited and it cannot be compared to the public sphere of the member states. Although collective actors have reacted to the emergence of new European-based institutions, due to internal constraints not all are in the same position to make the best of the EU opportunities. According to Marks and McAdam (1996) three areas should come under scrutiny:

1 *Labour movement.* The EU has had an important impact on industry, but while firms have become transnational, trade unions are still much constrained by being state-based. Multinational firms can out manoeuvre national unions by relocating all or part of their business to another country where the labour movement is less organized or less powerful. Attempts to create European-based trade union organizations led to the forming of the European Trade Union Confederation (ETUC) in 1973, representing more than 40 federations in over 20 countries. In practice, however, the ETUC has little power and, because of national constraints and idiosyncrasies (different legal frameworks in each country), it is not very effective.

2 *Regional movements.* Encouraged by the Maastricht Treaty and the principle of subsidiarity, regions and stateless nations are not only represented individually in Brussels but they have organized themselves on a European basis. They constitute an increasingly powerful pressure/lobbying group. The best known is perhaps the Association of European Regions. Ethnonations, that is, stateless nations, see in the EU of the future a guarantee for their survival as differentiated entities and an alternative to the issue of independence.

3 *New social movements.* Following on the Common Environmental Policy of 1972, the environmental movement has become ever more powerful. The policies of the EEC/EU have encouraged this kind of action. Both the Commission and the European Parliament have taken an active role in promoting environmentalism, often against the wishes of the states (**Baker, 2001**). Four major organizations have a base in Brussels: the European Environmental Bureau and the European offices of Friends of the Earth, WWF and Greenpeace. They operate at a European level, lobbying, gathering information, educating and using the European Court.

There is little doubt that different collective actors will play an increasing role in European affairs. How far this will create a level playing field in the EU is still open to contention. During the 1980s almost all socialist parties made a serious commitment to the European community. This represented a major change of orientation for many of them, having hitherto shown varying signs of euroscepticism; the British Labour Party was a case in point. However, following the Brussels meeting of 1989, the socialist parties of the EEC/EU intensified their collaboration and established a variety of cultural and organizational networks which meant an important affirmation of Europeanness. The Treaty of Maastricht was endorsed by all social democratic parties, despite some factual reservations expressed by the British Labour Party. It was obvious to them that socialism needed to operate at the EU level or it would lose power within each individual state (Melò, 1993).

As for the Western European communist parties, they were originally strongly against European unification. This was particularly true of the French Communist Party. By the 1970s the gap between communist and non-communist support for the EEC began to narrow. The Italian Communist Party took the lead in this movement. More recently, communist and ex-communist parties have manifested their commitment to the EU, though in some countries (Greece, France and Spain) there still persists rhetoric against what they call the 'Europe of capitalists'.

Finally, a word of caution in relation to the convergence of the European élites. Although it has been assumed that the area of industry and business is the most Europeanized one, important differences still persist between different EU countries. In a comparison between business élites in three major European countries (France, Germany and the UK), Bauer and Bertin-Mourot (1999) have shown that the national models of business leadership are still firmly entrenched in their respective countries, making it difficult for a European model to emerge (see also **Dent, 2001**). While European integration is strongly visible in the marketplace, the élite in big business is still reproduced in ways specific to each nation state. In their study, the authors emphasized that while in France they have compartmentalized hierarchical ranks, in Germany there is a high degree of differentiation of the ruling class along with low horizontal circulation among élites. The British system exhibits a degree of social openness, in which there are opportunities for upper-level white-collar workers. In the French system the validation of merits before entering work is the result either of inheritance or of academic achievement; in Germany the authority of the business head has to be legitimated all along, hence the importance of ongoing education and training. In Britain, occupational mobility is turned toward short-term financial earnings.

Summary

- The process toward European unification was initiated by top political élites in France, Italy, Germany and the Benelux countries after the Second World War.

- New collective actors are progressively being engaged in European affairs, among them the Labour movement, regional movements and new social movements such as the environmentalism of groups like Greenpeace and Friends of the Earth.

- European élites, although engaged in a convergence process, are still reproduced in ways specific to each nation state.

5   European identity

Ray Hudson (Hudson and Williams, 1999) has maintained that the formation of a true community of Europeans is important and desirable, and that it will not follow automatically from the converging of linguistic and cultural practices. It is difficult to envisage the disappearance of national differences, though they may be less pronounced in the future. What seems to be clear for Hudson is that only by looking at the future can a European identity be created; the past, unless highly sanitized, is likely to remain controversial and divisive. Europe, in his view, has to be invented; it is essential to construct an imagined community. This will inevitably make some people part of the in-group and others of the out-group; where to draw the boundaries is another matter. In reply to his critics, Hudson has suggested that increasing Europeanization will not necessarily lead to a 'fortress Europe'. It could equally, and perhaps even more likely, have the opposite effect, that is, make life easier for immigrants, asylum seekers, and so on. It is probable that the existence of a strong European citizenship will contribute to an increase in all kinds of rights for a variety of 'alien' groups.

There is another way of creating unity: from bottom to top. According to Borneman and Fowler (1997) a number of areas can be mentioned.

- Teaching of foreign languages. There are at least 70 languages spoken in Europe, and 15 of them are official in the EU. Although English dominates in a number of areas (popular music, science, business, tourism, and so on), multi-linguistic competence will still be required. It is open to argument whether English domination will lead to Europeanization (it is, after all, a global language).

- Increased exchanges at all levels (educational, cultural, and so on).

- Teaching an agreed curriculum on European history.

- Development of common European symbols – community of destiny (avoiding wars, preserving environment, and so on); community of values (tolerance, freedom, human rights, solidarity, and so on); community of life (active role of individuals in the making of Europe).

- Presence of Europe in the world arena (common defence, common foreign policy, and so on).

- Encouraging cultural tourism. Unlike mass tourism, which reinforces stereotypes, cultural tourism can help to dismantle prejudices and contribute to the creation of a genuine respect and appreciation for other cultures and languages.

- Some authors maintain that sport can help in the process of creating unity, even if they acknowledge that it can be a way of venting national passions. It can be argued, however, that the increased Europeanization of sport will promote a certain amount of European consciousness.

- Marriage and other unions across European nations are on the increase. In these cases the family unit becomes a microcosm of diversity, mirroring the wider European dimension and creating a space in which cultural, religious and other identities coexist and have to be negotiated.

- Europe as a cultural actor is an option defended mostly by French intellectuals as a way of opposing the penetration of American culture, particularly in the area of the audio-visual. In fact, this is a rather élitist position that is not shared by the people of Europe who vote with their feet concerning cultural products: 70 per cent of the market is dominated by American movies. Another concern about the so-called European cultural market is the fact that 93 per cent of European movies stay within their countries of origin. Furthermore, it is difficult to see how a continent so diverse linguistically and culturally can present a united front, unless it is to defend national cultures.

Summary

- The development of a European identity will be the outcome of a long process in which bottom-up as well as top-down initiatives are likely to be employed.

6   High culture and education in the making of Europe

Two factors which will have an important bearing on the creation of a European identity are high culture and education.

6.1   High culture

It has been said that high culture unites Europeans, while low culture separates them. Another way of putting it is to say that the European élites share a considerable amount of culture, while the masses do not.

For Mike Featherstone it is legitimate to talk about European culture in the sense of a 'symbolic representation, a historic idea which has developed above that of the nation state, yet does not entail the elimination of national cultural affiliations' (Featherstone, 1996, p.34). In this he follows the German sociologist Georg Simmel who envisaged European culture as the reworking of a tradition (Judeo-Christian and Greco-Roman) by a variety of cultural specialists (writers, painters, priests, and so on). From this perspective, European culture is what people like Dante, Shakespeare, Michaelangelo, Goethe, Mozart, Beethoven, Goya, Dostoevsky and many others produced.

An area that unites Europeans is literature. Most genres of literary discourse are pan-European; this includes poetry and the theatre. But if there is one genre that is quintessentially European, it is the novel. For Milan Kundera (1988) the novel has accompanied *Homo europaeus* for the past four centuries; it reflects a common experience which is the 'passion to know'. And this feature is typical of European civilization. With the novel was born the 'imaginative realm of tolerance ...; a dream many times betrayed but none the less strong enough to unite us' (Kundera, 1988, p.164). In Europe the respect for the individual has not followed a lineal path, but has rather progressed in leaps and bounds. The history of the European novel encapsulates the right of the individual to a free life.

There are some individuals who assert their Europeanness whole heartedly, and perhaps it is not surprising to find that many of them are intellectuals of sorts. This is the case, for example, with the originally Dutch writer Cees Nooteboom. Born in 1933, he has lived in Amsterdam, Berlin and the Balearic Islands. Widely travelled in Europe, he believes that Europe can only be the incredible diversity and richness of its peoples. In his book *De Ontvoering van Europa* (Nooteboom, 1993) he asserts that it is in the realm of the spirit that Europeans will find the currency that will allow the contact between the big and the small nations. Nooteboom's recipe for Europeanness presupposes an education which emphasizes the European heritage, a knowledge of other European languages, travelling in different countries and living in, and being familiar with, a number of European cultures. Another committed pro-European is the Czech writer and politician Václav Havel, who has written extensively on this topic.

6.2 Education

Education is obviously one of the crucial dimensions in any attempt to develop a future European identity or at least more understanding and convergence among Europeans. If the school made the nation, it should also be a key factor in promoting Europeanness. Observers of the school scene in Europe acknowledge the existence of a growing sentiment of interest for European themes (institutions, politics, peoples, languages). Furthermore, the EU-based exchange programmes have recognized the importance of emphasizing what is common about Europeans, as well as what is distinctive of each nation, region and locality. However, until the school curriculum reflects the importance of fostering links among European countries, of knowing each other better and of developing a common project for the future, the European ideal will remain the province of the few and the eurosceptics will continue to have the upper hand.

The Council of Ministers of the European Community, in its meeting of 24 May 1988, resolved to develop among children the awareness and knowledge of being European. The most important objectives of the decision were to:

- Strengthen in young people a sense of European identity and make clear to them the value of European civilization and of the foundations on which the European peoples intend to base their development today – in particular the safeguarding of the principles of democracy, social justice and respect for human rights.

- Prepare young people to take part in the economic and social development of the EU and in making concrete progress toward European integration, as stipulated in the Single European Act.

- Make them aware of the advantages which the Union represents, but also of the challenges it involves, in opening up an enlarged economic and social area to them.

- Improve their knowledge of the Union and its member states in their historical, cultural, economic and social aspects, and bring home to them the significance of the co-operation of the member states of the EU with other countries of Europe and the world.

How can these objectives be translated into action? At the level of the formal curriculum, teaching about the environment, the media, information technology, business, and so on can be used to enhance European understanding. Furthermore, the curriculum can also not only provide information about economic and monetary union, but also reinforce cross-cultural appreciation. Pupils should be made aware of the advantages of speaking European languages. An important thing recognized by educational experts is the development of a school environment which promotes a sense of respect and appreciation of other Europeans. In this context, the encouragement of contacts of all sorts across Europe is of paramount importance if integration is to be achieved.

An area of education that is enormously divisive, however, is the teaching of history. The European Commission, for example, gave support to a project which involved the creation of a kind of 'Eurohistory'. One of the results of this initiative was the publication in 1990 and in eight different languages of *Europe: A History of its Peoples*. Written by the French historian J.B. Duroselle, it was criticized for being somewhat francophile, but more importantly for not covering the totality of Europe; the Greeks were particularly annoyed that the contribution of Ancient Greece was left out. Other critics suggested that Duroselle only emphasized the positive in European history, while non-Europeans were depicted negatively. It must be noted, however, that the book also had enthusiastic supporters, including the prestigious British historians J.M. Roberts and Keith Robbins.

Another book which has tried to break the mould of the narrow nationalistic perspective is *The Illustrated History of Europe* (1992), an initiative of the French historian Frederic Delouche. The text is a collective enterprise in which twelve historians of different nationalities have aimed to present a common and balanced history of Europe. Published in most of the official languages of the EU, the book is aimed both at schoolchildren and the general public; it tries to understand, explain and educate. The common European themes that run through the text are predictable: Greco-Roman heritage, Christianity, the Renaissance, the Reformation, world expansion, scientific revolution, Enlightenment, industrialization, modernization and totalitarianism.

No doubt historians have a crucial role to play in recovering a balanced vision of the European past. The collapse of communism from 1989 to 1991 meant the 'return' to Europe of the Central and Eastern European peoples. Their histories have also to be reflected in any Eurohistory; the publication of Norman Davies's *Europe: A History* (1996) is a good example of this desired change of focus.

By the year 2000 there was a convergence within the EU in the direction of a rather broad curriculum centred on four main areas: national languages, foreign language(s), mathematics and science; other subjects were also gaining ground, namely information technology, citizenship and learning skills. However, educational systems continue to reflect their long-standing association with the nation state and continue to play a key role in the creation and transmission of national identities. At present, it is still true that the main function of an education system is to reproduce the national culture. Furthermore, the labour force is exclusively prepared for the national or even the sub-national market – the very small percentage of EU members who work outside their countries/regions attest to that. It is obvious that to increase labour mobility across Europe the educational systems must widen the horizon of the pupils well beyond the purely national/regional horizons (see Box 6.2).

Box 6.2 Suggestions for integration of a European dimension in the teaching of language and communication (secondary level)

Cultural awareness

- use authentic materials such as magazines, newspapers, satellite and other television programmes

- meet native speakers such as language assistants or visitors

- continue to learn about the customs and traditions of the country of the community of the target language

- experience a wide range of song and music from other cultures

- gain insights into some prose or poetry from European writers

- gain insight into conflict in other European societies

Vocational skills

- use the target language in a real or simulated vocational context

- take part in work experience schemes involving the use of target language

- understand the links between modern European languages and access to post-sixteen educational provision, training and occupations

- analyse and interpret information in advertising in the single market

- adapt to the culture and way of life in another European country when necessary

Summary

- High culture tends to unite Europeans.

- Education plays a key role in the construction of national identity. A common curriculum shared by all European peoples will be crucial in fostering the development of a European identity.

7 Toward a European civil society?

The EU is an economic, juridical and, to an extent, political reality. But is it a public space in the sense of an arena in which groups and individuals vigorously exchange symbolic messages of different types? It would appear as if, while the public of most EU countries are willing to accept ever closer economic union (including a common currency and even political convergence), when it comes to historical memories, social organization and cultural ideas (including religion), they are mostly recalcitrantly national in their attitudes.

From its inception to the present, the unification of Europe has proceeded unevenly to consolidate the economic dimension, and with more difficulty the legal and political ones. The real difficulties have always been encountered when attempts have been made to progress along the issues of cultural identity. The explanation is simply that they clash with the entrenched national realities that still dominate the European world. This is where there is presently an unbreachable gap between the growing, but still small group of intellectuals, politicians, civil servants, entrepreneurs, media people, academics, syndicalists and others who are committed pro-Europeans, and the public opinion of the different European countries who espouse national perspectives, often accompanied by negative stereotypes and xenophobic attitudes toward other European nationals. In spite of the elections to the European Parliament, or perhaps because of the limitation of such an institution, public opinions and especially political ideas are largely formed by the national media; this is also the chosen arena where politicians expend most of their energies.

Dominique Wolton (1993b) and Victor Pérez-Díaz (1998) have pointed out that there are a number of major differences between the national public space and the proposed European one:

- It is a fact that national public spaces have developed over a long period of time (at least since the French Revolution). The EU is not only young, but it has hitherto had mainly an economic basis.

- National public spaces were created within rigid state borders (even allowing for the existence of multinational states). The way in which the EU is evolving seems to prefigure a vast space 'from the Atlantic to the Urals', to use de Gaulle's well-known expression. Borders may be on the way out, but it is not clear how to build the 'common house'.

- While national identities are still strong, European identity is still in the making. The creation of a European citizenship may be a step in this direction, but Europe is still an aggregate of polities, not a new, fully shaped one.

- The question of a European commonality of values is becoming more difficult to achieve because the values *either* are becoming actually or potentially universal (democracy, liberalism, human rights, market economy, and so on) *or* can no longer function as European (Christianity, anti-Communism).

- The majority of national public spaces are constituted by the presence of a common language. This is not the case of Europe as a whole, where more than 70 languages are spoken. The absence of a lingua franca makes it difficult to participate in a political dialogue and makes the appearance of common ways of thinking and common attitudes more difficult. It is true that English is becoming the most commonly used language among Europeans, but it is difficult to see this development in other than purely instrumental terms.

- Within the EU a sphere of free public debate is little developed. As a consequence, it is difficult to know whether individuals are engaged citizens. In Europe most debates are about domestic issues.

Having a European passport, being able to freely travel around Europe (at least for the citizens of those countries which have signed the Schengen Agreement) and a few more trappings do not make for what Ralph Dahrendorf calls 'hard citizenship'. It is true that the members of the EU may feel that they belong to a community of sorts and that they share, to a certain extent, certain ideas and aspirations. But to move to something more substantive, to develop a more meaningful kind of citizenship, institutional and symbolic developments will have to be accompanied by educational ones. Even if European identity is not meant as a substitute for regional and national ones, but rather as complementary to both, history teaches us that it would be naive to think that it can grow quickly and without hurdles.

Not all authors are so pessimistic about the possibility of a European civil society. John Keane, for example, believes that the idea of European citizenship consecrated in 1992 will slowly but inevitably lead to the creation of a new political animal: the European civilian. He thinks that this person 'can take advantage of an emerging civil society comprising a mixture of personal contacts, networks, conferences, political parties, social initiatives, trade unions, small businesses and large firms, friendships and local and regional forums' (Keane, 1998, p.111).

There are even those who, like Shaw (1998), think that the EU, conceived as a supranational community, is anchored in the idea of citizenship which implies the rights and duties of the citizen as expressed in the treaties of the EEC/EU. Following T.H. Marshall's classical formulation in *Citizenship and Social Class* (1950), we can distinguish three kinds of rights:

- Civil or legal rights. The European Court of Justice supersedes national law in any matters concerning situations of national discrimination on grounds of race, religion, gender, and so on.

- Political rights. Here the emphasis is not only on democratic participation in the EU institutions, but also the right to information about the different levels of the EU.

- Social rights. These affect areas of employment, consumption, and so on.

On the whole, this bundle of rights may appear as limited, but there is no reason why the idea of European citizenship could not be taken much further even within the existing institutional framework. European citizenship and the rights and duties associated with it hold the potential to encourage greater engagements with the European project. It is in this sense that individuals could feel motivated to participate in governance processes shaping the EU.

Summary

- The EU is an economic, juridical and, to a certain extent, a political reality but a single European public space has not emerged yet.

- The establishment of European citizenship could play a crucial part in fostering a common European public space.

- European citizenship could encourage Europeans to play a more active role in EU affairs and participate in governance processes.

8   The future of the EU

The next ten years are likely to be momentous for the history of Europe. However, in the same way that no social scientist was able to predict the collapse of the Soviet order, it is pointless to speculate on possible but improbable scenarios. At this point it is only possible to project toward the future on the basis of the existing parameters; the more accurate and detailed our knowledge of the present trends is, the more likely our forecasts are to have some success.

Europe is at a crossroads in several different respects.

- Which way will Economic and Monetary Union (EMU) go? Will it contribute to cementing the EU *or* will it paralyse it for years to come? If EMU is reasonably successful, will it lead to further political and military integration? If EMU fails, what are the likely effects?

- When the expansion (mostly eastwards) of the EU comes, will it be accompanied by a thorough revision of its organizational and decision-making structures (which inevitably means more 'federative mechanisms'), *or* will it rather tumble along like a cumbersome, overbuilt contraption?

- Will NATO's expansion go ahead, incorporating not only 'central' European countries, but also the Baltics and possible others, *or* will the Russian veto stop or greatly curtail this project?

- What is the likely scenario in Russia in the years to come – a descent into further political chaos and economic decline *or* a slow but progressive move toward the consolidation of liberal democracy and sustained economic development?

- Will the EU be able to keep up technologically and economically with other world areas (USA, Japan, 'Asian Tigers') *or* will it lag behind and lose its competitive edge?

- Will future conflicts (including violent ones) be likely to originate at the cultural and religious levels *or* will more classical formulations, which emphasize the divisiveness of economic and social differences, be the shape of things to come?

- Is the trend toward the waning of the functions of the traditional European states likely to continue *or* will states reassert their sovereignty?

- Will stateless nations find satisfactory levels of autonomy within the framework of their respective states and within an overall, modified political structure of the EU *or* is it likely that separatist tendencies will prevail because of the rigidity of the existing state and communitarian political structures?

- Will the process of immigration continue at an accelerated pace *or* will the concept of a 'fortress Europe' prevail?

- What will be the fate of Third World immigrants in the EU? Will they be assimilated/integrated *or* will they maintain their original cultures?

Summary

- A variety of factors will decide the future of Europe, including the success or otherwise of EMU, the results of expansion, and the evolving global situation.

9 Conclusion

If we try to recapitulate what we have done in this chapter two main areas need to be considered: is there likely to be a European identity in the near future? and how important are national sentiments going to be?

While it could be said that by the end of the twentieth century the EU had become a reasonably integrated economic space politically, and especially at the cultural level, progress was limited. But even at the economic level, areas like labour mobility were still very low in the best of cases and commodity exchange was mainly developing along a number of clusters of countries (Germanic, Latin, Anglo-Scandinavian). A major difference among EU countries is the persistence of linguistic diversity. Many observers have stated that, at the practical level, English has become the lingua franca of the EU, even if at the political and administrative level there are as many languages as member states. But languages have not only an instrumental but also an emotional dimension and people's sense of national identity is often tied up with their mother tongue. Furthermore, language has vast implications for work, education, high and low culture and many other aspects of social life.

There is another obstacle to the development of a sense of European identity. It is the fact that intercultural communication is still largely conducted in terms of stereotypes and prejudices. If competence in at least two foreign languages is the precondition for the creation of a fluid linguistic environment, being aware that there are serious cultural barriers to productive communication and understanding is the first step toward recognizing that culture and language cannot be separated. If the EU takes its own slogan 'unity in diversity' seriously, it must acknowledge that without the mutual understanding and acceptance of this diversity the project of European unification will not travel very far. On the other hand, it has also been argued that the European project lacks an emotional dimension; it is too cold and bureaucratic. Without sentiments and without signs of identity it is impossible to generate a popular response in favour of the EU.

In relation to this issue we can close the argument by saying that there is not likely to be in the near future an entity that we can call 'Europe', at least not in the strong sense of the term. The political problems and approaches people take, their social concerns and their cultural habits and consumption patterns are still very much nation- and state-based, if not regionally coloured. Europe is bound to remain what Ralph Dahrendorf has called 'a figment of statistics'. However, if Europe cannot be a 'real' community perhaps it can become a 'virtual' one (Delanty, 1998). As we are entering the knowledge society, it is not unthinkable that Europe could be built on the growing interaction between the EU and its citizens through the electronic media.

As to the second question – how determinant or important are national sentiments, national identity and national assertion (national movements) likely to be in Europe in the next ten years? – many social scientists, following Hobsbawm's (1990) conclusions in *Nations and Nationalism Since 1780*, are claiming that the end of nationalism is in sight. Whatever may happen elsewhere, Hobsbawm's conviction is that in the Western world the days of nationalism are numbered due to the processes of cultural homogenization that are taking place all over. However, it is possible to argue that this is just a mirage that has repeated itself in history at least since Marx and Mill predicted the decline of national identity in favour of cosmopolitan, universalist ideologies. The strength of nationalism is not undermined by the existence of a growing transnational élite who exhibit multiple levels of identity according to situational parameters.

National identities are here to stay. Any forward-looking perspective has to come to terms with the persistence of some very basic categories such as kinship, language, culture, religion and historical memory. The importance of any of the categories may vary from place to place; what matters is the specific combination that occurs in each nation, and which makes it different from others. It is probable that a kind of 'European identity' will be on the increase along with, but not against or as a substitute for, national identities.

References

Ashcroft, S. and Timms, N. (1992) *What Europe Thinks*, Aldershot, Dartmouth.

Baker, S. (2001) 'Environmental governance in the EU' in Thompson, G. (ed.) *Governing the European Economy*, London, Sage/The Open University.

Bauer, M. and Bertin-Mourot, B. (1999) 'National models for making and legitimating élites', *European Societies*, vol.1, no.1, pp.9–31.

Borneman, J. and Fowler, N. (1997) 'Europeanization', *Annual Review of Anthropology*, vol.26, pp.487–514.

Davies, N. (1996) *Europe: A History*, London, Pimlico.

Delanty, G. (1998) 'Social theory and European transformation', *Sociological Research Online*, vol.3, no.1, pp.1–21.

Delouche, F. (1992) *The Illustrated History of Europe*, London, Seven Dials.

Dent, C.M. (2001) 'Governing the EU economy as a whole' in Thompson, G. (ed.) *Governing the European Economy*, London, Sage/The Open University.

Duroselle, J.B. (1990) *Europe: A History of its Peoples*, Harmondsworth, Penguin Books.

Featherstone, M. (1996) 'The formation of a European culture' in Dukes, P. (ed.) *Frontiers of European Culture*, Lampeter, Mellen Press.

Goddard, V., Llobera, J. and Shore, C. (1994) 'Introduction' in Goddard, V., Llobera, J. and Shore, C. (eds) *The Anthropology of Europe*, Oxford, Berg.

Hayward, J. (1996) 'Conclusion: European Union of stealth' in Hayward, J. (ed.) *Elitism, Population and European Elites*, Oxford, Oxford University Press.

Hobsbawm, E. (1990) *Nations and Nationalism since 1780*, Cambridge, Cambridge University Press.

Hudson, R. and Williams, A.M. (1999) *Divided Europe: Society and Territory*, London, Sage.

Inglehart, R. and Reif, K. (1991) 'Analyzing trends in West European opinion' in Inglehart, R. and Reif, K. (eds) *Eurobarometer*, London, Macmillan.

Keane, J. (1998) *Civil Society*, Cambridge, Polity Press.

Keyder, C. (1993) 'The dilemma of cultural identity on the margins of Europe', *Review*, vol.16, no.1, pp.19–33.

Kundera, M. (1988) *The Art of the Novel*, London, Faber and Faber.

Marks, G. and McAdam, G. (1996) 'Social movements and the changing structure of political opportunity in the European Union' in Marks, G., Scharpf, F.W., Schmitter, P.C. and Streeck, W. (eds) *Governance in the European Union*, London, Sage.

Marshall, T.H. (1950) *Citizenship and Social Class*, London, Pluto Press.

Melò, M. (1993) 'La social-démocratie entre nation et Europe' in Melò, M. (ed.) *De la Nation à l'Europe*, Bruxelles, Bruylant.

Nooteboom, C. (1993) *De Ontvoering van Europa* (Spanish translation *Cómo ser Europeos*, Madrid, Siruela, 1995).

Pérez-Díaz, V. (1998) 'The public sphere and a European civil society' in Alexander, J. (ed.) *Real Civil Societies*, London, Sage.

Seton-Watson, H. (1985) 'What is Europe, where is Europe?', *Encounter*, vol.377, pp.9–17.

Shaw, J. (1998) 'A concept of EU citizenship' in Kershen, A. (ed.) *A Question of Identity*, London, Ashgate.

Shore, C. (1993) 'Inventing the people's Europe', *Man*, vol.28, no.4, pp.179–200.

Wilson, F. (1999) *European Politics Today*, New York, Prentice-Hall.

Wolton, D. (1993a) 'La nation. Il n'y a pas d'espace public européen' in Compagnon, A. and Seebacher, J. (eds) *L'Esprit de l'Europe*, vol.2, Paris, Flammarion.

Wolton, D. (1993b) *Naissance de l'Europe Démocratique*, Paris, Flammarion.

Further reading

Seton-Watson, H. (1985) 'What is Europe, where is Europe?', *Encounter*, vol.377, pp.9–17.

Steiner, G. (1995) 'Culture: the price you pay' in Kearney, R. (ed.) *States of Mind*, Manchester, Manchester University Press.

Paxman, J. (1998) *The English: A Portrait of a People*, London, Michael Joseph, especially Chapter 2 'Funny foreigners'.

Chapter 7
The media in Europe

Denis McQuail

1 Introduction

The mass media, meaning all extensive public means of communication, play a significant part in many economic, social, cultural and political processes. This role appears to be expanding and becoming more central in forms of society that have been described as 'information societies' (see, for example, Webster, 1995) or 'network societies' (Van Dijk, 1999). The media comprise only one part of the communication activities in a society, but they are essential to the construction and dissemination of shared meanings, perceptions and understandings without which there is no common identification or orientation of action. This applies to the emerging regional political entity of Europe as much as to each national society.

The term 'mass media' identifies a very loosely constructed social institution that has few clear objectives, despite its apparent centrality and importance for society. It is common to attribute a number of public roles to the mass media, including those of collecting and disseminating information, explaining and interpreting events, helping to form and express public opinion and acting as a check on those in power. However, there is little if any obligation attached to these roles and most of the time most media are concerned with making profits by entertaining and diverting the mass of people and providing channels for information and influence.

The main aim of this chapter is to shed light on the contribution that media do or could make to the formation and definition of Europe as a political or cultural entity. Four over-arching questions are tackled. First, there is the extent to which the term 'the media' stands for a co-ordinated social order and set of activities. Second, there is the question of whether media contribute to conflict or to integration in Europe. Third, there is the issue of the extent and ways in which the media contribute to social exclusion or inclusion. Fourth, there is the issue of whether the media are a force for change in Europe or a conservative influence. I shall return to these questions at the end of the chapter and try to answer them on the basis of the information presented. But I shall start with a description of the general structure of media systems and the main forms of regulation.

2 General aspects of media structure in Europe

What are now called the mass media have quite distant historical origins. It is conventional to date their beginning to the invention of printing and book production in Europe in the mid-fifteenth century. Books began to circulate publicly and widely, leading to a diverse market and the rise of a reading public. The newspaper appeared in the early seventeenth century, and was connected with trade and city life. Its central component was and remains 'news' – reports of current events of relevance to potential readers. It also claimed a degree of independence from church and state. During the modern period, it has played an essential part in politics and the rise of democracy, as well as in commerce, nationally and inter-nationally. Film was the third medium to appear (at the close of the nineteenth century) and its main function has remained much as at the beginning: popular entertainment, although with cultural and propa-ganda aspects.

Radio broadcasting was added to the spectrum of media in the 1920s and the concept of mass media dates from this period, in recognition of the fact that in industrialized countries the media now reached the majority of the population, with much the same content. The high point of mass communication was attained in the 1970s when broadcast television was universally recognized as the dominant medium in terms of audience appeal and amount of use. Despite a certain 'demassification' of media and 'fragmentation' of audiences, the recent development of new electronic media, based on telecommunications and computers (es-pecially the internet), has accentuated rather than undermined the general significance of 'the media'. There was and remains a widespread belief that popular media must also be very influential, even powerful in society. This explains why media are relevant to the theme of the development of 'Europe' and accounts for the extensive regulation that has been applied to media, despite the claims of free publication and expression.

There are many basic similarities between the media systems of modern societies, including those of Europe. They all use the same technologies, they have the same general functions (entertainment, information, publicity and so on), and much the same economic basis and sources of finance. Their purposes include an inextricable mix of ideal (social, cultural and political) and material (utilitarian and economic) goals. They are all essentially *national* institutions, with their activities and aims largely bounded by national frontiers. They respond to the same pressures and opportunities from technology and market circumstances.

From a certain distance, European media systems look much the same in their essential components. In every country, even those small in size, there is a quite diverse and extensive newspaper and periodical press. There is also a national television and radio distribution system, usually dominated by two or three television channels. In addition there are regional and local media, plus the many new forms of electronic media.

BBC Television Centre, London

The variations in the basic structure of mass media provision can best be understood by looking at the main factors that underlie inter-country differences: size; degree of centralization; language and culture; and economic level.

The most obvious difference is that of *size*. The larger countries of Western Europe, namely Germany, France, the UK, Italy and Spain, are more likely, other things being equal, to initiate new trends in media, have more influence on other countries, be more self-sufficient themselves and be resistant to cross-border influences. They have cultural and linguistic advantages through size, and some historical advantages of media innovation (for instance, the early development of national film industries). They are likely to provide a larger and more diverse range of media. They also have more weight in pan-European or other transnational policy making.

The position of most small countries is defined by the same considerations. They are forced to import content and cultural influences and to be more protective of their own media industries. In some cases they are overshadowed by larger neighbours that disseminate media directly across frontiers: for example, Germany to Austria and Switzerland, the UK to Ireland, and France to Wallonian Belgium.

The *degree of centralization* of media structures does not necessarily correspond to the level of political centralization. This factor is mainly expressed in the relative significance of local or regional media as opposed to metropolitan or all-national media. In these terms, the UK has probably the most centralized media system in Europe, with a very strong national newspaper press that circulates throughout the state in numbers unmatched elsewhere. In general, with the exception of Scotland, the regional or local media are additional not alternative to the national press and television channels. By contrast, France and Germany have strong regional and city newspapers and an undeveloped central press. Television in Germany is also much more regionalized in organization. Spain and Italy both lack a large circulation national newspaper press, partly accounted for by much lower newspaper circulation in general. Most of the smaller countries of Europe also have a fragmented and diverse press, especially the Scandinavian countries, Holland and Belgium. On the other hand, these small countries are not in a position to have extensive national or regional television provision. It is worth noting that even where a large circulation national press is missing, most countries have one or more national titles, published in capital cities, that are considered to be influential, authoritative and close to the centre of political power. Examples include the Dutch *NRC Handelsblad*, Finland's *Helsingi Sanomat* and *Le Monde* in France.

Differences of *language and culture* also shape the map of the European media landscape. We can see certain competing and overlapping areas of influence, approximately as follows. First, we can point to an area of German influence, the largest single language group, that extends into Austria and Switzerland directly and now goes further into Central and Eastern Europe. Second, there is the UK, whose influence extends beyond the British Isles because of the relatively widespread knowledge of the English language and the success of the UK as a producer and exporter of audio-visual media (especially music and television) to the Continent. Third, we can see something like a Mediterranean media cultural area, comprising Spain, Italy and Portugal. Although they do not export much content to each other, they seem to share certain cultural tastes and habits and their media structures are similar. France stands out as more or less autonomous, although it too seeks to extend its influence by international transmissions and partnerships. Finally, the Nordic (Scandinavian) countries share common cultural and linguistic features (except Finland) and together form a critical mass of modest but useful proportions in maintaining their own distinctive media-cultural features.

Such differences can even be captured by a general North–South cultural dimension, although economic and historical factors also play a large part. Northern Europe has a more flourishing newspaper press and higher readership. Its television systems are 'less commercial' (according to various indicators), more educational and informational in content, more innovative in technology, and less inclined to import content from the USA. There is less time devoted to television viewing (although the UK is an exception to the 'Northern' norm in this respect). At an earlier stage, aside from relative wealth and higher educational standards, the countries of Northern Europe were more urbanized, more Protestant (read puritanical) and had more developed social welfare and democratic political systems. A comparative study of European television news programmes by Heinderyckx (1993) led to the suggestion that many variations could be captured by the existence of two distinct groups: a *'Romance-culture'* group and a *'Germanic-culture'* group. The former includes Spain, Italy, France, Switzerland and French Belgium, while the latter includes Germany, the UK, Holland and Flemish Belgium. 'Romance' news programmes were generally longer with fewer events covered, were more domestic in content and had more studio locations. The 'Germanic' news culture favours unobtrusive presentation, short and sober information and somewhat more objectivity.

As always, *economics* plays a key role. European countries have been converging in economic terms, but media systems reveal historical differences, mostly reflected in the North–South divide. Wealthier countries have more newspapers and higher readerships, plus more advanced television delivery systems. In these respects, Portugal, Italy, Spain and Greece are low in rank order, while the Scandinavian and Benelux countries plus Germany rank highly. Convergence of media systems is slower than the pace of new innovations. Currently, the old gaps show up in relation to the dissemination of domestic personal computers and the use of the internet (Table 7.1).

Table 7.1 The penetration of personal computers and the use of the internet (n/a = data not available)

Country	Ownership of computers (%)	Online access (internet) (%)
Austria	43	11
Belgium	34	11
Denmark	56	44
Finland	45	37
France	26	8
Germany	44	9
Greece	n/a	5
Ireland	19	12
Italy	22	13
Luxembourg	n/a	22
Netherlands	53	35
Portugal	16	6
Spain	17	8
Sweden	52	44
UK	39	2

(Computer ownership: *The Economist*, 19 February 2000;
internet access: *Eurobarometer* 51, July 1999)

One last but interesting feature of differentiation that has a mixed economic and social origin is the variable appearance of the mass circulation popular newspaper (sometimes called 'tabloid' or 'boulevard'). Only in Britain is there a very sharp divide between a 'quality' (or broadsheet) sector and a 'popular' (tabloid) sector of the national press. This has an economic base and is fostered by media centralization. Some other countries have examples of a popular national tabloid, such as *Bild* in Germany or *Neue Kronenzeitung* in Austria, but it is not a general feature of the newspaper press.

Several of the points made in these comments are reflected in the comparative data about media structure and use shown in Tables 7.2 and 7.3. Table 7.2 is organized to show the North–South division, by grouping countries according to newspaper development.

Table 7.2   Aspects of newspaper structure and use in Europe

Country	National versus regional balance of circulation	Press share of advertising expenditure (%) (1995)	Circulation: copies per 1,000 (1996)	Number of newspapers* (1994)
Denmark	M	63	311	40
Finland	R	59	456	56
Norway	N	60	592	84
Sweden	M	63	438	94
Switzerland	R	58	357	116
Netherlands	M	58	307	39
UK	N	42	330	88
Germany	R	49	318	383
Austria	N	46	230	17
Belgium	M	27	163	32
France	R	25	182	92
Ireland	N	57	157**	14
Portugal	N	17	93	23
Spain	R	32	105	125
Italy	R	21	105	79
Greece	N	13	78	48

* A newspaper is defined as a general paper published at least four days a week.

** Excludes papers based in the UK.

N = National, R = Regional, M = Mixed.

(Gustafson and Weibull, 1997)

Three groups of countries are distinguished in Table 7.2, with high, medium or low levels of newspaper penetration respectively, as measured by the number of newspapers and circulation per 1,000. One group consists largely of 'Northern' countries, although in fact they share other attributes: all were strongly affected by the Protestant Reformation;

several have known strong republican or social-democratic tendencies; and all have become relatively wealthy through industrialization or trade. Another group (all Southern countries) are mainly identifiable by Catholicism and relatively late industrialization. The variable of regionalism does not seem to relate to the level of newspaper development, although (not surprisingly perhaps) it does go with there being relatively more newspapers (as in Switzerland, Germany and France). In general, this promotes press diversity. The index of press share of advertising is intended to indicate relative economic importance, and it follows rather closely the ranking by circulation levels. It is noticeable that country size does not in itself make a difference. Finally, the figures in Table 7.2 are consistent with the view that newspaper press development virtually ceased at a certain point in the 'modernization' process (in fact, at about the middle of the twentieth century). Thereafter, audio-visual media were developed to meet the public and commercial communication requirements of late modernization. If so, there is little reason to expect any fundamental change to occur in the overall picture of inter-country differences. Although the figures shown are now somewhat dated (mid-1990s), the overall picture was much the same 10 or 20 years before and no fundamental shift can yet be discerned.

Table 7.3 (overleaf) provides some crucial information about different aspects of television structure and use in Europe. One interesting point to note is that in all the countries listed in Table 7.3, the number of TV households is almost identical to the number of households. Everywhere, much time is devoted to television viewing, nowhere less than 142 minutes per day on average (as in Austria). However, the amount of viewing does vary a good deal, up to a maximum average of 228 minutes in the UK, without there being any obvious explanation. On the other hand, aside from the case of the UK, the high-viewing countries are mainly those identified as lower in newspaper penetration (Spain, Italy, Greece and France), and vice versa for the low-viewing countries (such as Norway, Sweden, Finland, the Netherlands and Denmark). This is logical enough and raises the suspicion that the UK's standing in the 'newspaper league' may be due to high-circulation tabloids that have more in common with entertainment television than serious journalism. It does not look as if the number of national TV channels has any influence on the relative amount of viewing, and in fact the large expansion of television provision in Europe has not led to much increase in overall levels of viewing. For the most part the relative share of advertising going to television is a mirror image of the newspaper situation. The figures in Table 7.3 show how variable has been the spread of the new distribution technologies of cable and satellite. The latter is very much a minority facility, with only Germany much advanced. With the exception of Germany again, extensive cabling is still largely confined to small countries. This partly reflects the relative ease of installation, and partly the greater need in small countries for choice of provision, given the limited domestic production capacity. Despite current developments in digital television, there is unlikely to be any early dramatic change in a situation that has been quite static for several years.

Table 7.3 Television structure and use in Europe

Country	Number of national TV channels	TV adspend as a percentage of the total media adspend	Homes connected to cable (%)	Homes with direct satellite reception (millions)	Average TV viewing by individual (min. per day)
Austria (2.98)*	2	21	36	1.17	142
Belgium (3.66)	8	31	100	0.14	185
Denmark (2.37)	5	21	48	1.15	162
Finland (2.2)	4	21	40	1.66	150
France (22.16)	6	33	11	2.07	193
Germany (36.33)	14	22	48	10.40	196
Greece (3.3)	8	68	–	0.18	212
Ireland (1.13)	3	25	50	0.06	188
Italy (19.0)	9	58	–	1.10	217
Netherlands (6.4)	9	20	90	0.25	157
Norway (1.88)	5	18	37	0.38	144
Portugal (2.9)	4	50	13	0.28	173
Spain (11.8)	6	37	3	1.66	218
Sweden (3.7)	4	18	52	–	149
UK (23.9)	5	33	10	2.36	228

* The figure in brackets after the country name is the number of TV-owning households in millions.

(European Audiovisual Observatory, 1999)

By now there is something familiar about the media league table. The 'high newspaper' countries are again leading the way in computer and internet use, reflecting a head start in educational level and economic terms. However, it is also likely to have quite a lot to do with the dominance of the English language in internet content and thus relative national familiarity with English. Larger population non-English-speaking countries such as France, Italy and Spain have lagged in this respect and there must be considerable uncertainty about how far and how quickly this gap will be narrowed.

Summary

- The media serve much the same functions in each national society.
- There are considerable differences in the structure of national media systems (especially the newspaper press), due to the influence of historical, cultural, geographical and linguistic factors.

- These inter-country differences tend to be rather stable over time.

- The paradox of mass media is that they are at the same time strongly national in character and also one of the main gateways for transnational influences on ideas, culture, lifestyles and behaviour.

3   The regulation of mass media in Europe

The media occupy an ambiguous zone in respect of government regulation because of the widely recognized claim to freedom of publication (guaranteed by Article 10 of the European Convention on Human Rights), which rests not only on political but also on artistic and cultural foundations. Nevertheless, there remains a good deal of regulation, with forms and principles already quite similar across most of Europe. Three main foci of regulation can be found: *technology and infrastructure*, *ownership and control* and *content*.

Regulation of technology applies to virtually all electronic media in one form or another, but not at all to printing, and has various bases of legitimation. The motives for regulation of technology and infrastructure include: the need for development and investment; the need for standardization and inter-connectivity (this also applies internationally); reasons of national strategic interest (economic and military); the need for universal provision of basic communication needs (for consumers and industry); and the management of scarcity.

The regulation of ownership also has several aims and motivations. The central concern has usually been to prevent concentrations of ownership, with varying motives: to promote diversity and access and limit the political power of media; to give choice to consumers; and to promote economic efficiency and development through competition. Other motives for regulation of ownership include the wish to limit foreign ownership of media and to assist in media accountability by requiring transparency in respect of ownership.

The direct regulation of content is the most sensitive area, for reasons noted above, but even so the ultimate aim of most regulation is to influence the content of what is transmitted or published. A limited number of legitimate grounds for regulating content can also be found nearly everywhere. These have mainly to do with the protection of minors, issues of health and matters of taste and decency on which there is a broad consensus. In addition, advertising is generally excluded from any unconditional right to free expression and its content is subject to control nearly everywhere. The remaining main motive for content regulation of some media has to do with the protection of national culture and language.

3.1 Models of regulation of European media

Three main 'models' of regulation continue to exist in some form or another.

- The *media product* model. This applies to single items of content, such as books, films, music records, certain advertisements, internet sites and so on. While books, magazines and newspapers enjoy the freedom of the press (no advance censorship), some items can be judged illegal on a number of grounds (for example, obscenity or libel) and forbidden or censured after publication. Other media have less protection. The mechanisms of regulation are very diverse, but often involve some sort of supervisory board that may be statutory or self-regulatory (by the industry). France's Conseil Superieur de l'Audiovisuel (CSA), for example, supervises all aspects of television and radio, including content. In the UK, the statutory Broadcasting Standards Commission, the Board of Film Censors and the Press Complaints Commission deal with problematic content issues arising from television, films and newspapers respectively. And in the Netherlands, an independent government-appointed Media Council deals ultimately with problematic content issues arising from all mass media in principle. In the case of films and video recordings, rating systems (classifications) are widely applied by regulatory bodies to control distribution and exhibition. The grounds for control are to be found primarily in the sphere of content regulation and relate to potentially harmful effects. So far there has been little effective control of internet content, although it is unclear how much freedom it can claim. It falls within the scope of various laws, but there are severe practical problems of implementation by any regulatory authority and there is no example of any such body in Europe at the time of writing. The European Commission and Council of Europe favour self-regulation and an example often cited is that of the Internet Watch Foundation (IWF), founded in the UK in 1996, and broadly supported by government and industry. Ratings systems and software to filter out unwanted content are also being advocated and developed (see Slevin, 2000). Otherwise, content issues have been dealt with, as in the case of the press, mainly by recourse to the courts and by applying existing laws concerning publication.

- The *common carrier* model. This has traditionally applied to telephony and all public electronic services, cable services or air transport (it also applies to the postal service). The shared feature of these media is the carriage (transmission) of private messages from one sender to a receiver (point to point), as opposed to public dissemination. In general, the new electronic media such as the internet fall under this model, although, as noted above, content issues are rapidly attracting attention. The main focus of regulation has been on issues of infrastructure, ownership and access, but issues of privacy and security of data also arise. Until recently, the main means of control in Europe was by way of national public monopoly ownership and/or control of the post and telecommunication industries. Laws governing wireless and telegraphy dating back more than a century have provided basic tools of regulation in most European countries, although they have been modified by recent privatizations. In practice this has allowed the government of the day to regulate more or less at will. However, under increasing private ownership, control has shifted to self-regulation and some form of national regulatory agency.

- The *broadcasting* model. This was developed to allow close control of technology, ownership and content after the introduction of public wireless services in the 1920s, followed by television. The means of control adopted in Europe was typically a public monopoly account-able to government and to the public through parliament (public service broadcasting). The regulation of broadcasting is still very close at national and also European level, and in nearly every country there is a specific and detailed law governing radio and television. However, as a result of the changes described in the following section, it is giving way to looser forms of control and market discipline.

In general, the foundations for these separate 'models' are also weakening and the lines between media have become much less clear due to various forms of 'convergence' (especially the use of computers by all media).

Summary

- Regulation of media is held back by the need to respect freedom of the press and public expression and also by the fact that media are to a large extent part of the free-market system.

- The regulations that exist at the level of national societies are very fragmented and diversified, with complex procedures and agencies that have grown up differently according to local circumstances and political culture.

- There are three main models of regulation, differentiated according to the basic technology in use: print, broadcasting and electronic transmission.

- However, *convergence* of technology and organization is undermining the legitimacy of regulation in general and of this tripartite division in particular.

- Regulation of the internet is presenting new problems, since its content can claim protection under freedom of the press or communication privacy rules, but its technology and some of its uses make it akin to the highly regulated broadcasting sector.

4 Trends and changes in European media

The history of European mass media (effectively beginning in the 1930s) has been marked by several phases of change, leaving aside the impact of the Second World War (suppression and commandeering of media) and the post-war Sovietization of Eastern European media.

The first phase was one of reconstruction in countries directly affected by the war. In Germany, the press was de-Nazified and a new, decentralized broadcasting system was installed, with a strong public service element modelled on the BBC. In the formerly occupied countries, especially France, Holland, Belgium and Denmark, the press was purged of its collaborationist past and new titles were founded with their roots in resistance publications. In general, (radio) broadcasting was returned to its pre-war status and the initial development of television was encompassed within the same framework of regulation and public control as was radio. These events are a clear sign of the centrality of the media to the political culture of the nation states of Europe.

The second phase was a delayed readjustment to new conditions and new technologies once post-war recovery was under way in the 1960s. The central event was the rise of television to the position of dominant medium as measured in terms of popularity and time devoted by the audience. The same period saw large challenges facing the newspaper press, although the connection with the rise of television is uncertain. In a number of countries, some established newspapers failed and there was a general trend to concentration (fewer firms and titles) and a reduced diversity of content and type.

After a plateau of relative stability, the winds of change began to blow again at the start of the 1980s. An indication of the fragility of the reigning order was provided by events in Italy in 1976. A decision of the Constitutional Court casting doubt on the broadcasting monopoly opened the way for private local broadcasting. This was quickly followed by an explosion of local stations both out of control and competing with public broadcasting (RAI) and the emergence of a *de facto*, although not fully legal, commercial broadcasting sector which directly challenged the RAI (this was the start of Berlusconi's Fininvest media empire). All over Europe during the 1970s the broadcasting monopoly was seen as increasingly stifling, not only by commercial interests wanting to make money but also by many new political and social movements. These were keen to use the emerging advances in communication technology to liberate and expand public communication, especially at the local and regional level.

Since 1980, the process of change has been virtually continuous, although less driven by idealistic visions of active and participant societies than by commercial companies looking for profitable opportunities and by governments alert to the industrial and economic potential of the new information and communication technologies. Three main technological innovations provided the driving force for change. The first was the application of communication satellites to public broadcasting, made possible by international agreement at the World Administrative Radio Conference (WARC) in 1977. Satellites could transmit over a much wider area than traditional terrestrial transmitters, crossing national frontiers but requiring expensive receiving equipment (large dish aerials) as well as expensive launches.

The second innovation was the harnessing of telecommunications, the computer and the television set for the public dissemination of all kinds of information. The early systems were known by the generic name of *videotex* (as distinct from the contemporary invention of *teletext*, which was a way of using TV broadcasting for similar purposes). This was the forerunner of today's internet. The third innovation was the installation and upgrading of cable for local distribution of TV and radio.

Another new medium, that of home video-recording (the VCR), was widely available from the late 1970s and accustomed the viewer to greater freedom of choice, serving as an indirect challenge to the monopoly control of audio-visual media. By 1997, 73 per cent of European households were equipped with a VCR.

The Open University Call Centre

The impact of new technology

These different technologies all undermined the main legitimation of public monopoly and close regulation of broadcasting, which was primarily based on a scarcity of channels that no longer existed. Much regulation of broadcasting was exposed as a limitation on freedom of communication and a restraint on legitimate economic activity as well as on trans-border commerce. Claims to national sovereignty for broadcasting were judged inconsistent with the Treaty of Rome. Local radio and cable had already led the way in challenging regulation, and at the end of the 1970s the potential of communication satellites proved an irresistible argument for reform and expansion of the whole system of public electronic communication.

International satellite broadcasting made a shaky and unprofitable start in Europe in the early 1980s, but gained momentum after the launching in 1989 of the first commercial Astra satellite, dedicated to broadcasting rather than telecommunications. The ability of satellite transmission to cover a much larger area proved to be a liability in the end. Although it was theoretically possible to reach a very large audience in different countries from one transmitter, the ability to receive depended either on having a large and expensive satellite receiver dish or on being connected to a cable system that would take the transmission and redistribute it to households. Without a large or homogenous audience, it was (and remains) difficult to get advertising revenue. In addition, the barriers of language were not fully appreciated by the early commercial satellite channels.

By the mid-1980s several European governments were beginning to see the advantage and even the necessity of encouraging change, although they chose to encourage the free market rather than rely on state planning. This new liberalism showed up in legislation and deregulation that permitted controlled alternatives to public broadcasting, especially by way of cable and satellite. The result has been not only an expansion of television but also a large shift in the forms of ownership and financing, as is shown in Table 7.4.

Some current trends

- Audience patterns have changed as a result of greater channel choice. Attention is fragmented across a range of channels, and audiences for any given transmission are smaller on average.

- The average amount of time spent watching television has only increased to a small extent despite the expansion of supply. Differences between countries in media use have not changed.

- The digitalization of television transmission is gathering pace and will accelerate the multiplication of channels, cross-border communication and audience fragmentation.

- The availability of personal computers and connection to the internet are increasing, although there are large differences within Europe (see Table 7.1).

Table 7.4   Change in the structure of television in Europe, 1980 to 1998

System type	1980	1990	1998
Public monopoly/ licence fee only	Belgium Denmark Norway Sweden		
Public monopoly/ mixed revenue	Austria Finland France Germany Greece Iceland Ireland Netherlands Portugal Switzerland	Austria Denmark Iceland Ireland Netherlands Portugal Switzerland	Austria Ireland Switzerland
Private monopoly/ advertising only	Luxembourg	Luxembourg	Luxembourg
Dual system	Italy UK	Belgium Finland France Germany Greece Italy Norway Spain Sweden UK	Same as 1990 plus: Denmark Iceland Netherlands Portugal

(McQuail and Siune, 1998, p.27)

Summary

- Fundamental changes in the media have been brought about by innovations in communication technology, but also depend on supportive political and economic conditions.

- The newspaper press has remained relatively unchanged in ownership, structure and its main forms (types of publication).

- There has been a large expansion of radio and television provision in virtually every country.

- There has been a shift of balance from public to private (commercial) funding and control following the disappearance of the public monopoly in virtually all countries (Table 7.4). Much more television is financed by advertising than used to be the case, while direct public funding has stagnated.

- The *potential* for receiving television across national frontiers, mainly via satellite but sometimes via cable, has greatly increased.

- Current trends include changes in audience patterns and the use of new technologies, but the average watching time for television has only increased slightly.

5 Issues of European cultural autonomy and dependency

The question of cultural autonomy is a complex one, involving several issues and a variety of levels. In pre-mass media modern times it was connected with nationalism, and a number of countries in Europe were concerned to establish the primacy of a national language and culture with the aim of cementing the unity of the nation state (as in Italy and Germany). Elsewhere the main aim was to assert independence in the face of imperialist domination (as in Finland or Ireland). Sometimes the aim was to promote the autonomy of a distinct national and cultural region within a larger state (as in Flanders or Catalonia). A general concern was to maintain the integrity of national language and culture in the face of foreign influences in a time when nationalism was a dominant ideology. The point here is to underline the deep roots of debates about the cultural influence of mass media, while the rise of global audio-visual media and cross-frontier transmission has revived older fears.

In the post-war period in Western Europe the main source of external cultural influence (of all kinds) was the USA, partly from choice as a breath of fresh air and democracy but partly from necessity given the low state of European cultural industries. The rise of television increased the reliance on imports from the USA, reducing the element of choice. As Europe prospered, concern about this dependence was widely expressed, especially in smaller European countries. Research into the flow of media content, as early as the 1970s, showed the extreme *imbalance* of flow between the USA and Europe in television content. This was only part of a more general dominance of global communication flow by the USA, not least due to the operation of international news and television news film agencies. The dominance of the USA extended to popular music and film, for reasons that pre-dated the Second World War (see Tunstall, 1977).

In this phase, the dominant motive was often as much anti-USA and its alleged 'media imperialism' as it was nationalistic or cultural in origin. However, a new phase was initiated, from the early 1980s onwards, by the accelerating pace of the 'European project', following the enlargement and expanded scope of the European Community during the 1970s. For the first time, certain cultural goals of a supranational kind were being openly discussed and the concept of a 'European cultural identity' was being aired in the influential circles of European politics, despite a good deal of vagueness about its meaning (Schlesinger, 1991). It was also an ambiguous and ambivalent notion since it was a potential new threat to *national* cultural sovereignty, especially in the field of broadcasting. The idea of a 'European identity' was much more a construction deployed in political circles than one arising from popular sentiment, as Llobera has shown in Chapter 6. European concerns were certainly motivated as much by economic as by cultural considerations. The lowering of communication barriers within Europe, allowing free cross-border trans-missions, were viewed by some as a Trojan horse for the increased domination of imports from the USA.

5.1 The main issues and the current state of affairs

Six main issues dominate the debate.

- *Protecting national language and culture from excessive foreign influence.* There is little or no evidence that the mass media have actually undermined national language or culture, or that it has actually been undermined at all. The general prosperity of Europe has protected cultural industries as well as exposed people to new and external influences. There is a more or less common international news agenda, but international or foreign events are still presented (and interpreted by audiences) according to a predominantly domestic perspective and relevance. Foreign language media have made no real advances. The domain of sports, entertainment and celebrity is also very internationalized (and Europeanized) as a result of mass media, but national perspectives also shape the presentation of content and 'global' content is fitted into home-grown forms. The format and genres of popular fiction and entertainment have been borrowed and adapted to suit local tastes rather than simply imported in their original forms (Biltereyst, 1991, 1992; Liebes and Livingstone, 1998). European audiences have become used to 'American' media products and styles since the early days of cinema at least, and they have always been popular. Nevertheless, they are rarely quite as popular as the best 'national' productions, and the television audience in Europe seems quite able to appreciate the difference.

- *Ensuring a viable space within the nation states of Europe for national minorities with their own historic language and culture.* For national minorities, the circumstances vary considerably from case to case (see Section 10), but in general the climate for a greater degree of autonomy has improved. The expansion of television systems and break-up of monopoly control has made it technically and politically easier to meet demands for provision for minority languages without offending majorities. More diversity can be accommodated within the greater capacity.

- *Developing some degree of European cultural identity that is based on inter-communication and on independent and viable cultural production resources able to compete with the USA.* There has not been great progress on the idea of a European cultural identity. Surveys carried out for the European Union (EU) continue to show a rather variable and low adoption of the idea of a European identity (see Chapter 6). This notion is more an external construct applied to Europe than a home-grown idea.

- *Maintaining an adequate national cultural sovereignty in relation to the EU, without undermining European identity.* In the light of the above comments, it is not surprising that fears of a 'European' domination of national cultures have not been realized, and are indeed not as strongly expressed as fears of the influence of the USA.

- *Supporting regional and local identities in relation to the nation states in which they are embedded.* Regional and local identities within countries do not seem to have been adversely affected by the potentially homogenizing trends and changes described. New technology has assisted rather than hindered local and smaller-scale production, and regional and local media generally look quite prosperous.

- *Handling the integration of diverse minority cultural identities within a nation state, while respecting their right to some autonomy (multiculturalism).* There is great variability in the fate of ethnic and other minorities in Europe, especially those resulting from migration and asylum seeking (as Layton-Henry has discussed in Chapter 3). The general climate of opinion toward such minorities has not changed much, although there is more emphasis on restricting the growth of minority populations and on gradual integration. Cable television has been successfully used in many local instances to provide some autonomous communication channels for minorities (for example, Migranten TV in Amsterdam). There have also been developments in print media for dispersed other-language communities. However, the main provision for maintaining cultural identity has been through better access to television and other 'home' media by way of satellite, video and the internet.

Summary

- The issue of cultural and national autonomy is an old one, deeply rooted in different ways to national histories, but reactivated by the seeming potential of new communication technologies and new global tendencies.

- In general, both the impact of technology and the vulnerability of national (and regional) autonomy and diversity in the face of external influences have been much overestimated.

- The new technologies have a potential for increasing cultural independence and diversity as well as for reducing it.

6 National media policy in Europe

A quite general policy shift occurred across Europe during the 1980s, essentially delivering the task of new media development into the hands of the private sector. In general, for reasons already given, smaller countries with more concern for their cultural vulnerability were much more resistant to change, provided they could afford to pay for the retention of a strong public sector. Media policy generally took the form of legislation that effectively broke the broadcasting monopoly, by allowing new commercial channels to be offered on cable systems. The new television providers were often subjected to close regulation on certain matters of content and in relation to advertising and public channels. In many countries, new regulatory agencies were set up to deal with issues arising from the liberalization of cable and television, sometimes with a wider remit covering electronic media generally (for instance, the CSA in France).

Public broadcasting bodies have retained certain privileges, for instance by way of 'must-carry' rules on cable and exclusive coverage rights to certain events of national significance. Such privileges support the role of public service and also reflect the vested interests of political élites. However, the main protection has been the retention of public funding as a major source of income and often the freedom to engage in advertising. The position of public broadcasting has, nevertheless, remained vulnerable because of the need to compete for audiences with commercial television in order to fulfil its wider role (since it involves similar programming). Despite the support of the EU for public service broadcasting (for instance, in the protocol to the 1997 Amsterdam Treaty, which recognizes the essential social role of public broadcasting), there are also pressures from commercial operators, on the grounds of free competition. Public media policy thus moved from one of direct control and accountability to one of licensing and a mixture of central supervision and self-regulation.

The policies of national governments in relation to the newspaper press have been much more limited in scope. Policy can really only be directed at the structure of the press, and most European governments have adopted the maintenance of diversity as the main goal. This has two main aspects – having a choice of newspapers (if possible representing different political or cultural streams) in a given media market, and preventing the domination of the market (or a sector of it) by one owner. In practice, public policy can do little to ensure that there is a choice of newspapers in a given market (let alone influence the kind of newspapers). Newspapers have always appeared and died according to the changing circumstances and demands of the audience.

The freedom of the press?

In most countries there are measures to protect the general economic health of newspapers, on grounds of public interest, by way of postal rate and transportation concessions and remission of tax. In some places (especially in Scandinavian countries), subsidies are available for the protection of weaker newspapers facing competition or to help launch new ones, but this model is in decline. More significant are measures to prevent dominance of the newspaper market and limit cross-ownership between print and other media. In general, about 25 or 30 per cent of a given market is regarded as the upper permissible limit for any single firm to own. This limit is sometimes legally binding, as in France, but more often it is dealt with under discretionary rulings of anti-trust bodies (as in the UK) or by the industry's informal self-regulation (as in the Netherlands). Rules limiting media cross-ownership are easier to apply since all forms of radio and television are subject to regulation. However, it will not be easy to prevent newspapers extending their interests into the internet and other media that are provided by way of the telephone network or transnational satellites.

There are some other policy goals, especially a limitation on foreign ownership (as in France), incorporated into legislation in some countries. However, these cannot apply to other member states of the EU. There are also some legal requirements affecting transparency of ownership to make it possible to identify responsible publishers and apply rules concerning concentration of ownership.

Summary

- The main thrust of national media policy has been a shift away from cultural and toward commercial and industrial goals. This has involved the abolition of the public broadcasting monopoly and extensive deregulation and privatization.

- In general, media policy has been an exclusive preserve of national cultural politics, but it is now subject to strong external and international pressures.

- Public policy attempts to protect newspapers are increasingly marginal in their scope and impact.

7   The media policies of the EU

The main aims of the media policy of the EU have been essentially economic: to ensure the free movements of goods and services and a level playing field for the economic activities that make up a key aspect of mass media; to enlarge the European media market so that European firms could enjoy some of the advantages of scale and homogeneity that underlay the success of the USA's media; and to promote media industries, especially in the audio-visual sector.

A succession of programmes and policies has been issued from Brussels since the early 1980s, with an extending range of targets. Despite the early economic aims it was found that in order to pursue these it was necessary to tackle a number of related matters, including the freedom to communicate, issues of information property rights, questions of ownership, concentration and diversity, and certain issues of human rights and cultural values. In many of these social and cultural matters, the EU has been proceeding on a parallel path with the much wider Council of Europe.

Although European policy initiatives have steadily increased in number and range, the cornerstone can be considered to be the 1989 Directive, *Television Without Frontiers*, which is the main instrument of European media legislation and embodies the main principles of a common European policy for the electronic media. Its origins lie in the liberalizing and market harmonizing tendencies that have been described. The aim is to ensure for television the same freedom of communication across the frontiers of member states that is enjoyed by print and other cultural forms, and to lay the foundation for a single market in media goods and services.

Aside from considerations of technical feasibility and national cultural sovereignty, the main obstacle to cross-border television was a great variation in national legislation for broadcasting, especially as it affected advertising. In fact, it was the advertising lobby that drove the legislation forward, although there were also influential voices urging the new regulations as a necessary condition for achieving pan-European television channels.

The central feature of the 1989 Television Directive (made binding in 1991 and revised in 1996) is a set of basic or minimum rules that are acceptable to all member states. In respect of advertising, the limit set to the amount of advertising as a percentage of transmission time is a good deal higher than applies in most national regulation. There is also a limit on the frequency of advertising breaks in films. Certain categories of advertising are prohibited, following regulations widely in force nationally, and there are prohibitions on certain kinds of content that might be offensive or harmful to minors (especially pornography). One clause in the Directive requires 10 per cent of content to be made by independent producers, one of the attempts to stimulate audio-visual production.

The clause that has caused most controversy is that which stipulates a minimum 50 per cent of European content (leaving aside news and sport), but only 'where practicable'. Despite subsequent efforts, this has not been made binding. This rule has been interpreted as a protectionist move directed against the USA and designed to reduce the large trade imbalance in audio-visual products between Europe and the USA. Certainly, the motives were and remain mixed. They reflect a genuine concern about the USA's cultural 'imperialism' in the form of a flood of cheap programming filling the many new cable and satellite channels to the detriment of the national language and culture, and undermining the cultural and social goals of public broadcasting. The 50 per cent 'quota', as it came to be seen, was actually below the existing norm for nearly all established European television channels. In addition, little account was taken of the limited scope for, and appeal of, cross-border television then and now and the 'natural' limits set by audience preferences for imported content. However, the quota was resented in the USA. The row reflects the different notions of 'culture' on either side of the Atlantic and also illustrates the strength of global free-market forces and the difficulty of having either national or European media cultural policies that are seen as restricting international competition.

In practice, the Directive seems to have worked quite well in its main aims of maintaining some distinctive features of European broadcasting, despite the greater commercialization and internationalization. There has been quite a high degree of compliance, even with the non-binding 'quota' rule, and the domestic production of television content in fiction and entertainment has been stimulated. There have been only limited disputes about the content transmitted across European frontiers (mainly relating to pornography). However, the overall trade gap has not diminished and the new regime has not done a great deal to stimulate genuinely pan-European content in any form.

The European Commission has been very active and successful in opposing concentration of media ownership arising from mergers and takeovers within and across frontiers. There is a record of blocking proposed deals by major media firms (for example, the projected Bertelsmann–Kirch pay-TV merger in Germany in 1999). Such activities are undertaken by the powerful Competition Directorate of the Commission. In these aims it is generally in line with influential sentiment and with policies within countries.

Policy moves to safeguard the diversity of the press were initiated in 1992, with the publication of a discussion Green Paper that did little more than pose the question of whether something needed to be done, and if so what – for instance, a harmonization of existing national anti-concentration measures. It seems unlikely that effective action will be taken, given the political sensitivity of the issue. It is an issue on which politicians do fear the power of the media.

Throughout the period under review, the EU has launched a series of initiatives designed to support European cultural production in the audio-visual field, mostly grouped under the MEDIA I and MEDIA II programmes. Subsidies were given for film and television production, meeting cultural and artistic criteria as well as involving co-operation between countries and across sectors. The EU also extended its attention to regional linguistic minorities during the 1980s. The BABEL (Broadcasting Across the Barriers of European Languages) Programme was launched in 1988 and later integrated into MEDIA II. The aim was to support multi-lingualism in the audio-visual field. In general, such efforts have promoted the legitimacy of demands by linguistic minorities.

The EU is struggling, as are national governments, with the problems of regulating the internet and it has produced a number of documents and policy ideas. No policy has yet been formulated, but the general lines of thinking by the European Commission have been summarized by Slevin (2000) as: creating a European network of hotlines to stimulate the exchange of information and regulatory consistency and transparency; encouraging self-regulation and guidelines for codes of conduct; developing filtering and rating systems suitable for European conditions; and promoting co-ordination with other international initiatives.

Summary

- European media policy has been driven primarily by the economic goals of enlarging and harmonizing the European media market, encouraging competition and promoting audio-visual industries and new technology.

- A secondary goal has been to promote European self-sufficiency in media and, indirectly, to contribute to a common sense of European identity.

- There has been some success in promoting market expansion, European media production and unification, and competition, but the aims are sometimes contradictory and counter-productive. The media trade imbalance with the USA has not been reduced.

- European media policy has made little progress in dealing with the thorny problem of press diversity and concentration of ownership on a Europe-wide basis, but the overall situation remains stable and the level of press diversity has not markedly declined.

- Film production and minority languages have received help.

- A start has been made in formulating European policy in relation to the internet.

8   Media at the European level?

At an early stage of speculation about the development of a European 'cultural' identity, corresponding with the start of the satellite era (circa 1980), there were high hopes that pan-European television services could make a significant contribution to the greater 'unification' of Europe in social and cultural terms. This was already being pushed forward on the economic and political fronts. The institution of a European Parliament and the first direct elections for this in 1979 highlighted the absence of common means of public communication on matters affecting all of Europe. At that time and since, voluntary efforts were made by the European Broadcasting Union (EBU), the association of European Public Broadcasters, to facilitate the flow of news across frontiers by way of conventional broadcasting. In the end, however, such efforts depended on local editorial news judgements, which generally did not favour news from other European countries per se.

The first real test of the pan-European potential of television was made for commercial purposes by Rupert Murdoch's Sky Channel, starting in 1983. However, because of limitations on cross-border advertising, barriers of language and the small audiences equipped to receive satellite television, the concept of a general (commercial) television channel for a multinational audience was not much advanced by this pioneering initiative. An attempt was also made by a group of public broadcasting organizations in 1984 and 1985 to establish a pan-European satellite channel (Europa TV), financed out of their own resources but with the aim of being self-financing by way of advertising. After a relatively short period, the experiment was abandoned, for much the same reasons that limited commercial satellite television.

Since then, however, there has been much more experience of transnational television in Europe, following the extension of cable and the relaxation of policy, aided by the Television Directive. However, the concept of pan-European media has still made little progress. Obstacles remain, some practical, others rooted in culture and society. Although cable television has expanded, most television in Europe is still sent and received by terrestrial broadcasting, even if with some help from satellites (see Table 7.3). Barriers of language and culture remain, as do limited sources of advertising revenue and the limited willingness of consumers to pay for more television. The evidence is clear enough that the media public likes its own national and language content first of all, with Hollywood content a second choice, especially for fiction and drama. There is little reason to expect this to change, and a similar rule applies to news. It has to be timely and relevant to its audience, and this almost by definition rules out much demand for cross-national news transmissions that cannot economically (and cost is a big factor) be as up-to-the-minute as national news and equally relevant to the concerns of all audiences. These barriers are there even before we consider the question of language. As a result, international news services such as CNN, BBC World and Euro News do not have much of an audience or impact and are not really viable on their own. There are other examples of partial success in cross-border transmission, including the Franco-German arts channel Arte and the French satellite channel TV5 that provides a focus for French language speakers in Europe as well as in the rest of the world.

The main exceptions to this generally negative assessment are to be found in respect of sport and music, which also appeal to some definable minority tastes (here large minorities). At least one pan-European sport channel (Eurosport) has been generally successful, and MTV Europe was one of the first transnational channels to acquire a large audience. However, it has also proved vulnerable to local, own-language competition and has been forced to regionalize its transmissions and diversify its language away from English, even though English retains an advantage as the preferred language of song lyrics (see Wieten et al., 2000).

There are other media besides television, but little evidence elsewhere of their Europeanization. A European newspaper (*The European*) was initiated by Robert Maxwell in 1985, but it was limited by the usual factors of only appearing in the English language and having to be relevant to such a disparate and ill-defined readership. Certain English newspapers (for example, *The Financial Times* and *The Guardian*) are printed and published on the continent in European editions, although without aiming to be European in content. *The Financial Times* has also started a German language version (*FT Deutschland*). English-language magazines also circulate to a limited extent in the capitals of Europe, but they testify to the cosmopolitanism of a certain class rather than any awakening of European identity, as has been mentioned in both Chapter 1 and Chapter 6.

All in all, it looks as if there is neither a commercial nor a cultural base for significant pan-European media, however much technology, on the one hand, and policy and regulation, on the other, might have moved toward facilitating such developments. Even so, one should not underestimate the greater exposure to European neighbours by way of media coverage of sport, entertainment and celebrities, as well as by coverage of the same political and economic events and circumstances.

Summary

- The technological basis for pan-European broadcasting has been provided by satellite and cable for almost unlimited transnational media transmission.

- However, experience as well as theory shows that there is little consumer demand for such media provision under normal circumstances, aside from a few specialist services.

- Print media have shown almost no new capacity to travel, even by way of foreign ownership.

- It is still unclear if new media such as the internet will provide an exception to these conclusions.

9 Media and politics in Europe

The European newspaper and periodical press, and subsequently broadcasting, have always been related to politics, either by assisting in the exercise of power or challenging it on behalf of the public (their audiences). The relationship between politics and the media is close but complex and not always transparent. In general, the news media support the working of democratic political institutions and give much access to parties and politicians, who are often important sources of news. Some degree of access is generally required by broadcasting regulations. In many European countries leading newspapers have links with a political party or ideology; these are sometimes formal links, but more often they are not. In some countries, for instance Italy and Belgium, journalists are likely to act as political advocates as much as reporters. Even public television has been affected, with a formal or informal division of influence between channels, as in France, Italy and Belgium. The Dutch broadcasting system has openly legitimated direct political influence and other influences. However, there has been a growing tendency for media to adopt a non-aligned or neutral position toward government and politics in general. Deregulation and privatization of television have strengthened this model, although there is evidence of political parties and figures, irrespective of political colour, seeking informal alliances with the new media magnates.

In fact, television has continued to be inescapably politicized (although indirectly through policy and various pressures) as a result of continuing belief in its 'power' and the intense focus of attention of many different political interests in the opportunities and dangers represented by the medium. This is expressed in two main forms: one is a concern on the part of politicians about how they or issues and events are presented in the news; the second relates to questions of ownership and control, with politicians fearing concentrations of media power in private hands (with unpredictable consequences). As a result, many decisions affecting the media that would elsewhere be left to the market have become politically contentious. Examples abound in all countries, but the political decision in the UK in 1999 to block the takeover of Manchester United Football Club by Murdoch's Sky Broadcasting was illustrative, as was the political debate in the UK over the re-timing of a television news programme (*News at Ten*).

Despite the continuing grip of politics on most forms of mass media, there have been changes in the political and cultural climate as well as in the media themselves that threaten to undermine media politicization. Many observers of social trends recorded a general 'secularization' of European politics and society in the late twentieth century, especially after the decline of 1960s and 1970s radicalism. The secularization and relative 'depoliticization' of the media have taken several forms. One is the rise of the norm of news 'objectivity', meaning the separation of opinion from facts and the attempt to be informative and impartial. This is supported by the greater professionalization of journalism, the reliance on news agencies that have to sell the same 'news' in different markets, and the commercialization of media generally.

Another aspect of change in the media has been the general triumph of 'media logic' over 'political logic', or of form over content. Most centrally this means that media selection and attention is more governed by appearance, presentation and audience appeal than significance or substance. Critics have alleged a decline of serious journalism and pointed to the rise of 'infotainment' (see Brants and Siune, 1998). There is some evidence of a decline in interest and trust in politics among the general public, but no strong evidence that media are a cause. According to Brants (1998) there is no clear sign of any reduction in the flow of political news and information on television, and there has generally been some convergence of practice between public and private television channels.

Summary

- The media have always been very politicized in Europe, although in degrees and forms that varied between countries.

- Politicization is now taking new forms, with the decline of strong ideological and mass-based parties and the general secularization of society.

- The 'commercialization' of media is suspected of encouraging a decline and dilution of politics and the quality of the 'civic culture', although the evidence is not clear on this point.

10   Issues of language

The question of language has already been raised in connection with European and national identity. Several countries have taken some cultural policy steps to protect the national language. France is the foremost example, with a systematic set of policy and legal measures designed to promote the French language which also affect the media. The 1994 'loi Toubon' that requires the exclusive use of French words in advertising in France is only one expression of an enduring policy goal (Machill, 1997). The French media are also constrained by quotas for the broadcasting of French songs and showing of French films in the cinema, and in other ways. Such measures can be interpreted as protectionist in the trade sense, and in practice they are directed at 'Anglo-Saxon' media hegemony, but they can only be understood in terms of national culture and history.

The direct protection of a national language by legal means can be difficult to reconcile with other principles of European law, especially those concerning freedom of competition and freedom of expression. Seen from the perspective of linguistic minorities in various countries, including France, it is the official language of the centralized nation state that is both problematic and generally promoted by the mass media. As we have noted, in all countries, language has been and remains the 'ultimate barrier' to foreign cultural subversion by way of mass media (Biltereyst, 1992). But within national frontiers the same language is the main engine of subversion for linguistic minorities, and there is no linguistic defence.

The question of language is often connected with that of region, since most indigenous minority languages coincide with a region that can also be a basis for some media provision. The most apparently successful modern attempts in Europe to develop media in national minority languages relate to areas that have some regional and political identity. The following, for example, all have their own television channels: Wales (S4C), Catalonia (TV3) and the Basque Country (ETB), the Irish Gaeltacht (TG4) and Friesland (Omrap Fryslan). Other regions with a different language from the national one are not so successful in getting provision. An example is the Breton language: despite 24 per cent of Basse Bretagne (about 370,000 people) being Breton speakers, there is very little media provision. This is not primarily due to the French language policy of the state, but reflects social and economic factors. The Breton-speaking population is ageing and not likely to support financially viable media. Leaving language aside, the success of regional and local media (especially radio or television) in Europe has been very variable and unpredictable. The availability of the technology (for instance, being interconnected by cable) is a necessary but far from sufficient condition.

Minority language situations vary enormously from case to case, leaving aside regionalism and the survival of ancient indigenous languages. They include the results of history and past colonization (like the Swedish minority of Finland or the German-speaking community in Belgium), and the federal division of Switzerland, not forgetting recent waves of immigration in Europe. According to Cormack (1998) the chances for minority language media depend not only on obvious things like the absolute *number* of speakers (as is the case with Catalonia) but also on the degree of political support, the symbolic value of the minority language (for example, in Ireland), and the mounting of effective mass campaigns of support. International trends also play a part. At the present time within Europe, there is a helpful stress on a 'Europe of the Regions' (see Chapter 2), partly as a way of circumventing national(istic) resistance to 'Europeanization'. Cormack notes that regional language movements have often been led by intellectuals (sometimes within the national media) and this has not always reflected the degree of popular demand for the minority language media, without which they are not viable. While it is always possible to implement such media provision as an act of policy (as in Ireland) it is not possible to guarantee success in the market. In the competitive and globalizing media climate that pertains in much of Europe, the chances of doing more than preserving certain remnants of early country languages are not especially good, even though established small-country languages look quite safe.

Summary

- The developments in media described in this chapter can be seen as both negative and positive for sub-state and regional languages.

- In general, the conditions for minority language survival are provided by factors other than technology and media systems.

- International media trends (globalization) are more of a challenge to *national*-level media than regional, local or minority media. These same trends can also help foreign ethnic communities by keeping them in touch with their countries of origin.

11   Europe in the news

There is little systematic evidence about how the news media of Europe report each other's affairs or report 'Europe' as a concept, supranational entity or set of institutions. The matter is generally considered of some importance in influencing European opinion toward the EU in general or any particular EU initiative (for instance, the European single currency). There is a tendency to believe that if only 'the media' were more positive toward 'Europe', especially in countries with a reputation for being awkward, such as Britain and Denmark, the whole project would move forward more smoothly. Even greater attention of any kind to the EU would be welcomed by its political élites. It would also seem that for the EU to become a more clearly identifiable political entity, some kind of 'European public opinion' has to come into being, and this seems to call for some basis in public communication. Similarly, it has been supposed, certainly in the early days, that the occasion of the European election would be constructed as a significant transnational event by the media as well as by politicians (Blumler, 1983). Later experience showed that this was scarcely the case. The European election, like European 'public opinion', is little more than the sum or average of the different national 'parts'. In general, it has the status of a 'second order' election, symbolically about Europe, but in practice more of an interim test of national opinion.

There is plenty of fragmentary evidence on the matter of news selection and quite a lot is known about the general tendencies at work. These seem to operate in much the same way in different countries. Events tend to be selected if they are genuinely 'news' (very recent and about interesting topics) as well as directly relevant to the given news audience. It always helps if they have a dramatic, conflict-laden, exciting or personal character. On nearly all these points, most news about other European countries and about the doings of political 'Europe' does not qualify. Where it does, it tends to be 'bad news' about disputes, disagreements with other countries or criticism of EU institutions. As a result, most of the time, the citizens of European countries are not exposed to much news of their neighbours and only selectively to 'Europe' as such.

BBC News 24

The main pathway of entry for news about Europe is by way of the national political institution that defines some particular issues as relevant, significant, positive or negative. In addition, certain more or less symbolic and pre-planned occasions, apart from elections, such as the regular meetings of the European Council (heads of government), provide a routine focus of attention. In fact, because of the steady extension of the range of the activities of EU institutions, news about Europe in every sense has tended to rise gradually in absolute and relative terms because it is objectively more relevant (at the cost, for instance, of news about domestic matters in the USA). It has also gradually become harder to distinguish European from 'home' political news, and this has helped to create a sense of normality and greater propinquity. It remains the case that news about other countries in Europe and about Europe itself continues to be treated by the great majority of news media everywhere from the perspective of the home country. It is unrealistic to expect this to change much as a result of any action that the media themselves could take. In this matter the media overwhelmingly follow the lead of their own politicians and their perception of domestic opinion.

Summary

- There is generally more European news and news about other European countries in today's media, compared with 25 years ago.

- This news is still chosen on grounds of relevance to the 'home country' and presented according to the national perspective of the 'home' media.

- In practice, a good deal of news relating to Europe has everywhere become 'domesticated', rather than being treated as 'international' or 'foreign'.

12   Conclusion

The time has come to answer the broad questions about the media and Europe posed in the introductory section.

First, there is the question of whether 'the media' can be considered as a coherent institution in modern Europe. The first answer that comes to mind is a negative one, given the degree to which the particular media institutions and operations are so rooted in the national history, shaped by the political culture and guided by national priorities. Above all, they are governed in practice by *spatial* considerations, and the primary space is always nearer to home. However, a second answer would be much more qualified. The space in which we live is certainly expanding and the media themselves are increasingly able to bridge spatial gaps. The media institutions all have their local peculiarities, but they operate according to the same basic logic, and they deal with the same general categories of content everywhere. It has proved possible to make policy for European media and there is every reason to expect the range of policy to expand in due course. There are also many ties and interconnections of co-operation, exchange and ownership between European media, and these are likely to grow in number and strength. There are some features of European media that are distinctive and are likely to continue (for instance, public service broadcasting).

Do the mass media contribute more to conflict than to integration in Europe? There will be somewhat different answers depending on where one lives. In Britain, one might be inclined to think that the media predominantly contribute to conflict about and with Europe. If all European countries had the same experience it is unlikely that there could be an EU at all. However, it would be a mistake to assume that the media, even in Britain, are really so autonomous (despite press freedom) or so one-directional. Even Britain has come a long way toward accepting its European future, through necessity. Here, as elsewhere, the media are more likely to reflect and give voice to dominant and conflicting currents of opinion. This is part of their business in serving audiences and also serving political institutions. We can also be misled by considering the media only in respect of their political role. Ideas about Europe are as much, maybe more, shaped by other content, especially sport, entertainment and advertising. All of these are following a Europeanizing (and globalizing) trend, without any guiding policy and without any conflict or public resistance. Whatever else, we can dispense with the idea that the media could ever be an effective means of propaganda for (or against) Europe, guided by some political élite with its own agenda.

The media are not, in general, a great force for equality or fairness. They mainly exist to make money by satisfying majority tastes in a national society, especially the tastes of the more prosperous sections of society. They are mainly a product of members of the same classes they seek to serve, and often reflect their prejudiced and limited understandings. Media professions are still dominated by middle-class men and under-represent women and ethnic minorities as well as those of working-class origin. This situation changes only slowly as society changes. Despite this, as an institution of public life, giving access to diverse points of view, adhering to laws and certain conventions, the media are not generally and deliberately racist or unfair. Their range is wide enough to allow attention to injustice and some minority needs, if only sporadically. A more positive conclusion can be drawn about the newer (non-mass) media that have been made possible by new technology. It is easier than in the past for minorities of all kinds to provide for their own communication needs or to keep in touch with their homelands (if this applies). What remains problematic is the bridge between the self-sustaining minority and the wider society, without which genuine multiculturalism is hard to realize. The media in Europe seem now to serve exclusion and inclusion about equally, but working on non-convergent paths.

The fourth question has almost been answered by the preceding remarks. Mass media are generally a force for change because of their dedication to all things new, impelled by their own logic. They are also still linked to political systems and provide a conduit for political change as well as a reflection of public opinion (albeit imperfectly). Again, we should look at the outlook and interests of the people who typically make up the media professions. They are more likely to be young, prosperous and liberated rather than reactionary and resistant to change. But the media dedication to novelty and change (aside from the input of political and social élites) is inspired more by technological fantasy, futurism and the lure of new consumer markets than by commitment to progress or social change as a value in itself. It is quite probable that the 'European idea' belongs to the category of innovations that are favoured by the media professions and their dominant culture. Whether or not we should take comfort from this I'll leave to the reader.

References

Biltereyst, D. (1991) 'Resisting American hegemony: a comparative analysis of the reception of domestic and US fiction', *European Journal of Communication*, vol.6, no.4, pp.469–97.

Biltereyst, D. (1992) 'Language and culture as ultimate barriers', *European Journal of Communication*, vol.7, no.4, pp.517–40.

Blumler, J.G. (ed.) (1983) *Communicating Politics: Television and the First European Parliamentary Elections*, London, Sage.

Brants, K. (1998) 'Who's afraid of infotainment?', *European Journal of Communication*, vol.13, no.3, pp.315–36.

Brants, K. and Siune, K. (1998) 'Politicization in decline' in McQuail, D. and Siune, K. (eds) *Media Policy: Convergence; Commerce; Concentration*, London, Sage.

Cormack, M. (1998) 'Minority language media in Western Europe: preliminary considerations', *European Journal of Communication*, vol.13, no.1, pp.33–52.

European Audiovisual Observatory (1999) *Statistical Yearbook – Film, Television, Video and New Media in Europe*, Strasbourg, Council of Europe.

Gustafson, K.E. and Weibull, L. (1997) 'European newspaper readership: structure and development', *Communications*, vol.22, no.3, pp.249–73.

Heinderyckx, F. (1993) 'TV news programmes in West Europe: a comparative study', *European Journal of Communication*, vol.8, no.4, pp.425–50.

Liebes, T. and Livingstone, S. (1998) 'European soap operas: diversification of a genre', *European Journal of Communication*, vol.13, no.4, pp.147–80.

Machill, M. (1997) 'Background to French language policy and its impact on the media', *European Journal of Communication*, vol.12, no.4, pp.497–500.

McQuail, D. and Siune, K. (eds) (1998) *Media Policy: Convergence; Commerce; Concentration*, London, Sage.

Schlesinger, P. (1991) *Media, State and Nation*, London, Sage.

Slevin, J. (2000) *The Internet and Society*, London, Sage.

Tunstall, J. (1977) *The Media are American*, London, Constable.

Van Dijk, J.A.G.M. (1999) *The Network Society*, London, Sage.

Webster, F. (1995) *Images of the Information Society*, London, Routledge.

Wieten, J., Dahlgren, P. and Murdock, G. (eds) (2000) *The Changing Landscape of European Broadcasting*, London, Sage.

Further reading

Blumler, J.G. (ed.) (1992) *Television and the Public Interest: Vulnerable Values in West European Broadcasting*, London, Sage.

Euromedia Research Group (1997) *The Media in Western Europe: A Handbook*, London, Sage.

D'Haenens, L. and Saeys, F. (1998) 'Media dynamics and regulatory concerns in the digital age', *Communications Monograph*, vol.1, Berlin, Quintessenz Verlags.

Hoffman-Reim, W. (1996) *Regulating Media*, New York, Guildford Press.

Robillard, S. (1995) *Television in Europe: Regulatory Bodies*, European Institute for the Media, Monograph 19, London, John Libbey.

Schlesinger, P. (1991) *Media, State and Nation*, London, Sage.

Thompson, K. (ed.) (1997) *Media and Cultural Regulation*, London, Sage.

Van Dijk, J.A.G.M. (1999) *The Network Society*, London, Sage.

Chapter 8
Drugs and European governance

Eugene McLaughlin and Karim Murji

1 Introduction

The usage, control and regulation of illicit drugs play a significant part in the political, cultural and economic processes of European societies and European Union (EU) collaboration. In political terms, the issue of how drug use should be treated is often a matter of dispute between governments that advocate a crackdown and pressure groups that believe drug use should be a matter of individual choice not legal regulation. Conventional distinctions of the political left and right tend to break down when drug controls are considered, particularly given the degree of concordance witnessed between all the main political parties across Europe. In cultural terms, illegal drugs are closely connected with various forms of European popular culture, including film, music festivals, fashion and tourism. And there is evidence for the increased acceptability of certain illegal recreational drugs among younger people in Europe. This so-called 'normalization' of drug use underpins arguments for a 'cultural shift' in which drugs have become part of the mainstream, rather than a deviant aspect of everyday life. In economic terms, the drugs trade is part of the 'hidden economy' of illicit transactions; but, given the amount of drugs money circulating the globe, it is also embedded into key sectors of the legal economy. An estimated $120 billion from the drugs trade was laundered through the world's financial system in 1999 and 2000, although – as with much else where illicit transactions are concerned – this is a 'guesstimate'. Some economists argue that the illegal drugs 'multinationals' are among the most profitable actors in the international economy, helping to drive economic and cultural globalization.

This chapter will not consider the ongoing debate about whether there should be a controlled legalization of drugs in Europe. Its main aim is to examine the ways in which illicit drugs are governed 'from above', in the form of the nation state and transnational bodies, and 'from below', in the form of popular culture and new urban networks. In addition to a brief assessment of the state of the illegal drugs trade in Europe, the chapter addresses three main questions.

- To what extent is there harmony or diversity in the drugs laws and penalties of EU countries?

- How has the threat of drugs served to enhance the establishment of a pan-European law-enforcement complex?

- How do drugs and popular cultural forms – in particular, the drug ecstasy and 'rave culture' – suggest different notions of the place of drugs in Europe, and different ways of governing drug use?

What do we mean by the word 'drugs'? The World Health Organization Expert Committee on Drug Dependence (1993) defines drugs as 'any substance that, when taken into a living organism, may modify its perception, mood, cognition, behaviour or motor function'. This definition therefore covers legal substances such as nicotine and alcohol, as well as prescribed drugs such as tranquillizers. However, in this chapter 'drugs' refers to those substances that are cultivated, produced, processed, trafficked and supplied unlawfully and used illicitly. Legal substances are not part of this discussion, although it is widely recognized that they can be the cause of more health-related and social problems than the illicit drugs (Robson, 1999).

Another definitional issue is to distinguish between drug *supply* or trafficking, which is often linked with organized crime and transnational criminal networks, and drug *use*. Of course, there are areas where the two overlap; for instance, when one person buys a quantity of drugs to supply to a group of friends or associates. In legal terms, this could be considered a supplying offence, although it is sometimes thought of as 'social supply' and EU countries regard it in different ways. There is a confusing and changing array of terminology surrounding drugs and drug problems, but this chapter will use the most neutral term 'drug use' rather than 'addiction', 'dependence', 'abuse' or 'misuse'.

The significance of the preceding issues is that they underline the distinction and bifurcation in law and policy between serious organized crime and minor drug sellers, and between the 'problematic' and 'recreational' (or casual) use of drugs.

Summary

- Drugs are linked into and across the political, economic and cultural spheres of Europe.

- The term 'drugs' as used here refers to illicit drugs, and their regulation covers everything from minor use and possession to serious organized crime.

2 Assessing the state of drug use in Europe

In order to gauge the response to drugs by European governments it would be useful to have a comprehensive picture of the following: the prevalence of drug use; the main drugs involved; the changes in the types and quantities of drugs to be found in Europe; the identity of the drug takers; the numbers of people employed in the business; and the trends in production, trafficking, distribution and consumption. The range of data on drugs collected on a routine basis by governments and a multitude of national and international agencies, think tanks, working parties and pressure groups is considerable, although there are difficulties with comparing data collected by different agencies and different governments, a problem recognized by the recently established European Monitoring Centre for Drugs and Drug Addiction (EMCDDA, 1999).

It is important to be aware that there are serious gaps in the knowledge base about drugs. The criminalized status of drugs across Europe means that there is a very good reason for people not to be honest about drug use. This makes it difficult to establish reliable figures that can be compared across countries and over time. Related indicators – for example, the numbers of people in treatment for drug problems – do not solve the problem. Not all people with a drugs problem wish to, or are able to, access existing treatment facilities; for example, services for heroin users may not be suitable for cocaine users. In other cases, some or many users of drugs such as cannabis, amphetamines and ecstasy may not see themselves as having a 'drug problem'. Thus data on the usage of drugs is inevitably incomplete (Figure 8.1 overleaf).

Other indicators, such as the quantities of drugs seized by law-enforcement officials, or the numbers of people arrested and convicted for drugs offences, or the retail price of drugs, are also problematic. Whatever the quantity of drugs interdicted, an unknown percentage still gets through, and what that percentage is can only be guessed at. The type and quantity of drug seizures may reflect the nature of enforcement activity as much as it indicates any 'real' changes in illicit activity. Law-enforcement 'pressure points' on particular routes and drug types undoubtedly influence where and what types of drugs will be seized. For example, in the 1990s a lot of attention centred on cocaine smuggling into various parts of Europe because of concerns about the spread of crack-cocaine use and supply. But in the space of a few years, it became apparent that the concentration on cocaine had led to a large increase in heroin availability. If we apply market-based economic models to understanding drug trafficking, drug smugglers will always seek to use forms of importation that carry the lowest risk. As enforcement pressure bears down on particular drugs, routes, amounts or methods of importation, drug importers are likely to change or modify their methods. These 'modelling adaptations' indicate that drug markets and law enforcement are interlinked and help to shape one another. Consequently, there is a problem in separating the effects of

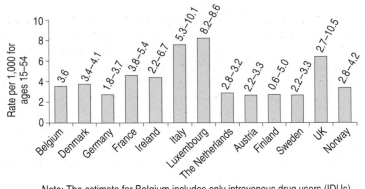

National prevalence estimates of problem drug use in some EU countries and Norway

Note: The estimate for Belgium includes only intravenous drug users (IDUs) and thus underestimates problem drug use. Some member states were unable to provide data.

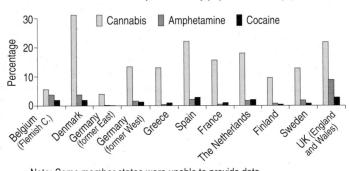

Lifetime experience of cannabis, amphetamine and cocaine use in some EU countries (measured by population surveys)

Note: Some member states were unable to provide data.

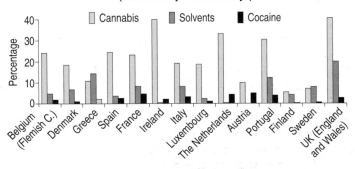

Lifetime experience of cannabis, solvent and cocaine use among 15- to 16-year-old schoolchildren in some EU countries (measured by school surveys)

Note: Some member states were unable to provide data.

Figure 8.1 Estimates of drug use in European countries, 1999 (EMCDDA, 1999)

supply reduction efforts on price from the other factors that affect price, such as demand (Murji, 1998).

A word of caution about the commonplace or taken-for-granted ways in which drugs are thought about is also worth including. Drugs are often represented as coming into Europe from 'outside'. This is seen in maps that depict the flow of drugs from South America, South-East Asia, the Middle East or North Africa into 'the West', with arrows that chart the movement of drugs such as cocaine and heroin (Figure 8.2). Note that the arrows are all one way. But what about synthetic drugs, such as ecstasy and amphetamines, that are produced in laboratories and are not derived from plants? If we took these drugs into account, the arrows would be rather different and the two-way flows of drugs across national boundaries would look much more complex (Figure 8.3 overleaf).

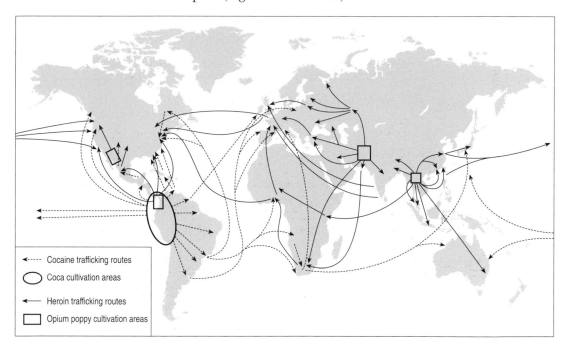

Figure 8.2 Global trafficking routes for heroin and cocaine

It is relatively unusual to see maps such as Figure 8.3. Our purpose in including it is to begin to problematize some of the dominant discourses about where drugs come from, and to introduce the idea of internal trafficking within EU member states.

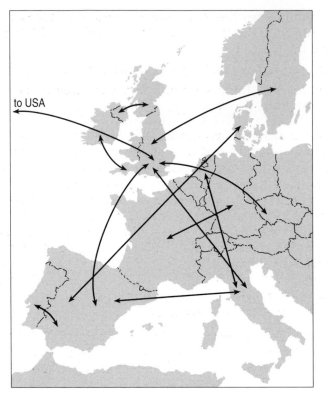

Figure 8.3   Ecstasy and amphetamine flows in Europe

Summary

- There are difficulties in establishing and comparing rates of drug use in different EU countries, just as there are difficulties in estimating the amounts of drugs entering individual European countries.

- Drugs are linked into a discourse of 'otherness', which imagines that they come into Europe from 'outside'.

3   Drug control and legal diversity within the EU

In common with almost every country in the world, the nation states of the EU agree that illicit drugs are a serious social problem. The main reasons stated for tackling the illicit drug trade are because it fuels serious organized crime, generates acquisitive forms of criminality and compounds other social problems.

European governments share a common vision of member states progressively freed from the harm caused by the misuse of illicit drugs. This entails a combination of:

- national and international legal penalties for dealing in drugs

- treatment and rehabilitation programmes for drug users

- education and preventative initiatives for 'at-risk' groups.

However, there remain significant differences within the EU in how member states classify and deal with drugs in legal terms, and in the precise mix of enforcement, treatment and prevention used. Some countries make more use of criminal justice deterrents and penal sanctions than others, and there are considerable differences in the extent to which drug users are processed through the criminal justice system and in the penalties attached to the possession of particular drugs. Some member states make a distinction in policy and practice between trafficking and selling and the use of drugs, and between 'soft' and 'hard' drugs. In each jurisdiction the blend of drugs policies and practices can be affected by the varied and shifting relationship between competing welfare and law-enforcement agencies.

An Independent Inquiry into the Misuse of Drugs Act 1971 by the Police Foundation (2000) used the categories of drug *use*, *possession* and *trafficking* to summarize the position in six EU countries (Table 8.1 overleaf).

As we saw in Figure 8.1, cannabis is the most commonly used illegal drug in Europe. Cannabis remains illegal across Europe, although member states adopt a variety of responses to it: some tolerate certain forms of possession and consumption, some apply administrative penalties or sanctions and some use penal sanctions. This range of responses creates a heterogeneous legal map for the regulation of cannabis in Europe (Figure 8.4 on page 238).

Hence, as a whole, diversity rather than commonality marks the ways in which European governments regulate drug use and supply. The question of whether the EU should seek to harmonize the approaches or opt for a particular 'model' has not been broached. Drug control is an increasingly important part of intergovernmental activity, but it may be that the specific methods employed in individual EU countries reflect the subsidiarity principle, which states that supranational EU action is justified only when:

- there are transnational considerations

- a lack of action would be in contravention of an EU treaty

- action would be beneficial for reasons of effect and scale

- there is a need to harmonize norms and standards to achieve treaty objectives.

Table 8.1   Drug-related acts that are allowed, prohibited, administratively responded to or criminally punished in six European states

	Italy	France	Spain	The Netherlands	Germany	Sweden
Use						
Drug use *per se* (i.e. in private).	Not prohibited after 1993 referendum. (Prohibited only between 1990 and 1993; never criminalized.)	Prohibited and criminalized. Up to 1 year in prison or fine or diversion to medical treatment.	Unlawful, but not punishable.	Not prohibited, but see below.	Not prohibited.	Prohibited and criminalized. Law provides maximum sentence of 3 years, but in practice fine or 6 months.
Public drug use.	As above (not differentiated).	Not differentiated.	A serious administrative offence (fine, forfeiture etc.).	A 'lesser offence' in some local jurisdictions.	Not an offence. Administrative order against nuisance, or treated as possession or supply.	Not differentiated.
Possession						
Possession *per se* (i.e. in private).	Prohibited. Administrative infringement regardless of quantity (unless seen as trafficking, when criminalized).	Possession for own use has no legal definition in French law. Possession is seen in connection with either use or supply.	Unlawful but not an administrative offence, unless in public (c.f. below).	Prohibited and criminalized, but expediency principle means no prosecution in practice.	Criminalized, but prosecutorial or pre/post-verdict de-penalization is possible for small amounts.	As for use, although prison more likely (up to 3 years) if quantities indicate supply.
Possession in public places.	As above.	As above.	Serious administrative offence.	As above.	Not differentiated.	As above.
Obtaining a prohibited drug.	As above – except for cultivation, which is criminalized.	As above.	No criminal offence if for personal use; criminal offence if for resale or trafficking.	Criminal offence. Includes cannabis cultivation, which leads to confiscation.	Criminal offence. Includes cultivation of cannabis or psychoactive mushrooms.	As above.

Trafficking					
Small/retail: giving or selling to a drug user.	Criminal offence. Up to 4 years in prison for soft drugs, 6 years for hard drugs (unless, say, sharing between users in a group, which is an administrative infringement, like private possession).	Misdemeanour. Up to 5 years in prison.	In general, a criminal offence. Soft drugs mean 1 to 3 years in prison, hard drugs 3 to 9 years plus fines.	Giving or exchanging may be treated as supply, which means up to 2 years in prison.	For users and others selling small amounts, a 'drug trade' misdemeanour. Up to 5 years in prison.	Up to 3 years in prison.
Medium/distribution: non-small amounts (e.g. not retail sale).	Criminal offence. Up to 6 years in prison for soft drugs, up to 20 years for hard drugs.	Intermediate between above and below. Up to 10 years in prison (includes users bringing drugs into the country).	Intermediate between above and below.	Up to 12 years in prison (the maximum under the Opium Act). Expediency principle: coffee shops a special case (non-application of criminal law).	For possession or traffic of 'non-small amounts', up to 15 years in prison.	Intermediate penalties (see above and below).
Big or organized crime, or otherwise aggravated offences.	Up to 30 years in prison for aggravated circumstances of trafficking, 20–24 years basic penalty for directing an organized trafficking group.	Up to 30 years or life for being a manager, or for taking part in organized importation, exportation or production.	First degree aggravations, for big quantities or members of crime groups: soft drugs 3–4.5 years, hard drugs 9–13.5 years. Second degree aggravations, for leaders or extreme gravity: soft drugs 4.5–6.75 years, hard drugs 13.5–20.25 years (plus fines).	Parallel organized crime charges almost always applied in cases of international trafficking, adding a third to Opium Law penalty: total then up to 16 years in prison.	Minimum 5 years in prison for trafficking within a gang, up to a maximum of 15 years.	Up to 10 years if involving criminal organization, unscrupulous behaviour or large amounts.

(condensed and adapted from Dorn and Jamieson, 2000)

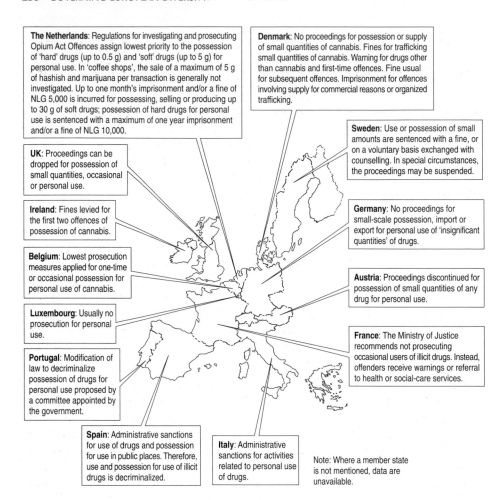

The Netherlands: Regulations for investigating and prosecuting Opium Act Offences assign lowest priority to the possession of 'hard' drugs (up to 0.5 g) and 'soft' drugs (up to 5 g) for personal use. In 'coffee shops', the sale of a maximum of 5 g of hashish and marijuana per transaction is generally not investigated. Up to one month's imprisonment and/or a fine of NLG 5,000 is incurred for possessing, selling or producing up to 30 g of soft drugs; possession of hard drugs for personal use is sentenced with a maximum of one year imprisonment and/or a fine of NLG 10,000.

Denmark: No proceedings for possession or supply of small quantities of cannabis. Fines for trafficking small quantities of cannabis. Warning for drugs other than cannabis and first-time offences. Fine usual for subsequent offences. Imprisonment for offences involving supply for commercial reasons or organized trafficking.

Sweden: Use or possession of small amounts are sentenced with a fine, or on a voluntary basis exchanged with counselling. In special circumstances, the proceedings may be suspended.

UK: Proceedings can be dropped for possession of small quantities, occasional or personal use.

Germany: No proceedings for small-scale possession, import or export for personal use of 'insignificant quantities' of drugs.

Ireland: Fines levied for the first two offences of possession of cannabis.

Belgium: Lowest prosecution measures applied for one-time or occasional possession for personal use of cannabis.

Austria: Proceedings discontinued for possession of small quantities of any drug for personal use.

Luxembourg: Usually no prosecution for personal use.

France: The Ministry of Justice recommends not prosecuting occasional users of illicit drugs. Instead, offenders receive warnings or referral to health or social-care services.

Portugal: Modification of law to decriminalize possession of drugs for personal use proposed by a committee appointed by the government.

Spain: Administrative sanctions for use of drugs and possession for use in public places. Therefore, use and possession for use of illicit drugs is decriminalized.

Italy: Administrative sanctions for activities related to personal use of drugs.

Note: Where a member state is not mentioned, data are unavailable.

Figure 8.4 EU responses to minor drug-related offences, 1999

(EMCDDA, 1999)

Summary

- EU countries classify and regulate drugs in diverse ways, and there are differences of emphasis between competing medical, educational and enforcement approaches.

- The ways in which EU states regulate cannabis – the most widely used illicit drug – produce a heterogeneous legal map.

- While drug control is an important part of intergovernmental activity, the extent of the diversity among EU states is an example of the subsidiarity principle in action.

4 Governance from above: the international drug-control system

The application of terms such as 'globalization' and 'transnationalization' to describe drug trafficking is relatively recent, although it is the case that drug control has been part of an 'international system' of control for nearly a century. Four aspects of this control are considered here, and taken together they illustrate global and transnational dimensions of drug control that transcend the EU as a geopolitical entity.

First, in considering the international origins of drug controls it should be noted that for most of the nineteenth century there were no controls on the production, sale, import and export or possession of drugs. At this time, the opium trade played a major role in the economic, political and military strategies of the major colonial powers. This highly sophisticated and profitable trade formed the basis for the development of a specifically capitalist transnational trading system. Britain, the main drug producer and trafficker, fought the 'Opium wars' against China in the name of 'free trade' because China wanted to stop British companies importing opium (Goodman et al., 1995; Berridge, 1999).

Misgivings about the forced trade of opium to China and the lack of regulation came from a number of sources in different jurisdictions. Doctors and pharmacists sought to extend their professional power by seeking the authority to control the availability of drugs. Moral crusaders saw drugs as linked to vice and worried about the deleterious and demoralizing effects of drugs. In the USA, Netherlands and the UK, for example, the problem of opium was said to be linked with the small Chinese communities in these countries, through fears about the effect of 'opium dens' on the rest of the population. This is one of many instances in which the threat posed by drugs has been associated with particular minority groups, and in particular with racialized minorities, 'foreigners' and 'outsiders' (Kohn, 1992).

The pressure for prohibitionist policies and criminalization built up through a number of international conventions from the first decade of the twentieth century. The deliberations of the meeting of the International Opium Commission in Shanghai in 1909 resulted in the Hague Opium Convention of 1912, the first treaty to attempt to control opium and cocaine on an international basis. In 1920, the League of Nations assumed responsibility for the Hague Convention and a second international opium convention came into force in 1928. The United Nations assumed responsibility for the League of Nations' drug control strategies in 1946 (McAllister, 1999).

Second, the contemporary global framework of drug control is set by the United Nations. All the member states of the EU are signatories to three mutually supportive and complementary United Nations international drug conventions:

- The Single Convention on Narcotic Drugs (1961)
- The Convention on Psychotropic Substances (1971)
- The UN Convention against Illicit Traffic in Narcotic Drugs and Psychotropic Substances (1988).

These conventions form part of the international system of drug control that ties nation states together, and they are one of the main reasons why no individual state can move all the way toward legalizing drugs. The conventions set out agreements on drug controls and require states to limit drug use to medical and scientific purposes; to establish sanctions or punishments for actions contrary to a law or regulation following from the conventions; and to prohibit and criminalize drug supply. However, this does not mean that all the signatories have harmonized their drug control policies. Some countries have opted not to accept some parts of the UN conventions. For instance, Article 3(2) of the 1988 Convention asserts that every state should: 'establish a criminal offence under its domestic law, when committed intentionally, [for] possession ... for personal consumption'. But, in practice, this Article is interpreted in the light of national laws and constitutional principles, which is why there is so much diversity in the legal responses of EU countries, as we saw in Section 3.

Third, all the EU nations are members of the International Criminal Police Organization (Interpol), which was established in 1923 to promote mutual assistance between police forces, within the limits of the laws existing in different countries. As drug trafficking has come to be seen as a transnational criminal activity, Interpol has sought to position itself as a key player in intergovernmental law enforcement. However, Interpol is not founded on an international treaty and it is an intelligence communications network, not an executive law-enforcement agency operating across national borders. In the field of drugs control, Interpol plays a role in transmitting information on crime, drug trafficking and seizures to the law-enforcement agencies of the 177 states that subscribe to it, assembling criminal intelligence on drug trends and the modus operandi of traffickers, and working with other international and regional organizations.

Fourth, although this book is concerned with Europe, it is important to mention, albeit briefly, the pivotal role of the USA in international law enforcement. There are several significant aspects to this role. The US Drug Enforcement Administration (DEA) is responsible for enforcing the country's controlled substance laws and regulations, and is unequivocally opposed to the decriminalization or legalization of drugs. In addition to its law-enforcement duties, it promotes the message that drugs are inextricably linked to crime, violence and social disintegration. It has a network of over 200 operational agents located in 60 countries around the world. Terms such as 'narco-diplomacy' and the 'narco-enforcement complex' have been used to suggest the ways in which the USA's highly militarized global 'war against drugs' has driven law enforcement abroad, for instance into parts of South America and South-East Asia. In the name of reducing drug consumption in the USA and in western nations, the DEA aims to reduce drug cultivation, destroy laboratories, disrupt drug cartels and the flow of drugs, and interdict drug shipments in source and transit countries. The drugs and foreign policy interests of the USA have sometimes coincided and sometimes clashed, producing a strange and complex picture of drugs in international politics (Belenko, 2000). For instance, it has been suggested that US governments have supported various authoritarian regimes thought to have been involved in drug trafficking. Another point is that the transatlantic axis has sometimes been important to UK governments, partly as a counter-weight to the EU. This causes problems for Europe because the UK's criminal justice initiatives have had a tendency to emphasize a tough public 'law and order' stance that stresses enforcement above treatment and prevention as the best way to deal with drugs. Through meetings of the world's biggest economies, the UK and the USA have promoted international co-operation on measures involving asset seizure and anti-money laundering strategies, both of which have been closely connected with the proceeds of drug trafficking. Finally, in the post-Cold War era an expansive new US-driven 'security politics' has developed, combining the domestic and global with police forces and military concerns. NATO remains the cornerstone of transatlantic security, but a broader and widening agenda for international security has emerged, with various agreements between the USA and the EU committing both sides to co-operate on international crime, terrorism, drug trafficking, mass migration, environmental issues and nuclear safety concerns.

So, locating drugs and drug trafficking in the international arena means that it is difficult to disassociate the drugs agenda from discussions about money laundering, terrorism, immigration and so on. The precise place of drugs in all of this is open to debate, and there is a view that the official discourse linking these issues together may obscure more than it reveals. However, it certainly seems to be a central part of the agenda of building a transnational law-enforcement complex.

Summary

- Drugs have been the focus of an international system of drug control for nearly a century.

- United Nations conventions form a framework for international drug control, but individual nations can interpret these conventions in terms of their own constitutional principles.

- There is a historic and developing transatlantic axis between the USA and individual European countries and, more recently, between the USA and the EU in the field of drug control.

5   Governance from above: the European law-enforcement complex

This section looks at various ways in which drugs have helped to drive a European law-enforcement agenda. Drugs have often been at the forefront in making the case for new and far-reaching changes in law enforcement, producing innovative legislation for asset seizure and forfeiture, and an array of international assistance treaties between governments that authorize mutual powers of search, seizure and assistance between law-enforcement agencies. Drugs have driven the nationalization of certain police functions across Europe and their transnationalization through Europol. In the post-Cold War 1990s, the intelligence services also began playing a more formal role in drug enforcement. For these reasons drugs have been second only to terrorism as the major stimulus to developments in law enforcement. While these developments are mainly at the level of intelligence collection, analysis, control and dissemination (as distinct from operational law enforcement), Dorn et al. (1992) have stressed the role of intelligence as a 'Trojan horse' for operational innovations in European policing.

5.1   'Fortress Europe'

Part of the developing identity of the EU has been constituted through constructing barriers against various 'out-groups' or 'others', including migrants and drug traffickers; indeed, the two have sometimes been treated as coterminous or identical. Within Europe there were fears that the post-1992 opening up of internal movement within the EU would facilitate the movement of various groups seen as threatening the stability of Europe. Calls for pan-European measures against drug trafficking and a high-tech 'ring of steel' around Europe have heightened the spatial conception of a Europe menaced on all sides by the excluded and the 'other' (Cohen, 2000). In the last two decades, the groups and nationalities labelled as prime movers of drugs include the Colombian cocaine cartels, 'yardies' from Jamaica and Nigerian/West-African drug couriers. Following the collapse of the former Soviet Union, the fall of the Berlin Wall and the wars in the Balkans, new threats have been identified. Drugs, crime and corruption are seen as problems that originate in the Russian Mafiosi from the East, while at the southern borders of the EU there are concerns about Turkish heroin and Albanian and North-African drug sellers entering through Italy, Spain and Portugal.

The racialization of drugs is integral – not incidental – to the development of controls. It is part of the construction of an idea of 'the West' that is threatened by and has to stand against the forces of barbarism that make up 'the rest' (Hall, 1992). Consequently, as with discussions about immigration and, increasingly, refugees and asylum seekers, drugs are discursively constructed in terms of an invasion or flooding metaphor. Drugs are seen to be 'pouring' into the EU, so that it is at risk of being 'awash' with or 'swamped' by them. The 'dangerous otherness' of drugs has been connected with both terrorism and illegal immigration in a discursive chain that enables politicians and others to call for enhanced border controls to contain and counter these external threats. National and transnational security discussions tie together various demands for controls to monitor and prevent the movement of all 'undesirables'. Critics have called this the creation of 'Fortress Europe', in which all such groups are categorized together in order to keep everyone, from refugees to terrorists, out of the 'safe European home'. This has been described as a form of racism, 'which cannot tell one black from another, a citizen from an immigrant, an immigrant from a refugee – and classes all Third World peoples as immigrants and refugees, and all immigrants and refugees as terrorists and drug dealers' (Sivanandan, 1988, p.9).

5.2 The Europeanization of law enforcement

As has been noted already, arguments for enhancing law enforcement to combat the threat of what is seen as an increasingly transnational and organized criminality and drug trafficking have a long history. Throughout the late 1980s chief police officers were active in calling for more co-ordination of policing across Europe and the creation of federal investigative organizations. The need to control transnational criminal networks was almost always cited as the main reason for these measures.

The idea that drug markets and drug trafficking are organized in tiers or in a pyramidal structure controlled by a few at the top is commonplace, and it is suggested that law enforcement needs to match or 'mirror' this organizational structure in order to be effective. But there are at least three questions or problems with this model. First, the notion of tiered or highly organized drug trafficking has been questioned by research that indicates that drug markets are fluid and messy, and do not necessarily conform to a pyramidal structure. Intense competition in drug markets produces fragmentation rather than cohesion. Second, there are reasons to at least question the assumption that crime and drug trafficking are becoming global phenomena. The most obvious reasons given for this belief – ease of movement, profitability and the search for new markets – are not new. Indeed, it could be argued that developments such as bilateral extradition, asset seizure and enhanced co-operation in world banking against money laundering all make cross-national operations more difficult and therefore more dangerous. The idea that globalization provides new opportunities for global crime and criminal networks has almost become a part of common sense. But it may be that crime itself drives globalization – of enforcement networks, laws, treaties and so on. Hence, third, there is an in-built 'logic of escalation'. If drug trafficking is truly a transcontinental enterprise, why stop at the nation state, or at Europe?

An approach to drugs based upon law and policing is a cornerstone of the Justice and Home Affairs pillar of European co-ordination. Member states have agreed to extensive international co-operation between law-enforcement agencies in seeking to combat drugs and drug trafficking. And the threat of drugs has been the basis for exceptional developments in policing, the law and penalties. This can be seen in the nationalization and transnationalization of policing functions and agencies, such as the formation of Europol, the passing of legislation to seize financial assets and the introduction of heavy penalties for serious drugs offences.

Allied with debates about globalization, the growth of transnational law enforcement and policy making have been seen to mark the limits of nation states, which have become 'stretched' or 'hollowed out' in their capacity to govern within national boundaries. However, in law enforcement, there has been a 'thickening' of state regulation alongside the development of more intrusive and more punitive measures, through intergovernmental co-operation, information sharing and mutual assistance between states. Within the EU a period of building institutional capacity has seen the spread of a network of overlapping and discrete organizations (see Figure 8.5). The lines of accountability between them are unclear, and the lack of accountability, control and public debate over some of these developments is commonly referred to as the 'democratic deficit' (McLaughlin, 1992).

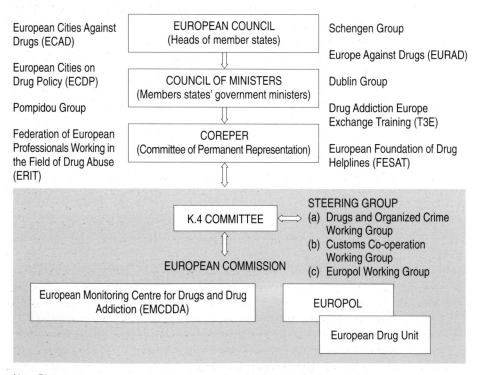

Note: Diagram shows groups inside (attached) and outside (detached) the formal EU structure.

Figure 8.5 Drug-related organizations in Europe

International police co-operation is not a new phenomenon, but since the 1970s there have been several significant developments that have set the context for the unfolding framework.

First, an early example of collective collaboration was the organization of European police co-operation known as TREVI (Terrorism, Radicalism, and Violence International). Established in 1975, TREVI – which strictly speaking existed quite separately from European Community institutions – sought to assist the interior and justice departments of member states to work together more effectively to combat terrorism. Soon the remit was expanded to include serious crime, including drugs.

Second, as we have seen, the case for the opening up of internal borders in the EU to facilitate the free movement of labour has gone hand-in-hand with the argument that this must be balanced by increased powers to track and monitor the movement of various individuals and groups. A specific mechanism for this is the Schengen Treaty, although not all EU nations subscribe to it. In June 1985, at Schengen in Luxembourg, five EU member states (Germany, France, Belgium, Luxembourg and the Netherlands) signed an agreement for the gradual elimination of frontier controls between these countries and, in doing so, to increase police co-operation and information exchange. Thus, alongside a discourse of freedom the agreement also articulated the need for compensatory measures to guarantee that 'external' borders were adequately policed. This triggered a joint European internal security project, justified by the threat posed by increased organized crime, terrorists, drug traffickers and illegal immigrants. The signatories of the Schengen Treaty granted each other's police forces the right of pursuit and arrest across frontiers. They backed the creation of the Schengen Information System, a computerized service that would give police and immigration officials a multinational database, notably on suspect persons, stolen vehicles and forged money. The system was deemed to be particularly important for policing the movements of 'third country' nationals entering the EU at the external borders of 'Schengenland'.

Third, the 1991 Maastricht Treaty sanctioned the development of an EU-wide policing agency. In 1993 Europol was established as an information base to provide a mechanism to pass sensitive criminal intelligence from one police force to another, to analyse intelligence across member states and to support police operations directed by national police forces. Because it was deemed politically sensitive – it might be seen to undermine the actions of national police agencies – Europol was prevented from intervening in police operations within member states. The first stage of the Europol project was to establish a European Drugs Unit, based in The Hague, to tackle the trade in drug smuggling through the co-ordination of the information and intelligence emanating from national police forces. The 1994 Essen Summit decided to expand the terms of reference of the European Drugs Unit to encompass illegal immigration, trafficking in human beings, car theft and the smuggling of nuclear materials. It also agreed to closer co-operation with former Eastern European states. The Europol Convention was published in July 1995 and the Europol Treaty was launched for ratification later that year.

As part of that process there is a renewed commitment within the EU to closer co-operation on international crime, particularly the drugs trade, involving the harmonization of sentencing for drugs, a crackdown on cross-border drugs trade and the transformation of Europol into a federal FBI-style police force with the power to operate across national frontiers. By June 1998 the fifteen EU member states had ratified the Europol Treaty.

Subsequent developments have consolidated both the broad outlines and finer points of these three developments. The EU summit in Tampere, Finland in October 1999 was the first held specifically to discuss the harmonization of justice and home affairs policies and practices across the EU. It agreed to adopt far-reaching and long-term common plans on policing, immigration and asylum designed to improve co-operation. These included a task force to crack down on criminal gangs taking advantage of the abolition of border controls, sort out the jumble of national criminal laws and address the lack of co-ordination between police forces.

5.3   Some problems with governance from above

Before leaving this section let us consider a few problems associated with governance from above and the view that drugs are driving an increasing tendency toward political and legal homogeneity in the EU.

First, the emphasis on erecting and maintaining stronger external border controls has gone hand-in-hand with the argument for greater freedom of internal movement. But member states are divided about whether they can trust each other to maintain the barriers that are supposed to act as a control. The idea that there are easy points of entry for global drug cartels, especially through Greece, Turkey, Spain, Portugal and Italy, presents these countries as the 'weak links' or the 'soft underbelly' in the European security cordon. Hence some northern European countries such as Germany and the UK see themselves as unable to rely on the border controls of southern European states. Indeed this was one of the reasons why the UK held out against the 'borderless Europe' that was supposed to have been initiated at the end of 1992. So it can be seen that there are serious political fault lines in the building and the realization of a common European approach to drugs.

Second, there is the distinction between supranational and inter-governmental policies and strategies. The former are characterized by joint working and sharing of sovereignty; the latter place more emphasis on co-operation between individual nation states (**Bromley, 2001**). The law-enforcement measures against drugs agreed at EU level are often couched in terms of increased co-operation between the police forces of member states. While this suggests that law enforcement is increasingly intergovernmental, we should recall that there are tensions between this approach and the moves toward a pan-European police force. The heated argument about whether there should be a joint European military force can be seen as a prototype of the argument there would be if a genuine European police force with operational powers to act in any member state was proposed, although there may well be more support for it in some EU countries (for example, those in Schengen) than in others. In this sense, the Schengen countries have already initiated the 'two-speed' development of European institutions. For 'eurosceptics', the need for action on organized crime and drugs is balanced against concerns about the creation of a European super-state, in which individual nation states are reduced to little more than regional status.

Third, it may be that advances in technology will raise unprecedented problems for supranational or intergovernmental modes of regulation. While we should be wary of 'technological determinism', the growth of the internet has raised new and unprecedented regulatory problems. For governments, there is a problem that what they may wish to control or prohibit operates outside of their political and legal jurisdictions; and the same problem applies to intergovernmental bodies. Beyond that, there are the additional problems that the internet proliferates very quickly (so shutting down one site may only displace the problem). It is not surprising that the internet has been identified with changing drug cultures. While there is little research on what is, in any case, a fast-moving scene, one 'guesstimate' is that there are around 17,000 sites concerned with drugs. It has been suggested that some of these are sites used by drug traffickers, while others facilitate the purchase of drugs online.

Summary

- A 'Fortress Europe' mentality has informed the strengthening of controls at the boundaries of the EU in the name of controlling and preventing the movement of undesirable goods and commodities.
- The emphasis on law enforcement as the means to control drug supply has led to the development of a Europeanized policing network.
- Differences between EU nations, as well as new technologies, are responsible for gaps in the 'Fortress', both in discursive terms and in practice.

6   Governance from below

There are tensions and conflicts associated with drugs, and an emphasis on transnationalization and law enforcement can neglect the fact that drug use is governed in other ways. This section looks at a variety of governance mechanisms 'from below'. These include public opinion about drug control in Europe; the spread of a Euro (and global) youth drugs culture, particularly associated with 'club cultures'; and, finally, the role of key European cities in responding to and managing drugs. As with law enforcement, these forms of governance from below produce harmonization and differentiation within Europe.

6.1   Drugs and public opinion

To what extent can it be argued that the EU-wide innovations on drugs are based on and driven by public demands for politicians to take action? This question is more difficult to answer than it may seem at first sight. How do public concerns get translated into political programmes and policies? And which concerns are taken up: the most pressing ones, the ones where something can most easily be done, or the ones where it is easiest to suggest action, even if that action will not have much impact on the ground? These questions suggest that we should not simply take at face value claims that drugs policies reflect public priorities.

The European Commission's regular surveys of public opinion in all member states are published in *Eurobarometer* (Figure 8.6). Few of the questions are explicitly about drugs, but the subject does come up in citizens' fears and concerns and in the extent of support for joint decision making. In 1997, the increase in drugs and organized crime came second in a list of fears that people had about the building of Europe. Under the Justice and Home Affairs heading, respondents were asked about the extent of their support for joint EU action on drug trafficking, immigration policy and rules for asylum. Across the EU as a whole, seven out of ten people supported joint EU action against drug trafficking, and of the three issues raised this was the one that had the most support, although the extent of the support varied across member states.

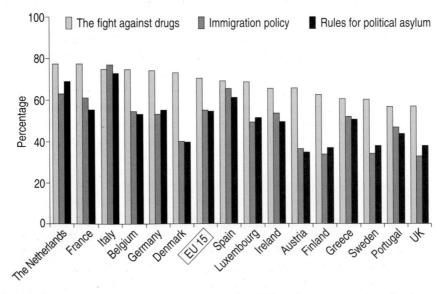

Figure 8.6 Amsterdam Treaty: support for EU action concerning Justice and Home Affairs, 1997

(European Commission, 1997)

A 1998 *Eurobarometer* survey asked about priorities for action by the European Parliament (European Commission, 1998). The survey found that the fight against drug trafficking and crime was among the top four priorities in all member states, but, again, the extent of the support varied within Europe. It came top in two countries, Sweden and the UK, where support for it was almost twice that in Spain and Italy. There were substantial majorities for the views that the fight against drugs is more an EU than a national responsibility and that fighting organized crime and drug trafficking should be priorities for the EU.

However, we should note that these questions frequently combine drugs with organized crime, and that they focus on drug trafficking. It is possible that questions about ways of dealing with and responding to drug use and users would reveal more variation, perhaps including a greater stress on treatment and prevention than on law enforcement.

6.2 The emergence of a European drugs and dance culture

Politicians, police officers and drugs agencies periodically point out that the majority of people do not take illicit drugs and do not approve of drug taking and stress that firm policies are required to protect young people. However, we must also acknowledge the evidence that an increasing percentage of people have tried drugs, and that young people in particular are willing to both tolerate and experiment with illicit drugs for 'recreational purposes'. As we saw in Figure 8.1, over 30 per cent of people in Denmark and over 20 per cent in Spain and the UK have tried cannabis at some time. The figures are even higher if we focus on young people.

One way of accounting for the rise in drug consumption can be found in this quotation from the UN International Drug Control Programme.

> Perhaps the most striking aspect to emerge from studying drug abuse trends among young people is the increasing homogenization of drug behaviour patterns around the world – that is, the gap between patterns of drug taking in western industrialized countries and those in developing countries, or those in transition, seems to have narrowed. While western youth continues to provide a model that other nations follow – in drugs as in many aspects of socio-cultural behaviour – the basic trends seem remarkably similar. This is evident in the pervasiveness of a consumer driven youth drug culture, in the falling of age of first drug use and in the increasing availability of drugs and different drug types, all of which point to a 'normalization' or apparent acceptability of drug taking behaviour around the world. ... Drugs are just one ingredient of

an irreverent, image-conscious culture which embraces music, fashion, films, and a language which is incomprehensible except to those in the know.

(United Nations, 1997, p.85)

Here we see a different kind of harmonization and, perhaps, Europeanization from that witnessed at the law-enforcement level. Youth cultures are intertwined and each is marked, in terms of authenticity, by the locality and conditions of its production. Cultural flows, commercial and otherwise, carry the key representations of any given subculture, including music, clothes, language, literature and politics. It is through these continually evolving flows that drug use has become an embedded, 'normalized' part of local and transnational youth cultures and the broader 'ways of life' of popular culture. These cultures provide alternative understandings of the meaning and significance of drugs and suggest alternative ways of governing drug use. Since the 1960s, youth cultures and recreational drugs have been interlinked across Europe. The changes in popular culture and the expansion of new media outlets have meant that drugs have become an almost routine part of public discourse. Accompanying this, there is certainly evidence of increased drug taking, although, as we have seen, public attitudes to drugs remain mixed. Nonetheless, some observers believe that the acceptability of drug use among key groups means that supranational measures are out of step with the normalization of drugs within an emergent Euro youth/popular culture.

In the 1990s, there was a lot of news media attention about crack-cocaine, but the drug of the decade was undoubtedly ecstasy (the popular name for the chemical substance MDMA). Ecstasy surfaced in Spain in the early 1980s, when young people across Europe coming home from holidays in Ibiza reported a new, vague and elusive dance culture that was mixing different musical genres to produce what became known as 'Acid House' or the 'Balearic Sound'. At the same time, innovative musical formats such as 'House', 'Garage' and 'Trance' were moving from New York, Chicago and Detroit into clubs in various European cities. Musicians and DJs in European cities sought to reinvent this sound and feeling and to forge the disparate strands together (Garratt, 1998; Reynolds, 1998). A key feature of the emergent dance culture that resulted was the affiliation between electronic dance music, the gay club scene and the 'designer' drug ecstasy. Places such as Ibiza became symbolic reference points in contemporary youth culture (mirroring the role conventionally accorded to the city of Amsterdam), and they came to represent sites of relative deregulation and permissiveness.

The popularity of ecstasy in the 'rave' and club scenes introduced a generation of young Europeans to the pleasures and risks of taking drugs. The distinction between the consumption and supply of drugs blurred as young people engaged in forms of 'social supply' (buying drugs to pass on to friends) that could legally be regarded as drug trafficking. At its height, the popularity of the 'rave culture' provided a clear example of the disjunction between political and law-enforcement rhetoric about winning the 'war' against drugs and the experiences and attitudes of the so-called 'Chemical Generation'. What followed, in the UK at least, was a period that included the 1988 'Summer of Love' and the propagation of 'Smiley Culture', in which a yellow circle with a face became a ubiquitous part of popular culture. Indeed, at this time rave culture seemed to be regarded as largely harmless, and it was claimed that ecstasy and club culture helped to break down class, gender and racial boundaries. Ecstasy seemed to find some surprising outlets, and it was even thought that a decline in football hooliganism was due to the 'chilled out' effects of the drug.

Ecstasy production increased, and as supply expanded the price came down.

> In the late 1980s, Ecstasy production was a relatively expensive process and very little production was actually being carried out in the UK, but by the early 1990s European and British Ecstasy laboratories had become highly commercial drug factories pumping out more and more of the drug. As a result, the price of Ecstasy fell dramatically from £15–20 in 1987 to as little as £7 in 1996.
>
> (Joseph, 2000, p.43)

Here we can begin to see the ways in which a DIY club culture and ecstasy became an increasingly commercial concern. And for some of the earliest participants in the scene, this process signalled the 'beginning of the end' of a culture that had still not fully crystallized in the public consciousness. 'Abby', a young gay man who first took ecstasy in 1987, felt that: 'When it [ecstasy and Acid House] grew people saw a chance to make a lot of money – clothing, records, clubs and drugs. ... Once the entertainment industry saw there was money to be made, Acid House died ...' (cited in Dorn et al., 1992, p.9).

In subsequent years, a new generation of entrepreneurs promoted 'raves' in fields and disused land. A complex system was initiated to inform would-be ravers about the time and location of such events, including messages on pirate radio stations and telephone numbers that could be called to obtain details of the venue. Advances in technology – especially mobile phones – also helped to drive the movement. At first, the authorities became aware of raves in fields through the build up of traffic jams on motorways at unusual times, often the early hours of the morning, and a barrage of sound that was audible several miles away.

> To the unattuned ear, it can sound at best numbingly repetitive, and at worst mindless. It usually begins with a dissonant shudder and builds, often in the space of one ten-minute mix, into something relentlessly bombastic, a noise that is brutally technological and utterly primal. These records are designed purely for the dance-floor and, increasingly, seem structured to

enhance the Ecstasy experience, becoming an integral part of the extrasensory overload that is the very essence of the rave experience.

At the centre of the maelstrom, when the rave is in full flow and you are surrounded by 5,000 similar souls, with the smoke machines billowing dry ice and the strobes slowing every movement down to mass un-coordinated robotics, there is no escape. You simply abandon yourself to the barrage, as one record melts seamlessly into another. Some experts are now suggesting that, once undergone, it is the rave experience, rather than Ecstasy, that can become addictive. Perhaps this is true. What is certain, however, is that the rave scene would not have happened on such a scale without Ecstasy, and Ecstasy would not have become so enormously popular without the rave scene.

(O'Hagan, 1992, pp.10–11)

Raves became a leisure activity, 'seamlessly integrated into the fabric of the weekend ritual. From 1990 onwards, as the fall-out from Acid House germinated across the country, its sounds, signs, symbols and slang had become all pervasive, part of the everyday landscape' (Collin, 1997, p.267)

Official and public concerns about illegal raves and widespread drug taking led to changes in legislation and policy. For example, in 1990 the UK government made it illegal to hold a rave in a field without a licence, and clubs were driven underground into warehouses and other disused premises. But, paradoxically, within a few years the liberalization of the licensing and club laws brought British cities roughly into line with their European counterparts, enabling a new generation of promoters to organize legal raves.

In what sense can we see raves as forms of governance from below? First, we have mentioned the complex co-ordination involved in getting thousands of people to attend a rave. Second, the advent of legalized raves and the growth of massive 'super-clubs' can be seen to have altered the site and form of the regulation of drugs. These clubs operated restrictions on the selling and use of drugs, and the police had the power to call for them to be closed down if this policy was not observed. In this way, the clubs were given much greater responsibility for managing drugs. Third, and most significantly, there was the regulation of drug use through the dissemination of 'harm reduction' messages. These messages may be issued by state-funded agencies (or by governments), but they are just as likely to come from club owners, voluntary workers, dance and music magazines or websites. All of this is undoubtedly different from the law-enforcement approach discussed earlier, but it cannot be called deregulation. Rather it is a form of regulation or governance without the state. Harm reduction can symbolize several things. One of its common meanings is that a policy of harm reduction entails an acceptance by various authorities that drugs will be used in spite of the existence of prohibitions. In these circumstances, the aim of harm reduction is to promote safer forms of drug use by, for example, informing users of possible consequences and of ways of dealing with – and avoiding – these consequences. This involves a key shift in the ways that drug users are conceived of. Instead of thoughts of 'helplessness' or 'dependency', harm reduction invokes a conception of 'controlled' and 'informed' drug use. For O'Malley (1999), it makes drug use 'thinkable in new ways', and these new ways are part of a strategy of 'governing at a distance', in which individuals are 'responsibilized' to become 'skilled and informed' decision makers governing their own actions.

> The process requires no *political* intervention other than the enabling steps of governance to provide information and skills for the subject to deploy as they see fit ... government through harm minimalization presents itself as neither condemning nor condoning drug use, and while individuals are 'responsibilized' this appears to have none of the punitive connotations that apply to fields of criminal activity with which illicit drug use overlaps. At face value this is founded in the fact that the information about drug risks, appearing as objective and accurate, will present itself as no more than mapping out a *quasi-natural order of risks* rather than imposing an order formed and policed by political governance. The risks appear as probabilistic events triggered by the failure of the user to take necessary avoiding steps.
>
> (O'Malley, 1999, pp.203–4)

6.3   The European Cities network

One potentially significant development in alternative approaches to governing drugs in Europe is the European Cities on Drug Policy (ECDP) network. Established in 1990, this initiative highlights the increasing role that European cities are playing in furthering Europeanization and constructing new forms of regional and local governance. The background to the formation of the ECDP is that, during the 1990s, lobbying for resources for urban regeneration projects led a dialogue on best practice in urban governance. The re-imagining of key European cities as regional capitals led to metropolitan co-operation and the establishment of various inter-city networks. These networks perform symbolic and instrumental roles, including managing the changing status of the European city and attempting to regulate city rivalry by stimulating collaboration rather than competition. In so doing they are attempting to construct the notion of 'the city' as a prime organizer of a vibrant, progressive European culture. Drugs are just one feature of city life, and they may be regarded as a social problem or a social benefit. In the former view, drugs are connected to criminal activity, urban decline and problematic drug users; alternatively, in the latter view, drugs are part of a diverse and tolerant cityscape based on pleasure and consumption. The first view may be more widely held (remember the public opinion surveys we looked at earlier), but the balance between the two views is never fixed, as attitudes shift. Conflict and consensus about drugs will continue to exist alongside each other.

City governments can be thought of as mediating – or standing in-between – these two positions. In this sense we can see the ECDP as an *intermediate* level of governance, positioned between the national and transnational on the one hand and the popular cultural forms on the other. The city authorities are also largely responsible for the delivery of policy in terms of overseeing the police, education, welfare and medical facilities. The ECDP's starting point is that cities need to adopt local and pragmatic means of addressing drug use.

> ... it happens rather frequently that national or international drug legislation and guidelines prove to be instruments unsuited for the development of pragmatic approaches at communal level. Therefore, we observe a clear discrepancy between international conventions, their realization at governmental level, and local solutions. In this respect we had to recognize that we are unable to delegate the problem to the governments of the states. Instead we are being called to develop local strategies in collaboration and exchange with other cities and regions.
>
> (European Cities on Drug Policy, 1998)

The ECDP network has to manoeuvre within national, EU-wide and global regulatory frameworks. Nonetheless, the network signifies an acknowledgement of at least two key points. One is that there are 'drug flows' across and within European cities. Consequently, if any one city is to avoid becoming a magnet for drug dealers and users, co-ordinated action will be required. The other point is that cities such as Barcelona, Frankfurt and Manchester may have more in common with each other than with their surrounding regions. This relatively novel development suggests a proliferation of the actors involved in drug policy and of the variety of forms and levels of governance involved in managing drugs across Europe. The ECDP Declaration (1998) states:

> We, the local politicians concerned with drug policy, realize that we have to assume the greatest and direct responsibility in approaching drug problems. In order to handle these drug problems we search for co-ordination and co-operation with other cities and also with national and international bodies. We observe legislation and international conventions in force. Given this legal context, we also feel obliged to look for possibilities and approaches of making allowance for pragmatically coping with the reality in our communities, broaching necessary changes, and to make these necessities heard.

The view that repression alone can solve drug related problems proved to be false a long time ago. Even if some cities and countries still adhere to this policy, we emphasize that this approach – often based on the utopian idea of a drug-free society – did not, and will not, bring about, in practice, any sufficient improvement of the situation.

We, the cities call for the necessary freedom and legal framework which [will] allow us to implement a well balanced pragmatic policy – as it is laid down in this declaration as well as in the Frankfurt Resolution of 1990 – according to our local needs, based on the particular characteristics of drug-related problems, social and cultural settings, and political priorities in our communities. In this process, all local bodies and authorities concerned with drug related problems should collaborate.

Human Rights, and every person's basic right to receive unbiased help to survive and to live in human dignity – with or without drugs – have to be the basis of international, national, and local drug policy. At the same time, the citizens of our communities must be protected effectively from drug related problems.

The Declaration seeks to develop and support a pragmatic, multi-agency approach based on a shift away from criminal justice interventions and toward harm reduction measures. For the ECDP, this would involve differentiating between cannabis and other illegal drugs; legally regulating the trade in cannabis; ensuring that criminal justice sanctions do not apply to the purchase, possession and consumption of small quantities of cannabis for personal use; creating a legal basis for the establishment of facilities in which drugs can be consumed under supervision; and allowing the medically controlled prescription of drugs to long-term users.

The signatories argue that establishing inter-city agreements and strengthening co-operation and co-ordination are vital, because if only a few cities implement such a policy they 'will attract drug users like magnets and soon be overwhelmed by the problems with which they are confronted'.

Summary

- Public opinion provides support for joint EU action against drug trafficking, but this may not mean that the public favours only law enforcement.
- The drug ecstasy was widely used across Europe in the 1990s and, perhaps, became a normal part of youth culture.
- The 1990s also saw the expansion of 'harm reduction' measures as a popular, non-stigmatizing response to drug use.

- Governance mechanisms 'from below' operate through the 'responsibilization' of drug users.
- Some European cities are providing another network and a different level of governance in relation to managing drug use.

7   Conclusion

One way of reading this chapter is to see it as contrasting a 'zero tolerance' legal and punitive framework with a 'maximum tolerance' deregulative, harm reduction approach. In support of the 'zero tolerance' position, we have seen that the EU has been developing its policy competencies and capacities and expanding the scope of its authority. A complex and dense network of overlapping policy initiatives and practices is producing a multi-tiered system of drug governance. Intergovernmental and transnational measures have stressed strict law enforcement and tough penalties as the primary means of controlling the supply and limiting the use of illicit drugs, and a variety of judicial and policing measures are being developed to further those ends. Drug control has been one of the key justifications for developing new and enhanced networks of regulation and surveillance in EU member states. And it can be plausibly argued that drugs are at the leading edge of European harmonization on judicial and policing matters.

In support of the 'maximum tolerance' position, we have seen that evidence of 'normalized' drug taking casts doubt on law-enforcement strategies. It also suggests a cultural and generational shift toward drug consumption as a regular and routine 'life-style choice'. For some observers, the cultures associated with the drug ecstasy signal this decisive shift, which over time can lead only to disillusionment with 'out of touch' politicians and the political rhetoric of a 'war' on drugs.

However, this chapter has also suggested that these neat dichotomies are untenable. Neither the 'Euro law enforcement' nor the 'Euro youth cultures' approach is monolithic or without its own contradictions. Governments that 'wave the big stick' of law enforcement may also support light sanctions for minor drug use and dealing. Countries that appear to be tolerant and permissive toward drug use may have stiff penalties for drug trafficking. And the EU, for all its activities under the heading of Justice and Home Affairs, also has a European Drug Promotion Week and disseminates models of good practice – including harm reduction. It is true that these approaches receive less news media attention than law-enforcement initiatives, but their very existence suggests a diversified picture of drug policy at the EU level. Beyond that, in terms of individual nation states, there is, as we have seen, diversity in the ways in which penalties and sanctions for drug offences are defined and implemented. And it is still possible to state that, for all the talk of a

'Chemical Generation', most surveys still suggest that the majority of young people do not take or try drugs. Whether a crucial and significant cultural shift on drugs occurred in the 1990s is something that will become clear only with the passage of time.

In terms of regulatory mechanisms, governance 'from above' entails the building of institutions with a global and pan-European perspective and remit. Governance 'from below' seeks to make drug users autonomous and responsible for their decisions and actions. In terms of its concern with drug users and harm reduction, the European Cities on Drug Policy network may be more an example of governance 'from below' than governance 'from above'. For the foreseeable future, drugs and drug policies are likely to remain a matter of controversy and contestation, and arguments for greater harmonization and diversity will persist.

References

Belenko, S.R. (ed.) (2000) *Drugs and Drug Policy in America*, Westwood, Greenwood Press.

Berridge, V. (1999) *Opium and the People*, London, Free Association Books.

Bromley, S.J. (ed.) (2001) *Governing the European Union*, London, Sage/The Open University.

Cohen, R. (2000) 'Europe's love–hate relationship with foreigners', *New York Times*, 24 December, Section 4, pp.4–6.

Collin, M. (1997) *Altered State: The Story of Ecstasy Culture and Acid House*, London, Serpent's Tail.

Dorn, N. and Jamieson, A. (2000) *Room for Manoeuvre*, London, DrugScope.

Dorn, N., Murji, K. and South, N. (1992) *Traffickers: Drug Markets and Law Enforcement*, London, Routledge.

European Cities on Drug Policy (ECDP) (1998) *Declaration of the European Cities on Drug Policy*, http://www.ecdp.net/

European Commission (1997) 'Support for key policy areas: the road from Maastricht to Amsterdam', *Eurobarometer*, no.47, pp.25–36.

European Commission (1998) 'Trends in public opinion of the European Union', *Eurobarometer*, no.49, pp.18–42.

European Monitoring Centre for Drugs and Drug Addiction (EMCDDA) (1999) *1999 Extended Annual Report on the State of the Drugs Problem in the European Union*, Luxembourg, Office for Official Publications of the European Communities.

Garratt, S. (1998) *Adventures in Wonderland: A Decade in Club Culture*, London, Headline Books.

Goodman, J., Lovejoy, P.E. and Shernatt, A. (eds) (1995) *Consuming Habits: Drugs in History and Anthropology*, London, Routledge.

Hall, S. (1992) 'The West and the rest: discourse and power' in Hall, S. and Gieben, B. (eds) *Formations of Modernity*, Cambridge, Polity Press.

Joseph, M. (2000) *Ecstasy*, London, Carlton Books.

Kohn, M. (1992) *Dope Girls: The Birth of the British Drug Underground*, London, Lawrence and Wishart.

McAllister, W.B. (1999) *Drug Diplomacy in the Twentieth Century*, London, Routledge.

McLaughlin, E. (1992) 'The democratic deficit: the European Union and the accountability of the British Police', *British Journal of Criminology*, vol.32, no.4, pp.473–87.

Murji, K. (1998) *Policing Drugs*, Aldershot, Ashgate.

O'Hagan, A. (1992) 'A place in the solstice sun', *The Independent*, 21 June, pp.10–12.

O'Malley, P. (1999) 'Consuming risks: harm minimalization and the government of "drug-users"' in Smandych, R. (ed.) *Governable Places*, Aldershot, Dartmouth.

Police Foundation (2000) *Drugs and the Law: An Independent Inquiry into the Misuse of Drugs Act 1971*, London, Police Foundation.

Reynolds, S. (1998) *Energy Flash: A Journey Through Rave Music and Dance Culture*, London, Picador.

Robson, P. (1999) *Forbidden Drugs*, Oxford, Oxford University Press.

Sivanandan, A. (1988) 'The new racism', *New Statesman*, 4 November, pp.8–9.

United Nations (1997) *International Drug Control Programme World Drug Report*, Oxford, Oxford University Press.

World Health Organization Expert Committee on Drug Dependence (1993) *Twenty-Eighth Report*, Geneva, World Health Organization.

Further reading

O'Malley, P. (1999) 'Consuming risks: harm minimalization and the government of "drug-users"' in Smandych, R. (ed.) *Governable Places*, Aldershot, Dartmouth.

United Nations (annual) *International Drug Control Programme World Drug Report*, Oxford, Oxford University Press.

Chapter 9
Conclusion: One Europe? The democratic governance of a continent

Salvador Giner and Montserrat Guibernau

1 Introduction

The previous chapters have explored different dimensions of Europe's social and cultural diversity by focusing upon seven major themes.

- Regionalism and the analysis of different types of regions within the European Union (EU), ranging from geographical regions to regions with a strong sense of identity and culture and a considerable degree of political autonomy. This theme has included some speculation about the role of nations without states in the EU of the foreseeable future, and an examination of the different initiatives and associations created by regions in seeking greater participation in the EU structure and institutions (Chapter 2).

- The rising diversity experienced by European societies as a result of the wide range of ethnic groups they contain and the significant increase in the number of immigrants entering the EU. This theme has also involved some discussion about citizenship issues, discrimination against migrants and ethnic groups, and an analysis of the challenges posed by defining the EU as a multicultural society (Chapter 3).

- The great variety of new social movements emerging within European societies, reflecting not only a rising awareness of peoples' right to develop individual and collective identities, but also exemplifying how 'cultural' and 'life-style' demands acquire political meaning. This often results in the articulation of bottom-up mechanisms, challenging the status quo and entering governance processes at a national and transnational level (Chapter 4).

- Transformations in family life and sexual politics throughout the EU, such as lower fertility rates since the 1960s, the rise in the number of births outside marriage, the upsurge in divorce rates, the percentage of married women in paid employment and an increase in life expectancy.

Unifying trends have been contrasted with persisting North–South differences based upon culture, socio-political factors and economic variation (Chapter 5).

- The different images of Europe envisaged by the founding fathers of a united European community, as well as different initiatives toward the construction of a common European identity (Chapter 6).

- The study of the European media, which reveals the existence of different structures in national media systems that show a strong national character while remaining the main gateway for transnational influences and are one of the most important agents in the promotion of a European identity (Chapter 7).

- Differences in drug regulation in various EU countries as an example of legal systems that reflect the specific cultures of each European state. But also, and more importantly, current trends toward the harmonization of the law, and the creation of a dense network of overlapping policy initiatives and practices that is producing a multi-tiered system of drug governance (Chapter 8).

The study of each of these areas has provided specific examples of how both individuals and groups seek to express and reassert their identity at various levels. These examples encompass national, regional and ethnic forms of identity. But they also include notions of class, gender and environmental movements, as well as drug use and regulation, as representatives of specific concerns closely tied up with 'identity politics'. Further to this, the study of the media and its role in shaping people's identity has opened up the question of the eventual development of a truly European media, free from American influence and capable of instilling a shared sense of 'Europeanness' among EU citizens. In addition, consideration has been given to the study of those features that unite Europeans and could act as a basis for the emergence of a shared identity. The idea that the EU is primarily a trans-European élite project that is now in its early stages should help to account for the weak sense of identity shared by most EU citizens.

The great diversity which lies at the heart of the EU opens up questions about the plausibility of turning an economic and political space generated by a political institution, the EU, into a coherent and governable society. The main challenges to this process are associated with the following questions: Who will be allowed to be different? What types of difference will be tolerated? And what principles are going to determine the regulation of difference?

Conflict exists, and it is likely to continue to play a key part in the future development of the EU. Conflict expresses itself through tensions between traditional and new forms of life, work and habits. It is also a defining feature of the relations between the nation states forming the EU, its regions and ethnic groups, and all those social movements, most of them transnational in character, that challenge national and/or EU regulations. As we have seen, conflict has often resulted in the creation of alternative governance mechanisms which pose a challenge to traditional top-down forms of government (see Chapters 4, 5 and 8 in particular). The quest for identity that seems to pervade the lives of Europeans has encouraged them to generate various types of networks, adding to civil society's dynamism and resulting in the rise of new forms of governance destined to preserve and enhance different forms of identity.

The EU provides a new environment within which individuals and groups seek recognition and organize their participation in politics. The big question is whether the development of a political institution such as the EU and the harmonization of Europe through the implementation of EU Directives will result in the emergence of a common identity accompanied by sentiments of loyalty and attachment to the EU or, on the contrary, whether national loyalties and interests will prevail and prevent the emergence of a European identity.

2   Unity and diversity

Probably no other continent-sized part of the world has been the subject of such a prolonged discussion about its essential unity or disunity. There are other large parts of the world – India, Latin America, Africa – where there has been heated discussion about similar issues. In those areas, however, the debate has arisen only after the advent of modernity. In Europe, discussions about its nature and inner diversity, together with attendant, more practical, disputes about the material implications of Europe's existence as a shared 'homeland', all go back to antiquity. And no one is willing to deny the fact that this common heritage is a crucial feature in Europeans' sense of identity or *raison d'être* (see Chapter 1). Thus more than mere lip service is paid to that legacy. After all, most of the terms that define our civilization, and several of those that legitimize current efforts toward unification, were forged in antiquity and consciously revived in modernity.

The debate about Europe's inner unity or lack of it has often remained dormant, or been limited to the influential few for long periods of time (see Chapter 6). Yet it flared up again with great force in modern times with the rise of nationalism and the nation state. It gathered strength precisely at a time when the shared bonds differentiating Europe from the rest of the world, bar some of its own overseas colonies, were overshadowed in Europe itself by the overpowering claims of nationalism and nation – that is, state – sovereignty. These bonds included Christendom, Roman Law, an inherited body of classical culture, a trans-European educational network, capitalism and, eventually, the industrial mode of production. It was precisely when the strength of these common bonds weakened, and European wars ceased to be fought between social classes or religious factions (Catholics and Protestants) and became wars between states with overseas empires or ambitions, that Europeans began to reflect in earnest about their now increasingly problematic unity. This mood lasted roughly from the French Revolution to the aftermath of the Second World War.

The discussion ceased to be purely ideological or academic with the development of a European Community on the west of the continent shortly after the Second World War. After the initial failure of a European military alliance and the subsequent subordination of the European West to NATO and the East to the Warsaw Pact, each led by a 'non-European' hegemonic power, and the creation of the incipient but successful European Coal and Steel Community, the years after 1957 saw something more than mere co-operation between states. The nascent EU, with its initially weak Council, Parliament, Commission and Court, soon began to encompass most European countries, in various degrees of integration (see **Bromley, 2001**). It was then that the discussion about 'one Europe' (the existence of one European society, one body of citizens, one single political and economic unit) ceased to be idle speculation. By the late 1960s the early European idealists had become respected visionaries, and their notions no longer seemed far-fetched. Even before the year 2000, the EU and the countries on their way to accession had almost become coterminous with the conventional frontiers of what had always been defined geographically and culturally as Europe. Switzerland, with its special ties and agreements with the surrounding Union, and some adjacent countries claiming varying degrees of 'Europeanness' do not represent glaring exceptions to the growing political, economic and administrative unity.

As a result, 'Europe' today is already much more than an abstract notion, or a mere geographical expression. It is now also much more than an aspiration – although it remains that as well for the always present 'euromaximalists'. It is, finally, a fact in every sense (albeit a complex one, with a jigsaw of states whose sovereignty has been only partially eroded and whose powers have been only partially relinquished in various degrees to the common institutions of the Union). Europeans being what they are, however, such a 'fact' is bound to continue to be looked at with some reservations from every possible angle. 'Europe' will continue to be denied, affirmed and qualified by many. Some will reconsider their initial integrationist views one way or another; others will advocate outright federalism, thus circumventing the problems posed by several of the current member states. Finally, there will be the 'eurominimalists', those who prefer a set of bilateral agreements with 'Brussels' in order to cope with the 'European fact', so bowing to the realities of the Union without losing, at least formally, any semblance of sovereignty or autonomy. Yet none of these various arrangements appears to be able to undermine the ultimate force of what has finally materialized on the continent.

In spite of such developments there will continue to be 'eurosceptics' in our midst. Yet they, too, are an essential part of the culture of disagreement on which the European mind thrives. And, with all the necessary provisos and qualifications, the most elementary evidence points to the consolidation of an economic, political, administrative and cultural entity covering most of Europe outside Russia. The transnational and trans-state ties at all levels are now too strong to be denied: a point of no return might have already been reached in many areas, and it is now too late for Europe to go back to its former fragmentation.

Resistance by eurosceptics in many countries – especially in several Nordic states and the UK – stems from the fact that it will be increasingly hard to 'opt out' of any arrangements with the EU once they have been entered into. In this context, interestingly, serious consideration of what constitutes Europe, or even European civilization, is still far from idle. The 'civilization' issues are too important to be dismissed as superfluous or as the result of the whimsical entertainments of hair-splitting philosophers and academics. Nor are those issues today, as has all too often been the case in the past, the sole manifestation of unavowed ideological interests and nationalistic and other passions. An awareness of the timeless debate about the problematic nature of Europe as a unit has become part of our culture as Europeans. Yet on a more practical level, and under the conditions of advanced modernity and the considerable progress already made in terms of European unification, this debate may be put aside for the moment. The fact is that, for all practical purposes, Europe today – the EU, that is – is underpinned by two elements: citizenship and a shared consciousness of belonging to the EU. The first element is institutional, and the second element, although seemingly more abstract or even vague, is equally relevant.

Wars, religious and ideological conflicts, massive economic imbalances and a network of sovereign states thriving on mutual hostility have divided Europeans for a very long time (see Chapter 1). In recent history, the essence of the grave and repeated confrontations between European countries must be partly found in their efforts at national differentiation (and a parallel assimilation of minorities) combined with the divergent economic or political interests of each state. Throughout time, different European countries have sought hegemony over the entire European space (Charles V, Napoleon, Hitler) or over a sizeable part of it (the Austrian Empire, Prussia). Only in the latter part of the twentieth century has a serious effort been made to create a common ground with equal rights for all and no single hegemonic state.

This recent effort has taken place despite de facto alliances between governments to develop a 'hard core' of nations leading the process of European unification. This has been the case with France and Germany, helped since 1957 by constant British misgivings, doubts and lack of enthusiasm. (The lack of a third major partner in the development of the core has only made its existence more obvious.) This new 'bicephalous' form of incipient intra-European 'hegemony', however, is much milder than any past expression of internal predominance by a single monarchy or nation. Moreover, large countries such as Italy or Spain have not allowed it to threaten the European project to any great extent.

The possibility of an advanced and powerful Europe geographically centered on the Netherlands, surrounded by a weaker, even 'backward', periphery, has rightly been seen as a dangerous element. Efforts to distribute structural development funds toward the periphery, combined with the extraordinary economic expansion undergone by the western and southern peripheries (Ireland, Portugal, Spain, southern Italy and Greece) have eliminated the danger. It now looms in the East, however, as the collapse of Communism after 1989 opened the way for that part of the continent to join the Union. Yet the crucial fact remains that trans-European regional imbalances no longer seriously threaten the rise of a shared citizenship in the already existing Union. This is not to say that economic, cultural and political imbalances will not continue to exist between parts of Europe, creating differences and tensions between formally equal citizens. For example, there are economic imbalances between northern and southern England, between the Italian 'Padania' and the Mezzogiorno and between western and eastern Germany, and there are political imbalances between France and Corsica and between Spain and the Basque Country. We should also remember that similar internal tensions have always occurred and will continue to occur within individual European states.

3   On European citizenship

Ethnic, linguistic, religious and economic differences are not always, per se, sufficient sources of confrontation or disunity unless they are made so by those who seek to mobilize the people concerned for their own purposes. The firm bonds of a shared citizenship can, often enough, hold together a complex and variegated society. There is increasing evidence that such may be the situation in the EU in the not too distant future. Europe, of course, is as much of a mosaic today as it was yesterday, although the legal and political bonds between EU citizens are slowly moving them toward the development of a shared citizenship. In this matter the EU may not be unique. Thus other large political units and internally differentiated parts of the world may be further along this path than the EU is. The internal cultural, economic and socio-structural differences in India, for instance, are arguably greater than those in the EU, yet India is one country and one state.

A crucial fact for the rise of a European citizenship is that the *Pax Europaea* now in the making is not the result, as the *Pax Romana* once was, of a central, conquering power. Despite the lack of a democratic notion of the body politic, Roman subjects became citizens through an effective process of detribalization and legal integration in the imperial order. The historical parallel is instructive precisely because of the vast differences in technology, knowledge and belief that separates us from that remote period. The EU is undergoing both legal and political integration and, to a considerable extent, cultural convergence at many levels, starting with the media culture of today. These developments underpin the legal and political arrangements of European citizenship.

The intensification of ethnic militancy, moves toward local and regional autonomy and the proliferation of new cultural identities do not entirely invalidate such assertions. A number of studies have emphasized the fact that today's expressions of localism, particularism and differentiation are, to a large extent, reactions against homogenization, against the levelling trends of the rise of 'mass society'. Yet the generalization of European citizenship need not mean homogeneity nor 'massification'. Obviously, many will perceive this supposedly insidious process to be at work in the EU of today, and will deem a truly united Europe to be a danger to their deeply rooted national loyalties. Multiple political loyalties are common enough in the world, but they are not always seen to be acceptable.

Citizenship is a slow process: legally, it may be bestowed overnight, but it takes time to seep in, to become an everyday and widespread practice. Not every observer of this phenomenon has been capable of grasping it, or has been willing to do so. There were heated discussions about the desirability of a common European citizenship as late as the year 2000, when proposals were made by some for a European constitution and a single citizenship (for example, Joschka Fischer's speech in Berlin on 12 May 2000). For some prominent pro-Europeans (such as Jean-Pierre Chevènement), any form of federation – and therefore shared citizenship – was still anathema, as was any serious consideration of meso-government, ranging from political decentralization to shared sovereignty, in relation to minority nations within nation states. (In fact, Chevènement tended his resignation as a minister over the issue of granting Corsica a degree of autonomy within France.) Pro-European 'Jacobins', in favour of a centralist and unitary view of the nation state, are in a quandary over a shared citizenship that devolves power and authority to regions and nationalities, undeterred by the fact that some countries, Spain clearly so, and the UK to a lesser extent, have been moving in that direction for some time.

At the turn of the century, perhaps both those in favour of a more or less immediate European citizenship and those against it failed to grasp its essential nature as a historical process, not just a legal or constitutional decision, which will take time to become established and will affect different people in different ways.

4   Toward a governable Europe?

'Governance' refers to styles and methods of governing, and more often than not to those outside the formal political structure of the state. Civil society, frequently a self-regulatory sphere, is therefore considered an essential part of governance. It should be obvious by now why such notions are important for the current and future development of a Europe-wide polity. The previous chapters have already given some consideration to this topic.

Democratic states command widespread loyalty. Their governments govern. In the EU, the law-abiding citizens' allegiance is to the state, and often to the European authorities as well – no matter how remote – although only because their respective countries have transferred power to the European Parliament or, in the case of the single currency, to the European Central Bank (see **Thompson, 2001**).

It would be surprising if the European project did not arouse misgivings about the viability of governance across its many lands and large population, especially considering the enormous prestige and quasi-religious allegiance and, indeed, devotion and affection felt by Europe's people to their native lands, languages and traditions. Moreover, every conflict which involves two or more different European states is immediately viewed as a weakness in the nascent European polity and as a serious hindrance to its governance. When French fisherman blockade their ports, directly affecting British imports, or French farmers burn Spanish lorries carrying fruit and produce into France or across it, the conflicts are seen by the people concerned as international, although neither French farmers nor French fishermen see any difficulties in getting financial help from Brussels on the basis of the Common Agricultural Policy or other protectionist measures.

The emergence of the EU as a governable entity will depend on the strengthening of the Union's institutional network and its dialogue and interaction with a still incipient European civil society. (*Eurobarometer* figures continue to emphasize the fact that most people see themselves first as, for example, Italian, Dutch or Danes, and only secondarily as Europeans – see Chapter 6.) During the early stages of integration (and still today) governance depended on negotiations between governments, multilateral agreements and the consent of national authorities. The rotating national presidencies and the regular meetings of heads of governments and ministers are still paramount, and governing Europe depends largely on the functioning of this arrangement. However, the European Parliament, the Commission (despite the odd crisis) and the rise of single European officers with special powers continue to point toward integration. So, of course, does the consolidation of a single European currency. The value of the latter in terms of symbolic integration may be greater than its merely financial and economic significance. To say that governance in Europe is likely to encounter difficulties is to say little, since governance is a transnational problem, taking place in many parts of the world and with vastly different degrees of intensity. It is more useful to see integration the other way around, as a *solution* for governance in Europe under conditions of globalization, continued European prosperity and international competition. A disunited Europe may be far more ungovernable than a united one.

Such reflections do not allow us to ignore some serious governance problems that are likely to arise precisely as a consequence of unification. Take, as an example, a crucial issue that is hardly mentioned, perhaps because it makes us so uncomfortable: Europe's future borders in the east. Russia's accession has not yet been contemplated, but it may be one day, once the country recovers from its present state of prostration. Its enormous extension over the northern part of the Asian continent, let alone its population of 125 million people, will pose serious problems of governance for a European Parliament already strained by the coexistence of very large countries (Germany and France) and very small ones (Luxembourg and Ireland). Further to this, a more serious and even more rarely mentioned question concerns Turkey, an official candidate for accession since 1999. Greek hostility is seen by some as a marginal problem, but it is also seen by many to be very convenient, as are continued reports by Amnesty International and other independent groups on the deficiencies of Turkish democracy. The real question is: Will the EU wish to maintain an open or partially open frontier with countries such as Iraq and Syria? Will the EU's immigration policies and targets be controllable under these circumstances, when the Schengen and non-Schengen nations of today can hardly contain the flow of immigrants across the Straits of Gibraltar, or from Albania into southern Italy, or avoid the gruesome trade in human beings over the Channel into England?

None of the governance problems facing Europe in 2001 appears to be wholly untreatable, however. Neo-Nazi hooliganism and ethnic terrorism in several areas are deeply worrying, almost as worrying as was the shameful war in the Balkans in the late 1990s, but a sober look at our history over the last century shows that they are minute in comparison with the cataclysms of that period. Beyond any rhetoric, it is evident that the EU is being built so that they do not happen again. And for that purpose its governance as a single unit (whether on a federal, quasi-federal or confederal basis) is a necessary thing. Yet the Union's institutional framework on its own will not be sufficient. The Union will hold as a durable and viable polity only if governance at the social level, that is, only if a strong and healthy civil society, underpins the entire edifice.

5   Toward a European civil society?

It was not long ago that some observers worried about a possible crisis of civil society. A term of classical, liberal origins – rooted in the Scottish Enlightenment and then in the works of Hegel – the notion of 'civil society' has been kept alive by the Marxist tradition, in which it has never been devoid of pejorative undertones, for it has been seen as almost synonymous with 'bourgeois society'. Be that as it may, the rise of large corporations, the expansion of bureaucracies and the costly welfare state, the powerful agreements between employers and trade unions ('corporatism' and 'neo-corporatism'), together with the constant growth of the public sector, inclined many to think that civil society, as an autonomous sphere in which citizens were free to pursue their interests unmolested, was facing hard times from rather unexpected quarters. Thus far, only totalitarian regimes had been openly hostile to the notion.

The last decades of the twentieth century saw a considerable reaction against state intervention and a parallel interest in the autonomy of civil society, both on the right and the left of the political spectrum. On the right, 'neo-liberalism' under Thatcher and Reagan rediscovered civil society as the proper realm of private initiative, untrammelled competition and possible de-bureaucratization. (Yet neo-liberalism sang the praises of private initiative and individualism while doing little or nothing against the large multinational corporations and institutions that were hardly strengthening it.) On the left, a rediscovery of the people's sovereign autonomy was seen as a timely substitute for a rapidly disappearing proletariat. Civic associations with altruistic aims proliferated, in Europe, North America and elsewhere, restoring lost hopes among the more libertarian and progressive elements of the left.

Without going into an analysis of the causes of this phenomenon, it is sufficient to say that Europe soon became one of the major world centres of its development, so much so that a vigorous civil society is now a powerful structural component in each of its component countries. Civic associations, social movements, altruistic organizations and production and consumer co-operatives form a vast network of citizens' bodies. Taken together, both their sheer volume and quality forbid any consideration of this dimension of civil society as merely marginal. The new civil society must be taken seriously in looking into European governance, since most citizens' associations – even local ones – now possess a markedly transnational character, and often see themselves as such. This is especially true of both altruistic civic organizations (often called non-governmental organizations or NGOs) and of the co-operative and non-profit sector of the economy, the so-called 'Third Sector'.

The notion that Europeans can now more readily accept democracy because they no longer believe in politics is a catchy phrase, and there is a grain of truth in the notion that a relative disappointment with large-party politics has been largely compensated for by an active involvement in the more specific pursuits of civic associationalism and non-party social involvement. This favours the proliferation of the bottom-up governance mechanisms considered in some of the previous chapters. After many years of an increasingly powerful public sector, many people are seeking greater control over their lives, and they often do so without opting for entrepreneurial capitalism or concentrating on a private career. Citizens' associations and movements offer public (altruistic) involvement without party manipulation. Moreover, the pursuit of single issues yields palpable results and stands as an example of the tensions usually emerging between top-down and bottom-up regulatory processes, calling our attention to the significant impact of civil society's initiatives in the development of new forms of governance.

The liberal and constitutional polity which protects us all (the state and the nascent European proto-state) stimulates such activities within civil society and, in turn, keeps political parties on their toes, forcing them to heed their promises, mostly in those areas, such as environmental protection, where politicians are prone to forget their electoral programmes. In this sense, Immanuel Kant's notion of 'rational civil associations' fits them better than any other group. Civic and voluntary associations, both in Europe and elsewhere, strengthen the current shift from government to governance without destroying the former.

Government does not have to rule and administer everything. By avoiding violence and accepting negotiation, pressure, altruistic ideals and good public behaviour, civic associations spread democracy horizontally, and generate a permanent flow of inputs from 'down upwards' that are slowly changing the face of politics in the European continent. Although their members often pretend otherwise, civic associations are not apolitical, although they may be non-party. They represent the public dimension of the private realm.

The civil society underpinnings of European democracy are increasingly obvious as time passes. Precisely because of such welcome developments it is necessary to emphasize that they are not sufficiently strong to support the entire European edifice, nor would it be convenient for a future European polity if parties and institutions were undermined by the private sphere of the public realm represented by civic associations and initiatives. The 'Third Sector' represented by this dimension of civil society – along with the public sector and the entrepreneurial and profit sector – has become important throughout Europe without being confined to any single country or region. It is now a distinctively European feature.

6   The tradition of the new

Western societies have always been restless and innovative. Innovation is part of their tradition. No idealization is involved in this notion: the exceptions to this trend are too glaring (and often too painful) to be ignored. Effort to prevent innovation or maintain obsolete orthodoxies by force have repeatedly caused much suffering and even terror in many parts of Europe. To complicate matters, barbarous innovations such as fascism and Nazism justified themselves during the twentieth century through the ideological invention of a fictitious past. Some innovations in weaponry, state control and ideological nihilism (an extreme form of scepticism that systematically rejects all values) have tried to arrest the flow of new ideas, and have done the peoples of Europe no good at all.

With all these provisos, it seems fair to assert that European civilization has been based on a humanistic interpretation of progress as an unending flow of innovations. Greater religious freedom, the abolition of slavery, the universalization of citizenship, the granting of equal rights to women and men, the universal right to education or medical treatment and so on have all materialized, one after another, as moral innovations. Overcoming the narrow limits of the national community must be included in this impressive list of innovations, from which the obvious scientific and technological developments have been purposefully excluded. The Europe of the future cannot possibly aspire to witness the final stage of this progression, nor to monopolize it. For one thing, the tradition of innovation long ago ceased to be confined to our continent.

The rise of the first industrial nation in the world, England, also marked the last historical moment at which systematic and relentless innovation was practically confined to Europe. The innovatory mood had already spread to Europe's own overseas colonies, and then to the world. Modernization (that is, systematic innovation), once a European invention, travelled well, and is now the legacy of mankind.

Europe's place in the world system, and in the current stage of the globalization process, although bound to shift and change, will be firmer under a united Europe. This does not seem to be a matter of opinion. Besides, all the developments point in that direction. Western Europe's investments abroad are increasingly 'European' and involve more than one EU country. Of course, massive investments by single countries – such as those of Spain in Latin America over the last two decades – may still be seen as 'national'. But many of the investing companies are in turn multinational, or are partly owned by companies from other EU countries. As for internal European economic integration, the process advances at a pace that outstrips all rhetoric by the eurosceptic lobby: fusions between hallowed institutions – the London and Frankfurt stock exchanges, for example – illustrate the measure of the process. This is also innovation: the local bourse – Milan, Paris, London – as a national institution, and as the epitome of the financial power of a national bourgeoisie, will soon be no more. Likewise, it is inconceivable that the goods and merchandise that now flow freely across Europe will cease to do so, or that intra-European migrations or intermarriages will stop. It does not look as though transnational property markets will be dismantled – for example, English dwellers in the Dordogne and south-eastern Spain, and Germans in Majorca.

There is no sign that Europeans are prepared to abandon their leading role as innovators. They are only understandably worried that they may lag behind Americans, Japanese and others in the great modern conspiracy to base social change on discovery, research and free enquiry. They were not slow to realize that in some fields European collaboration was absolutely necessary – nuclear research, as exemplified by the Euratom laboratories at Saclay; the Concorde works at Toulouse; the astronomical observatory in the Canary Islands; and the development of the Airbus. They have been more sluggish in the creation of other programmes – for example, Erasmus exchange programmes across universities, and the Rectors and Vice-Chancellors Conference. But on the whole, integration and synergy are growing apace. A reverse of the European brain-drain to the USA has not occurred, but there is no longer evidence of any massive setbacks (cataclysms, rather) such as the exodus of the Central European Jewish intelligentsia under the Nazis, or that of the Spanish scientists, artists and intellectuals who, having rescued their country from a period of decay, perished or were forced into exile during the same dark period of our common history. For those interested in the maintenance of the democratic framework which guarantees that such events will not happen again, the European project can only be seen as the necessary solution.

7 From conflict to consensus

The Soviet Union finally collapsed only a few weeks after the Maastricht Treaty of 1991, which set ambitious plans for further integration and political expansion to the East. With the disappearance of a rival and utterly different Europe, the political formula of liberal democracy, market capitalism, the welfare state and a civil society became entirely unchallenged throughout the continent.

The event, accompanied by the rightful claims of Poles, Hungarians, the Baltic peoples and other nations to join the Union, permitted a certain amount of optimism about the prospects for peace and prosperity throughout the EU. With the collapse of the Stalinist corruption of socialism and communism, the era of violent conflict and war opened by the rise of fascism seemed to come to a definite close. Ideologies were far from dead – in fact, a consensus ideology about the need for market capitalism and, in Europe, the necessity to maintain and improve the achievements of the welfare state became paramount. Much complacency about this could be perceived in many countries, and there was little vigorous opposition to the aggressive pronouncements of neo-liberals with their blunt idealization of the free market. (They had little or nothing to say about multinational monopolies and oligopolies, that is, market situations in which control over the supply of a commodity is held by a small number of producers, which, by definition, distort the markets.)

A long cycle of growth and prosperity in the 1990s came to reinforce the economic formulas of the moment, as well as the feeling that we were all on the right track. Labour disputes and other conflicts were sometimes quite serious (in declining industries or in transport) but the zero-sum view of all manner of conflicts became a thing of the past, with the notable exception of political terrorism in Northern Ireland, the Basque Country and Corsica. On the whole, the trend has been toward the territorialization of political violence – from Kosovo to Northern Ireland.

All this must be acknowledged if we are to put in the right perspective the social problems and attendant conflicts that loom increasingly large in European societies. Immigration – essentially a solution not a problem for a stagnant and ageing population and economies in dire need of workers – is a case in point. The European nations have undergone a long process of ethnic concentration on given areas (ethnic territorialization), especially after the end of the First World War in 1918. With the notorious exception of the Balkans, where ethnic concentration and expulsions took place at the end of the century, and perhaps Transylvania in Romania, with its Hungarian population, the tendency has been to concentrate ethnic groups in a given territory. Now, with the influx of immigrants, the multicultural and multi-ethnic map of Europe begins to approach that of the USA, whose huge 'minorities' are interspersed over a single territory. The ethnic components of non-European origin are not regularly distributed: for example, Turks in Germany, Indonesians in

Holland, Moroccans in Spain, Algerians in France, and Pakistanis in the UK. On the whole, their political integration has been smooth. The violence so far has been as ugly and barbarous as it has been circumscribed, and it has been initiated by hoodlums and neo-Nazi groups. There is no evidence that it will be eradicated – only contained – in the coming years, and its existence shows us that no bucolic view of European society is permissible.

Historically, European societies were the first to witness the rise of social classes as the main units of inequality, as they grew out of the crumbling feudal system. (Other forms of stratification and hierarchy predominated elsewhere in the world until the arrival of capitalism.) The imagery, language and politics of class conflict became a constant and crucial part of life in Europe from 1789 onwards. Neither increased social mobility brought about by the Industrial Revolution and overseas expansion nor the relentless growth of the middle classes throughout the continent managed to entirely drive out the logic of class inequalities and class conflict. The late decades of the twentieth century, however, finally saw the considerable attenuation of this situation. The continued presence of the welfare state (despite latter-day criticisms) and other factors (such as the ideological collapse of communism and the decline of the trade unions) prompted the demise of class conflict in its traditional form. The new situation did not represent the disappearance of privilege or other, often insidious, kinds of inequality. Yet class confrontation as such ceased to be an item on the agenda of the subordinate classes and their representatives. Many intellectuals and ideologues – always important in European political life – who had been favourable to the notion of class confrontation for their own reasons also abandoned it and analysed contemporary events in a different vein, even when they remained broadly on the left.

With the diminution of class exclusion and confrontations, other social collectives and groups have, during the second half of the twentieth century, especially after 1968, come to the fore as marginalized, unjustly exploited and generally excluded. They range over a very large spectrum and do not form a compact social class, as in the obvious case of women. Some – the chronically unemployed, for instance – tend to cluster more around a social class or set of classes (the subordinate ones in this case), but even they appear across the entire stratification. Under such circumstances, there is little or no chance that an effective solidarity movement may one day crystallize among groups as diverse as the poor, the middle class and upper working class unemployed, women in general and ethnic minorities (for instance, the numerous gypsies of Eastern Europe). Even social-class alliances – when they were in fashion – were often unstable and certainly always hard to launch effectively.

The main distributor of social integration and exclusion in Europe is still the market. Continuing with the example of women, it has been their participation in the economic power of the middle classes that has allowed them to gain access to the job market through higher education.

In turn, discrimination in the workplace has intensified their consciousness through the well-known process of relative deprivation leading to collective social action. Yet while integration processes such as these take place in contemporary Europe, others increase inequalities or set up barriers.

The arrival of immigrants has increased the number of the excluded, at a pace that probably exceeds the flow of Europeans entering the world of inclusion. Social services and school facilities still leave much to be desired, and the perennial class-based tendencies toward social closure and reproduction maintain levels of exclusion that clash with the universal principle of citizenship so cherished by the common culture of Europeans.

8   A conclusion

Is Europe a society? The answer is 'not yet' or, simply, 'no'. There is some abstract agreement among social scientists about what constitutes 'a society'. It is far easier to describe a nation, and even more so a state. The EU is a complex and unique political and economic unit that is certainly not devoid of a shared culture and tradition. Its peoples have been unevenly converging in levels of education, standards of living, technology, attitudes toward everyday life and many other dimensions, but they have not reached that point of fusion at which we might speak with assurance of a single society. How could we, when some countries – Italy, for instance – are still said to harbour several societies?

The process toward unification and efforts at governing the novel European polity – the production of effective governance – have taken place with a high degree of self-consciousness. Many people are involved in it and they are conscious of what they are doing. Europe is now essentially a project being carried out consciously by realists, and it is a clear example of social reflexivity on a very large scale. It is impossible to predict that Europeans today will finally produce the kind of society – within a globalized world – they aim to build. Time and again the unexpected consequences of human social action raise their, often ugly, heads. All we can say is that, contrary to inveterate custom, this time we have learned much from the past, and social change and decision often follow the rules of democracy, debate, criticism, tolerance and rationality. We may not be as environmentally minded as we ought to be, our solidarity with the poorer surrounding world is not as high as it should be, and our own handling of our minorities – whether ethnic, or migrant, or poor, or indigent – is not what ought to be expected. But there is an undeniable and effective effort being made by contemporary Europeans toward the establishment of a society worthy of our civilization and the best traditions of our history. At least this much must be conceded.

References

Bromley, S.J. (ed.) (2001) *Governing the European Union*, **London, Sage/The Open University.**

Thompson, G. (ed.) (2001) *Governing the European Economy*, **London, Sage/The Open University.**

Further reading

Arbós, X. and Giner, S. (1993) *La Gobernabilidad: Ciudadanía y Democracia en la Encrucijada Mundial*, Madrid, Siglo XXI.

Donati, P. (2000) *La Cittadinanza Societaria*, Bari, Laterza.

Giner, S. and Archer, M.S. (eds) (1978) *Contemporary Europe: Social Structures and Cultural Patterns*, London, Routledge.

Guibernau, M. (1999) *Nations Without States*, Cambridge, Polity Press.

Hall, J.A. (ed.) (1995) *Civil Society*, Cambridge, Polity Press.

Haller, M. and Richter, R. (eds) (1994) *Toward a European Nation? East and West, Center and Periphery*, London and New York, ME Sharpe.

Kaelble, H. (1987) *Auf dem Weg zu einer Europäischen Gesellschaft: eine Sozialgewschichte Westeuropas, 1880–1980*, Munich, C.H. Beck.

Leonard, M. (2000) *The Future Shape of Europe*, London, The Foreign Policy Center/BSMG Worldwide.

Therborn, G. (1995) *European Modernity and Beyond: The Trajectory of European Societies, 1945–2000*, London, Sage.

Index

abortion 151
Adenauer, Konrad 172, 180
advertising, and European Union media policy 216
ageing population 141, 148–9
agriculture, Common Agricultural Policy (CAP) 15, 51, 266
Amsterdam Treaty (1997) 98, 213
aristocracy, decline of the 10
Armenia 2
Ashcroft, S. 173
Asia, division between Europe and 2
associations, and governance 29–30
asylum seekers 18, 66
    'bogus' 69, 93
    in Britain 78, 92–3
    defining 69
    and the European Union 183
    in France 81, 82, 92
    in Germany 86, 87, 90, 92, 96
    and the Schengen Agreement 98
    see also refugees
Athenian democracy, and the 'idea of Europe' 6, 13
Austria
    births outside marriage 142, 143
    and the Committee of the Regions 54
    divorce rates 146
    and drugs
        drug-related offences 238
        illegal drug use 232, 238
        public opinion on 248
    fertility rates 142
    foreign population 67
    married women's employment 146, 147
    media in 197, 198
        newspapers 200
        television 202, 209
Azerbaijan 2

BABEL (Broadcasting Across the Barriers of European Languages) Programme 217

Baker, S. 107, 110, 131, 132, 133
Baltic Republics 2
Basque Country 271
    and EU regional policies 52
    and regional nationalism 17, 37, 40–1, 42, 43, 44, 45, 56, 58
    television 222
Bauer, M. 182
Belgium
    attitudes to European identity in 175
    births outside marriage 143
    Catholic Church in 14
    childcare in 152, 153
    divorce rates 146
    and drugs
        illegal drug use 232
        public opinion on 248
        responses to drug-related offences 238
    fertility rates 142
    foreign population 67
    married women's employment 147
    media in 198, 206, 223
        computers and the internet 199
        and politics 220
        television 202, 209
    regionalism in 45
    and the Schengen Agreement 245
Berath, Jean 169
Bertin-Mourot, B. 182
birth rates
    in Britain 142
    and childcare 152
    European 16–17, 142–3, 164–5
births outside marriage 17, 142, 143, 144, 164
book production in Europe 196
border controls, and drug trafficking 246
Borneman, J. 183
bourgeoisie
    and childcare 158
    rise of the 10
Brants, K. 221

Breton language 222
Britain
    anti-nuclear protests in 108
    Arts Council 26
    attitudes to Europe
        identity in 175
        integration in 174
    births outside marriage 142, 143
    business élites in 182
    and the Commonwealth 23
    and drugs
        and border controls 246
        illegal drug use 232, 249
        public opinion on 248, 249
        rave culture 251–3
        responses to drug-related
            offences 238, 241
        trafficking 239, 241
    environmental movement 122–3
        and green consumerism 135
        Green Party 127
    ethnic minority population 76–7,
        78–9
    and Europe 171
    and European citizenship 265
    and European unification 180, 263
    family life in 141–2
        ageing population and pensions
            148–9
        and child poverty 162–3
        and childcare 152
        and cohabitation 144
        divorce rates 145, 146
        fertility rates 143
        gay and lesbian households 156
        and governance 160, 162–3
        and teenage pregnancies 145,
            160–1
        and women in employment
            154–5
    and the Industrial Revolution 25
    labour market and employment
        rights in 120
    Labour Party and the European
        community in 181, 182
    local government and ethnic
        minority councillors in 78–9
    lone parents in 144–5
    married women's employment 147
    media in 197–8
        computers and the internet 199
        and the English language 198
        newspapers 200, 214
        regulation 204
        television 202, 209
    migrants in 65, 69, 74–9, 91–3
        and anti-discrimination
            legislation 78, 91
        asylum seekers and refugees 78,
            92–3
        and campaigns against racial
            violence 79, 91–2
        and citizenship 78, 91
        colonial (New Commonwealth)
            72, 73, 75–6, 77–9, 141
        displaced persons 75
        and European citizenship 99
        European workers 75
        foreign population 66, 67, 87
        and immigration policies 66, 78,
            79, 91
        integration policy 77–9
        Irish 75
        and multiculturalism 76, 78–9
        post-war 72, 73, 74–6
        and the term 'immigrant' 68
    regions and regionalism in 36, 40,
        44
        and centralism 47
        and a 'Europe of Nations' 37
        and a 'Europe of the Regions' 58
        and the European Union 51,
            53–4
        federalization 45, 54
    and town twinning 170
    trade unions in 113, 115, 116, 120
broadcasting
    cable 208, 210, 212
    national policy in Europe 213
    pan-European 218–19
    public service 226
    radio 196, 197, 206
    satellite 208, 210
    see also television
Bromley, S.J. 28, 35, 262
BUND (German Federation for
    Nature Protection) 125
Burgess, A. 8, 11, 12

cable television 208, 210, 212, 216,
    218–19
CAP (Common Agricultural Policy)
    15, 51, 266

capitalism, and industrialism 11–12
Catalonia
    regionalism in 17, 39, 40–1, 42, 43,
        44, 56
        and the European Union 53, 54
    television 222, 223
Catholicism 14, 19
    divorce and birth rates in Catholic
        countries 17, 145
    and the franchise 10
    and language 179
Central Europe
    and the Cold War 22, 26
    collapse of communism in 187
    and the Enlightenment 10
    and EU enlargement 177–8
    and the Industrial Revolution 11
    media in 198
Chechnya 22
Chernobyl incident 131
Chevènement, Jean-Pierre 265
child poverty, government policies
    in the UK 162–3
childcare 152–3, 158
China, and the opium trade 239
Christianity
    and European culture and values 6,
        7–9
    separation of Eastern Orthodox and
        Western European 14, 18–19
    see also Catholicism; Protestantism;
        religion
Churchill, Winston 180
cities
    concentration of European
        populations in 16
    European Cities on Drug Policy
        (ECDP) network 253–5, 256, 257
    migrants in 67, 69
citizenship 10, 32, 68, 73, 100
    in Britain 78, 91
    European 98–9, 183, 189, 190, 263,
        264–5
        and the Eurobarometer 173
        and social exclusion 273
    in France 82, 83, 93–4, 97
    in Germany 67, 88, 89, 90, 95
civil rights 190
civil society
    and environmental issues 134

    and governance 29–30, 265
    and social movements 105, 106,
        121
    towards a European 188–90, 267–9
Club of Rome report, The Limits to
    Growth 130
cohabitation 144, 145, 156
Cold War
    and the cultural frontiers of Europe
        12–13, 14
    legacy of the 19, 21–2, 26
    and religion 14, 19
colonialism, end of European 20,
    22–4
Common Agricultural Policy (CAP)
    15, 51, 266
communist parties, and European
    union 182–3
contraception 151, 157, 165
    and teenage pregnancies 161
Corfu, Kalamas campaign in 127,
    128–9, 136
Cormack, M. 223
corporatism
    and civil society 267
    and environmental movements
        122
Corsica 17, 44, 48, 265, 271
Council of Europe, and media
    regulation 204, 215
Council of European Municipalities
    169–70
Crouch, C. 15, 147
cultural autonomy, and the media
    210–12
cultural divisions in Europe 14–19,
    262–4
    ethnic minorities 17, 18, 19
    gender and family life 16–17
    high and low culture 16, 19, 25–6,
        27
    linguistic 192
    national minorities 17–18
    religion 14
    social class 16, 19
    socio-economic 15–16, 19
    welfare systems 15, 19
cultural frontiers of Europe 1, 2–14,
    171, 179, 261–2

and the Cold War 12–13, 14
and the Enlightenment 9–11, 12,
13, 24, 25, 179
and EU enlargement 177–9
and geographical boundaries 2–6,
178
and the Industrial Revolution 11–12,
13, 25
and religion 6, 7–9
cultural tourism 183
cultural unity in Europe 19–27,
169–93, 260, 261–2
and *acquis communautaire* 172
and the Cold War 19, 21–2
cultural homogenization 20, 25–6,
27
and education 184–5, 188
and the end of the 'European
Empire' 20, 22–4
and European civil society 172,
188–90
and the European ideal 171
and European political culture 20,
24
and high culture 184–5, 188
and the idea of Europe 176–9
and memories of war 19, 21
and new social movements 20,
24–5, 26, 27
and town twinning 169–70
see also European culture; European
identity
Czech Republic 2–3, 66
Czechoslovakia 2, 25

Dahrendorf, Ralph 189, 192
Davies, Norman, *Europe: A History*
187
Dawson, G. 114
De Gasperi, Alcide 172, 180
Delors, Jacques 58, 180
Delouche, Frederic, *The Illustrated
History of Europe* 186–7
democracy
Athenian, and the 'idea of Europe'
6, 13
and civil society 268–9
'democratic deficit' in Europe 35,
131–2, 244

Denmark
attitudes to Europe in 174, 175
births outside marriage 142, 143
childcare in 153
divorce rates 145, 146
and drugs
illegal drug use 232
public opinion on 248
responses to drug-related
offences 238
fertility rates 142
gay and lesbian households 157
married women's employment 147,
152
media in 206
computers and the internet 199
newspapers 200, 201
television 201, 202, 209
regions and regionalism in 47
young people and contraception
161
disabled workers, and employment
rights 120–1
divorce
European differences in rates of 17,
145–6
and lone parents 144
and women's employment 146, 148
Donzelot, Jacques, *The Policing of
Families* 158
Dorn, N. 242
drugs 229–57, 260
cannabis 232, 235, 238
defining 230
drug use in Europe 32, 231–4
and the economy 229
ecstasy and dance culture 230,
249–53, 257
and the European Cities on Drug
Policy (ECDP) network 253–5,
256
in European Union countries
illegal drug use 32, 229, 234–6
responses to drug-related
offences 236–8
and harm reduction policies 252–3,
256
'maximum tolerance' approach to
256
'normalization' of drug use 229
problematic use of 230, 231, 232

seizures by law-enforcement
officials 231
trafficking 32, 230, 231
and border controls 246
and the European law-
enforcement complex 242–7
global routes 233–4
international drug controls
239–41
public opinion on 248–9
'zero tolerance' approach to 256
Duroselle, J.B., *Europe: A History of its
Peoples* 186

Earth Summit (1992) 113, 132–3
Agenda 21 132–3
Local Agenda 21 133
Eastern Europe
and the Cold War 22
collapse of communism in 187
and the Enlightenment 10
and EU enlargement 177–8, 178–9,
263–4
and the Industrial Revolution 11
media in 198
migration to Germany from 67, 87
EBU (European Broadcasting Union)
218
ECDP (European Cities on Drug
Policy) network 253–5, 256, 257
economic growth, and trade unions
114–15
economic integration 270
education
creation of national systems of 10
and European identity 185–7, 188
higher education in Europe 144
history teaching 183, 186–7
EEC (European Economic
Community) 13, 171, 180, 262
employment patterns
changes in 154–5, 157
diversity of European 15–16
employment rights, and the labour
market in Europe 117–21
EMU (Economic and Monetary
Union)
future of 191
and regionalism 50, 57

England, regions and regionalism in
40, 58
English language 183, 192
magazines 219
and the media 202
Enlightenment
and civil society 267
and European culture 1, 9–11, 12,
13, 24, 25, 179
environmental movements 104, 105,
109–10, 111, 121–36
and Agenda 21 136
and the Chernobyl incident 131
and corporatism 122
and eco-coporatism 130–4, 181
sustainable development 131–2
in France 122, 134–5
and the German Green Party 122,
123–7, 133
Greenpeace 133, 135, 181, 182
Kalamas campaign 127, 128–9, 136
and party politics 110
and the Rio Earth Summit (1992)
132–3, 133
in the UK 122–3, 127
and green consumerism 134–5
ERDF (European Regional
Development Fund) 51, 164
ethnic minorities in Europe 17, 18,
19
see also migrants
ethnic terrorism 267, 272
ethnonations, and the European
Union 181
ETUC (European Trade Union
Confederation) 181
Eurobarometer
and European identity 173–6, 266
survey on drugs 248–9
European Broadcasting Union (EBU)
218
European Central Bank 265
European Cities on Drug Policy
(ECDP) network 253–5, 256, 257
European Coal and Steel
Community 180, 262
European Commission 172
and the environmental movement
181

and the *Eurobarometer* 173, 175, 176, 248–9
and gender issues 159
and governance 266
and history teaching 186
and the media 204, 217
and regional policies 50, 52
European Convention on Human Rights 203
European Court of Justice 98, 190
European culture
  high culture 184–5, 188
  promoting 183–4
  and values 5–7, 189
European Economic Community (EEC) 13, 171, 180, 262
European identity 260
  'bottom-up' process of creating 172, 183–4
  and civil society 188–90
  cultural identity 6–7, 19, 26, 27, 211, 212
  and education 185–7, 188
  and the European Union 1, 7, 13, 27–8, 170–1, 260, 262
  and high culture 184–5, 188
  measuring (the *Eurobarometer*) 173–6, 266
European Parliament
  and drug trafficking 249
  and environmental issues 126, 134
  and the environmental movement 181
  and governance 165, 265, 266
  and the media 218
  public opinion on European government responsible to 174
  and regional policies 50, 51
  and trade unions 120
European project 13, 26, 27, 28, 211, 266, 270
European Regional Development Fund (ERDF) 51, 164
European Trade Union Confederation (ETUC) 181
European Union (EU)
  action programmes on the labour market and family life 163–4
  conflict in the 27–8, 260–1
  criteria for joining 176–7

and the 'democratic deficit' 35, 131–2, 244
and drugs
  European Drug Promotion Week 256
  illegal drug use 32, 229, 234–6
  international drug control 239–40, 241
  law-enforcement complex 242–7
  responses to drug-related offences 236–8
enlargement 1, 3, 22, 177–9
  and Eastern Europe 177–8, 178–9, 263–4
  future of 191
  and migration 99
  and Turkey 8, 177–8, 266–7
and the environmental movement 130, 131–2, 133–4, 181
European élites and the unification of Europe 180–2
and European identity 1, 7, 13, 27–8, 170–1, 260, 262
and the 'European project' 13, 26, 27, 28, 211
European Social Policy, and employment rights 120–1
and 'fortress Europe' 183, 191, 242–3, 247
future of the 190–1
governance problems 266–7
integration 1, 7, 13, 24
  economic 270
  and the end of the Cold War 22
  and family life 165–6
  and gender equality 150
  and regionalism 57, 62
  support in for different countries 174
and the labour movement 181
media policies 215–18
migrants and refugees 66, 97–9, 100, 183, 259, 267
and national loyalties 265
and new social movements 181
and the news media 223–5
requirements for membership 1
Social Charter 120
see also regions and regionalism
Europol 242, 244–5
eurosceptics 262–3

family life 139–66, 259–60
    and childcare 152–3, 158
    and gender roles 139, 140
    and governance 139, 140–1, 157–64
        organizations involved in 159–61
        and public/private spheres 158,
            159, 161–4
        tradition and transformation 165
    and paid employment 139–40
    recent trends in 16–17, 28, 32, 139,
        141–9
        ageing population 141, 148–9
        births outside marriage 17, 142,
            143, 144, 164
        cohabitation 144, 145, 156
        divorce rates 17, 145–6, 165
        factors influencing 139, 150–7
        fertility rates 16–17, 142–3, 164–5
        lesbian and gay households 140,
            156–7
        lone parent households 142,
            144–5, 156
        married women's employment
            146–8, 148–9
        teenage pregnancy 145, 160–1
    and the regulation of working
        hours 163
    and reproductive rights 150, 151
    unity and diversity in 165
    and the women's movement 150–2,
        157
Featherstone, M. 184
federalism
    and the construction of the
        European community 172
    and the European Union (EU) 35,
        37, 54, 59, 61, 62
    and the growing importance of
        regions 36, 45–7
fertility rates *see* birth rates
film 196
Finland
    births outside marriage 142, 143
    and the Committee of the Regions
        54
    divorce rates 146
    and drugs
        illegal drug use 232
        public opinion on 248
    fertility rates 142
    married women's employment 147

    media in 198, 223
        computers and the internet 199
        newspapers 200, 201
        television 201, 202, 209
First World War 23
Fischer, Joschka 265
Flanders 17
'fortress Europe' 183, 191, 247
    and drug trafficking 242–3
Fowler, N. 183
France
    anti-nuclear protests in 108
    births outside marriage 142, 143
    business élites in 182
    Communist Party 182
    divorce rates 146
    and drugs
        illegal drug use in 232
        public opinion on 248
        responses to drug-related
            offences 236–7, 238
    enfranchisement in 10
    environmental movement in 122,
        134–5
    and European culture 184
    and European unification 263
    family life in
        and childcare 152–3
        cohabitation 144, 156
        fertility rates 143, 152
        gay and lesbian households 157
        and the gender division of labour
            156
        and governance 160, 161
        married women's employment
            147
        and reproductive rights 151, 160
        and unemployment 144
    immigrant communities 18
    and the Industrial Revolution 11
    labour market 118
    media in 197, 198, 206
        computers and the internet 199
        and the French language 222
        newspapers 200, 214
        and politics 220
        regulation 204
        television 201, 202, 209
    migrants in 65, 66, 69, 80–4, 93–4
        asylum seekers 81, 82, 92
        and citizenship 82, 83, 93–4, 97

and discrimination 94
foreign population 67
and the *Front National* 81, 84, 94, 97
and immigration policies 80–2
integration policy 82–3, 84
and multiculturalism 94, 96
post-war 70, 72, 73, 80, 141
and the term 'immigrant' 68
regions and regionalism in 47–8
and the European Union (EU) 51, 52
religion in 14
'revolution' in Paris (1968) 25
and the Schengen Agreement 98, 245
and town twinning 170
trade unions in 113–14, 115, 117
franchise, and citizenship 10
freedom, and European values 6, 9
French Revolution 9

Galicia 40–1
GATT (General Agreement on Tariffs and Trade) 90
Gaulle, Charles de 58, 181, 189
gay and lesbian households 140, 156–7
gender, and attitudes to European identity 175–6
General Agreement on Tariffs and Trade (GATT) 90
geographical boundaries of Europe 2–6, 178
Georgia 2, 22
Germanic media culture 199
Germany
    births outside marriage 142, 143
    business élites in 182
    divorce rates 146
    and drugs
        border controls 246
        illegal drug use 232
        public opinion on 248
        responses to drug-related offences 236–7, 238
    and European unification 263
    family life in
        and childcare 152, 153
        and cohabitation 144

    and governance 160
    married women's employment 147, 148
    and unemployment 144
    fertility rates 143
    Green Party 122, 123–7, 133
    labour market 118
    media in 197, 198, 206
        computers and the internet 199
        and language 198
        newspapers 200
        television 201, 202, 209
    migrants in 18, 65, 66, 69, 72, 84–90, 94–6
        asylum seekers 86, 87, 90, 92, 96
        and citizenship 67, 88, 89, 90, 95
        ethnic Germans 67, 87, 90, 94–5
        foreign population 67, 87, 88, 90, 95
        guestworkers 68–9, 72, 85–6, 89, 90, 95
        integration policy 88–9, 96
        nineteenth-century immigration 84–5
        post-war 70, 72, 73, 85–6, 141
        and the Second World War 70, 85, 88–9
        Turkish youths 95–6
    regions and regionalism in 39, 47, 53, 56, 58
    religion in 14
    reunification of 2, 22, 87, 95, 96
    Romanticism 25
    and the Schengen Agreement 98, 245
    social movements in 108
    and town twinning 170
    trade unions 114–15, 115–16, 117
globalization
    and drug trafficking 229, 239, 243
    and the media 223
    and migration 90
    and regions and regionalism 32, 36, 48–9, 50, 56, 60, 62
    EU regional policies 51, 55
governance 28–31, 265–7, 273
    and changes in family life 139, 140–1, 157–64
    and drugs in Europe 229–57
    eco-coporatism 130–4
    and New Public Management 162
    regional 49

government, and governance 28–9, 30–1
Grahl, J. 114, 120
Greece
    births outside marriage 142, 143
    Communist Party 182
    divorce rates 145, 146
    and drugs
        border controls 246
        illegal drug use 232
        public opinion on 248
    fertility rates 143
    industrial relations in 120
    and the Industrial Revolution 11
    Kalamas campaign in Corfu 127, 128–9, 136
    married women's employment 146, 147
    media in
        computers and the internet 199
        newspapers 200
        television 201, 202, 209
    migrants in 65, 66
    regions and regionalism in 48, 56
    and Turkey 177, 267
Greenpeace 133, 135, 181, 182
Grote, George 6
gypsies 66, 272

Hague, William 93
Hattersley, Roy 78
Heffernan, R. 132
Hegel, G.W.F. 267
Heinderyckx, F. 198
high culture, and European identity 184–5, 188
history
    historical origins of Europe 3–5, 7
    teaching 183, 186–7
Hobsbawm, E., *Nations and Nationalism* 193
Holland *see* Netherlands
Hudson, R. 183
humanism, and European values 6, 9
Hume, John 58
Hungary, European claims of 2–3
Huntington, Samuel, *The Clash of Civilizations and the Remaking of World Order* 7

Iceland, television in 209
'idea of Europe' 6
identity politics, and regionalism 36
immigration *see* migrants
incomes, gender inequality in 155
Industrial Revolution 1, 11–12, 13, 25
information societies, and the media 195
Inglehart, R. 174
innovation, and European civilization 269–70
International Criminal Police Organization (Interpol) 240
internet 196, 202, 207, 208, 212
    and drugs 247
    and newspapers 214
    regulation of the 204, 205
Internet Watch Foundation (IWF) 204
investments, European 270
Iraq 267
Ireland
    attitudes to European identity in 175
    births outside marriage 143
    divorce rates 145, 146
    and drugs
        public opinion on 248
        responses to drug-related offences 238
    economic growth in 15
    environmental movements in 133
    family life in 144
    fertility rates 143
    illegal drug use in 232
    Irish immigrants in Britain 75
    married women's employment 146, 147
    media in 197, 223
        newspapers 200
        television 202, 209
    migration to Europe from 70
    and the nation state 37
    regions and regionalism in 39, 40, 44
        and the European Union 51, 53
    religious decline in 14
    television 222
    see also Northern Ireland

Islam
    and European culture 7, 8
    in France 83, 94, 97
    in Turkey 177
Italy
    attitudes to European identity in
      175
    births outside marriage 143
    Communist Party 182
    divorce rates 145, 146
    and drugs
      border controls 246
      illegal drug use 232
      public opinion on 248, 249
      responses to drug-related
        offences 236–7, 238
    Emilia Romagna 49, 57
    and European unification 263
    family life in 144
    fertility rates 143
    immigrant communities 18
    and the Industrial Revolution 11
    married women's employment 146,
      147
    media, television 201, 202
    media in 197, 198, 206
      computers and the internet 199
      newspapers 200
      and politics 220
      television 209
    migrants in 66
    regions and regionalism in 44, 47,
      49
      and the European Union 51
      Lombardy 53, 54
    socio-economic changes 15, 19
    trade unions in 113–14, 120
IWF (Internet Watch Foundation)
    204

Jenkins, Roy 73
Joseph, M. 251

Kant, Immanuel 268
Keane, John 189
Keynes, John Maynard 26
Kohr, Leopold, *The Breakdown of
    Nations* 57
Kundera, Milan 185

labour market
    discrimination in the 118
    and employment rights 117–21
    and EU regional policies 52
    and family life 139–40
    migrant workers 18
    and the regulation of working
      hours 163
    restructuring 116–17
    secondary 118
    and trade unions 116–21
    transnational links and
      dockworkers 119
    women in employment 16, 19, 150,
      154–5, 157
      European Union action
        programmes 163–4
      and integration 272–3
      married women 146–8, 148–9,
        152, 159, 165
      wages of 155
language
    creating unity in Europe through
      183
    groups in Europe 179
    linguistic diversity in Europe 192
    and the media in Europe 198, 211,
      222–3
Lawrence, Stephen 79, 92
Le Pen, Jean Marie 81
legal rights 190
Lenin, V.I. 23
lesbian and gay households 140,
    156–7
liberal-democratic political systems,
    and European unity 22
life expectancy 148
Lister, Ruth 162
literature, European 185
local government in Britain, ethnic
    minority councillors 78–9
lone-parent households 142, 144–5,
    156
Lord, C. 132
Lovering, John 49
Luxembourg
    and the Committee of the Regions
      54
    and drugs
      illegal drug use in 232

public opinion on 248
responses to drug-related
offences 236–7, 238
foreign population 66, 67
media in
computers and the internet 199
television 209
and the Schengen Agreement 245

Maastricht Treaty (1992) 24, 54, 99
and the collapse of the Soviet
Union 271
and Europol 245
and regional movements 181
and social democratic parties 181–2
and town twinning 170
McAdam, G. 181
Machiavelli, N. 9
Macpherson Report (on the murder
of Stephen Lawrence) 79, 92
Marks, G. 181
marriage
across European nations 184
age at 141, 142
births outside 17, 142, 143, 144,
164
married women's employment 146–8,
148–9, 159, 165
and childcare 152
Marshall Plan/Aid 21, 70, 85
Marshall, T.H., *Citizenship and Social
Class* 190
Martel, Charles 8
Marx, Karl 193
material progress, and European
values 6, 9
Maxwell, Robert 219
media 195–227
MEDIA 1 and MEDIA II programmes
217
media
and conflict in Europe 226
and environmental movements
122
and European cultural autonomy
210–12
and the 'European idea' 227
and European Union policies 215–
18
film 196

on illegal immigrants 66, 93
impact of new technology on 207–8
and information/network societies
195
and language 198, 211, 222–3
and multiculturalism 212, 226
as national institutions 196
national media policy in Europe
213–15
new electronic 196, 203
news media 223–5
pan-European 218–20
and politics 220–1
radio broadcasting 196, 197, 206
regulation 28, 32, 203–5
broadcasting model of 205
common carrier model of 204–5
content 203–4
impact of new technology on
207–8
media product model of 204
ownership 203
technology 203
and space 225–6
structure in Europe 196–203
and culture 198–9
degrees of centralization 197–8
and economics 199–201
and language 198
trends and changes in European
206–10
video-recording (VCR) 207
see also newspapers; television
Mediterranean countries
economic growth 15
welfare systems 15
Melucci, Alberto 107
Middle Ages, and the concept of
Europe 7, 9
migrants 18, 32, 65–100, 141, 191,
259, 271–2
direct and indirect integration
policies 74
drugs and illegal immigration 243
economic migrants 65, 68
and economic recession (1970s)
65
and the European Union 66, 97–9,
100, 183, 259, 267
and family life 140
and family reunification 65

and globalization 90
gypsies 66
and immigration policies 66, 67–8,
    74
and labour migration 65, 66
post-war migration 69–71
and the Schengen Agreement 98
and social exclusion 273
strategies for integration and
    exclusion 73–4
see also asylum seekers; Britain;
    citizenship; France; Germany;
    refugees
Mill, J.S. 193
Mitchell, Juliet 151
Mitterand, François 81
Monnet, Jean 172, 180
multiculturalism 18, 68
in Britain 76, 78–9
and France 94, 96
and the media 212, 226
Muslims *see* Islam

nation states
and the European Union 35, 37,
    56
and illegal drugs 230, 244
and international migration 65
and public spaces 189
and regionalism 28, 56, 60, 61, 62
rise and consolidation of 10
and unity in Europe 261
national identities
and the *Eurobarometer* 173–4
future of 192–3
national minorities in Europe 17–18,
    19
and drugs 239
and the media 211–12
    and language 222–3
National Trust 123, 125
nationalism 10, 261
and cultural autonomy 210
regional 25, 28, 32, 44–5
NATO (North Atlantic Treaty
    Organization) 21, 177, 191, 241,
    262
neo-liberalism, and civil society
    267–8

Netherlands
attitudes to European identity in
    175
births outside marriage 143
divorce rates 146
and drugs
    illegal drug use 232
    public opinion on 248
    responses to drug-related
        offences 236–7, 238
environmental movement in 122
and European unification 263
fertility rates 143
foreign population 67
gay and lesbian households 157
labour market 118
media in 198, 206
    computers and the internet 199
    newspapers 200, 201, 214
    and politics 220
    television 201, 202, 209
regions and regionalism in 47
religion 14
and the Schengen Agreement 98,
    245
young people and contraception
    161
networks
European Cities on Drug Policy
    (ECDP) network 253–5, 256,
    257
industrial relations 105
network societies and the media
    195
regional networking and alliances
    52–3.
self-organizing 29–30
    social movements as 104–11
New Public Management 162
new social movements *see* social
    movements
new technology, and the media
    207–8
news media 223–5
newspapers 196, 197, 206
    European Union policies on 217,
        218
    and national media policy 213–15
    pan-European 219
    structure and use in Europe 198,
        200, 201, 202

NGOs (non-governmental
    organizations)
        and civil society 268
        and environmental issues 134
        women's 150, 159
Nooteboom, Cees 185
North–South divide in Europe 264
    and birth rates 16–17
    and births outside marriage 17
    and divorce rates 17
    and immigration policies 66
    and the media 198–9, 200–1
    and religion 14
    socio-economic 15, 19
    and women in paid work 16
Northern Ireland 271
    and European Union regional
        policies 51
    Labour government and
        constitutional reform in 58
    and regional nationalism 17, 40,
        44, 45, 47, 58
Norway
    births outside marriage 142, 143
    divorce rates 146
    fertility rates 143
    gay and lesbian households 157
    illegal drug use in 232
    married women's employment 147
    media in
        newspapers 200, 201
        television 201, 202, 209
novels, and European civilization
    185

O'Hagan, A. 252
O'Malley, P. 253

paid employment *see* labour market
parenthood, and lesbian and gay
    couples 140
pensions, in the UK 148–9
Pérez-Díaz, Victor 188
Phillips, Trevor 79
Piachaud, D. 162–3
Poland 2–3, 75
police, international co-operation
    242, 244, 245–6, 247

political culture, European 20, 24
political parties
    Christian Democrats 14
    and environmental movements in
        the UK 122–3
    and European union 182–3
    Green parties 104, 109, 122, 123–7,
        130, 133, 135
    and social movements 104
    and trade unions 104–5
political rights 190
political violence, territorialization
    of 271
politics, and the media 220–1
Portugal
    African colonies 23
    attitudes to European identity in
        175
    births outside marriage 143
    divorce rates 145, 146
    and drugs
        border controls 246
        public opinion on 248
        responses to drug-related
            offences 236–7, 238
    fertility rates 143
    growth in incomes 15, 19
    immigrant communities 18
    and the Industrial Revolution 11
    married women's employment 147
    media in 198, 199
        computers and the internet 199
        newspapers 200
        television 202, 209
    migrants in 66
    Reconquista 42
    regions and regionalism in 41, 42,
        47, 48, 56
poverty, and lone parents 144, 162
Powell, Enoch 78
Protestantism 14, 19
    and language 179
public opinion
    on drugs 248–9
    and the *Eurobarometer* 173–6
    and the news media 224
public space, emergence of a
    European 172, 188–90
Pujol, Jordi 54

racism, and colonialism 23
radio broadcasting 196, 197, 206
Reagan, Ronald 267–8
refugees 18, 28, 66
    Convention refugees 69
    and 'fortress Europe' 243
    in Germany 88
    status 69
    see also asylum seekers
regional movements, and the
    European Union 181
regions and regionalism 35–62
    defining 38
    diversity of 35–6, 38–44
    and the European Union 35, 36–7,
        49, 50–9, 181, 259
        Committee of the Regions 50,
            53–5, 56
        cross-border regions 38, 53
        and a 'Europe of Nations' 35, 37,
            58
        and a 'Europe of the Regions' 35,
            37, 49, 55–9, 62
        and federalism 35, 37, 54, 59, 61,
            62
        and the 'Four Motors' 46, 53, 57
        integration 57, 62
        regional networking and
            alliances 52–3
        regional policies 50, 51–2
        'subsidiarity' principle 54
    and federalization 36, 45–7, 59
    future of 59–61
    and globalization 32, 36, 48–9, 50,
        51, 55, 56, 60, 62
    growing importance of regions 36
    and the media
        and language 222–3
        and regional identities 212
    and nation states 28, 56, 60, 61, 62
    'national' and 'non-national'
        regions 39
    and nationalism 25, 28, 32, 44–5
    and 'new regionalism' 49
Reif, K. 174
religion
    and birth rates 16–17
    and the cultural frontiers of Europe
        6, 7–9
    decline of 14
    diversity in 14, 18–19

and the franchise 10
    and language groups in Europe 179
    separation of church and state 10
    see also Catholicism; Christianity;
        Protestantism
reproductive rights 150, 151
Rio Earth Summit (1992) 132–3, 133
Robbins, Keith 186
Roberts, J.M. 186
Romance media culture 199
Romania 2–3, 66
Russia 171, 178, 191, 266

satellite broadcasting 208, 210, 212,
    216, 218
Scandinavian countries
    media in 198, 199, 214
    welfare systems 15
    see also Denmark; Finland; Norway;
        Sweden
Schengen Agreement 90, 98, 99, 189,
    244, 245, 247, 267
Schmitter, P.C. 29
Schumacher, E.F., Small is Beautiful
    57
Schuman, Robert 172, 180
Scotland
    Labour government and
        constitutional reform in 58
    media in 198
    and regional nationalism 17, 39,
        40, 44, 47
        and the European Union (EU) 50,
            52, 57–8
SEA (Single European Act), and
    environmental policies 132
Second World War
    and the European ideal 171
    legacy of the 21, 26
    and migration 65, 69–70, 100
        Irish immigration to Britain 75
        to Germany 70, 85, 88–9
secularization, and the media 221
self-organizing networks 29–30
    social movements as 104–11, 135–6
SEM see Single European Market
    (SEM)
Seton-Watson, Hugh 179
Shaw, J. 190

Simmel, Georg 184
Single European Market (SEM), and
    regionalism 36, 50, 51, 55, 57, 62
Slevin, J. 217
Slovak Republic, European claims of
    2–3
Smith, Anthony 8
social change, and industrialism 11
social class
    and attitudes to childcare 158
    changes in class structure 122
    class conflict 272
    divisions in Europe 16, 19
social movements 20, 24–5, 26, 27,
    28, 103–36, 259
    and the European Union 181
    explaining 106–9
    gay pride movements 104
    and governance 28–9, 30–1, 32
    Green parties 104, 109
    as insiders or challengers 108–9
    old and new 104–6, 109, 121,
        135
    peace movement 105
    and post-materialism 107–8, 121,
        122, 135
    and the resources mobilization
        approach 108–9
    as self-organizing networks 104–11,
        135–6
    and social and economic change
        106
    women's movement 105, 150–2
    see also environmental movements;
        trade unions
social regulation, and self-organizing
    networks 30
social rights 190
socio-economic diversity in Europe
    15–16, 19
solidarity, and common European
    culture 6, 7
Soviet Union, collapse of the 2, 22,
    178, 242, 271
Spaak, Paul 172, 180
Spain
    ageing population 148
    attitudes to European identity in
        175
    births outside marriage 143

Communist Party 182
divorce rates 145, 146
and drugs
    border controls 246
    illegal drug use in 232, 249
    public opinion on 248, 249
    responses to drug-related
        offences 236–7, 238
and Europe citizenship 265
and European unification 263
family life in 144
fertility rates 143
Franco dictatorship 38, 41, 43, 44
growth in incomes 15, 19
immigrant communities 18
and the Industrial Revolution 11
married women's employment 146,
    147
media in 197, 198
    computers and the internet 199
    newspapers 200, 201
    television 202
migrants in 66
Reconquista 42
regions and regionalism in 36,
    40–3, 44, 47, 56
    federalization 45
support for European integration in
    174
see also Basque Country; Catalonia
Spinelli, Altiero 180
sport
    Europeanization of 183
    and pan-European television 219
stateless nations, and the European
    Union 181, 191
Strange, Susan 60
Streeck, W. 29
sustainable development 131–2
Sutherland, H. 162–3
Sweden
    ageing population 148
    births outside marriage 142, 143
    and the Committee of the Regions
        54
    divorce rates 145, 146
    and drugs
        illegal drug use in 232
        public opinion on 248, 249
        responses to drug-related
            offences 236–7, 238

fertility rates 143
foreign population 67, 69
gay and lesbian households 157
media in
    computers and the internet
      199
    newspapers 201
    television 201, 202, 209
social movements in 108
Switzerland
    births outside marriage 143
    divorce rates 146
    and the European Union 262
    family life in 144
    fertility rates 143
    foreign population 66, 67, 141
    and the franchise 10
    married women's employment 147
    media in 197, 198
      newspapers 200
      television 202, 209
    religion 14
Syria 267

tax credits 163
teenage pregnancy 145, 160–1
television 196, 197, 198
    cable 208, 210, 212, 216, 218–19
    digital 208
    and European cultural autonomy
      210
    and European Union media policies
      215–17
    and national minorities in Europe
      212
    news programmes 198–9, 219, 221,
      224
    pan-European 218–19
    and politics 220–1
    satellite 208, 210, 212, 216,
      218–19
    structure and use in Europe 201,
      202
Television Directive (1989) 216–17
Thatcher, Margaret 47, 58, 181,
    267–8
Thompson, G. 15, 265
Tilly, Charles 108
Timms, N. 173

tourism, cultural 183
town twinning 169–70
trade unions 104–5, 109, 110,
    111–21, 121–2, 135
    and environmental protection
      113
    and the European Union 181
    in France 113–14, 115, 117
    in Germany 114–15, 115–16, 117
    in Italy 113–14, 120
    and the labour market in Europe
      116–21
    in the UK 113, 115, 116, 120
    and working-class identity 112
TREVI (Terrorism, Radicalism and
    Violence International) 245
Truman Doctrine 21
Turkey
    drugs and border controls 246
    and EU membership 8, 177–8,
      266–7
    European claims of 2–3
    and the geographical boundaries of
      Europe 2, 171
Turner, Victor 179

UN Convention on Asylum and
    Refugees 90
unemployment
    in the European Union 120
    of immigrants 80, 81, 83, 89
    and lone parents 144
United Kingdom (UK) *see* Britain
United Nations, and international
    drug control 239–40, 249–50
United States
    and cultural homogenization in
      Europe 26, 27
    and the division of Europe between
      West and East 21
    Drug Enforcement Administration
      (DEA) 240–1
    and the media in Europe 210–11,
      212, 216, 218
    and post-war reconstruction in
      Europe 21, 70
    young people and contraception
      161

wages, of women 155
Wales
    Labour government and
      constitutional reform in 58
    regionalism in 40, 44, 47
      and the European Union (EU) 53,
        58
    television 222
wars
    and divisions in Europe 7–8, 261,
      262
    memories of the two world wars 7,
      19, 21
Waterman, P. 119
welfare systems 15, 19
Wilson, Woodrow 23
Wolton, Dominique 188
women
    ecofeminism and the German
      Green Party 125, 126
    and the franchise 10
    and the governance of family life
      158, 159–60
    in paid work 16, 19, 272–23

    and carers 162
    and changes in employment
      154–5, 157
    European Union action
      programmes 163–4
    and gender equality 150, 159
    married women 146–8, 148–9,
      152, 159, 165
    wages of 155
    and reproductive rights 150, 151
women's movement 105, 150–2,
    157, 159, 161, 164
World Trade Organization (WTO),
    demonstrations against the 109,
    110
WTO *see* World Trade Organization
    (WTO)

young people
    drugs and rave culture 230, 249–53,
      257
    and European identity 185–6
Yugoslavia (former) 22, 66, 67

Acknowledgements

Grateful acknowledgement is made to the following sources for permission to reproduce material in this book.

Figures

Figures 2.1 and 2.2: Wagstaff, P. (ed.) (1999) *Regionalism in the European Union*, Intellect Limited; *Figure 3.1*: Hammar, T. (ed.) (1985) 'Introduction', Chapter 1 in *European Immigration Policy*, Cambridge University Press; *Figure 4.1*: Chris Davies/Network; *Figures 4.2(a) and 42(b)*: John Harris/Report Digital; *Figure 4.3*: Marco Marianella/Olympia Publifoto; *Figure 4.4*: A. Maslennikov/Still Pictures; *Figure 4.5*: © Dieter Magnus, Environmental Artist; *Figure 4.6*: Courtesy of the German Green Party, Landesverband Niedersachen, Hannover; *Figures 8.1 and 8.4*: *Extended Annual Report on the State of the Drugs Problem in the European Union* (1999) European Communities; *Figure 8.2*: United Nations Department of Public Information (1998) *United Nations Chronicle*, no.21998, United Nations Publications; *Figure 8.5*: Stark, C. et al. (1999) 'European drug policy on supply and demand reduction', *Illegal Drug Use in the United Kingdom: Prevention, Treatment and Enforcement*, Ashgate Publishing Limited; *Figure 8.6*: *Eurobarometer* 47 (1997) © European Communities, 1995–2000.

Tables

Table 3.2: Professor Zig Layton-Henry; *Table 3.3*: 'Labour Force Surveys, 1998/99', National Statistics © Crown Copyright 2000; *Table 3.5*: *Trends in International Migration: Continuous Reporting System on Migration*, Annual Report 1999, Copyright OECD; *Table 3.6*: *Trends in International Migration: Continuous Reporting System on Migration*, Annual Report 1992, Copyright OECD; *Table 4.1*: Martell, L. (1994) 'The Green Movement', *Ecology and Society, An Introduction*, Polity Press/University of Massachusetts Press; *Table 4.2*: Cotgrove, S. and Duff, A. (1981) 'Environmentalism, values and social change', *British Journal of Sociology*, vol.32, reproduced by permission of Taylor & Francis Limited, PO Box 25, Abingdon, Oxfordshire, OX14 3UE; *Table 5.1*: McRae, S. (1999) *Economic Disadvantage and Family Change in Britain*, Occasional Paper 1, Oxford Brookes University; *Tables 5.2, 5.3, 5.4 and 5.5*: Crouch, C. (1999) *Social Change in Western Europe*, by permission of Oxford University Press; *Table 5.6*: Equal Opportunities Commission, *Annual Report 1998*; *Table 6.1*: *Eurobarometer* 49, September 1998, © European Communities, 1995–2000; *Table 7.1*: *Eurobarometer* 51, July 1999 (internet access), © European Communities/© *The Economist*, London, 19 February 2000 (computer ownership); *Table 7.4*: Reprinted by permission of Sage Publications Ltd from Siune, K. and Hultén, O. (1998) 'Does public broadcasting have a future?', McQuail, D. and Siune, K. (eds) *Media Policy: Convergence; Commerce; Concentration*, copyright Sage

Publications; *Table 8.1*: Dorn, N. and Jamieson, A. (2000) *Room for Manoeuvre*, Overview Report, March 2000, DrugScope.

Boxes

Box 4.2: European Press Agency; *Box 4.3*: Eleftheria, Corfu.

Photographs

Page 20: Antonio Guibernau; *pages 149, 153, 207 and 214*: Mike Levers; *pages 197 and 224*: BBC Stills Photo Library.

Every effort has been made to trace all the copyright owners, but if any have been inadvertently overlooked, the publishers will be pleased to make the necessary arrangements at the first opportunity.